Psychology and Human Performance in Space Programs

Psychology and Human Performance in Space Programs
Extreme Application

Edited by
Lauren Blackwell Landon, Kelley J. Slack, and
Eduardo Salas

CRC Press
Taylor & Francis Group
Boca Raton London New York

CRC Press is an imprint of the
Taylor & Francis Group, an **informa** business

First edition published 2021
by CRC Press
6000 Broken Sound Parkway NW, Suite 300, Boca Raton, FL 33487-2742

and by CRC Press
2 Park Square, Milton Park, Abingdon, Oxon, OX14 4RN

© 2021 Taylor & Francis Group, LLC

CRC Press is an imprint of Taylor & Francis Group, LLC

Reasonable efforts have been made to publish reliable data and information, but the author and publisher cannot assume responsibility for the validity of all materials or the consequences of their use. The authors and publishers have attempted to trace the copyright holders of all material reproduced in this publication and apologize to copyright holders if permission to publish in this form has not been obtained. If any copyright material has not been acknowledged please write and let us know so we may rectify in any future reprint.

Except as permitted under U.S. Copyright Law, no part of this book may be reprinted, reproduced, transmitted, or utilized in any form by any electronic, mechanical, or other means, now known or hereafter invented, including photocopying, microfilming, and recording, or in any information storage or retrieval system, without written permission from the publishers.

For permission to photocopy or use material electronically from this work, access www.copyright.com or contact the Copyright Clearance Center, Inc. (CCC), 222 Rosewood Drive, Danvers, MA 01923, 978-750-8400. For works that are not available on CCC please contact mpkbookspermissions@tandf.co.uk

Trademark notice: Product or corporate names may be trademarks or registered trademarks and are used only for identification and explanation without intent to infringe.

Library of Congress Cataloging-in-Publication Data
Names: Landon, Lauren Blackwell, editor. | Slack, Kelley J., editor. |
Salas, Eduardo, editor.
Title: Psychology and human performance in space programs / edited by
Lauren Blackwell Landon, Kelley J. Slack, Eduardo Salas.
Description: 1st edition. | Boca Raton, FL : CRC Press, 2020. | Includes
bibliographical references and index. | Contents: volume 1. Research at
the frontier — volume 2. Extreme application.
Identifiers: LCCN 2020026901 (print) | LCCN 2020026902 (ebook) |
ISBN 9781138339866 (volume 1 ; hbk) | ISBN 9781138339880 (volume 2 ; hbk) |
ISBN 9780429440854 (volume 2 ; ebk) | ISBN 9780429440878 (volume 1 ; ebk)
Subjects: LCSH: Astronautics—Human factors.
Classification: LCC TL1500 .P885 2020 (print) | LCC TL1500 (ebook) |
DDC 629.45001/9—dc23
LC record available at https://lccn.loc.gov/2020026901
LC ebook record available at https://lccn.loc.gov/2020026902

ISBN: 9781138339880 (hbk)
ISBN: 9780429440854 (ebk)

Typeset in Times
by codeMantra

"For my colleagues at NASA and beyond, from whom I am constantly learning. And always, for my family, who supports me in doing challenging and meaningful work." – Lauren Blackwell Landon, PhD

"For the BHP group at Johnson Space Center, and in particular for the women of OpPsy who work tirelessly to support our astronauts." – Kelley J. Slack, PhD

"To my countless 'team science teammates' who have made the journey (so far) impactful, fulfilling and fun – my gratitude and admiration!" – Eduardo Salas, PhD

Contents

Preface xi
Editors xv
Contributors xvii
List of Acronyms and Abbreviations xxiii

Chapter 1 Ethical Considerations Associated with Exploration and Analog Environment Research 1

Kristen Pryor, Cliff Haimann, and Eric Dunleavy

Chapter 2 Psychological Selection for Extreme Environments 17

Lacey L. Schmidt and Annette C. Spychalski

Chapter 3 Out Of This World Jobs: Alternative Work Analysis and Validation Methods in Extreme Environments 35

Laura Galarza, Julie A. Steinke, and Jamie D. Barrett

Chapter 4 Applying Research-Based Training Principles: Toward Crew-Centered, Mission-Oriented Space Flight Training 63

Donna L. Dempsey and Immanuel Barshi

Chapter 5 Team Training for Long-Duration Space Exploration: A Look Ahead at the Coming Challenges 81

Natalie Croitoru, Tiffany M. Bisbey, and Eduardo Salas

Chapter 6 Mitigating the Impact of Communication Delay 101

Ute Fischer and Kathleen Mosier

Chapter 7 Behavioral Health Adaptation in ICE Environments: Process and Countermeasures for NASA Astronauts 115

Walter E. Sipes, Kelley J. Slack, and Gary E. Beven

Chapter 8 Space Flight Operational Psychological Support for Astronauts and Their Families 133

Jessica L. Hughlett, Elizabeth T. Turner, Kelley J. Slack, and Walter E. Sipes

Chapter 9 Extremely Stressed and Extremely Bored: Team Self-Maintenance in Long-Duration Space Exploration 155

Deborah DiazGranados, Jessica L. Wildman, and Michael T. Curtis

Chapter 10 Working in Space: Managing Transitions between Tasks 179

Jessica Mesmer-Magnus, Alina Lungeanu, Alexa Harris, Ashley Niler, Leslie A. DeChurch, and Noshir Contractor

Chapter 11 The Human Factors of Design for Spaceflight 205

Kritina Holden, Gordon Vos, and Jessica J. Marquez

Chapter 12 Introduction: The Power of Higher-Order Goals for Space Exploration 225

Kathryn E. Keeton and David Musson

Chapter 13 Behavioral Health and Performance for Long-Duration Missions 235

Christopher F. Flynn

Chapter 14 The Canadian Space Agency and Human Behavior and Performance in Space: Historical Overview 253

Leena Tomi and Marvin Lange

Chapter 15 Astronaut Selection at JAXA – from the BHP Perspective 267

Natsuhiko Inoue

Chapter 16 Selected Russian Contributions to Spaceflight 279

Part 1: Russian Psychological Support, Monitoring, and Inflight Studies 280
Vadim Gushin, Dmitry Shved, Alla Vinokhodova, Yuriy Bubeev, Daria Schastlivtceva, Anna Yusupova, Olga Karpova, and Angelina Chekalina

Part 2: Russian Space Experiment "CONTENT" 284
Vadim Gushin, Dmitry Shved, Anna Yusupova, Natalya Supolkina, and Angelina Chekalina

Part 3: Russian Space Experiment "INTERACTIONS-2" 289
Vadim Gushin, Alla Vinokhodova, Anna Yusupova, and Gro Sandal

Part 4: Russian Space Experiment "PILOT-T" 293
Daria Schastlivtceva, Tatyana Kotrovskaya, Yuriy Bubeev, Alexander Dudukin, Angelina Chekalina, and Bernd Johannes

Chapter 17 The Blue Dot 301
Don Pettit

Index 305

Preface

INTRODUCTION TO VOLUME 2: EXTREME APPLICATION

During an expedition, astronauts cannot take a break from their workplace by returning home at the end of a challenging day. They live, work, and breathe in the same confined and extreme location, and the reason they are in that location is due to their work. Because of this, we have attempted to present these volumes more from an industrial-organizational (IO), or work, psychology model rather than a clinical model. One key distinction between the two models is the focus on the workplace. A second key distinction involves how people, in this case astronauts, are viewed and the approach taken to provide support. With the more traditional clinical approach, the underlying model is the medical one – healing the ill. Prevention, under the medical model, is for the purpose of avoiding future illness.

In contrast, IOs assume a normal, healthy workforce and from there, we seek to improve work, productivity, and performance. Part of that involves prevention, mitigation, and treatment, but the underlying lens through which IOs operate varies fundamentally from that historically used by clinicians. To that end, we hope we have succeeded in presenting these volumes with an emphasis on how to improve what is already strong rather than from a perspective of fixing what is broken. We strove to focus on how to enhance the strengths astronauts already bring to their missions and included insights into the medical model where necessary.

The overarching goal for the space program, regardless of country, is one of exploration, science, and discovery. This goal meets a basic human need to investigate the unknown. At NASA, and other space agencies, an even deeper, more basic goal than that of exploration is the goal of crew safety. Above all other goals, we work to keep the astronauts and cosmonauts safe. The majority of directorates at NASA achieve this by focusing on the physical health of the astronaut, be it designing more effective shields from radiation, developing tastier food with a longer nutritional shelf life, or testing a rocket launch system to get humans beyond low Earth orbit once again.

For psychologists and those involved closely with the crews, the psychological well-being of the crew is no less important than the physical health and often is more important. The interrelationship and interdependencies between psychological and physical health means that each is a necessary but not sufficient component of overall well-being. People can be in poor physical health yet in good psychosocial health. And we can have the opposite. But for an extreme trip with high-risk outcomes, one cannot be subservient to the other. A strong emotional self can overcome physical impairments that someone with a poor emotional self will not be able to. Taking care of the psychological health of crews, individually and collectively, is at least as critical as physical health. The two are intertwined, interdependent, and cannot always be separated.

Throughout all chapters in both volumes, the unremitting theme is the psychological well-being of individual crewmembers and the crew as a whole. This volume

Extreme Application focuses on what is being provided now to ensure their psychological well-being.

—**Kelley, Lauren, & Eduardo**

CHAPTER OVERVIEWS

We open this volume with an exploration of the ethics of human spaceflight. Pryor, Haimann, and Dunleavy provide a refresher on ethical guidelines associated with research with human subjects and compares those with NASA's current guidelines for human research. An issue, they point out, is that astronauts are employees and as such are not voluntary participants. They investigate the ramifications of this distinction from an ethical point of view.

Most of this volume effectively follows the life cycle of an astronaut, from selection, to training, to mission support before, during, and after spaceflight. Selecting astronauts begins the cycle. Schmidt and Spychalski detail the history of the psychological and psychiatric aspects of selecting astronauts, discussing how the process has evolved over the years, in part in response to the job of astronaut changing. Lessons they learned during their years selecting astronauts provide a basis for recommendations on strengthening the process.

Galarza, Barrett, and Steinke continue the discussion of challenges associated with astronaut selection. They summarize the last two job analyses and the anticipated changes to the work of astronauts that prompted them. Post job analyses, changes were made to the psychological and psychiatric aspects of astronaut selection. These require revalidating the system, which is difficult considering the small sample size, the infrequency of astronaut selection, and the lack of criterion data. They end with an examination of alternative means of achieving this validation.

Once selected, astronauts and cosmonauts spend years training before even being eligible to be assigned to a mission and then years more training for a specific mission. Dempsey and Barshi review the siloed nature of training of required technical skills that have been used to date. With long-duration exploration missions (LDEM), particularly to Mars, spaceflight training will need to shift to a crew-centered, mission-oriented design. This design calls for technical skills being introduced to a crew within the context of use. They provide vignettes on how training for Mars might look and discuss associated applied training principles.

Shifting more to the training of non-technical skills required for spaceflight, Croitoru, Bisbey, and Salas examine the challenges associated with training teams for LDEM. While much is known about teams training, less is known about how this knowledge will transfer to the LDEM context. They discuss the traditional teams training paradigm and LDEM implications for training content, context, delivery, and tools.

Compounding challenges of training a diverse, international crew for a novel mission is the ever-lengthening delay in communication that will occur as the spacecraft travels away from Earth. Fischer and Mosier begin their chapter with a telling quotation from an astronaut recalling how communication between crew and Mission Control Center (MCC) failed during a communication delay simulated during

Preface   xiii

NEEMO-16, a spaceflight analog environment. Fischer and Mosier highlight three aspects of the communication process that will require support during time-delayed conditions. They provide insight into lessons learned from development and evaluation of a communication protocol aimed at facilitating asynchronous communication.

Across the three chapters on training, there is an emphasis on the team, be it crew or the larger crew-ground system. It becomes apparent how a team functions will impact mission success. Thus, training the team, and not just the individual, becomes critical.

The next section focuses on supporting astronauts and crews. The first two chapters, written by current and former members of the Behavioral Health and Performance (BHP) group, relay NASA's approach to support.

Sipes, Slack, and Beven elucidate how the BHP group meets its mandate to protect the behavioral health and thus the performance of astronauts. They discuss the history and future of behavioral health support provided over the life of an astronaut.

Hughlett, Turner, Slack, and Sipes continue by detailing the operational psychology (OpPsy) support BHP offers to astronauts who are assigned to a mission. OpPsy is responsible for providing nonclinical countermeasures targeted towards supporting the psychological well-being of an astronaut. Countermeasures are tailored to the needs of each astronaut. How and what is provided will necessarily change when missions leave low Earth orbit.

The next three chapters focus on leveraging technology to provide better tools and support to spaceflight crews. The nature of a mission to Mars will force the crew to be more autonomous. Self-maintenance, which is currently done by the various mission control centers, will fall to the crew itself.

DiazGranados, Wildman, and Curtis provide findings and recommendations based on an operational assessment conducted with spaceflight experts. Mesmer-Magnus, Lungeanu, Harris, Niler, DeChurch, and Contractor examine factors affecting the perception of work and the ease of task transitions during spaceflight. They present CREST, a computer model of task switching designed to improve the design of astronaut schedules.

Human factors is a critical component in designing spaceflight systems that support crewmembers. Holden, Marquez, and Vos, examine research of human and environmental factors that impact the design and efficacy of space-based human-systems.

This volume then explores how other space agencies protect their crewmembers' psychological health. Keeton and Musson frame these chapters with a discussion on the power of higher-order goals to align values and actions. They set the stage for us to understand that regardless of the seemingly disparate nature of the chapters in this section, higher-order goals of exploration and well-being are a common element linking the efforts across the space agencies. A perspective further confirmed by the prevalence of collaborative international spaceflight research and evidenced by the inclusion of two European psychologists as authors within the Russian chapter.

Chris Flynn provides insights into the key role NASA's BHP group and its larger interagency counterpart, the Spaceflight Human Behavioral Health and Performance Group (SHBPWG), have had in protecting astronauts' psychological well-being. Each space agency's equivalent to NASA's BHP group is a member of SHBPWG and part of developing and advancing operational requirements and programs crucial to ensure the behavioral health and performance of astronauts and thus mission success.

Tomi and Lange provide an overview of how the interagency working group focused on human behavior and performance came into being and the Canadian Space Agency's (CSA) role within it. They go on to discuss the CSA's approach to selection, training, and support (for both the astronaut and family).

Inoue of the Japan Aerospace Exploration Agency (JAXA) focuses on selecting Japanese astronauts. JAXA's process shares commonalities with other space agencies but demonstrates that national culture naturally influences the specifics of the selection process. He focuses on the last two selection cycles for Japanese astronauts and details a key difference between JAXA's approach and that of other space agencies.

In four parts, Gushin and his colleagues provide insight into the Russian inflight medical support focused on psychophysiological control, support, and research. Part one explains the factors of spaceflight that indicated a need for psychological support and describes types of support offered to cosmonauts. The remaining three parts summarize experiments on trends in cosmonaut communication ("CONTENT"), the existence of values specific to cosmonauts and astronauts ("INTERACTIONS-2"), and the effect of spaceflight on the reliability in cosmonaut performance ("PILOT-T").

We conclude the volume with astronaut Don Pettit, veteran of two International Space Station expeditions and one Shuttle expedition. He writes of the successes and failures of human exploration over time and the human urge to go where no one has gone before. This innate urge, he says, is one reason humans continue to survive. Expanding our presence to another planet will increase our species' chances of survival. Pettit ends with a poem that captures the essence of the hope and uncertainty of future exploration missions. His essay evokes a need to continue to new frontiers. A fitting end to this volume and to the beginning of the next chapter in space exploration.

Throughout the entire two volume set, we have seen again and again how critical psychological well-being is to mission success. From selecting the most psychologically fit, to training focused on maintaining well-being, through prevention of decrements to psychological well-being while on expedition—all couched within the understanding that further exploration of space is the goal. These volumes provide evidence that integral to every space agency's overarching goal of exploration is the psychological well-being of those involved in that exploration. No mission can succeed without selecting, training, and supporting the most psychologically fit of us to be those explorers. And integral to that is the evidence and experience provided by those best suited to psychological well-being at work – industrial-organizational psychologists, those best suited for creating environments promoting well-being – human factors psychologists, – and those best suited to psychological well-being in general – clinical psychologists and psychiatrists.

Editors

Lauren Blackwell Landon, PhD, is the Team Risk Discipline Scientist in the Human Factors and Behavioral Performance (HFBP) Element, a division of NASA's Human Research Program. She is also a scientist in the Behavioral Health & Performance (BHP) Laboratory at NASA's Lyndon B. Johnson Space Center. Her research is focused on teams in extreme environments, examining the influence of individual team-oriented characteristics, teamwork processes, and interdisciplinary areas (e.g., human factors, sleep/fatigue), as it affects team performance and functioning. Dr. Landon enjoys being a member of the award-winning NASA Astronaut Selection Team and training team skills to astronauts and flight controllers. She is also an adjunct assistant professor in the Department of Psychological Sciences at Rice University. She previously worked as an Organizational Development Consultant at the Department of Energy's Oak Ridge National Laboratory and as a human factors researcher for the Federal Aviation Administration's Civil Aerospace Medical Institute (FAA-CAMI). She has worked on projects funded by the U.S. Army, the U.S. Navy, the U.S. military's Special Forces, Defense Advanced Research Projects Agency (DARPA), and National Science Foundation (NSF), among other organizations. She earned all four of her degrees from the University of Oklahoma including a PhD in Industrial-Organizational Psychology.

Kelley J. Slack, PhD, joined the Science and Research team at Birkman International after almost 20 years working as part of the Behavioral Health and Performance group at NASA's Lyndon B. Johnson Space Center. There, her work centered on the psychological and psychiatric selection of astronauts. At Birkman, her work is focused on maintaining the scientific rigor of their assessments and leading research to further understand the complex relationships between personality and work. Dr. Slack studied behavioral sciences at London School of Economics and graduated with honors from Rice University with double majors in business and behavioral science. After gaining international and domestic business experience, she returned to school and earned her PhD in Industrial and Organizational Psychology from the University of Houston with a minor in Statistics. She is a licensed psychologist in the State of Texas.

Eduardo Salas, PhD, holds the Allyn R. and Gladys M. Cline Chair of Psychology and he is Chair of the Psychological Sciences Department at Rice University. Previously, he spent 15 years at the University of Central Florida, where he was University Trustee Chair and Pegasus Professor, and the Program Director for the Institute for Simulation & Training. He also spent 15 years at the Naval Air Warfare Center Training Systems Division (formerly Naval Training Systems Center). Dr. Salas has published numerous books and scientific articles in the fields of applied psychology and human factors. He has received research funding from many agencies across the government as well as acted as a consultant in industry. His award-winning research focuses on uncovering what facilitates teamwork and team effectiveness in organizations; how and why team training works; how to optimize simulation-based training; how to design, implement, and evaluate training and development systems, and generate evidence-based guidance for those in practice. He is a fellow of the Human Factors and Ergonomics Society, the American Psychological Association, the Society for Industrial and Organizational Psychology, and the Association for Psychological Science, among others, and is one of the most cited researchers in the field of applied psychology.

Contributors

Clayton C. Anderson, MS
NASA Astronaut (retired)
Astro Clay, LLC
Houston, Texas

Brennan Antone, BS
Department of Industrial Engineering
 and Management Sciences
Northwestern University
Evanston, Illinois

Jamie D. Barrett, PhD
Federal Aviation Administration
Oklahoma City, Oklahoma

Immanuel Barshi, PhD
Human Systems Integration Division
NASA's Ames Research Center
Mountain View, California

Suzanne T. Bell, PhD
Behavioral Health & Performance
 Laboratory
KBR/NASA's Lyndon B. Johnson
 Space Center
Houston, Texas
and
Psychology Department
DePaul University
Chicago, Illinois

Gary E. Beven, MD
Space and Occupational
 Medicine Branch
NASA's Lyndon B. Johnson
 Space Center
Houston, Texas

Tiffany M. Bisbey, PhD
Department of Psychological Sciences
Rice University
Houston, Texas

Yuriy Bubeev, MD
SRC RF – Institute of Bio-Medical
 Problems of RAS
Moscow, Russia

C. Shawn Burke, PhD
Institute for Simulation and Training
University of Central Florida
Orlando, Florida

Bryan J. Caldwell, PhD
Research Operations and Integration
Human Health Operations Division
KBR/NASA's Lyndon B. Johnson
 Space Center
Houston, Texas

Dorothy R. Carter, PhD
Department of Psychology
The University of Georgia
Athens, Georgia

Angelina Chekalina, PhD
SRC RF – Institute of Bio-Medical
 Problems of RAS
Moscow, Russia

Noshir S. Contractor, PhD
Department of Industrial Engineering
 and Management Sciences
Northwestern University
Evanston, Illinois

Natalie Croitoru, BA
University of North Carolina at
 Chapel Hill
Chapel Hill, North Carolina

Ronita L. Cromwell, PhD
Baylor College of Medicine
Houston, Texas

E. Vincent Cross II, PhD
TRACLabs
Webster, Texas

Michael T. Curtis, PhD
Bonsai Institute, LLC
Richmond, Virginia

Leslie A. DeChurch, PhD
Department of Communication Studies
Northwestern University
Evanston, Illinois

Donna L. Dempsey, PhD
Human System Engineering &
  Integration Division
NASA's Lyndon B. Johnson
  Space Center
Houston, Texas

Deborah DiazGranados, PhD
School of Medicine
Virginia Commonwealth University
Richmond, Virginia

James E. Driskell, PhD
Florida Maxima Corporation
Orlando, Florida

Tripp Driskell, PhD
Florida Maxima Corporation
Orlando, Florida

Alexander Dudukin
SRC RF – Institute of Bio-Medical
  Problems of RAS
Moscow, Russia

Eric Dunleavy, PhD
DCI Consulting Group
Washington, DC

Jennifer Feitosa, PhD
Department of Psychology
Claremont McKenna College
Claremont, California

Ute Fischer, PhD
Georgia Institute of Technology
Atlanta, Georgia

Christopher F. Flynn, MD
Federal Aviation Administration
Washington, DC

Laura Galarza, PhD
Universidad de Puerto Rico
San Juan, Puerto Rico

Vadim Gushin, MD, PhD
SRC RF – Institute of Bio-Medical
  Problems of RAS
Moscow, Russia

Cliff Haimann, PhD
DCI Consulting Group
Washington, DC

Alexa Harris, MA
Department of Communication
  Studies
Northwestern University
Evanston, Illinois

Alice F. Healy, PhD
Department of Psychology &
  Neuroscience
University of Colorado Boulder
Boulder, Colorado

Kritina Holden, PhD
Human Systems Engineering and
  Integration Division
Leidos/NASA's Lyndon B. Johnson
  Space Center
Houston, Texas

Jessica L. Hughlett, BS
Behavioral Health and Performance
  Group
KBR/NASA's Lyndon B. Johnson
  Space Center
Houston, Texas

Contributors

Natsuhiko Inoue, PhD
Japan Aerospace Exploration Agency
Chofu, Tokyo, Japan

Bernd Johannes, PhD
Institute of Aerospace Medicine
 (German Aerospace Center)
Cologne, Germany

Justin M. Jones, MS
Department of Psychology
The University of Georgia
Athens, Georgia

Olga Karpova
SRC RF – Institute of Bio-Medical
 Problems of RAS
Moscow, Russia

Sadaf Kazi, PhD
Armstrong Institute for Patient Safety
 and Quality
The Johns Hopkins University School
 of Medicine
Baltimore, Maryland

Kathryn E. Keeton, PhD
University of Texas at San Antonio;
 Minerva Work Solutions
San Antonio, Texas

Deanna M. Kennedy, PhD
School of Business
University of Washington Bothell
Bothell, Washington

Salar Khaleghzadegan, BS
Armstrong Institute for Patient Safety
 and Quality
The Johns Hopkins University School
 of Medicine
Baltimore, Maryland

Molly P. Kilcullen, MS
Department of Psychological Sciences
Rice University
Houston, Texas

James A. Kole, PhD
Department of Psychological Sciences
University of Northern Colorado
Greeley, Colorado

Tatyana Kotrovskaya, PhD
SRC RF – Institute of Bio-Medical
 Problems of RAS
Moscow, Russia

Lauren Blackwell Landon, PhD
Behavioral Health & Performance
 Laboratory
Biomedical Research and
 Environmental Sciences Division
KBR/NASA's Lyndon B. Johnson
 Space Center
Houston, Texas

Marvin Lange, CD, MD, FRCPC
Canadian Space Agency
Longueuil, Quebec, Canada

Jamie Levy, PhD
The Group for Organizational
 Effectiveness (gOE)
Albany, New York

Alina Lungeanu, PhD
Department of Communication
 Studies
Northwestern University
Evanston, Illinois

Jessica J. Marquez, PhD
Human Systems Integration Division
NASA's Ames Research Center
Mountain View, California

John E. Mathieu, PhD
Department of Management
University of Connecticut
Storrs, Connecticut

M. Travis Maynard, PhD
Department of Management
Colorado State University
Fort Collins, Colorado

Jessica Mesmer-Magnus, PhD
Cameron School of Business
University of North Carolina Wilmington
Wilmington, North Carolina

Justine Moavero, MS
Institute for Simulation and Training
University of Central Florida
Orlando, Florida

Kathleen Mosier, PhD
Psychology Department
San Francisco State University
San Francisco, California

David Musson, MD, PhD
McMaster University and Northern
   Ontario School of Medicine
Sudbury, Ontario, Canada

Joseph Neigut, BS
Space Medicine Operations Division
NASA's Lyndon B. Johnson
   Space Center
Houston, Texas

Ashley Niler, PhD
Department of Communication
   Sciences
Northwestern University
Evanston, Illinois

Jensine Paoletti, MS
Department of Psychological Sciences
Rice University
Houston, Texas

Jacob G. Pendergraft, BS
Department of Psychology
The University of Georgia
Athens, Georgia

Don Pettit, PhD
NASA Astronaut
NASA's Lyndon B. Johnson
   Space Center
Houston, Texas

Kristen Pryor, MS
DCI Consulting Group
Washington, DC

Peter G. Roma, PhD
Behavioral Health & Performance
   Laboratory
Biomedical Research and
   Environmental Sciences Division
KBR/NASA's Lyndon B. Johnson
   Space Center
Houston, Texas

Michael A. Rosen, PhD
Armstrong Institute for Patient Safety
   and Quality
The Johns Hopkins University School
   of Medicine
Baltimore, Maryland

Eduardo Salas, PhD
Department of Psychological Sciences
Rice University
Houston, Texas

Gro Sandal, PhD
Department of Psychosocial Science
University of Bergen
Bergen, Norway

Daria Schastlivtceva
SRC RF – Institute of Bio-Medical
   Problems of RAS
Moscow, Russia

Contributors

Aaron Schecter, PhD
Department of Management
 Information Systems
The University of Georgia
Athens, Georgia

Lacey L. Schmidt, PhD
Minerva Work Solutions;
 PLLC/University of Houston
Houston, Texas

Vivian I. Schneider, PhD
Institute of Cognitive Sciences
University of Colorado Boulder
Boulder, Colorado

Julia M. Schorn, BS
Behavioral Health & Performance
 Laboratory
Biomedical Research and
 Environmental Sciences Division
KBR/NASA's Lyndon B. Johnson
 Space Center
University of California – Los Angeles
Los Angeles, California

Marissa Shuffler, PhD
Department of Psychology
Clemson University
Clemson, South Carolina

Dmitry Shved, PhD
SRC RF – Institute of Bio-Medical
 Problems of RAS
Moscow, Russia

Walter E. Sipes, PhD
Aerospace Psychology Consultants
Tucson, Arizona

Kelley J. Slack, PhD
Birkman International/Minerva Work
 Solutions PLLC
Houston, Texas

Annette C. Spychalski, PhD
ACS People Development

Julie A. Steinke, PhD
The MITRE Corporation
McLean, Virginia

Natalya Supolkina
SRC RF – Institute of Bio-Medical
 Problems of RAS
Moscow, Russia

Scott I. Tannenbaum, PhD
The Group for Organizational
 Effectiveness (gOE)
Albany, New York

Leena Tomi, MS, MA
Canadian Space Agency
Longueuil, Quebec, Canada

Hayley M. Trainer, MS
Department of Psychology
The University of Georgia
Athens, Geogia

Elizabeth T. Turner
KBR/NASA's Lyndon B. Johnson
 Space Center
Houston, Texas

Alla Vinokhodova, PhD
SRC RF – Institute of Bio-Medical
 Problems of RAS
Moscow, Russia

Gordon Vos, PhD
Human Systems Engineering and
 Integration Division
NASA's Lyndon B. Johnson
 Space Center
Houston, Texas

Jessica L. Wildman, PhD
Florida Institute of Technology
Melbourne, Florida

Anna Yusupova, PhD
SRC RF – Institute of Bio-Medical
  Problems of RAS
Moscow, Russia

List of Acronyms and Abbreviations

ABM	Agent-based model
AERA	American Educational Research Association
AMB	Astronaut Medical Board
ANAM	Automated Neurological Assessment Metrics
AO	Order of Australia
APA	American Psychological Association
ASB	Astronaut Selection Board
ASCAN	Astronaut candidate
ASG	Astronaut Spouses Group
ATTIC	Astronaut Team Training in Canada
AWAM	Alternative work analysis methods
BASALT	Biologic Analog Science Associated with Lava Terrains
BHP	Behavioral Health and Performance
BHPG	Behavioral Health and Performance Group
BP	Blood pressure
CAP	Contingency Action Plan
CAPCOM	Capsule communicator
CAST	Crew Autonomous Scheduling Test
CATP ITP	Canadian Aerospace Training Project International Training Programs
CAVES	Cooperative Adventure for Valuing and Exercising
CCD	Cursor control device
CCP	Crew Care Packages
CDE	Crew Discretionary Events
CDR	Commander
CMO	Crew medical officer
Col-CC	Columbus Control Center
CP	Core Panel
CREST	Crew Recommender for Effectively Switching Task
CSA	Canadian Space Agency
CSTR	Complex space-time reaction
CTA	Cognitive task analysis
DLR	German Aerospace Center
DNA	Deoxyribonucleic acid
DND	Canadian Department of National Defense
DO	Doctor of osteopathic medicine
DRM	Design reference mission
ECG	Electrocardiograms
EEP	Extreme environment positions

EPR	Engine pressure ratio
ESA	European Space Agency
EVA	Extra-vehicular activities (or spacewalk)
FMT	Fatigue Management Team
FOD	Flight Operations Directorate
FSE	Flight Systems Engineer
FSO	Family Support Office
FY	Fiscal year
g	Gravity
GCTC	Gagarin Cosmonaut Training Center
GIFT	Generalized intelligent framework for tutoring
GMT	Greenwich Mean Time
HabCom	Habitat communicator
HBP	Human behavior and performance
HCD	Human-Centered Design
HERA	Human Exploration Research Analog
HFBP	Human Factors and Behavioral Performance
HIDP	Human Integration Design Processes
HSI	Human Systems Integration
HI-SEAS	Hawai'i Space Exploration Analog and Simulation
HITL	Human-in-the-Loop
HTV	H-II Transfer Vehicle "KOUNOTORI"
IBMP	Institute for Biomedical Problems
ICE	Isolated, confined, and extreme
IM	Intramuscular
IOM	Institute of Medicine
IP	Internet protocol
IRB	Institutional Review Board
IRP	In-flight Resource Planning
iSHORT	Space Habitability Observation Reporting Tool
ISO	International Organization for Standardization
ISS	International Space Station
ISSP	International Space Station Program
ITCB	International Training Control Board
ITP	International Training Program
JAXA	Japanese Aerospace Exploration Agency
JCV	Job Component Validity
JEM	Japanese Experiment Module "KIBO"
JRM	Job requirements matrices
JRM	Job Requirement Matrix
JSC	Johnson Space Center
KSAO	Knowledge, skills, abilities and other characteristics
LCC	Launch Control Center
LDM	Long-duration mission
LDSE	Long-duration space exploration
LEO	Low Earth orbit

LSF	Long spaceflight
MCC	Mission Control Center
MCOP	Multilateral Crew Operations Panel
MMOP	Multilateral Medical Operations Panel
MMPB	Multilateral Medical Policy Board
MMSEV	Multi-mission space exploration vehicle
MPCV	Multi-purpose crew vehicle
MS	Mission specialist
MSMB	Multilateral Space Medicine Board
MTM	Multiple teams membership
MTS	Multiteam system
MTV	Mars Transfer Vehicle
NASA	National Aeronautics and Space Administration
NASDA	National Space Development Agency of Japan
NCME	National Council on Measurement in Education
NEEMO	NASA Extreme Environment Mission Operations project
NHV	Net Habitable Volume
NOAA	National Oceanic and Atmospheric Association
NOLS	National Outdoor Leadership School
NRC	National Research Council of Canada
NSBRI	National Space Biomedical Research Institute
NSEEV	Noticing salience effort expectancy value
NTRS	NASA Technical Reports Server
O*NET	Occupational Information Network
OSM	Operational Space Medicine Program
PAQ	Position Analysis Questionnaire
PFC	Private family conference
PLRP	Pavilion Lake Research Project
PO	*per os* (by mouth)
PPC	Private psychological conferences
PPRS	Psychiatric/Psychological Review Subcommittee
PSPA	Personal self-perception and attitudes
PWT	Posterior wall thickness
RATS	Research and Technology Studies
RMSSD	Root mean square of successive differences between normal heartbeats
RS	Russian segment
RSA	Russian Space Agency
RSP	Respiratory Support Pack
SDM	Short-duration missions
SE	Space experiment
SFTL	Single-flow-to-launch
SHBPWG	Spaceflight Human Behavior and Performance Working Group
SME	Subject matter expert
STS	Space transportation system
SV	Synthetic validity

SVMF	Space Vehicle Mockup Facility
SVMR	Simple visual motor response
TCOUP	Russian Mission Control Center
TKSC	Tsukuba Space Center
TRISH	Translational Research Institute for Space Health
TT	Test transportability
USAF	United States Air Force
VG	Validity Generalization
WMA	World Medical Association
μ-g	Microgravity

1 Ethical Considerations Associated with Exploration and Analog Environment Research

Kristen Pryor, Cliff Haimann, and Eric Dunleavy
DCI Consulting Group

CONTENTS

Introduction 1
    Evolution of Ethical Guidelines for Research Using Human Subjects 2
Existing Ethical Guidelines 3
    Nuremberg Code 3
    Declaration of Helsinki 3
    The Belmont Report 4
    Institutional Review Board at NASA 6
    Applying Ethical Guidelines to Human Exploration and Analog Research Environments 6
    Employees Versus Volunteer Research Subjects 7
    Sufficiency of Participant-focused Ethical Guidelines 9
    Sufficiency of Beneficence – or Risk/Benefit Analysis – Focused Guidance 11
Conclusion 13
References 14

INTRODUCTION

The journey of human discovery and exploration can be traced back as far as records of humans exist. While exploration is undertaken by all mobile animal species, humans engage in this activity with significantly higher frequency (Hughes, 1997; Kidd & Hayden, 2015). Evolutionary anthropologists have linked this apparently innate desire to understand and explore our environment to a gene variant possessed by approximately 20% of the population (Weaver, 2015), although the desire for exploration cannot manifest without the means and ability to do so.

Through the beginning of the 20th century, exploration involved discovering, observing, and mapping new lands and surface areas of oceans. During the

European Age of Discovery or Age of Exploration (15th–17th centuries) the "last frontier on our planet" – the oceans – was sailed and charted at an exponentially higher rate than ever before (Granath, 2015). Despite this increase and the technological advances since the mid-20th century that have provided the means for even more robust exploration of deep sea environments, the oceans, which comprise 70% of the earth's surface, remain mostly unobserved and unexplored (National Oceanic and Atmospheric Association [NOAA], 2018).

Conversely, the vast majority of the earth's land had been explored by the turn of the 20th century, and explorers began to turn skyward for the next challenge. Individuals participating in these feats accepted the hazards and risks, with Charles Lindbergh stating "I believe the risks I take are justified by the sheer love of the life I lead" (Granath, 2015). Within a relatively minimal timeframe, humans advanced from the initial aviation pioneers (e.g., Lindbergh's flight from New York to Paris in 1927) to testing the boundaries of flight at the edges of the earth's atmosphere (e.g., the German Rocket Team in the late 1940s). The dawn of official human space exploration followed shortly after, in 1961, when Yuri Gagarin circled the earth for 108 minutes.

Evaluating the ethics of an activity humans have been seeking out and engaging in for thousands of years is at once a deceivingly simple and incredibly complex task. As our means and ability to explore more extreme environments have increased through technological advances, so have our obligations for critically examining the proposed undertakings before proceeding with endeavors that inherently risk human life. The simplicity of this evaluation lies in the clear ethical guidelines that have been established and promulgated for research involving human subjects, resulting from lessons learned through unethical endeavors (e.g., Nazi experiments, the Tuskegee Syphilis Experiment). The complexity lies in determining how to analyze the various potential risks, costs, and benefits to determine if the proposed endeavor sufficiently outweighs risks and costs with benefits. At the outset, we will note that this endeavor was recently undertaken in part by a cross-disciplinary set of experts in the specific context of long duration and exploration spaceflights, resulting in ethics, principles, responsibilities, and a decision framework for these missions from a health perspective (*Health Standards;* Institute of Medicine [IOM], 2014); efforts have been made to avoid excessive repetition here, although there is an overlap. Below is a primer and refresh on the ethical guidelines and requirements for research involving human subjects followed by a discussion on the application of those guidelines and requirements to humans in exploration and analog research environments.

EVOLUTION OF ETHICAL GUIDELINES FOR RESEARCH USING HUMAN SUBJECTS

After the end of the Holocaust, the world had to face the reality that medical doctors in Germany had performed experiments on human subjects that were often cruel in nature. Unfortunately, at that time, there was little consensus in the scientific community regarding what constituted legitimate research as opposed to illegitimate, inhumane experimentation. During the latter part of the 20th century, scientists collaborated to formally codify standards that could guide ethical research, and these standards have since been applied to medicine and the social sciences; however, now as humanity's reach is extending further into space, new questions about the ethics of extreme environment research are arising, and researchers inevitably have to consider (1) whether this research can be evaluated using current ethical guidelines and (2) whether new ethical standards are required given the unique nature of emerging research streams (e.g., a manned trip to Mars).

EXISTING ETHICAL GUIDELINES

Nuremberg Code

The medical experimentation performed by the Nazis during World War II and the Holocaust greatly shaped ethical research standards. The Nazi's influence on medical ethics and research can partially be traced to the military tribunals that occurred after the war ended. In the case of USA vs Karl Brandt et al., multiple German doctors had to defend the actions they had undertaken in the concentration camps, which included human experimentation. According to these defendants, their experiments had not deviated from existing American and German research practices, and they argued that there was no clear differentiation between legal and illegal experimentation. This argument prompted two American doctors, Andrew Ivy and Leo Alexander, to articulate six points that defined ethical research. The military tribunal overseeing the case expanded upon these points to create ten, which were labeled as the Nuremberg Code (n.d.a) and are delineated in Table 1.1. This document would influence the ethics of research throughout the remaining part of the 20th century.

This Code focused heavily on medical research as opposed to psychological research, but many of the Code's tenets, such as voluntary consent and the ability to end an experiment, are the core elements of modern social science research standards, which are described later.

Declaration of Helsinki

The World Medical Association (WMA) added to international dialogue on research ethics when it created the Declaration of Helsinki in 1964. The document has been revised during the latter part of the 20th century, and the WMA made its most recent adjustments in 2013. NASA views this Declaration as a foundational document guiding research practices (Kovo, 2018). The Declaration is intended for the medical community, but many of its central provisions relate to research in various fields. Of note, the document stresses the importance of creating and submitting a detailed research protocol that describes factors such as affiliation, funding, sponsors, and conflicts of interest to a research ethics committee that should evaluate these for inappropriate research practices. The WMA emphasized that detailed assessments of risks and benefits must precede research. Echoing points from the Nuremberg code, the Declaration also described the significance of informed consent, which means that competent human subjects have to be informed of a study's goals along with

TABLE 1.1
Ten points of Nuremburg Code (Nuremberg Code, n.d.b)

S.No.	Nuremburg Code Points
1.	The voluntary consent of the human subject is absolutely essential.
2.	The experiment should be such as to yield fruitful results for the good of society, unprocurable by other methods or means of study, and not random and unnecessary in nature.
3.	The experiment should be so designed and based on the results of animal experimentation and a knowledge of the natural history of the disease or other problems under study that the anticipated results will justify the performance of the experiment.
4.	The experiment should be so conducted as to avoid all unnecessary physical and mental suffering and injury.
5.	No experiment should be conducted, where there is an a priori reason to believe that death or disabling injury will occur; except, perhaps, in those experiments where the experimental physicians also serve as subjects.
6.	The degree of risk to be taken should never exceed that determined by the humanitarian importance of the problem to be solved by the experiment.
7.	Proper preparations should be made and adequate facilities provided to protect the experimental subject against even remote possibilities of injury, disability, or death.
8.	The experiment should be conducted only by scientifically qualified persons. The highest degree of skill and care should be required through all stages of the experiment of those who conduct or engage in the experiment.
9.	During the course of the experiment, the human subject should be at liberty to bring the experiment to an end, if he has reached the physical or mental state, where continuation of the experiment seemed to him to be impossible.
10.	During the course of the experiment, the scientist in charge must be prepared to terminate the experiment at any stage, if he has probable cause to believe, in the exercise of the good faith, superior skill, and careful judgement required of him, that a continuation of the experiment is likely to result in injury, disability, or death to the experimental subject.

the potential risks and benefits (https://www.wma.net/what-we-do/medical-ethics/declaration-of-helsinki/).

THE BELMONT REPORT

The National Research Act of 1974 created the National Commission for the Protection of Human Subjects in Biomedical and Behavioral Research, which codified its work in the Belmont Report (HEW, 1979). This document described standards for ethical research practices, and it became the foundation for (1) research-related regulation in the United States and (2) the current procedures organizations use to review research protocols (Buelow, 2011). Moreover, unlike previous ethical guidance, the report did not have a focus that was clearly medical in nature. It stressed three core principles that could guide research in a wide range of fields: Respect for Persons, Beneficence, and Justice.

Respect for Persons

According to the report: "Respect for persons incorporates at least two ethical convictions: first, that individuals should be treated as autonomous agents, and second, that persons with diminished autonomy are entitled to protection." An autonomous person is capable of thinking about personal goals and acting in accordance with personal decisions. In order to respect such research subjects, a scientist cannot withhold information or deny a person the right to act on decisions. For those who are not capable of self-determination (potentially because of age or cognitive impairment), ethical standards require protecting them from harm.

This principle is particularly important for the concept of informed consent. Respecting individuals requires that human subjects are given the opportunity to decide what will happen to them. This can only occur if three elements are present. First, individuals must be provided with information about the research, such as the purpose, procedure, and potential risks and benefits. Second, research subjects must be able to comprehend the information that is provided to them. Research descriptions cannot be disorganized and must present research details at an appropriate level of complexity. Third, informed consent is possible only if research conditions are free of coercion or undue influence. Specifically, participants cannot be compelled to participate, and they cannot be presented with unreasonable rewards in return for compliance.

Beneficence

The second guiding principle outlined in the Belmont Report is Beneficence. As noted in the report: "Two general rules have been formulated as complementary expressions of beneficent actions in this sense: (1) do not harm and (2) maximize possible benefits and minimize possible harms." This principle requires researchers to consider not only the magnitude of a risk or negative event but also the probability that the event will occur. When discussing Beneficence, the report also notes that (1) brutal treatment of subjects cannot be justified, (2) risks should be reduced when possible, (3) the use of vulnerable populations needs to be thoroughly justified, and (4) risks and benefits need to be thoroughly described in the procedures that make up the informed consent process.

Justice

The final principle outlined in the Belmont Report is Justice, which addresses questions such as who should take part in research and who ought to benefit from it? This principle is particularly relevant to the selection of subjects for research. The report states that individuals should not receive potentially beneficial research because they are of means or in the good graces of researchers. Likewise, research involving risk should not be intended only for populations that are less fortunate. According to the report, certain disadvantaged groups (e.g., economically disadvantaged) should not consistently be used as research subjects because they are readily available in the setting where research occurs. Such individuals need to be "protected against the danger of being involved in research solely for administrative convenience, or because they are easy to manipulate as a result of their illness or socioeconomic condition."

INSTITUTIONAL REVIEW BOARD AT NASA

The Belmont Report and its central principles provide the ethical foundation for all of NASA's research. This report, in combination with Federal Regulations (Protection of Human Subjects, 2018), guides the mechanisms that NASA and others can use to review potential research and exploration endeavors. As the Agency notes on its website, the goal of its Institutional Review Board (IRB), which operates in accordance with the aforementioned federal regulations, is to review research to ensure the "ethical, safe, and equitable treatment of the subjects" (https://irb.nasa/gov/). Among other activities, this Board compares the risks of research to its benefits for the individual or society at large, identifies mechanisms that can reduce risks, and serves as the ethical committee that oversees all research. NASA specifically lists the three principles from the Belmont Report and its IRB ensures the four protections outlined in Table 1.2.

These direct references to the Belmont Report and its content demonstrate that the ethical implications of NASA's research and exploration can potentially be evaluated via the ethical standards that scientists have refined via the documents previously outlined.

APPLYING ETHICAL GUIDELINES TO HUMAN EXPLORATION AND ANALOG RESEARCH ENVIRONMENTS

Current exploration of the oceans and space are characterized by vastly different approaches compared with those of earlier explorers. One clear distinction is the use of analog research environments, particularly in the case of space exploration, to test specific scenarios, concepts, and technology in a more controlled yet similar environment prior to the intended space mission. Because no one analog (to date) can simulate all aspects of a human space mission, various analog environments have been established to simulate particular aspects of future missions. Another distinction

TABLE 1.2
Four Protections Ensured by NASA's IRB

S.No.	Protections
1.	Voluntary participation, without coercion in any form, and indicated by free and informed consent;
2.	Freedom for a subject to withdraw from an experiment at any time, for any reason, without penalty;
3.	An appropriate balance between potential benefits of the research to the subject or to society and the risks assumed by the subject;
4.	Fair procedures and outcomes in the selection of the research subjects.

relates to the nature and complexity of the technology required to undertake these endeavors – in that they are inherently extremely costly and new technologies require extensive testing and evaluation prior to use in operational environments. The most central and enduring alignment with earlier explorers is that humans who apply to participate in these endeavors (e.g., over 18,000 applications received for 14 or fewer NASA astronaut positions in the last open application period according to Lewin (2016)) are committed to the idea that benefits, both personally and for humanity more broadly, outweigh the very real risks, up to and including death.

Evaluating the ethics of human exploration and research in analog environments first requires determining the extent to which existing ethical guidelines sufficiently address the complexities involved in human exploration and analog research environments. Existing ethical guidelines and regulations require that, where humans are to be involved in research, several actions are taken. They further require those actions to have been independently reviewed and evaluated prior to implementation. NASA's IRB exists to ensure that research endeavors comport with the existing ethical guidelines and requirements, notably including:

- Establishing fair selection procedures for choosing research participants (Justice),
- Obtaining voluntary, informed consent to participate in the research (Respect for Persons), including:
  - Fully describing the research purpose, methods, potential risks and benefits,
  - Presenting the above such that the participant can comprehend the information, and
  - Avoiding coercion in any form
- Taking conspicuous efforts to maximize possible benefits and minimize possible harm (Beneficence), including:
  - Evaluating both the potential impact and probability of a risk or hazard,
  - Reducing, to the extent possible, the likelihood of risks, and
  - Ensuring the benefits outweigh the risks.

However, there are a number of nuances and questions involved in evaluating the sufficiency of the current ethical guidelines. First, what are the ethical implications associated with the fact that in many instances, astronauts voluntarily apply and are hired to take part in activities that may be risky (as opposed to simply being research volunteers)? Second, are the participant-focused requirements sufficient (e.g., requiring informed consent and fair selection) for NASA's endeavors? Third, to what extent are the beneficence-related requirements sufficiently defined for these endeavors? Finally, is there anything missing, from an ethical perspective, that should be considered?

EMPLOYEES VERSUS VOLUNTEER RESEARCH SUBJECTS

Astronauts straddle the line between research subjects and paid employees, and this fact impacts the ethical considerations that should be applied to human behavior in space. From one perspective, astronauts are paid employees who take part in work activities that could be quite dangerous; however, there are many other dangerous professions that individuals also consciously choose to enter (e.g., law enforcement, firefighting, logging, fishing, and the military). From this point of view, the aforementioned Belmont Principles would not often need to be applied to astronauts in the performance of their duties, just as they are likely not often applied to firefighters or loggers.

Even if astronauts should simply be treated similarly to those in all dangerous professions, NASA still adheres to the principles espoused by the Belmont Report as it works with these employees.[1] First, given the legal framework and requirements around recruitment and selection in the United States, arguably the Justice prong still holds for astronauts (e.g., fair selection process). Further, the extensive training required before being considered, let alone selected for a mission, indicates that the Respect for Persons prong would also hold (e.g., astronaut candidates are informed of the potential risks and benefits, to the extent they are known, and spend years gaining an in-depth understanding of these). Despite the fact that astronauts receive payment, they only make about half as much as a commercial airline pilot despite greater stress, risk, and effort required (Howell, 2017); this would tend to negate an argument that inappropriate rewards (i.e., pay) may act as coercion to participate. Finally, before money is allotted to fund a given exploration mission, there is extensive effort to quantify and demonstrate the expected benefits, risks, and costs, as well as associated research to identify and mitigate risks to the extent possible (see Kaplan & Mikes, 2012; Managing Strategy Risks – Independent experts); thus, the Beneficence prong holds as well.

However, as a result of their employment, astronauts also have plenty of opportunities to become research participants in medical and psychological experiments. This is one differentiator from other careers that also pose risk. Another important differentiator for astronauts, especially those under consideration for long duration spaceflight, involves the ability to withdraw from research. Although many of the other positions with inherent risk include an opportunity for individuals to end the employment at will (e.g., logger, firefighter), this may not be possible for astronauts because even those in low Earth orbit or shorter duration missions cannot easily return to earth if they decide that they no longer want to perform the job. Further, while an astronaut may choose to avoid voluntary participation in research or decide to cease active participation, personal medical data and monitoring information (e.g., video) are still gathered for the duration of the mission. Researchers can request the de-identified medical data of astronauts or utilize other publically available flight information. In effect, this allows astronauts to be removed psychologically from research (i.e., they believe they are not being actively studied for the research purpose); but, the reality remains that astronauts' data are still available in the research space. Current ethical guidelines (in the Belmont Report, for example) do not explore the idea of participant withdrawal in significant detail, and future thinking should consider physical removal as well as psychological withdrawal from research.

---

[1] For a more in depth evaluation of the considerations relevant for astronauts, see the *Health Standards*.

Ethical Considerations

SUFFICIENCY OF PARTICIPANT-FOCUSED ETHICAL GUIDELINES

Despite some variance in the specific requirements or tenets set forth across the existing ethical guidelines, they converge on the notion that human participants must be willing and informed parties to the research. Put differently, to the extent that the humans participating in a research or exploration endeavor are (1) voluntarily present; (2) competently informed about the research, the purpose, the potential benefits, and the potential risks; and (3) free to end their participation at any time without fear of retaliation, then existing ethical guidelines would suggest the endeavor is appropriate, assuming the other guidelines are also met. The question, then, is whether this represents sufficient consideration of ethical concerns. In Figure 1.1, we suggest a series of logical steps to determine if these ethical requirements have been met.

This set of circumstances seems logical and highlights an important assumption within existing guidelines that can apply to research in extreme environments: at some point, researchers must defer to the personal or individual judgement of a rational human as he or she decides what constitutes an acceptable cost benefit ratio and volunteers for that specific role.

In fact, idiosyncratic evaluations of risk and rewards have often been deemed acceptable motivations behind a willingness to take part in research in extreme environments. Frederick "Rick" Hauck, a retired astronaut, wrote an article after the Columbia tragedy articulating that (1) the job of an astronaut is not the only job with an inherent risk of death and (2) individuals who recognize their personal risk/reward ratio has tilted too far will leave that job. He further stated: "Please leave matters of risk up to the astronauts and their families. They've made their choice" (Hauck, 2003). Indeed, in discussions with others who have participated in

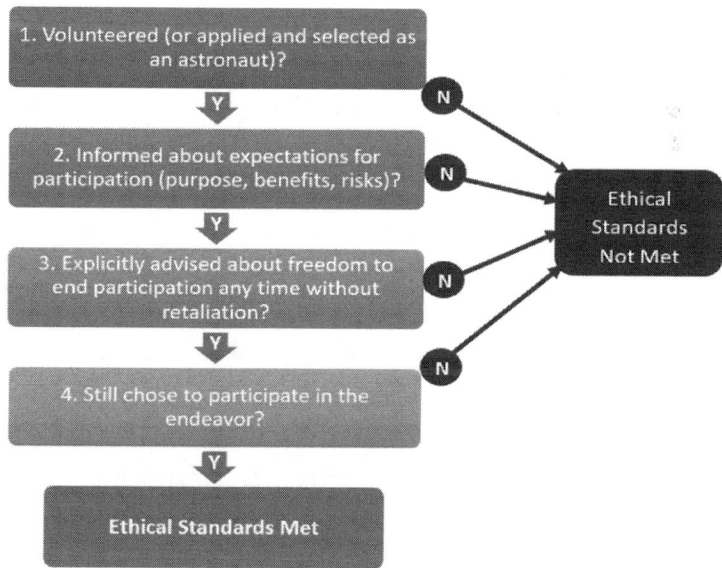

FIGURE 1.1 Ethical requirements decision tree.

assignments to extreme environments or analog research, these decisions are not made lightly.

As one example, Captain Dan Simon, a National Oceanic and Atmospheric Administration (NOAA) commissioned officer who has accepted assignments in extreme environments including both Antarctica and Greenland, said "There are certainly risks, but they are outweighed by the benefits to both my own senses of adventure and accomplishment and to the increase in human knowledge" (D. Simon, personal communication, March 7, 2019). He further indicated that changing life circumstances (i.e., fatherhood) have changed his personal risk/benefit analysis. In another example, Dr. Jocelyn Dunn, who participated in an eight-month Mars analog environment research study as part of the HI-SEAS Mission III, indicated not only that there were several personal benefits and risks or potential negative outcomes initially weighed before deciding to participate, but also that after agreeing to participate, other benefits, risks, outcomes, and scenarios were considered (J. Dunn, personal communication, March 14, 2019). In other words, the risk/benefit ratio is not a one-time evaluation for these individuals but instead a continual balancing of scales, based on changing conditions and circumstances. However, as noted in the *Health Standards*, in instances where individual risk taking imposes involuntary risk on others (i.e., space exploration), an entirely individual-centered decision is inadequate and requires additional action to promote a favorable risk to benefit balance.

With regard to the sufficiency of participant-focused research guidance, some considerations may impact the assessment of current guidelines as space exploration and analog environment research continue and prepare for potentially longer duration events. First, even if researchers can clearly articulate and define risks for research participants, awareness of these risks will never ensure complete safety, and space research (and research in other extreme environments) will inevitably continue to be one of humanity's most dangerous efforts. In other words, individuals who are often not directly benefitting from research in a measurable way (e.g., they are not receiving a treatment of some kind) will be subjected to inherently dangerous work. In 2013, NASA presented to the Institute of Medicine, a probabilistic risk assessment as well as ethics principles and guidelines for long duration and exploration spaceflights. Of note, estimates are refined over time, as additional data are gathered. However, one 6-month ISS mission (low Earth orbit) spaceflight was estimated to equate to approximately 14 years cutting timber – the most dangerous job by fatal work injury rate in 2018 (Blanchard, 2018) – or equivalent to being a firefighter on September 11, 2001[2] (Behnken, Barratt, Walker, & Whitson, 2013). Further, even if risks can be quantified, the likelihood that an unforeseen risk or hazard is encountered exists and is considerably higher in the first attempt(s). Also, the longer the event duration, the higher the likelihood that a detrimental risk is realized (Turner, 2014). To provide examples, in the analog research space, one such unforeseen complication for Dr. Dunn was unexpected media interest and attention both during and following participation; although the exposure was an unintended benefit, the level of interest was also an unintended consequence as an additional source of stress. For astronauts and others who accept assignments in extreme environments, not

---

[2] Long term medical considerations were excluded from the evaluations.

only should probabilistic risk assessment evaluations be clearly delineated, but also part of the decision to participate must include weighing a potential re-acclimation period after the assignment (e.g., Scott Kelly, who required a month of rehabilitation to regain strength after his spaceflight; Capt. Dan Simon, who experienced a re-acclimation period after extended time in an isolated environment; or Dr. Dunn, who in hindsight indicated that it would have been more prudent to allow for a re-acclimation period before attempting to return to all responsibilities).

Relatedly, the implementation of long-duration missions creates additional participation considerations that current ethical guidelines may not be able to address. During long missions to Mars, for example, astronauts will be monitored (e.g., participant health conditions) for extensive periods of time, which means they are potentially participating in some form of research (i.e. supplying medical data) for years. Such monitoring may become burdensome, especially if monitors are uncomfortable or heavy. Even though society now allows for more real-time monitoring of individuals (for example via iPhones and smart watches), existing research guidelines do not comment on the extensive monitoring that would occur on a multi-year research endeavor. Further, the extensive monitoring that could take place may skew data results, which weakens the argument that such monitoring is appropriate. To illustrate, individuals who have to continually complete the same set of questionnaires or surveys over extended periods of time in analog environments become fatigued or potentially just provide the same response for every research iteration because this response pattern is less burdensome (J. Dunn, personal communication, March 14, 2019). Given this reality, long-term research efforts requiring active subject participation may not be effective, which weakens the arguments in favor of this type of research.

SUFFICIENCY OF BENEFICENCE – OR RISK/BENEFIT ANALYSIS – FOCUSED GUIDANCE

This is the most complex aspect to evaluate regarding existing ethical guidance as applied to human exploration and analog research in extreme environments. The actual requirement is deceivingly simple: maximize the potential benefits and minimize the potential harm associated with an endeavor, ensuring that the benefits outweigh the risks. The complexity lies not only in the various levels of analysis available but also in the benefits and risks or costs appropriate to include at the various levels and the potential for different evaluators to weigh the benefits, risks, and costs in different ways. Three conceptual levels of analysis are discussed below, and the reader is directed to the *Health Standards* for a more detailed evaluation.

The discussion regarding the sufficiency of participant-focused ethical guidance touched on the individual level of this risk/benefit analysis. And if one were to stop at this individual level of analysis, the existing guidance would seem to be sufficient because it can be applied to current aspirations, such as sending humans to Mars. While such a long trip inevitably creates uncertainty and provides ample opportunity for unknown problems, researchers can currently describe the anticipated risks associated with this venture, which is required according to current ethical standards. For instance, such exploration increases risks to the physical health of those involved due to increased radiation exposure. Psychological health is also threatened because of limited social support and interaction; however, extensive research in analog environments to date has been seeking to further clarify, evaluate, and establish mitigation procedures for the anticipated psychological risks of such a mission, and researchers can emphasize this point to all research participants. Ultimately, at the individual level, scientists can likely provide potential subjects with sufficient information about costs and benefits.

However, as the level of analysis moves up from the individual to a group or societal level, the analysis process can become more nebulous. For example, NASA and other space agencies have created system-wide policies surrounding thresholds for acceptable exposure or risk levels relating to specific hazards (e.g., the amount of radiation exposure expected on a three-year Mars mission would equal or exceed the current thresholds set for lifetime radiation exposure), but those thresholds – or the extent to which individuals are allowed, if willing, to accept increased risks associated with exceeding those thresholds – may need to be re-evaluated in light of the change from low Earth orbit to longer range missions. In previous endeavors, one mitigation option has been to shorten the mission duration; however, as longer range missions are contemplated, other mitigation strategies are necessary. If thresholds cannot be changed because of human biological limitations, NASA may have to rely on enhancing protective technologies for its employees and research participants in order to continue with the endeavor.

When evaluating the cost/benefit analysis from a societal level, questions such as whether it is ethical to spend resources on exploration at all, given other potential uses for the funds, must be considered, in addition to potential risks to human life and equipment. These factors must then be balanced against the expected benefits from such exploration and research. The difficulty in a societal-level analysis is the extent to which different values or weights may be assigned to the costs, risks, and benefits included in the equation, even if those individual components are identical. This diversion of weighting can lead to two opposing viewpoints as to whether a particular endeavor meets the ethical guidance of benefits outweighing the costs/risks.

In a societal-level cost/benefit analysis, the literal cost of human exploration, particularly space exploration, is often the subject of intense scrutiny, arguably more so than any other potential risks on the negative side of the equation. One such consistent criticism centers around the notion that the money spent on space exploration and analog environment research could instead be put to better or more beneficial use. This particular criticism was raised by Sister Mary Jacunda, a nun working in Africa in 1970. In response to her inquiry as to why the funding for space exploration couldn't be better used to feed the hungry, one of the top rocket scientists at NASA, Ernst Stuhlinger, wrote, in part: "The voyage to Mars will certainly not be a direct source of food for the hungry. However, it will lead to so many new technologies and capabilities that the spin-offs from this project alone will be worth many times the cost of its implementation" (Siegel, 2017). In addition to that quote, the response also delved into the more nuanced issues of how the US federal budget is allotted, and how that money can be spent once appropriated through Congress. Note that NASA's annual budget since FY 2010 has hovered around 0.5% of the entire Federal budget and has been on a fairly slow but steady decline in percentage terms since the early 1990s (Kring, n.d.; Roberts, 2019).

The primary benefit of human exploration associated with analog environment research at a societal level is the acquisition of additional knowledge, skill, and technology advancements resulting from these endeavors. In terms of additional knowledge and skill, each new endeavor, whether or not the goals set are achieved, serves to add to the collective human understanding of the universe and the phenomena surrounding Earth. In fact, research has demonstrated that failing to achieve a goal actually results in greater knowledge gain and that knowledge is retained longer (Madsen & Desai, 2010). The exploration of space can inspire the next generation to consider becoming a scientist or an engineer while also helping humanity to increase the collective understanding of the universe surrounding us (Hedman, 2005). Regarding the new technologies that benefit society, some argue that these advances would have occurred absent the catalyst of space exploration, albeit potentially taking longer to fully develop and refine. Whether they would have been invented absent the space exploration angle, there is an entire publication and associated website (https://spinoff.nasa.gov/) dedicated to the myriad intended and unintended benefits related to technology, systems, and processes developed to provide the means for space exploration, but additionally leveraged to benefit society or commercial endeavors.

As demonstrated in the preceding paragraphs, while the direct cost of exploration is more consistently measurable, the implications of that cost, the assignment of value to the benefits realized or anticipated from a particular endeavor, and the appropriate weighting of the risks associated with that endeavor are not clear. It is outside the scope of this essay to define or determine the appropriate factors and weights to include in a societal analysis. However, the lack of clarity points to a potential gap in the existing ethical guidance – specifically relating to clarity around the level at which the cost/benefit analysis should be focused, and the point at which that ceases to be an ethical concern and instead becomes a societal value-based question or concern.

CONCLUSION

Over the course of the latter part of the 20th century, researchers have refined a set of ethical guidelines that provide the foundation for modern research practices. These research standards (e.g., Belmont Report) stress that principles including Respect for Persons, Beneficence, and Justice should guide ethical procedures. In many instances, existing guidance (1) can apply to research participants and astronauts alike and (2) is often sufficient for evaluating research in extreme environments because scientists can adhere to current ethical considerations by ensuring informed consent, defining risks and benefits, and mitigating risks where possible.

Given emerging exploratory endeavors (e.g., long duration mission to Mars), however, the broad nature of existing ethical guidance still leaves uncertainty. For example, according to current practices, research participants should be able to withdraw from studies any time, although an astronaut performing research on Mars would not have this luxury. Moreover, existing guidelines do not provide details about the nuances of risk analysis, and it is not entirely clear how risk and rewards should be considered from a societal perspective. This higher level of analysis is particularly important for research at NASA because spin-off technology and societal benefits are consistently used to justify space research.

The existing uncertainty should not prevent researchers from exploring new environments, but scientists must continue to be mindful of the ethical considerations that have arisen over the past century. Inevitably, this mindfulness will require thorough planning and detailed analysis of costs and benefits (where feasible). The *Health Standards* represent a concerted effort to identify a framework for ethical evaluations and decision making regarding human participation in long duration and exploration spaceflights, with implications for ethical considerations in analog research environments. Without continuing these types of actions, extreme environment research faces the possibility of creating the next cautionary tale that will be the driving force for revisions to documents such as the Belmont Report. That said, current research precautions, such as IRBs and risk mitigation procedures, suggest that modern-day researchers are mindful of ethical ramifications and will responsibly lead science to new frontiers.

REFERENCES

Behnken, R., Barratt, M., Walker, S., & Whitson, P. (2013, July). *Ethics principles and guidelines for health standards for long duration and exploration spaceflights.* Presentation to the Committee on Ethics Principles and Guidelines for Health Standards for Long Duration and Exploration Spaceflights, Washington, DC.

Blanchard, D. (2018). *Top 10 most dangerous jobs of 2018.* Retrieved March 21, 2019, from https://www.ehstoday.com/safety/top-10-most-dangerous-jobs-2018/gallery?slide=10

Buelow, P. A. (2011). The institutional review board: A brief history of attempts to protect human subjects in research. *Clinical Nurse Specialist, 25*(6), 277–280.

Department of Health, Education, and Welfare (HEW). (1979). *The Belmont report: Ethical principles and guidelines for the protection of human subjects of research.* Retrieved from https://www.hhs.gov/ohrp/regulations-and-policy/belmont-report/index.html

Granath, B. (2015). *The human desire for exploration leads to discovery.* Retrieved from https://www.nasa.gov/feature/the-human-desire-for-exploration-leads-to-discovery

Hauck, F. H. (2003, July). *Is it worth the risk?* Retrieved from https://www.airspacemag.com/space/is-it-worth-the-risk-4880471/

Hedman, E. R. (2005). *The politics and ethics of spending money on space exploration.* Retrieved March 21, 2019, from http://www.thespacereview.com/article/520/1

Howell, E. (2017). *For astronauts, crazy risks come with the job.* Retrieved March 13, 2019, from https://www.nbcnews.com/mach/science/astronauts-crazy-risks-come-job-ncna78445

Hughes, R. N. (1997). Intrinsic exploration in animals: motives and measurement. *Behavioral Processes, 41*(3), pp. 213–226. doi:10.1016/S0376-6357(97)00055-7

IOM (Institute of Medicine). (2014). *Health standards for long duration and exploration spaceflight: Ethics principles, responsibilities, and decision framework.* Washington, DC: The National Academies Press. doi:10.17226/18576

Kaplan, R. S., & Mikes, A. (2012). Managing risks: A new framework. *Harvard Business Review.* Retrieved from https://hbr.org/2012/06/managing-risks-a-new-framework

Kidd, C., & Hayden, B. Y. (2015). The psychology and neuroscience of curiosity. *Neuron, 88*(3), pp. 449–460. doi:10.1016/j.neuron.2015.09.010

Kovo, Y. (2018). *Declaration of Helsinki.* Retrieved March 21, 2019, from https://www.nasa.gov/ames/hrirb/declaration-helsinki

Kring, D. A. (n.d.). *NASA budget history & support for our future.* Retrieved March 21, 2019, from https://www.lpi.usra.edu/exploration/multimedia/

Lewin, S. (2016). *Over 18,300 apply to become NASA astronauts, smashing record.* Retrieved March 13, 2019, from https://www.space.com/31987-nasa-astronaut-applications-smash-record.html

Madsen, P. M., & Desai, V. M. (2010). Failing to learn? The effects of failure and success on organizational learning in the global orbital launch vehicle industry. *Academy of Management Journal, 53*(3), pp. 451–476.

National Oceanic and Atmospheric Administration (NOAA). (2018). *How much of the ocean have we explored?* Retrieved from https://oceanservice.noaa.gov/facts/exploration.html.

Nuremberg Code. (n.d.a). Retrieved March 21, 2019, from https://www.ushmm.org/information/exhibitions/online-exhibitions/special-focus/doctors-trial/nuremberg-code

Protection of Human Subjects, 14 C.F.R § 1230. (2018). Retrieved from https://www.govinfo.gov/app/details/CFR-2012-title14-vol5/CFR-2012-title14-vol5-part1230

Roberts, T. G. (2019). *History of the NASA budget.* Retrieved March 21, 2019, from https://aerospace.csis.org/data/history-nasa-budget/

Siegel, E. (2017). *Why exploring space and investing in research is non-negotiable.* Retrieved March 21, 2019, from https://www.forbes.com/sites/startswithabang/2017/10/26/even-while-the-world-suffers-investing-in-science-is-non-negotiable/#570c34a21647

The Nuremberg Code. (n.d.b) Retrieved March 21, 2019, from https://history.nih.gov/research/downloads/nuremberg.pdf

Turner, R. (2014, April). *Health standards for long duration and exploration spaceflight: Ethics principles, responsibilities, and decision framework.* Presentation at Space Weather Workshop, Boulder, CO. Retrieved from: https://www.swpc.noaa.gov/sites/default/files/images/u33/Turner.pdf

Weaver, S. (2015). *Exploring the final frontier.* Retrieved from https://blog.oup.com/2015/05/final-frontier-exploration-vsi/

2 Psychological Selection for Extreme Environments

Lacey L. Schmidt
Minerva Work Solutions, PLLC/University of Houston

Annette C. Spychalski
ACS People Development

CONTENTS

Introduction 17
What We Know from Assessing Astronaut Applicants 19
What We Learned from Assessing Astronaut Applicants 24
Conclusions and Recommendations 28
References 30

INTRODUCTION

Validating personnel assessments and selection systems for organizations (e.g., scientifically crafting fair and effective methods for choosing employees who can perform the job well) typically requires large samples of people who have either currently, or have recently, performed the job (Highhouse, Doverspike, & Guion, 2015). Thus, finding a sufficient sample of people to validate an assessment or selection system remains the first and one of the greatest challenges associated with selecting people to perform jobs in extreme environments (such as selecting astronaut candidates for spaceflight missions). Most of the challenges in psychological selection for extreme environments revolve around three central issues: (1) the jobs performed in extreme environments are largely unique and relatively few people are in or have performed those jobs (e.g., Astronaut), (2) there is a limited number of extreme environments and it is often difficult to compare them and extract their common elements, and (3) the unique nature of these jobs also makes it difficult to non-invasively identify reasonable and consistently measurable performance criteria (Shepanek, 2005).

Over the course of this chapter, we summarize what we know about using psychology to select workers for extreme environments, especially in relation to these three central issues. We also discuss how we use that knowledge to inform the psychological selection of astronauts, and the lessons learned from that application.

To conclude, we reflect on what the future of psychological selection for extreme environment work holds given new long-duration spaceflight mission concepts and the likely international flavor of future endeavors. Before proceeding, we would like to explicitly communicate our conceptions of extreme environments and reasons for applying psychological selection tactics in them.

What makes an environment extreme? Existing in it is dangerous because of constant physical, emotional, and/or mental threats to inhabitants' presence (e.g., Space, the Arctic Tundra, a war zone, a fire scene). An environment might also be extreme because it requires an exceptionally high level of performance and even small errors can be deadly (e.g., emergency rooms, fighter jets). Organizations functioning with small error margins are often called High-Reliability Organizations, and many of the organizations that operate in extreme environments (e.g., NASA) fall into this category and must perform to demanding standards. For such organizations and the employees working in them, the science of psychology (i.e., the study of human behavior) offers a means to create effective selection, training, and support systems to optimize their performance and sustain their viability under extremely challenging conditions.

Psychological selection practices applied to work in extreme environments are of interest to the world at large because what works well on the edge of these frontiers is likely to work in many other environments. These practices might be particularly helpful in circumstances involving a greater element of uncertainty than usual. For example, selecting individuals to work in the globally distributed, virtual, rotating/plug-and-play, ad hoc team environment necessary to support International Space Station (ISS) operations yields some novel opportunities to assess teamwork skills. They may also be of value to selecting and developing individuals for more traditional jobs in temporarily extreme contexts (e.g., international logistics coordinators, interdisciplinary research administrators, or regional incident commanders for natural disasters). Historically, many other extreme environments have been considered good analogs for spaceflight, and in return, spaceflight has become something of an ultimate test of psychological selection science and practices. Space analogs provide crucial "testbed" environments that allow exploration of theories about optimal methods for selecting individuals to serve in the astronaut corps, as well as selecting individuals to participate in actual space missions. Several important issues critical to spaceflight are illuminated by studying key analog environments. For example, they provide a relevant setting for learning how to manage complex, long-duration missions, while addressing key mission risks (MacCallum, Poynter, & Bearden, 2004). Because a human mission to Mars is lengthier and more complex than any space endeavor undertaken to date, we must continue leveraging space analogs as we work to set future missions up for success.

Analog environments include a subset of the features and dynamics that characterize spaceflight. For example, completing a scientific mission on Antarctica is similar to spaceflight in that the physical environment is hostile, communication options with those outside the mission are limited, and individuals are required to interact with other team members 24/7, whether they like one another or not (also, help is not close at hand and the crew must operate as autonomously as possible) (Palinkas, Gunderson, Holland, Miller, & Johnson, 2000; Tanaka & Watanabe, 1994;

Wood et al., 2005). However, spaceflight involves additional complications (e.g., high level of visibility with the general public, radiation exposure threats, no re-supply or evacuation options, and extremely long distances) (Leveton, 2014). Therefore, spaceflight remains a unique test of selection science and practice. In other words, if a selection method works in the supremely demanding and unforgiving context of spaceflight, it will likely work in other high-stakes environments as well.

Selection processes occur in extreme environments to replace individuals who have left the program and to meet crewmember requirements for current and future missions, as is the case at NASA. Astronaut selection requires the coordination of many Johnson Space Center elements, one of which is the Behavioral Health and Performance Group (BHP) within Space Medicine. BHP is mandated to assist in conducting psychiatric evaluations of the applicants to determine whether each individual meets NASA Medical Standard criteria for qualification and to report this determination to the Astronaut Medical Board (AMB). This mechanism is similar to what is used in other space agencies, special operations units in military organizations, and for many public safety jobs (e.g., law enforcement officers) throughout the world. Additionally, BHP is asked to provide information on candidates' psychological suitability for long-duration spaceflight to the Astronaut Selection Board (ASB) and to consult on psychological factors to inform both the AMB and ASB's interviews and decisions (This additional aspect of psychological selection is more unique to BHP). Due to the unusually high number of highly qualified applicants for a limited number of positions (e.g., over 8,000 for ten openings), the concept of psychological suitability is more pronounced in extreme environments than traditional environments, especially for spaceflight. The large number of strong candidates creates the opportunity to refine selection criteria and work to identify those likely to flourish, rather than just endure, in dangerous, uncertain, and demanding conditions. This mindset of identifying candidates most likely to thrive is a relatively recent evolution in psychological selection for spaceflight. Also, it is potentially an important concept to transfer to other jobs in the public safety domain. However, the goal of hiring those most likely to thrive generates more challenges in identifying reasonable and consistently measurable performance criteria needed to validate selection processes.

It is worth reiterating that the development of psychological selection practices for spaceflight continues to face the same three major challenges: (1) few past or present incumbents to help us define the job reliably, (2) disparate aspects of operating contexts and missions even among similarly extreme environments, and (3) inherently uncertain performance criteria. What we know about astronaut selection is largely defined by our efforts to address these three challenges.

WHAT WE KNOW FROM ASSESSING ASTRONAUT APPLICANTS

Psychological or psychiatric screening for an illness that might jeopardize a spaceflight mission is considered an obvious performance criterion, and has been a part of the original selection of astronauts and cosmonauts since the beginning of space agencies (Steimle & Norberg, 2013). Validation and standardization of selection practices were considered in Industrial-Organizational Psychology journals since that time. However, astronaut applicant psychiatric evaluations were perceived as purely medical judgements and conducted primarily by physicians who used varying styles and methods. In 1989, as psychologists became more regularly involved in astronaut selection, a method of providing well-grounded, standardized evaluations for psychiatrically qualifying or disqualifying astronaut applicants was initiated. Standardized selection methods lead to more consistent, higher quality selection decisions because they require all candidates to be evaluated against the same criteria, using the same "measuring stick." In addition, use of a standardized process helps to prevent perceived or actual discriminatory hiring processes as well as lay the foundation for continuous improvement of the process. During early and short-duration space missions (SDMs) (e.g., Space Shuttle); selection at NASA heavily emphasized the identification of psychopathology. Initially, it was most sensible and practical to focus on leveraging science to "select out" applicants who were likely to do harm in or be harmed by an extreme environment. Also, because SDMs lasted less than 3 weeks, astronauts free of psychopathology could reasonably be expected to handle the presenting stressors and challenges whether they had skills indicating that they would genuinely thrive during space flight or not. NASA's focus expanded to include long-duration missions with participation in MIR (i.e., the Russian Space Station) and the ISS in the 1990s. The unique demands of long-duration missions (>2 weeks and up to 3 years for future Mars missions) placed a greater emphasis on the qualities and skills that allow astronauts to safely and eagerly adapt to living and working in space for long periods of time (currently, 10–12 months on ISS at most) (Collins, 2003). The additional skills needed for successful adaptability to long-duration missions led BHP to update the tools and procedures used for psychological screening of astronaut applicants several times since 1998 (Fiedler & Carpenter, 2005; Galarza & Holland, 1999a, 1999b; Landon, Vessey, & Barrett, 2016). In addition to screening for psychological and psychiatric indicators of illness that might jeopardize missions, BHP also collects information regarding the clinical indicators of suitability for living and working in spaceflight conditions for months at a time.

The modern process involves a battery of appropriate psychometric tests, typically chosen by a group of qualified psychiatrists and clinically focused psychologists, and administered to a small group of qualified applicants. Then, semi-structured interviews (standardized across professionals engaged in the psychological and psychiatric screening of astronaut candidates) are conducted with an even smaller group of highly qualified applicants. Additional assessment activities (e.g., teamwork reaction exercises, work samples) have also been used during the last four selection cycles. Data is compiled and analyzed after each cycle to check the effectiveness and efficiency of the selection process… as much as the accumulated data, operational constraints, and accepted statistical practices of the day allow (Landon et al., 2016). All these assessment methods have evolved somewhat since their initial inclusion to reflect changes in the science of selection and changes in the astronaut job demands and job context (c.f., completion of Space Shuttle flights and the longer-duration missions of the ISS).

Continual evolution of both the assessment process and elements is an absolute must to accommodate new spaceflight mission concepts and preparations. For example, until June of 2008, the ISS program used a one-to-one backup scheme for training ISS crews. It required that a fully dedicated backup crewmember train alongside each prime crewmember. After the launch of the prime crewmember, the backup crewmember was then inserted into a prime training flow and the whole training sequence (i.e., from assignment as a backup to flight as a prime crewmember) typically required 4–5 years for inexperienced crewmembers. This schedule provided opportunities for crewmembers to interact with one another, build relationships, and develop effective teamwork habits together. Unfortunately, that training schedule was too long, complicated, expensive, and exhaustive to be practical. In 2007, the Expedition Training Requirements Integration Panel of the International Training Control Board outlined the single-flow-to-launch (SFTL) concept that, along with other economies, helped reduce the 5 years or more typically needed to train inexperienced crewmembers to 2 years or less. However, these gains in efficiency required astronauts to prepare for training much more extensively (e.g., network with instructors beforehand, build the appropriate level of proficiency in the training language and culture, complete pre-assignment work and review training materials independent of instruction prior to re-assignment or new mission assignment, etc.). Most importantly, SFTL also reduced the opportunity for crewmembers to train together as a team and this limited crews' ability to establish shared mental models and interpersonal experiences prior to flight. In fact, the modern ISS six-person crewmembers may not even meet one another prior to their mission. Although the training flow for the ISS spans 2.5 years, each astronaut or cosmonaut largely trains alone, traveling primarily between the US and Russia (Steimle & Norberg, 2013), and also to Canada (for Canadarm), Europe (for European module training), and JAXA (for Dextre robot on end of Kibo lab). This extensive travel, demanding learning schedule, and inability to bond as a team create a more acute need to select astronauts who learn quickly, demonstrate great resilience to constant travel, and exhibit exceptional teamwork knowledge and behavior. Thanks to current training efficiencies, rarely do all six ISS crewmembers train together (usually only for a total of 8–12 hours of emergency evacuation simulations), and even more rarely have any of the six lived together prior to launch. This means that it is now more important than ever to select astronauts who live well with strangers and in multi-cultural contexts. Since training provides less opportunity to test and foster effective teamwork or group living behaviors, changes like these have and will continue to raise new questions regarding how to select candidates already well suited to teamwork and cross-cultural group living.

Poor selection decisions for any job can result in significant costs related to errors made by weak performers, the need to find suitable replacements, and getting new incumbents up to speed. Typically, organizations invest in assessing psychological characteristics that cannot be developed through training and are developed over long periods of time or even a lifetime (e.g., personality traits, cognitive ability), and are often measured through tests. One important advantage of using tests is that individual applicants are treated consistently. Using standardized tests or assessments ensures that the same information is gathered on each individual and used in a similar way, and this helps to ensure the consistency and quality of selection decisions (Zedeck, 2011). Many psychological factors have significant face validity for work in extreme environments, so it is relatively easy to argue for the application of tests and assessment in psychological selection for these environments (Bell, 2007; Ones, Dilchert, Viswesvaran, & Judge, 2007). However, standardized tests are associated with several legal and practical concerns worth reviewing here.

As with any other method of making or informing employment decisions, tests can be legally and ethically scrutinized if there is a belief that unfair discrimination has occurred. Adverse impact exists when the selection rate of a given demographic group (e.g., females vs. males, whites vs. blacks, etc.) is substantially lower than the selection rate of the majority group. Any selection procedure may show score differences that result in exclusionary effects upon a group, but some types (e.g., physical ability tests, cognitive ability tests) are more likely to do so. However, these tests often accurately predict job performance and other outcomes of interest and they can significantly contribute to effective selection decisions. Before using a test, it is important to anticipate whether adverse impact might occur and to consider ways that minimize any exclusionary effects while preserving the ability to make valid inferences based on test scores. If an incidence of adverse impact does occur, it is important to demonstrate that the inferences made based on test scores are appropriate and that the constructs tested are bona fide job qualifications, especially when selecting for jobs as socially revered and desired as the astronaut role. For these jobs, we know that multi-method job analyses are especially critical in helping determine and document bona fide job qualifications and identifying fair and accurate ways to assess performance (i.e., for future use in validation research). The multi-method concept of job analysis (e.g., literature reviews, interviews, surveys, observations, cognitive task analysis, sociometric) is especially important in building sound psychological selection systems for extreme environments. This is because there is no other way to collect enough evidence to make reasonable decisions, given the first two of our three primary challenges: (1) small sample sizes of current and past incumbents, and (2) highly variable contexts for the exact same job titles.

Also, given our third challenge of continuously evolving performance criteria, we know that the only way to ensure effective selection systems is to conduct multi-method job analysis studies regularly. For this reason, competency modeling is another tool from the Industrial-Organizational Psychology tool box that makes good, practical sense. Effective selection processes are based upon the qualities and skills required to meet the organization's expectation for competent performance (e.g., a competency model). Many organizations use competency frameworks to select individuals (such as IBM, GE, Verizon, Waste Management, Hanover, Shell, 3M, the United States Office of Personnel Management) (Rodriguez, Patel, Bright, Gregory, & Gowing, 2002; Schmidt, 2008a, 2008b). There is both spaceflight- and ground-based job analysis evidence suggesting that teamwork, communication, leadership, and related competencies help predict individual and team performance and safety across many jobs that involve key elements of the astronaut role.

Several efforts have been made to identify factors that are important for selecting individual crewmembers for long-duration spaceflight (Barrett, Holland, & Vessey, 2015; Caldwell, 2005; Galarza & Holland, 1999; Manzey, Schwie, & Fassbender, 1995; McGrath, Arrow, & Berdah, 2000; Nicholas & Fouchee, 1990; Rose, Fogg, Helmreich, & McFadden, 1994; Vinograd, 1974). There have been and still are reoccurring attempts to use content-, construct-, and criterion-related validation approaches to link assessment tools to the competencies needed for short- and long-duration missions and ultimately to astronaut performance criteria (Musson, Sandal, & Helmreich, 2004; Rose et al., 1994; Santy et al., 1993).

Selection research within spaceflight is severely limited by the lack of job performance data available to researchers. This lack of performance data is due, in part, to the fact that there is such a limited number of astronauts actually selected (around 340 US astronauts over the life of the program) and that there is so much evolution in the job (from Mercury to ISS). Quantifying different levels of performance (optimal versus adequate versus inadequate) is unrealistic with such small sample sizes. Even when performance data are available, there is rarely much observable variance in performance (likely because incumbents have been so highly selected and trained by that point) and this makes criterion-related validation untenable. As a result, space agencies have heavily relied upon content validation methods when making changes to selection processes.

These issues are relevant for all space agencies, as they all suffer from a lack of performance data and small sample sizes. For example, the Russians have long collected personality data on cosmonauts (Kanas & Manzey, 2008), but the empirical linking of personality factors to specific performance levels necessary to provide cut-scores or norms for selection has still eluded Russian researchers. One exception to this lack of reporting on empirical selection data was a study published in relation to the European Space Agency's 2008/2009 selection cycle (Maschke, Oubaid, & Pecena, 2011). Maschke et al. (2011) documented some criterion-related validity evidence on at least one personality test used by the European Space Agency. Considering the critical need for additional methods of ensuring the quality of selection tools for the high-stakes astronaut position, Landon and colleagues (Landon et al., 2016; Landon, Rokholt, Slack, & Pecena, 2017) urge space agencies to make increased quality and quantity of astronaut performance data a priority. This will allow for more rigorous evaluation of current selection tools and their alternatives.

The current dearth of performance data makes conducting criterion-related validation particularly troublesome for space agencies. Messick (1995; 1998) proposed that validity can only be established once a preponderance of evidence has been collected (1) indicating that the test content is relevant to the construct; (2) there is theoretical rationale behind the test scores; (3) the test is scored in a manner that corresponds to the construct's structure; (4) the generalizability of the test is known; (5) test scores are related to similar constructs and not dissimilar constructs; and (6) the consequences of using test scores are well understood. At this point, many space agencies attempt to collect evidence in all six categories, but the scarcity of present and past job incumbents, unique contexts, and lack of performance data preclude them from establishing theoretical rationale behind specific test scores or adequately determining the consequences of using test scores. We do know that astronauts, and many who work in extreme environments, self-select and are so well screened before their initial psychological testing that they typically demonstrate little variability across most constructs. Range restriction is problematic and only likely to remain so as we reach for the stars in completely new ways and engage in longer-duration missions (that will likely require far more international collaboration to pull off than prior explorations).

WHAT WE LEARNED FROM ASSESSING ASTRONAUT APPLICANTS

Future research regarding selection for spaceflight must resort to more creative tactics for quantifying performance and validating predictors. For example, space agencies could conduct studies to generalize and validate predictors among samples of teams whose work approximates some portion of astronaut responsibilities or tasks. Synthetic validation tactics will also hold more appeal as collaborations between the commercial and international space agencies continue expanding to accomplish long-duration missions.

In the meantime, 50 years of ground-based research on individual selection for work done in teams, including small group research conducted in analog and/or extreme environments, should inform astronaut selection. Ground-based studies show that new teams choosing individuals who are skilled at training and articulating their roles to others, compromising, helping other team members take on their tasks, and who also understand effective team processes achieved better team performance than those ignoring these individual skills during selection (Jones, Stevens, & Fischer, 2000). Evidence suggests that individual characteristics (in addition to individual skills and values) influence performance in a teamwork setting. For example, Barrick, Stewart, Neubert, and Mount (1998) found that a team member with a very low score on Conscientiousness (as measured by the NEO PI-R) had an impact on team performance by acting as the "weakest link," constraining team performance. In assembly and maintenance work teams, team averages on three personality factors (Emotional Stability, Conscientiousness, and Agreeableness) and general mental ability were positively correlated with supervisor ratings of team effectiveness. In addition, team average general mental ability and two personality factors (Extraversion, Emotional Stability) were positively related to supervisor ratings of the team's ability to maintain itself over time (Barrick et al., 1998). One meta-analysis found that interpersonal facilitation was significantly predicted by three personality factors (Conscientiousness, Emotional Stability, and Agreeableness) (Hurtz & Donovan, 2000). Studies like these provide ample evidence that individual factors, such as personality and general mental ability, help predict the quality of performance in a teamwork setting.

Research on pilots offers further evidence that individual personality factors are relevant to selecting individuals capable of effective teamwork. In regards to interpersonal characteristics, a "right stuff" cluster based on the Personality Characteristics Inventory was composed of high levels of expressivity (warmth, sensitivity), low levels of negative instrumentality (arrogance/hostility), and verbal aggressiveness (complaining, nagging, passive-aggressive) (Chidester, Helmreich, Gregorich, & Geis, 1991; Gregorich, Helmreich, Wilhelm, & Chidester, 1989; Musson & Helmreich, 2005). A "wrong stuff" cluster included high levels of verbal aggressiveness and low levels of positive expressivity; whereas, a "no stuff" included low scores on expressiveness, instrumentality, mastery, etc. The "right stuff" cluster pilots were considered more effective by observers in a one-and-a-half-day simulated trip with crew than "low stuff" and "no stuff" pilots (Chidester, Kanki, Foushee, Dickinson, & Bowles, 1990).

Navy research in Antarctica suggests that while technical competence is necessary, it is also important to select individuals who exhibit "social compatibility or likeability, emotional control, patience, tolerance of others, self-confidence without egotism, the capacity to subordinate routinely one's own interests to work harmoniously as a member of a team, a sense of humor, and the ability to be easily entertained" as well as be practical and hardworking (Stuster, 1996, p. 268). NASA has historically used personality measures during astronaut selection as one source of data to capture key characteristics underpinning successful performance in the role. One challenge to evaluating the effectiveness of these tools is that there is a substantial delay (e.g., 10 years) between the time that these characteristics are initially measured and the time when astronauts are "tested" in actual space environments. Changes in personality may occur during that interval, which complicates the task of identifying the best predictors of astronaut mission success (Sgobba et al., 2018).

Another promising tool is biographical data questionnaires, which have been effectively used to predict success in military, government, and civilian training and job performance (Breaugh, 2009; U.S. OPM, 2018). Reviews indicate that biodata will predict a wide range of criteria (e.g., leadership performance, teamwork behaviors) in a wide variety of occupations and it typically yields cross validities between .30 and .40 (Bobko, Roth, & Potosky, 1999; Breaugh, 2009; Cook & Cripps, 2005; Schmidt, Ones, & Hunter, 1992). Strong research evidence indicates that empirically keyed biodata instruments can produce validities approaching or exceeding validities obtained with cognitive ability measures to predict a wide spectrum of performance criteria, ranging from leadership to absenteeism (Asher, 1972; Bobko et al., 1999; Hunter & Hunter, 1984; Mumford & Owens, 1987, Reilly & Chao 1982; Schmitt Gooding, Noe, & Kirsch, 1984). However, limitations on the use of biodata instruments include the large samples needed to develop valid empirical keys, low face validity for items (Smither Reilly, Millsap, AT&T, & Stoffey, 1993), potential of perceptions of invasiveness (Mael, Connerley, & Morath, 1996), and the possibility of faking or distortion by candidates (McFarland & Ryan, 2000). Given these limitations, effective use of biodata instruments during the psychological screening of astronaut applicants is extremely difficult. Organizations selecting for work in extreme environments cannot always manage the logistics of implementing biodata assessments with the larger applicant pools. For space agencies to benefit from biodata assessments, research will have to find ways to develop valid empirical keys with small, international samples.

Ground-based research also suggests that cognitive ability tests (both general and specific measures) are one of the most valid predictors of job performance, especially for more complex jobs (Hunter & Hunter, 1984). Despite their potential for disparate impact, given the strong validity associated with ability measures and the criticality of cognition-based skills and activities for successful astronaut job performance (e.g., identifying and gathering information, problem solving and decision making), cognitive ability measures remain a useful and legally defensible form of assessment in the selection processes for work in extreme environments. To this point, cognitive ability tests have only been introduced at a late stage of the astronaut selection process (i.e., for the final 200 to 50 applicants) and the limited range of the scores coming from such a small subset creates complications for conducting validation research. Cognitive ability test scores are one of the most robust predictors of job success, so a greater variety of cognitive ability tools could be used at an earlier stage in astronaut selection to more effectively select subsequent pools with greater diversity of sub-factors of general ability. Popular theories and ground-based studies suggest that well-roundedness among sub-factors or different conceptions of intelligence contributes to successful work performance in extreme environments. However, research is required to determine whether this is the case for the astronaut role before taking this approach to selecting individuals for that position.

A large preponderance of evidence from ground-based studies supports the general fairness, validity, and commonality of conducting structured interviews to screen applicants across industries and cultures (Carson, Carson, Fontenot, & Burdin, 2005; Fox & Spector, 2000; Huffcutt Weekley, Wiesner, Degroot, & Jones, 2001; Pulakos & Schmitt, 1996; Schmidt & Hunter, 1998). Additionally, the literature indicates that structured interviews increase the veracity of clinical judgments and screening decisions by standardizing practices across clinicians (and/or assessors) within spaceflight (Endo, Ohbayashi, Yumikura, & Sekiguchi, 1994; Fassbender & Goeters, 1994; Santy & Jones, 1994) and in other industries. For these reasons, NASA has adopted a semi-structured approach to interviews designed to evaluate whether applicants are psychiatrically qualified, as well as those evaluating candidates' level of psychological suitability for the astronaut role.

The likely multi-national nature of future long-duration spaceflight missions will increase the need to use interviewers/assessors from multiple cultures to jointly assess applicants for the astronaut role. Traditional work is also more global than ever before in the course of human history, so there is good motivation for doing more research to understand how to best train interviewers from different cultures to assess fairly together and how to build interviews that accurately assess qualified applicants from multiple cultures.

Finally, we consider simulations. Work simulations present "applicants with a task stimulus that mimics an actual job situation [including teamwork requirements] and elicit responses that are interpreted as direct indicators of how applicants would handle the task situation if it were actually to occur on the job" (Motowidlo, Dunnette, & Carter, 1990, p. 640). Simulations vary in the amount of fidelity with which they present a task stimulus and elicit a response. Among astronauts, teamwork has consistently been mentioned as an important task and remains an area of interest for creating relevant, validated work samples. Such samples or "teamwork reaction exercises" have great public face validity and are highly valued by many past and current job incumbents in extreme environments (e.g., NASA's Astronaut Office).

Selection tools with high face validity often improve selection decisions because they function as realistic job previews that help applicants make better informed decisions about whether to join the organization. In addition, when face validity is high, applicants are more likely to perceive the selection process as fair and less likely to initiate litigation claims. Relationships with other important outcomes, such as job satisfaction, organizational commitment, and tendency to recommend the employer to others have been identified when using selection tools with high face validity as well (Kelechi, 2012). Additionally, validity coefficients for work samples equal or exceed those of other predictors (Schmidt & Hunter, 1998) because they provide a realistic set of test conditions that generalize to those of the actual job (Lance Johnson, Douthitt, Bennett, & Harville, 2000). Work simulations also have been shown to exhibit less adverse impact than other selection tools (Cascio & Phillips, 1979; Hough, Oswald, & Ployhart, 2001; Motowidlo & Tippins, 1993).

The high validity, perceived fairness, and reduced adverse impact associated with work samples depend on the point-to-point correspondence between the simulation and job content (Asher & Sciarrino, 1974). However, high-fidelity work simulations are usually expensive and time-consuming to administer (Cascio & Phillips, 1979). Ground-based research suggests that low-fidelity simulations have validities comparable to those of high-fidelity simulations (Motowidlo et al., 1990; Motowidlo & Tippins, 1993). Thus, low-fidelity work (and teamwork) samples remain a very attractive option for building sound psychological selection systems for future long-duration spaceflight endeavors. NASA has already introduced some team exercises to provide additional data on candidate competencies that were not thoroughly evaluated in other parts of the selection process. In 2009, candidates were assigned to teams responsible for completing tasks designed to mimic many of the cognitive and social problem-solving challenges that behavioral health and performance experts expected crews to face during expeditionary missions to the moon or Mars (Sipes, Polk, Beven, & Shepanek, 2016). Psychologists observed candidates in real time and collected observations of their behavior. Review of the effectiveness of this selection method revealed that successful completion of the exercise was often characterized by an "aha" moment experienced by a single team member when he/she identified a method for successfully overcoming the technical task presented to the team. From that point, the exercise became primarily about successfully executing a plan to implement the solution identified by that team member and was less effective in providing a forum that fostered opportunities for all participants to demonstrate their team-related capabilities. In addition, the exercise had been chosen without extensive forethought regarding the competencies that were most important to evaluate in a real-time setting.

The team exercise was modified for the 2013 selection cycle to alleviate these limitations (Beven, Holland, Picano, Moomaw, Slack, & Vander Ark, 2018). First, critical team-related competencies that were not effectively evaluated in other parts of the selection system were identified. The design of the exercise was modified to create opportunities for all participants to demonstrate those skills as the team worked to execute its task and a peer review component was added to the end of the exercise. Further, a second source of peer feedback was added at the end of the selection week. After having spent multiple days working and living together in crew quarters, candidates provided feedback on one another regarding their experiences during the final stage of the selection process (e.g., can you live with this person?). Further, in 2017, the MARS team simulation and an individual, "day in the life of an astronaut" simulation was added (Beven et al., 2018). The latter simulation requires applicants to interface with "Mission Control" and to execute mission-related tasks and simulate the muti-team system conditions inherent in the role today.

The teamwork exercises and peer-feedback aspects of these work samples are innovative and promising, but remain difficult to validate because of our three recurring primary challenges. The samples sizes will likely remain small for both developing and validating such work samples. The specific teamwork contexts and performance requirements will continue to evolve as new vehicles, equipment, and systems are created to enable longer-duration space exploration by humans.

Other space agencies have looked to real-time exercises as a context for evaluating team skills as well. For example, ESA astronaut candidates complete group and didactic team exercises that provide opportunities to display their competency in interacting with others and personality traits suitable for future astronauts during the final week of selection at the European Astronaut Centre (Maschke et al., 2011). JAXA has observed candidates as they complete tasks in a group setting since the early 90s (Endo et al., 1994). More recently, the agency added a one-week stay in an isolation chamber to its selection process. Here, candidates are continuously observed as they perform group and personal tasks, providing a rich environment in which to assess their leadership, teamwork skills, and productivity. Although this selection activity has not been formally validated, JAXA's BHP experts have provided considerable positive feedback on its effectiveness. It provides critical information that confirms (or corrects) information gathered in earlier phases of the selection process regarding candidate's skill in critical intra-personal and interpersonal competencies (Inoue & Tachibana, 2013).

CONCLUSIONS AND RECOMMENDATIONS

Space agencies and other organizations hoping to leverage work samples to improve psychological selection for extreme environment work would benefit from cooperating to collect data in analogous jobs and contexts. Such data could be combined and generalized to better address our three recurring challenges. There is strong agreement among the international space agencies regarding the competencies most critical for success on LDMs (i.e., motivation, relevant biological experience, cognitive/psychomotor capabilities, coping with stress and interpersonal behavior, interpersonal/teamwork skills, and cross-cultural competence) (Maschke et al., 2011). The varied approaches each agency has taken to measuring these competences provide a valuable opportunity to compare their effectiveness and extract best practices and perhaps standardized methods of assessing such skills for future selection cycles.

The most critical aspiration to date is to provide evidence-based specificity and underpinning to the tests, scales, exercises, interviews and other assessment tools used in each selection cycle. Further, it is important to evaluate their ability to predict more than a single, traditional performance criterion (e.g., performance in the probationary year, training and mission performance, annual supervisory ratings of job performance, peer ratings) and look for more innovative and relevant outcomes of interest.

Also, the *Uniform Guidelines on Employee Selection Procedures* (Section 5.K) (EEOC & CSC, 1978) and other relevant professional standards suggest that validity, once demonstrated, does not necessarily endure. Whenever the requirements of a job change substantially, or another equally valid selection procedure with less adverse impact becomes available, users may be required to revalidate or reassess the use of tests in the organization. The conditions and circumstances under which revalidation may be necessary are not clearly specified by the *Uniform Guidelines*. This suggests that even if the astronaut selection process is traditionally validated, researchers must continue periodically collecting criterion data from applicants selected so that validity can be re-evaluated.

Given the challenges already discussed, traditional validation is very unlikely. Thus, validity generalization or synthetic validation research and tactics are extremely important to the future of psychological selection for extreme environments. Validity generalization depends on the similarity between jobs and performance criteria and requires regular and recurring assessment of the astronaut role, knowledges, skills, abilities, duties, tasks, and personal characteristics (Steinke Schmidt, Slack, & Keeton, 2013). Making this information explicit and public would help researchers identify jobs that perform similar tasks and duties and require similar knowledge, skills, and abilities in reasonable analogs here on Earth. Our hope is that by the time space agencies venture on the first human mission to Mars, there will be significant validity evidence on standardized psychological tests used to select personnel for analogous jobs that may then be combined and used to inform the creation of a highly effective psychological selection process for pioneers on this ultimate adventure.

Finally, a few other things could be done to maximize the fairness, accuracy, and legal defensibility of the astronaut selection process. Psychological selection for astronauts would greatly benefit from a general shift away from the current overwhelmingly clinical framework (i.e., to identify what is wrong with the candidate) to one more focused on the goal of identifying the candidates who are most likely to perform the role well. Shifting the framework would require a heavier focus on identifying clear behavioral anchors for evaluating candidates during all selection activities, grounding practices firmly in Industrial-Organizational Psychology in particular, and potentially moving responsibility for the process from its traditional home in Space Medicine to one in Human Resources/Talent Management. Shifting would also require space agencies to consider whether clinically trained assessors are in the best position to effectively observe, capture, categorize, and objectively use the candidate data coming from the selection process. Assessors with a stronger background in Industrial-Organizational Psychology or Talent Management may offer greater experience and facility with these tasks and be able to maximize the value of the data collected, as well as the way in it is combined and used to make selection recommendations.

There is also some limited potential to enhance psychological selection for the mission and the team; and this is where a more clinical framework could shine (e.g., given two or more qualified people for this role in this mission and team, what is potentially "wrong" with each of them and which represents the greater risk? What is the least risky/inflammatory mix of personality profiles or cultural norms for this group?).

The only certainty right now is that more contextual changes are on the way: to the job, to the missions, and to the organizations involved in spaceflight. For example, NASA used to distinguish between Mission Specialist (MS) and Pilot roles, but this changed when Shuttle missions terminated. Currently, all astronauts are classified as MS and they don't have responsibility for actively flying the ISS (Flight Controllers do that via programmed codes from Earth). Astronauts in the future will likely need to fly the spacecraft again, and it will be important to identify accurate methods of identifying those best suited for that task who also have good skills required for handling the newer teamwork and cross-cultural duties inherent in modern spaceflight. Major challenges for Martian crews are likely to include social isolation, physical confinement, a small and diverse crew, communication delays between crew and ground, extremely long duration, and a high consequence environment (Landon, Slack, & Barrett, 2018).

Although space analogs have allowed us to anticipate many key challenges involved in new endeavors such as Martian missions, it's impossible to anticipate the full scope of complexities. Some "educated guesses" must be made about the difficulties that these missions will present for the astronauts and agencies who will undertake them, and by extension, the skills and characteristics that will be required to succeed in this novel situation.

The opportunity to advance knowledge of best practices for selecting individuals for jobs that don't yet exist creates an alluring invitation to work on the "cutting edge." NASA's unique appeal to the general public and the unique and provocative nature of the astronaut role provide compelling reasons for researchers and practitioners to continue devoting time and energy to issues described in this chapter. Moreover, methods of overcoming these challenges can be applied to selection challenges in "mainstream" psychology. We believe that both the challenges and advances in psychology related to astronaut selection will benefit those operating in other extreme environments as well as those in more conventional applications (e.g., positions that involve exceptionally high reliability and/or high stakes work). The future starts here and now.

REFERENCES

Asher, J. J. (1972). The biographical item: Can it be improved? *Personnel Psychology*, *25*(2), 251–269.

Asher, J. J., & Sciarrino, J. A. (1974). Realistic work sample tests: A review. *Personnel Psychology*, *27*(4), 519–533.

Barrett, J. D., Holland, A. W., & Vessey, W. B. (2015). *Identifying the "Right Stuff": An exploration focused astronaut job analysis*. In 30th Annual Conference of the Society for Industrial and Organizational Psychology, Philadelphia, PA.

Barrick, M. R., Stewart, G. L., Neubert, M. J., & Mount, M. K. (1998). Relating member ability and personality to work-team processes and team effectiveness. *Journal of Applied Psychology*, *83*(3), 377.

Bell, S. T. (2007). Deep-level composition variables as predictors of team performance: A meta-analysis. *Journal of Applied Psychology*, *92*(3), 595.

Beven, G., Holland, A., Picano, J. Moomaw, R., Slack, K., & Vander Ark, S. (2018). Behavioral components of NASA's 2017 astronaut selection. Presentation at the 89th annual scientific meeting of the Aerospace Medical Association; 6–10 May 2018, Dallas, TX.

Bobko, P., Roth, P. L., & Potosky, D. (1999). Derivation and implications of a meta-analytic matrix incorporating cognitive ability, alternative predictors, and job performance. *Personnel Psychology, 52*(3), 561–589.

Breaugh, J. A. (2009). The use of biodata for employee selection: Past research and future directions. *Human Resource Management Review, 19*(3), 219–231.

Caldwell, B. S. (2005). Analysis and modeling of information flow and distributed expertise in space-related operations. *Acta Astronautica, 56*(9–12), 996–1004.

Carson, K. D., Carson, P. P., Fontenot, G., & Burdin Jr, J. J. (2005). Structured interview questions for selecting productive, emotionally mature, and helpful employees. *The Health Care Manager, 24*(3), 209–215.

Cascio, W. F., & Phillips, N. F. (1979). Performance testing: A rose among thorns? *Personnel Psychology, 32*(4), 751–766.

Chidester, T. R., Helmreich, R. L., Gregorich, S. E., & Geis, C. E. (1991). Pilot personality and crew coordination: Implications for training and selection. *The International Journal of Aviation Psychology, 1*(1), 25–44.

Chidester, T. R., Kanki, B. G., Foushee, H. C., Dickinson, C. L., & Bowles, S. V. (1990). *Personality factors in flight operations. Volume 1: Leader characteristics and crew performance in a full-mission air transport simulation.* NASA-TM-102259, A-90018, NAS 1.15:102259, United States. Retrieved from https://ntrs.nasa.gov/search.jsp?R=19900014054

Collins, D. L. (2003). Psychological issues relevant to astronaut selection for long-duration spaceflight: a review of the literature. *Journal of Human Performance in Extreme Environments, 7*(1), 1.

Cook, M., & Cripps, B. (2005). *Psychological assessment in the workplace: A manager's guide.* West Sussex, England: John Wiley & Sons Ltd.

Endo, T., Ohbayashi, S., Yumikura, S., & Sekiguchi, C. (1994). Astronaut psychiatric selection procedures: A Japanese experience. *Aviation, Space, and Environmental Medicine, 65*(10, Sect 1), 916–919.

Equal Employment Opportunity Commission, & Civil Service Commission. Department of Labor, & Department of Justice. (1978). Uniform guidelines on employee selection procedures. *Federal Register, 43*(166), 38290–38315.

Fassbender, C., & Goeters, K. M. (1994). Psychological evaluation of European astronaut applications: results of the 1991 selection campaign. *Aviation, Space, and Environmental Medicine, 65*(10, Sect 1), 925–929.

Fiedler, E. R., & Carpenter, F. E. (2005). Evolution of the behavioral sciences branch of the space medicine and health care systems office at the Johnson Space Center. *Aviation, Space, and Environmental Medicine, 76*(6), B31–B35.

Fox, S., & Spector, P. E. (2000). Relations of emotional intelligence, practical intelligence, general intelligence, and trait affectivity with interview outcomes: it's not all just 'G'. *Journal of Organizational Behavior: The International Journal of Industrial, Occupational and Organizational Psychology and Behavior, 21*(2), 203–220.

Galarza, L., & Holland, A. (1999a). Critical astronaut proficiencies required for long-duration space flight SAE Technical Paper Series 1999-01-2096, SAE International. doi: 10.4271/1999-01-2096.

Galarza, L., & Holland, A. (1999b). Selecting astronauts for long-duration space missions SAE Technical Paper Series 1999-01-2097, SAE International. doi: 10.4271/1999-01-2097.

Gregorich, S., Helmreich, R. L., Wilhelm, J. A., & Chidester, T. (1989). Personality based clusters as predictors of aviator attitudes and performance. International Symposium on Aviation Psychology, 5th, Columbus, OH, Apr. 17–20, 1989, Proceedings. Volume 2 (A90-26176 10-53). Ohio State University, Columbus, OH, pp. 686–691. Retrieved from https://ntrs.nasa.gov/search.jsp?R=19900039218

Highhouse, S., Doverspike, D., & Guion, R. M. (2015). *Essentials of personnel assessment and selection*. New York, NY: Routledge.

Hough, L. M., Oswald, F. L., & Ployhart, R. E. (2001). Determinants, detection and amelioration of adverse impact in personnel selection procedures: Issues, evidence and lessons learned. *International Journal of Selection and Assessment*, 9(1–2), 152–194.

Huffcutt, A. I., Weekley, J. A., Wiesner, W. H., Degroot, T. G., & Jones, C. (2001). Comparison of situational and behavior description interview questions for higher-level positions. *Personnel Psychology*, 54(3), 619–644.

Hunter, J. E., & Hunter, R. F. (1984). Validity and utility of alternative predictors of job performance. *Psychological Bulletin*, 96(1), 72.

Hurtz, G. M., & Donovan, J. J. (2000). Personality and job performance: The Big Five revisited. *Journal of Applied Psychology*, 85(6), 869.

Inoue, N., & Tachibana, S. (2013). An isolation and confinement facility for the selection of astronaut candidates. *Aviation, Space, and Environmental Medicine*, 84(8), 867–871.

Jones, R. G., Stevens, M. J., & Fischer, D. L. (2000). Selection in team contexts. *Managing selection in changing organizations: Human resource strategies*, (pp. 210–241). San Francisco, CA: Jossey-Bass.

Kanas, N., & Manzey, D. (2008). *Space psychology and psychiatry* (Vol. 22). El Segundo, CA: Springer Science & Business Media.

Kelechi, J. K., 2012. The importance of predictive and face validity in employee selection and ways of maximizing them: An assessment of three selection methods. *International Journal of Business and Management*, 7, 22, 115–122.

Lance, C. E., Johnson, C. D., Douthitt, S. S., Bennett Jr, W., & Harville, D. L. (2000). Good news: Work sample administrators' global performance judgments are (about) as valid as we've suspected. *Human Performance*, 13(3), 253–277.

Landon, L. B., Rokholt, C., Slack, K. J., & Pecena, Y. (2017). Selecting astronauts for long-duration exploration missions: considerations for team performance and functioning. *REACH: Reviews in Human Space Exploration*, 3, 33–56.

Landon, L. B., Slack, K. J., & Barrett, J. D. (2018). Teamwork and collaboration in long-duration space missions: Going to extremes. *American Psychologist*, 73(4), 563–575.

Landon, L. B., Vessey, W. B., & Barrett, J. D. (2016). *Evidence report: Risk of performance and behavioral health decrements due to inadequate cooperation, coordination, communication, and psychosocial adaptation within a team*. Houston, TX: NASA.

Leveton, L. B. (2014). *Review of isolated, confined extreme environment (ICE) studies*. Presented at International Congress on Medicine and Space, Berlin.

MacCallum, T, Poynter, J., & Bearden, D. (2004). Report #2004-01-2473 Paragon Space Development Corp. Lessons Learned from Biosphere 2: When Viewed as a Ground Simulation/Analog for Long Duration Human Space Exploration and Settlement.

Mael, F. A., Connerley, M., & Morath, R. A. (1996). None of your business: Parameters of biodata invasiveness. *Personnel Psychology*, 49(3), 613–650.

Manzey, D., Schiewe, A., & Fassbender, C. (1995). Psychological countermeasures for extended manned spaceflights. *Acta Astronautica*, 35(4–5), 339–361.

Maschke, P., Oubaid, V., & Pecena, Y. (2011). How do astronaut candidate profiles differ from airline pilot profiles? *Aviation Psychology and Applied Human Factors*, 1(1), 38–44.

McFarland, L. A., & Ryan, A. M. (2000). Variance in faking across noncognitive measures. *Journal of Applied Psychology*, 85(5), 812.

McGrath, J. E., Arrow, H., & Berdahl, J. L. (2000). The study of groups: Past, present, and future. *Personality and Social Psychology Review*, 4(1), 95–105.

Messick, S. (1995). Validity of psychological assessment: Validation of inferences from persons' responses and performances as scientific inquiry into score meaning. *American Psychologist*, 50(9), 741.

Messick, S. (1998). Test validity: A matter of consequence. *Social Indicators Research*, 45(1–3), 35–44.

Motowidlo, S. J., Dunnette, M., & Carter, G. (1990). An alternative selection procedure: The low-fidelity simulation. *Journal of Applied Psychology*, 75(6), 640.

Motowidlo, S. J., & Tippins, N. (1993). Further studies of the low-fidelity simulation in the form of a situational inventory. *Journal of Occupational and Organizational Psychology*, 66(4), 337–344.

Mumford, M. D., & Owens, W. A. (1987). Methodology review: Principles, procedures, and findings in the application of background data measures. *Applied Psychological Measurement*, 11(1), 1–31.

Musson, D. M., & Helmreich, R. L. (2005). Long-term personality data collection in support of spaceflight and analogue research. *Aviation, Space, and Environmental Medicine*, 76(6), B119–B125.

Musson, D. M., Sandal, G., & Helmreich, R. L. (2004). Personality characteristics and trait clusters in final stage astronaut selection. *Aviation, Space, and Environmental Medicine*, 75(4), 342–349.

Nicholas, J. M., & Foushee, H. C. (1990). Organization, selection, and training of crews for extended spaceflight-Findings from analogs and implications. *Journal of Spacecraft and Rockets*, 27(5), 451–456.

Ones, D. S., Dilchert, S., Viswesvaran, C., & Judge, T. A. (2007). In support of personality assessment in organizational settings. *Personnel Psychology*, 60(4), 995–1027.

Palinkas, L. A., Gunderson, E., Holland, A. W., Miller, C., & Johnson, J. C. (2000). Predictors of behavior and performance in extreme environments: the Antarctic space analogue program. *Aviation, Space, and Environmental Medicine*, 71(6), 619–625.

Pulakos, E. D., & Schmitt, N. (1996). An evaluation of two strategies for reducing adverse impact and their effects on criterion-related validity. *Human Performance*, 9(3), 241–258.

Reilly, R. R., & Chao, G. T. (1982). Validity and fairness of some alternative employee selection procedures. *Personnel Psychology*, 35(1), 1–62.

Rodriguez, D., Patel, R., Bright, A., Gregory, D., & Gowing, M. K. (2002). Developing competency models to promote integrated human resource practices. *Human Resource Management: Published in Cooperation with the School of Business Administration, The University of Michigan and in alliance with the Society of Human Resources Management*, 41(3), 309–324.

Rose, R. M., Fogg, L. F., Helmreich, R. L., & McFadden, T. J. (1994). Psychological predictors of astronaut effectiveness. *Aviation, Space, and Environmental Medicine*, 65(10, Sect 1), 910–915.

Santy, P. A., Endicott, J., Jones, D. R., Rose, R. M., Patterson, J., Holland, A. W.,... & Marsh, R. D. (1993). Results of a structured psychiatric interview to evaluate NASA astronaut candidates. *Military Medicine*, 158(1), 5–9.

Santy, P. A., & Jones, D. R. (1994). An overview of international issues in astronaut psychological selection. *Aviation, Space, and Environmental Medicine*, 65(10, Sect 1), 900–903.

Schmidt, F. L., & Hunter, J. E. (1998). The validity and utility of selection methods in personnel psychology: Practical and theoretical implications of 85 years of research findings. *Psychological Bulletin*, 124(2), 262.

Schmidt, F. L., Ones, D. S., & Hunter, J. E. (1992). Personnel selection. *Annual Review of Psychology*, 43(1), 627–670.

Schmidt, L. (2008a). *International space station human behavior and performance competency model: Volume II* (NASA Technical Report). Document ID: 20080018551. Retrieved from https://ntrs.nasa.gov/archive/nasa/casi.ntrs.nasa.gov/20080018551.pdf

Schmidt, L. L. (2008b). Competency modeling for the final frontier: Supporting psychosocial health and performance in low earth orbit. *Performance Improvement*, 47(3), 52–58.

Schmitt, N., Gooding, R. Z., Noe, R. A., & Kirsch, M. (1984). Metaanalyses of validity studies published between 1964 and 1982 and the investigation of study characteristics. *Personnel Psychology*, *37*(3), 407–422.

Sgobba, T., Landon, L. B., Marciacq, J. B., Groen, E., Tikhonov, N., & Torchia, F. (2018). Selection and training. In T. Sgobba, B. Kanki, J. Clervoy, and G. Sandal (Eds.), *Space safety and human performance* (pp. 721–793). Cambridge, MA: Butterworth-Heinemann.

Shepanek, M. (2005). Human behavioral research in space: quandaries for research subjects and researchers. *Aviation, Space, and Environmental Medicine*, *76*(6), B25–B30.

Sipes, W. E., Polk, J. D., Beven, G., & Shepanek, M. (2016). Behavioral health and performance. In A. E. Nicogossian, R. S. Williams, C. L. Huntoon, C. R. Doarn, J. D. Polk, and V. S. Schneider (Eds.), *Space physiology and medicine* (pp. 367–389). New York, NY: Springer.

Smither, J. W., Reilly, R. R., Millsap, R. E., AT&T, K. P., & Stoffey, R. W. (1993). Applicant reactions to selection procedures. *Personnel Psychology*, *46*(1), 49–76.

Steimle, H., & Norberg, C. (2013). Astronaut selection and training. In C. Norberg (Ed.) *Human spaceflight and exploration* (pp. 255–294). Berlin, Heidelberg: Springer.

Steinke, J. A., Schmidt, L. L., Slack, K. J., & Keeton, K. K. (2013). The synthetic validation of NASA's astronaut selection program. In J. Steinke (Chair), *Practical and legal considerations for alternative validation processes in organizations.* Presented at the Society for Industrial and Organizational Psychology Annual Conference, Houston, TX.

Stuster, J. (1996). *Bold endeavors: Lessons from polar and space exploration.* Annapolis, MD: Naval Institute Press.

Tanaka, M., & Watanabe, S. (1994). Overwintering in the Antarctica as an analog for long term manned spaceflight. *Advances in Space Research*, *14*(8), 423–430.

U. S. Office of Personnel Management (2018) Retrieved from https://www.opm.gov/policy-data-oversight/assessment-and-selection/other-assessment-methods/biographical-data-biodata-tests/

Vinograd, S. P. (1974). *Studies of social group dynamics under isolated conditions. Objective summary of the literature as it relates to potential problems of long duration space flight* (NASA CR-2496). Washington, DC: NASA.

Wood, J., Schmidt, L., Lugg, D., Ayton, J., Phillips, T., & Shepanek, M. (2005). Life, survival, and behavioral health in small closed communities: 10 years of studying isolated Antarctic groups. *Aviation, Space, and Environmental Medicine*, *76*(6), B89–B93.

Zedeck, S. (2011). *APA handbook of industrial and organizational psychology. Volume 2: Selecting and developing members for the organization.* APA Reference Books Collection. Washington, D.C.: American Psychological Association.

3 Out Of This World Jobs
Alternative Work Analysis and Validation Methods in Extreme Environments

Laura Galarza
Universidad de Puerto Rico

Julie A. Steinke[1]
The MITRE Corporation

Jamie D. Barrett
Federal Aviation Administration

CONTENTS

Challenges to Traditional Work Analysis Approaches 36
Alternative Work Analysis Methods 38
Alternative Validation Strategies 38
    Case # 1: NASA 1996–2001 Alternative Work Analysis and
    Selection Validation Projects 41
    BHP Decisions on Work Analysis and Validation in Response to Challenges 41
    Work Analysis of Long-Duration ISS Missions 44
    Recommendations for Using AWAM for EEPs 46
    Limitations and Caveats 47
Case Study #2: Synthetic Validation of Astronaut Selection Methods 48
    Challenges to Validating Astronaut Selection Measures 48
    Recommendations for Synthetically Validating the Astronaut
    Selection Process 49
    Limitations and Caveats 52
    Future Considerations 53
Case Study #3: Astronaut Job Analysis Project (2013–2014) 54

---

[1] The author's affiliation with The MITRE Corporation is provided for identification purposes only, and is not intended to convey or imply MITRE's concurrence with, or support for, the positions, opinions or viewpoints expressed by the author. Approved for Public Release; Distribution Unlimited. PRS Case 19-2710.

Work Analysis Methodology 54
Recommendations 57
Limitations and Practical Implications 58
Conclusion 58
References 58

Various methods can be applied to identify, analyze, and validate job competencies across numerous types of jobs. However, jobs that occur within extreme environments (e.g., the job of an astronaut) create a unique set of challenges that constrain the application of many of those methods, thereby making the process of identifying job competencies and validating selection measures much more difficult than it is for jobs in more traditional environments. In this chapter we review some of the challenges faced when conducting work analysis and validating selection measures within extreme environments, with a particular focus on astronaut work. We then utilize case studies to illustrate how NASA addressed some of these challenges within extreme environments using alternative work analysis methods, and provide recommendations for conducting similar work.

CHALLENGES TO TRADITIONAL WORK ANALYSIS APPROACHES

Recent innovations in approaches to job analysis have led various researchers to embrace more comprehensive concepts of "work," resulting in extended definitions of the term and to a deliberate use of wide-ranging concepts about work analysis. Morgeson and Dierdorff (2010) defined work analysis as "the systematic investigation of (1) work role requirements and (2) the broader context within which work roles are enacted." (p. 4). Their definition focused on work roles rather than the traditional focus on job tasks. This new focus has several advantages for how jobs are examined. For one, this approach provides a flexible language to describe work. This approach also enables the ability to integrate across job requirements. These benefits enable researchers to view jobs as dynamic rather than static, which creates an enhanced approach to better address the complexities of describing and analyzing work. This approach is particularly useful for astronaut positions where job requirements continually adapt to changes in extreme environments, technology, and other aspects of the work.

Work analysis information is used for a variety of purposes, such as the development of assessments (Sanchez & Levine, 2013), selection (Gatewood, Field, & Barrick, 2016), training, and performance management programs among other human resource systems (Morgeson & Dierdorff, 2010). A work analysis can impact the design and development of a job when combined with additional considerations (e.g., legal, financial, and quality control considerations). One of the most important and frequent uses of work analysis information is for the development and validation of employee selection measures. Jurisprudence on the topic of measurement at work, more specifically the Griggs vs. Duke Power (1971) case, established the requirement that employee selection measures must be job-related. Jurisprudence and the law require test developers and users to provide evidence of job-relatedness and validity (Hanges, Salmon, & Aiken, 2013). Authors such as Gatewood et al. (2016) argue that traditional validation strategies are practical for organizations that have large numbers of employees but that broader approaches to validity are needed for organizations with small sample sizes or other challenges. Therefore, organizations with unique jobs including extreme environment positions (EEPs) such as the astronaut job could face challenges in applying traditional validation approaches due to issues of sample size and job uniqueness, among other factors (Galarza & Holland, 1999a).

Professional guidelines regarding psychological and employment testing establish that validity and job-relatedness are the most important considerations in developing and evaluating employee selection procedures for any job. The Standards for Educational and Psychological Testing of the American Educational Research Association (AERA), American Psychological Association (APA), and the National Council on Measurement in Education (NCME) (2014) establish that validation begins with an explicit statement of the proposed interpretation of test scores, along with a rationale for the relevance of those interpretations. Thus, evidence must be accumulated to provide a sound scientific basis for the interpretation of test scores *and* for describing the relationship between test scores and the job in question. However, in the case of EEPs, accumulating such evidence poses its own challenges to the process. For example, gathering work-related evidence for a job that is performed in space is extremely difficult for several reasons. Whereas most jobs can be observed by subject matter experts (SMEs) or organizational psychologists, astronaut SMEs are few and far between and it is highly unlikely that SMEs or organizational psychologists can be in space alongside astronauts to observe job performance. Additionally, in cases where evidence from one job might be used to generalize knowledge about another job (e.g., to make inferences about the astronaut job based on a similar job such as expeditioners), such interpretations need to be scientifically based, although they are prone to high variability and error.

Traditional work analysis approaches face additional challenges that can impact the scientific soundness of such efforts. Typically, these constraints take the form of scientific, operational (i.e., business), financial, strategic, or legal constraints that can limit the application of traditional work analysis approaches (McPhail, 2007). In such cases, alternative validation strategies can supplement the use of traditional criterion-related (local) validation strategies (McPhail, 2007). Common scientific and organizational constraints to applying traditional work analysis and validation approaches to certain types of jobs and organizations have been identified by McPhail (2007). Scientific constraints include sampling concerns (e.g., sample availability and sample size), a lack of random selection and assignment, and the criterion problem, among others.

Organizations usually have limited options for addressing these scientific and organizational challenges and must identify alternative methods. However, EEPs face additional challenges. Galarza and Holland (1999a) identified several challenges to applying traditional work analysis methods associated with working in extreme environments. Many of these challenges reflect common problems for highly complex jobs in addition to those that occur in EEPs. These challenges include: job uniqueness, task dynamism, mission diversity, impact of work context and working conditions of long-duration space missions, and rapid technological change. Several alternative work analysis and validation methods have been identified to address these challenges with an emphasis on the application of alternative methods to EEPs. The following sections discuss the alternative methods in more detail.

ALTERNATIVE WORK ANALYSIS METHODS

Alternative work analysis methods (AWAM) do not follow the traditional work analysis models where the focus is on specific tasks performed and work responsibilities specific to those tasks. They also do not rely on the use of standardized job analysis questionnaires. Instead, AWAMs focus on worker requirements and the broader work context and working conditions in which jobs are performed. Several AWAMs exist and are applied in a variety of circumstances, including: worker-oriented work analysis (Morgeson & Dierdorff, 2010) (that we classify as "alternative" when used as replacement for task-based analysis), analysis of work context (McPhail et al., 1995), competency modeling (Campion et al., 2011), strategic work analysis (Sackett, Walmsley, & Laczo, 2012), personality-oriented work analysis (Goffin et al., 2011; Hogan, Davis, & Hogan, 2007), cognitive task analysis (Sackett et al., 2012), video-based ergonomic work analysis (Paquet, Mathiassen, & Dempsey, 2006), and a blended work analysis strategy (Lievens, Sanchez, & De Corte, 2004). Table 3.1 provides a brief summary of the aforementioned AWAMs and their relevance to EEPs and we refer readers to the provided citations for further details.

AWAMs address organizational constraints (both scientific and operational) and the practical realities of traditional validation research. Furthermore, there is a relationship between the AWAM and validation methods, where the decision about which method to use could be driven or impacted by the validation strategy. AWAMs enable organizations to collect relevant work information that is difficult to obtain through more traditional methods. As described by McPhail (2007), alternative methods provide concrete methods and techniques for evaluating inferences made using a selection measure to predict future performance in situations where traditional (criterion-related) validation research is not possible or practical. These methods contribute work and validity evidence for the job(s) in question.

ALTERNATIVE VALIDATION STRATEGIES

Depending on the context and purpose of a selection procedure, current progress in the development of alternative validation strategies suggest that sufficient validity evidence is available to justify the appropriateness of applying a selection system to a new setting without conducting a local validation research study (McPhail, 2007). The use of a selection procedure can be based on validity evidence generalized from other selection procedures – or from meta-analytic evidence – if it is deemed applicable to the job in question. Strategies for generalizing validity evidence have been delineated in the organizational research literature and include (1) validity generalization (Hunter & Schmidt, 2004; McDaniel, 2007), (2) test transportability (Gibson & Caplinger, 2007), and (3) synthetic validity (Johnson, 2007; Primoff,

TABLE 3.1
Alternative Work Analysis Methods as Applied to Extreme Environment Positions (EEPs)

Alternative Work Analysis Approaches	Definition	Challenges Faced in Analyzing EEPs Addressed by Use of Alternative Methods	Advantages (A), and Limitations (L) of Alternative Approach
Worker-oriented work analysis	Identifies worker characteristics needed for successful performance. Worker requirements include KSAOs needed to perform the work (Morgeson & Dierdoff, 2010).	Task dynamism, mission variety, lack of feasibility for analyzing all job tasks, relatively small number of SMEs.	A: KSAO identification L: Requires an inferential leap regarding job-relatedness if task analysis is not conducted.
Analysis of work context	Analysis of the psychosocial, structural, and physical environment in which work is performed by examining three higher order dimensions of work: interpersonal relationships, physical work conditions, and structural job characteristics (adapted from McPhail et al., 1995)	Extreme working conditions, diverse teams, challenging physical working conditions, positions with challenging psychosocial and physical environment	A: Work context is critical to the understanding of EEPs L: Requires an inferential leap. Must document relationship to worker requirements and/or competencies required to perform in EEPs
Competency modeling	Collections of knowledge, skills, abilities, and other characteristics (KSAOs) needed for effective performance. Competency modeling links the KSAOs required for the job to organizational strategy to generate a set of competencies required for job performance (Campion et al., 2011)	Changing jobs, future job, relatively small number of SMEs, strategic alignment	A: Cost-effectiveness; distinguishing top performers from average performers, descriptions of how competencies progress with employee level, the need to consider future job requirements either directly or indirectly, and ways to present competencies in a manner that facilitates ease of use (Campion et al., 2011) L: Requires an inferential leap regarding job-relatedness if task analysis is not conducted
Strategic work analysis	Focuses on analysis for changing job situations and projections about future work (Sackett et al., 2012)	Changing jobs, new positions, future jobs	A: Can be used to analyze future positions L: Prediction effectiveness potentially limited

(Continued)

TABLE 3.1 (Continued)
Alternative Work Analysis Methods as Applied to Extreme Environment Positions (EEPs)

Alternative Work Analysis Approaches	Definition	Challenges Faced in Analyzing EEPs Addressed by Use of Alternative Methods	Advantages (A), and Limitations (L) of Alternative Approach
Cognitive task analysis	Consists of the identification and analysis of cognitive processes that underlie task performance (Sackett et al., 2012)	Use for modeling cognitive processes of work; cognitively complex jobs	A: Use to understand work-related cognitive processes L: Considered a supplement (not a replacement) to traditional job analysis. No agreed-upon methods for conducting CTA; effortful
Personality oriented job-analysis	Direct identification of personality characteristics required to perform specific jobs; authors (e.g., Goffin et al., 2011) have presented evidence of its criterion-related validity. Personality oriented job analysis has been recommended as part of the process of converging validity generalization evidence for the use of personality tests (Hogan et al., 2007)	Use of information for developing or validating personality measures	A: Allows for the direct identification of personality characteristics required for the job L: SMEs might engage in self-serving bias when rating personality requirements
Video-based job analysis and video-based ergonomic job analysis	Use of live or recorded video to analyze work. A sub-set of this approach, video-based ergonomic job analysis, is used to identify risk exposure and hazardous work situations (Paquet et al., 2006)	Use when there is lack of feasibility for direct observation	A: Used for analyzing work for EEPs when direct observation is not possible or feasible L: Lacks direct observation. Requires trained and reliable coders
Blended approach	Blends task analysis and competency modeling and incorporates organizational strategy into the derivation of broad worker attributes or competencies combined with the methodological rigor of task analysis (Lievens et al., 2004)	Use when the combination of traditional task analysis and competency modeling is feasible	A: Incorporates strategy into the identification of competencies while maintaining the rigor of task analysis L: Use only when the combination of traditional and alternative methods is feasible

1957; Primoff, 1959, Peterson & Bownas, 1982), including the JRM (J-coefficient) Model and Job Component Validity (JCV) approaches (Hoffman, Rashkovsky, & D'Egidio, 2007). Table 3.2 summarizes the definitions and characteristics of these methods.

It is important to note that the approaches to synthetic validity summarized in Table 3.2 are not mutually exclusive and the use of any methods should lead to a convergence in results. Further, combining alternative methods would be beneficial in that doing so enables a broader analysis of how various test scores relate to identified competencies associated with specific jobs. Alternative validation strategies prove useful when faced with the scientific and operational constraints that present challenges to many traditional work analysis approaches. In the next section we demonstrate how NASA used various alternative methods to analyze the astronaut job and attempted to validate those findings and provide insights into how these approaches can be applied to other EEPs.

To demonstrate the value of alternative methods for studying EEPs, we present three case studies that illustrate NASA's use of alternative work analysis and validation methods. Together, these case studies demonstrate a progression (over several years) of job analysis approaches involving alternative work analysis and validation methods. The case studies present the decisions and methods used by the NASA Behavioral Health and Performance Group (BHP) to address the challenges of analyzing and validating selection measures for the astronaut job. Each case study is unique in the focus and methodology. Case Study #1 presents alternative work analysis methods used to examine astronaut competencies and work demands required for long-duration (versus short-duration) space missions. Case Study #2 explored possible alternatives for conducting synthetic validation that could be applied to future validation efforts. Case Study #3 examined the linkage between a comprehensive work analysis and the validation approaches.

CASE # 1: NASA 1996–2001 ALTERNATIVE WORK ANALYSIS AND SELECTION VALIDATION PROJECTS

Case Study #1 summarizes a NASA BHP project conducted from 1996 to 2001 on alternative work analysis with results applied to astronaut selection, training, and support. The project built on prior NASA analysis of the astronaut job conducted by Jeanneret (1988) using the Position Analysis Questionnaire (PAQ). The first main objective was to examine and document work differences and worker competencies required for long-duration space missions. The second objective was to update, develop, and validate selection measures and training countermeasures for International Space Station (ISS) missions.

BHP DECISIONS ON WORK ANALYSIS AND VALIDATION IN RESPONSE TO CHALLENGES

In response to the challenges inherent in the analysis of EEPs, BHP made various decisions in 1996 regarding work analysis approaches and methods. The first decision was to use a *worker-oriented job analysis* with characteristics similar to what

TABLE 3.2
Alternative Validation Approaches, EEP Challenges Addressed and Requirements and Advantages of Alternative Approaches

Alternative Validation Approaches	EEP Challenges Addressed	Requirements (R), Advantages (A), and Limitations (L)
Validity Generalization (VG) is "the conclusion that validity generalizes across common situational variables that might differ from one setting to another" (Gibson & Capliner, 2007, p.35). It involves the "application of meta-analysis to the correlations between an employment test and a criterion, typically jobs or workplace training performance." (McDaniel, 2007, p. 159)	Task dynamism, mission variety, lack of feasibility for local validation, relatively small number of SMEs, changing job, jobs that do not exist	**R:** Availability of validity evidence, job similarity in major work behaviors, evidence of fairness, substantial similarity in the job performed **A:** cost-effectiveness **L:** job similarity with EEPs would be required
Test transportability (TT) refers to the extent to which tests validated in one location can be used in other locations (Gibson & Capliner, 2007). Test transportability is likely to provide support for the use of previously validated tests in jobs that share specific characteristics with the EEP	Lack of feasibility for local validation, relatively small number of SMEs, new jobs, changing job	**R:** Availability of validity evidence, job similarity in major work behaviors, evidence of fairness, substantial similarity in the job performed **A:** Cost-effectiveness **L:** Job similarity with EEPs would be required. According to Hoffman and McPhail (1998), validated tests can be used without conducting a local validation study provided there is substantial similarity in the job performed, applicants, and incumbents
Synthetic Validity (SV) "describes the logical process of inferring test-battery validity from predetermined validities of the tests for basic work components" (Mossholder and Arvey, 1984, p. 323). These techniques involve predicting test scores from job component scores (Johnson, 2007)	Task dynamism, mission variety, lack of feasibility for local validation, relatively small number of SMEs	**R:** Availability of validity evidence, similarity in job components, evidence of fairness, substantial similarity in the job performed **A:** cost-effectiveness **L:** similarity in job components would be required. Mossholder and Arvey (1984) also compared synthetic validation with validity generalization (VG), noting that SV requires more detailed analysis of the job(s) than Validity Generalization

(Continued)

TABLE 3.2 (Continued)
Alternative Validation Approaches, EEP Challenges Addressed and Requirements and Advantages of Alternative Approaches

Alternative Validation Approaches	EEP Challenges Addressed	Requirements (R). Advantages (A), and Limitations (L)
Synthetic Validity: **JRM/The J-coefficient Model** is a method for determining an index of agreement between elements within jobs and tests expected to relate to those job elements (Primoff, 1957, 1959). Thus, if it is known that a test is valid for an element, it is then possible to estimate the value of the test to the job. Peterson and Bownas (1982) referred to this method as the Job Requirement Matrix (JRM)	Changing job, jobs that do not yet exist, Future work, and a relatively small number of SMEs	**R:** Commonality of job components, similar inferences across situations and jobs **A:** Practical, legally defensible. One advantage to the J-coefficient is that any set of elements can be evaluated as a pattern. The J-coefficient formula represents the degree to which individual elements uniquely contribute to a test score and provides a rating of the "relative importance of job elements for people who work at a job" (Primoff, 1957) compared to traditional validity coefficients, which provide ratings of relative job proficiency for people working in a job. Job elements (requirements) are demonstrative of aptitudes and abilities and are identified by experts knowledgeable of the job who rate the importance of various job elements. Assuming these relationships are stable, overall performance can be predicted by job elements, which can then be translated into validity coefficients. **L:** Similarity in job elements required
Synthetic Validity: **Job Component Validity (JCV)** is a technique that determines the extent to which incumbents' test scores (or test validity coefficients) relate to an attribute/component's importance to a job (Hoffman et al., 2007; McCormick, 1959)	Changing job, jobs that do not yet exist, future work, and relatively small number of SMEs	**R:** Commonality of job components, similar inferences across situations and jobs. A basic assumption behind JCV is that common behaviors shared by different jobs require the same individual attributes to carry out such behaviors (McCormick, DeNisi, & Shaw, 1979). This information indirectly links test scores and job components across jobs **A:** Practical, legally defensible, compatible with the Uniform Guidelines **L:** Similarity in job elements required

is today called *competency modeling* (Campion et al., 2011), an alternative work analysis methodology defined in Table 3.1. NASA decided to integrate into the work analysis process elements of what is now called *strategic work analysis* (Sackett et al., 2012) consisting of asking SMEs to describe competencies needed for the ISS astronaut job not yet identified by NASA. NASA also analyzed the work context by examining psychosocial, physical, and structural job demands unique to the work of long-duration space station astronauts. The decision was made to combine qualitative focus groups and administration of quantitative questionnaires completed by SMEs chosen with strict inclusion criteria regardless of the resulting sample size. Technological integrations also were included, particularly the use of group decision support systems and computer technology for collecting data and administering questionnaires. NASA relied on content and construct validation of selection measures and training countermeasures. The NASA BHP examined the relationship between selection measures and qualitative judgments of the applicants' competency level, and examined meta-analytic evidence in the published literature for validity generalization of some measures. The alternative method of validity generalization was used due to lack of availability of quantitative performance data. During the 1996–1998 period it was not possible to conduct a local validation study to examine the criterion-related validity of selection measures for ISS missions that began years later. The first International Space Station mission, ISS Expedition 1, began on October 31, 2000 (NASA, 2015).

WORK ANALYSIS OF LONG-DURATION ISS MISSIONS

To address work analysis challenges, NASA developed a data-driven qualitative and quantitative examination of unique environmental demands and astronaut proficiencies required for long-duration space station missions (LDM) that lasted more than 30 days (excluding potential future Lunar and Mars missions) and short-duration missions (SDM) space that lasted less than 30 days (e.g., shuttle missions). This effort was designed to guide ongoing revisions to astronaut selection and training for space missions. A worker-oriented analysis (i.e., competency analysis) was combined with elements from a strategic work analysis to examine the proficiencies needed for LDMs while work context was explored by examining the environmental demands of the missions.

NASA conducted extensive literature reviews and debriefings with astronauts and mission support experts at NASA in addition to experts from ISS partner agencies with experience in flying or supporting non-NASA missions (e.g., *Mir* Space Station missions) who served as SMEs for the project. Strict criteria were used to identify SMEs with direct flight experience or support roles on LDMs. The criteria for inclusion were favored over use of a larger sample to ensure that SMEs were as qualified as possible to provide the necessary insights. The project team developed a list of potential proficiencies and job demands to be validated by a focus group of SMEs consisting of management, astronauts, and mission support experts. The SMEs reviewed and revised questionnaire items through qualitative discussions and the use of a computerized group decision support system. Part I of the questionnaire consisted of 47 proficiencies and behavioral indicators of each proficiency. SMEs were asked to rate the importance of each proficiency for long- and short-duration missions. Part II consisted of 42 job and environmental demands associated with LDMs and SDMs. SMEs rated the importance and probability that each demand occurred. Questionnaires were completed by 20 astronaut and mission support SMEs from NASA, the Russian Space Agency (RSA), and the European Space Agency (ESA). Results of this effort, described in more detail by Galarza & Holland (1999a), indicated statistically significant differences in average ratings of importance across proficiencies (KSAOs), with some KSAOs demonstrating higher importance than others. Furthermore, results indicated that KSAOs differed in terms of importance ratings for SDM and LDM.

Critical Astronaut Competencies

The primary aim of this work was to understand proficiencies needed for LDMs and how those proficiencies differed from SDM proficiencies. Forty-seven KSAOs were classified by five SMEs into ten factors. The average criticality rating was calculated for astronaut proficiencies within each of the ten factors. These calculations resulted in ten-factor criticality ratings for LDMs and ten factor criticality ratings for SDMs. The most critical factors for LDMs (in order of criticality) were mental and emotional stability, group living, working under stress, teamwork, and family issues. The results of the study provided an empirically based categorization of critical non-technical skills required for adaptability to LDMs. Despite the evidence showing that the astronaut proficiencies identified in the study are relevant to human adaptability to both SDM and LDM, the results revealed differences between the criticality ratings for both types of missions. The findings indicated a different criticality order for the factors when sorted by criticality for SDMs (Galarza & Holland, 1999a).

Work Context

The understanding of work context is critical in the analysis of EEPs, particularly for the astronaut position. The second part of the study described in Case Study #1 consisted of an examination of critical working conditions of ISS missions. The most critical job and environmental demands of LDMs to the ISS were categorized as: separation from family and friends; difficult living circumstances, habitability issues in confinement (e.g., crowding); work load, work tasks, and recreational issues; health, safety, and risk issues; composition and dynamics of heterogeneous international crews; demands for interactions with external groups; high visibility of work/human errors; and interactions with complex systems, and artificial life support systems.

Application of Work Analysis Information

Based on the empirical results of this operational study, and the judgment of SME raters, unique space station mission job demands and working conditions that could significantly affect an astronaut's adaptability and performance during missions were identified. These critical astronaut proficiencies and environmental job demands were used as the basis for developing psychological selection, training, and support tools for astronauts. BHP used proficiency and environmental demands information to upgrade psychological selection measures, psychological and expeditionary training, and psychological support countermeasures for astronauts.

Astronaut Selection

Astronaut selection measures for LDMs to the ISS were upgraded and new measures were developed as need identified (Galarza & Holland, 1999b). Given the ISS was not yet operational, performance data was not available – or not feasible to obtain – so BHP collected evidence on various types of validity inferences (construct and content validity, validity generalization, and other alternative validation strategies discussed in this chapter) as well as expert judgments. Internal BHP qualitative and quantitative reviews integrating results of published meta-analytic studies (e.g., Hunter & Hunter, 1984; Mumford & Owens, 1987; Reilly & Chao, 1982) examined the relationships between selection measures and job performance and contributed to the accumulation of validity generalization evidence (Galarza & Holland, 1999b). BHP examined the statistical relationship among selection tools and tests that measured the same competencies (construct validation), provided evidence of SME linkages between competencies and selection tools (content validation by five selection SMEs, three of whom were external to NASA), and the relationships between selection measures and interview ratings of competencies (convergent validity). These results provided insights into the relationships between test scores and required competencies for LDMs that would inform future selection procedures.

Expeditionary Training

The ten required competencies for space missions were further categorized by BHP SMEs in three main training themes: self-care/self-management, teamwork, and leadership (Hysong, Galarza, & Holland, 2007). A team of SMEs from BHP and members of the Astronaut Office collaborated on the design, field testing, and revision of expeditionary training activities for astronauts which consisted of didactic and experiential components. A peer-rating checklist form was developed to measure expeditionary training performance in the three main training themes.

Recommendations for Using AWAM for EEPs

The AWAM used in Case Study #1 led to the collection of data about work-related proficiencies and demands that informed improvement of astronaut selection and training processes. The valuable alternative methods provided work-related information and evidence when traditional methods were not viable. The following recommendations based on lessons learned from Case Study #1 could be implemented in future applications of alternative work analysis methods for the astronaut job and other EEPs.

Recommendation 1
Worker oriented, competency modeling approaches combined with aspects of strategic work analysis and analysis of the work context should be used to address the

challenges of analyzing work in EEPs. These approaches address the challenges of applying traditional task-based approach to the analysis of EEPs. Organizations with EEPs could use one or a combination of these approaches to analyze recently created jobs, jobs that do not yet exist, or when task-based job-analysis is not feasible. Authors such as Lievens et al. (2004) have recommended blended approaches.

Recommendation 2

To address sample size limitations, we recommend using focus groups and SMEs chosen with strict inclusion criteria. Lievens et al. (2004) empirically demonstrated the importance of expertise in making more reliable and accurate work-related judgements and argued that SME selection is a critical aspect of applying alternative work analysis methods. Subject matter expertise is important for addressing concerns regarding legal defensibility of SME inferences of job relevance. In summary, SMEs should be selected very carefully to address the challenges of the inferential process inherent to competency modeling in the absence of task-based or standardized job analysis techniques.

Recommendation 3

Integrate technology in competency modeling and work analysis processes where appropriate. Technology can be integrated at various phases of the project including the use of group-decision support systems and computer versions of questionnaires. Mason and Lin (2008) advocate for the integration of technology in these processes and propose the use of web-based focus groups, online data warehouses of competency models, and online surveys to gather data from SMEs and incumbents, as well as leveraging the use of existing online databases of job information such as the Occupational Information Network (O*NET). However, implementation must consider the limitations of automation and technology use including cultural, access, job, and organizational variables.

Recommendation 4

When EEP performance data is not available or not easy to obtain, evidence for various types of validity inferences should be collected. Consistent with Case Study #1 and with previous publications (e.g., McPhail, 2007), it is highly recommended that enough evidence be accumulated through construct validation, content validation, and through alternative validation strategies discussed in this chapter.

LIMITATIONS AND CAVEATS

Case Study #1 did not include insights from a task analysis because the task-level analysis was replaced with an alternative work analysis method. Additionally, 20 SMEs were used, representing a less than desirable sample size that increases the likelihood of problems associated with sampling error. However, only a few NASA astronauts and mission-support experts had lived and worked on *Mir* missions. Because the aim of the study was to identify the LDM critical skills required of NASA astronauts and the associated job demands and working conditions for LDMs on the ISS, BHP preferred the inclusion of individuals who had direct participation or support experience on LDMs. The inclusion of behavioral experts, mission support experts, and astronauts from a variety of space agencies helped maximize the number of available SMEs. Further, although NASA updated its selection measures in this work, these measures lacked local criterion-related validation evidence.

Despite the insights and gains developed from the work described in Case Study #1, NASA's mission continued to progress and with it, the demands and needs of the astronaut job were altered. The space shuttle program ended in 2011 as NASA was charged with working toward manned missions to Mars. Thus, the job of astronaut fundamentally changed and further work was necessary to determine how previous work analysis information, in addition to other alternative methods, could be used to identify and validate astronaut core competencies for Mars missions. Case Study #2 explores this work.

CASE STUDY #2: SYNTHETIC VALIDATION OF ASTRONAUT SELECTION METHODS

As noted earlier, specific circumstances (e.g., small samples, rapidly changing jobs, or insufficient resources) mitigate the extent to which traditional validation approaches are useful in some organizational contexts (McPhail, 2007). Under these circumstances validity generalization techniques can be used to validate selection procedures (EEOC, 1978). NASA continually faces such circumstances concerning its astronaut selection process and as a result, in 2012 explored how synthetic validation could be applied to develop a method that identified comprehensive astronaut characteristics and their relationship to space flight suitability and job performance. Several synthetic validation approaches were considered to identify an effective method (or combination of methods) to validate its astronaut selection process. Although the synthetic validation approach has not yet been applied directly to astronaut selection methods, its potential for usage is outlined in this case study.

CHALLENGES TO VALIDATING ASTRONAUT SELECTION MEASURES

To understand behaviors that encompass attributes expected to relate to successful performance as an astronaut, BHP identified core competencies important for successful astronaut performance in LDMs (Bessone et al., 2008). These competencies represent individual characteristics that appear vital to successful astronaut job performance and include: emotional stability, performance under stress, communication skills, group living, and team skills, among others. These competencies are expected to result in high performance and success within the astronaut role and can be evaluated across many activities. The collection of competency data and evaluation of the core competencies' relationships with predictor tests and levels of performance would provide validation evidence for the use of psychological measures for selection purposes. However, traditional approaches to performance measurement and evaluation are not possible. Thus, astronaut job and mission performance data that could help determine and rank salient personality characteristics and behaviors of high performing astronauts is unavailable.

A lack of quantitative data on astronaut performance in space missions and several other factors limit the criterion-related validity of selection measures, leaving psychometric characteristics of astronaut selection measures unvalidated through traditional methods. A significant limitation to the validation of selection measures is the fact that few people experience the highly unique position of astronaut. Prior to the 2012–2013 astronaut selection cycle, only 330 individuals had served as U.S. astronauts, reflecting a selection ratio of approximately 0.006%, drastically different from most jobs. A relatively small proportion of the applicant pool that progresses to the psychological testing stage of the selection process, and range restriction of predictors and possible range restriction of potential criteria, can affect validity coefficient sizes (Cascio & Aguinis, 2018).

Criterion identification also limits the use of traditional validation strategies. Evaluating astronaut performance is difficult for several reasons. Time demands of astronauts are highly constrained as they almost constantly train for mission-specific requirements. Most importantly, not only does NASA lack consistent performance data from astronauts, but most job performance activities occur in space and are not easily observed and the limited performance data that do exist do not provide enough variability within or between astronauts. These limitations make it difficult to identify the range in performance needed to demonstrate test-criterion co-variance. In spite of these limitations it is crucial to provide validity evidence consistent with scientific, legal, and professional standards (e.g., AERA et al., 2014; EEOC, 1978; SIOP, 2003). These challenges and constraints limit the use of traditional validation approaches for measures used in astronaut selection. Alternative validation strategies, however, can provide insight into the usefulness of psychological measures for selection practices despite these constraints.

Evaluating predictors of astronaut core competencies (e.g., tests or activities to evaluate team skills) increase understanding of how competencies combine to represent the appropriate mix of attributes for successful spaceflight performance. Ultimately, combining information about each identified core competency could help formulate an overall validity coefficient summarizing the relationship between various psychological predictors and all astronaut job competencies. Synthetic validation is an alternative approach that could enable increased use of psychological measures to aid astronaut selection procedures.

Recommendations for Synthetically Validating the Astronaut Selection Process

Case Study #2 focused on the examination of alternative validation approaches to astronaut selection methods. The BHP conducted a review of synthetic validation procedures to make specific recommendations and inform future applications of this validation process for astronaut selection measures. Based on a review of synthetic validation procedures and existing information regarding the astronaut selection process (e.g., BHP reports), recommendations were identified for how to synthetically validate psychological measures used to select astronauts or other EEPs. These recommendations describe how to create an integrative approach for synthetic validation and identify potential knowledge or data gaps in the validation process that should be addressed before applying alternative validation methods, as well as identify techniques to assess reliability through cross-validation.

Recommendation 1

Organizations with EEPs should conduct an updated work analysis whenever the job (e.g., type of mission) changes. Updated work analyses form the basis for the identification and future measurement of updated competencies (e.g., behavioral markers).

Recommendation 2

To gain a full understanding of EEP performance (e.g., astronaut performance), performance standards for all levels of overall performance must be defined. For example, BHP should continue to examine existing sources of performance data and identify new methods for defining and collecting additional performance data. Ideally, BHP should be able to distinguish between high, medium, and low levels of astronaut performance. As LDMs change, slight variations in performance among astronauts could impact crew safety and mission completion.

Recommendation 3

A database of research identifying relationships between job components (e.g., competencies) and associated psychological measures should be developed. This database should include research on similar EEPs (e.g., those facing extreme weather or isolation), as well as other occupations where incumbents are expected to demonstrate similar desired competencies (e.g., pilots, policemen, arctic expeditioners). Such empirical knowledge is useful for the evaluation of relationships between psychological measures and overall performance across a variety of occupations and settings that share characteristics with the astronaut position. This information can form the basis for research questions and hypotheses concerning how similar findings might generalize across populations. Empirical evidence from other occupations could be weighted based on shared characteristics with astronauts and be combined with existing data available from testing sources to further evaluate weighting schemes. Test source validation data would provide an overall coefficient for how each test relates to specific competencies and to performance indicators. A database of similar occupations makes it possible to determine the extent to which relationships differ across particular jobs, further refining the relationship between specific tests and identified competencies. In other words, a predictor test carrying similar weights across occupations could become stronger in extreme environments, indicating that the test should potentially be weighted differently under certain circumstances despite being valid across a wide range of occupations. Additionally, some competencies might be more important than others. For instance, those high in perseverance are likely to work through problems, a beneficial trait in extreme environments. But the ability to make sound judgments could be more important in dynamic situations (e.g., when the crew needs to abandon a task in order to stay alive). This information would support further synthetic validation approaches by providing guidance for how to formulate component weights when calculating overall validity coefficients.

Recommendation 4

Multiple synthetic validation methods should be used to determine which identified relationships exist among a sample comprised solely of EEPs (e.g., astronauts). Two specific models are recommended: JCM and J-Coefficient/JRM (assuming overall performance measures are subsequently defined). Combined results from these approaches provide evidence of how psychological predictors relate to various competencies desired among astronauts, as well as indicators of astronaut performance. Results from these approaches should converge, demonstrating consistencies across examined relationships.

JCV can be used to determine the importance of each competency to the occupation. Regression equations, using data from meta-analysis described earlier, combined with data from current astronaut populations can identify regression weights (betas) that signify the importance of the component to overall performance. These weights should be calculated on the basis of perceived judgments to examine agreement between the two methods. Judgments of a competency's importance should be obtained from several sources to fully define job behavior. Sources should include supervisors, training managers, peers, and others (e.g., management astronauts who demonstrate significant understanding of job demands). This information could be supplemented by results from other research efforts, such as BHP's video job analysis, which used video-taped examples from NASA missions to evaluate astronaut behavior in space. Thus, weights should be informed by various sources. However, it would be helpful to determine the extent to which certain sources might be more important than others (e.g., a supervisor's perceptions of competency importance might need to be weighted more than a training manager's perceptions of those competencies). JCM provides information about the specific weights each competency should carry in relation to overall job performance. Once weights are obtained, they can be summed, resulting in a larger regression equation for predicting performance. The fact that multiple ways to calculate larger regression equations exist provides support for the use of multiple methods (e.g., they converge), and can identify further knowledge gaps or questions to be answered (e.g., why methods might fail to converge). However, it is important that an increased potential for error does exist with this method and should be considered by researchers before making any final conclusions, particularly in cases of small sample sizes, smaller regression weights, too much variance unaccounted for due to summing of weights, or, alternatively, not enough astronaut performance data to accurately test the model. The limitations could further contribute to the existing range restriction problem in validation where a ceiling effect might already exist for many of these competencies. The JRM (J-coefficient) model enables ranking of job components by importance. This method is an alternative to regression analyses, whose standardized coefficients inform importance ratings. Ideally, conclusions from these methods would converge with components following the same rank order, if not having similar importance weights. Trained raters can determine if weights need to be more succinct (on target with each other), thereby addressing variance across raters (e.g., training managers rating astronauts differently than management astronauts). This process should be used at least until reliability in the rating process is demonstrated (e.g., people consistently rate others similarly, or the most consistent raters are identified).

Recommendation 5
Simulated data that models the psychological characteristics of astronauts identified using the above methods should be used to replicate findings. Replicating procedures with similar data sets determines the consistency of approaches across various samples. These comparisons provide a way to test method reliability and provide insight into potential methodological changes that could result in a more fine-tuned approach to calculating synthetic validity coefficients (e.g., conduct model comparisons of various weighting procedures).

LIMITATIONS AND CAVEATS

Several limitations potentially influence the results of any synthetic validation approach to astronaut selection. The first group of limitations of the application of synthetic validity are related to technical aspects. First, the lack of variability in outcome measures is likely to impact obtained results. Determining consistent and conceptually sound objective and/or quantitative measures of performance would help minimize this problem, although the extent to which competencies prove useful for predicting astronaut performance for future missions might remain unclear. Second, there are some technical limitations related to the application of the JRM Model. The JRM (J-coefficient) model was identified as potentially useful for BHP. However, to use JRM for the development of synthetic validity coefficients, BHP needs to further substantiate definition of overall astronaut performance. Until then, the JRM method could be difficult to use because no clear definition of astronaut performance exists, currently limiting a synthetic validation approach to using only the JCV method. It should be noted that Hollenbeck and Whitener (1988) identified one advantage to the JRM approach that could prove useful for NASA and similar EEP organizations. These authors suggest that an integrated approach to synthetic validity using sampling theory and matrix algebra did not need to fix the order of aggregation in validation, enabling the use of synthetic validation techniques in circumstances where organizations faced small sample sizes. This model for evaluating job elements' relationships with performance might provide BHP with a way to account for the relatively small sample size of astronauts available for evaluation. Further, it would be useful to determine which statistical manipulations are potentially applicable to the JCV approach, allowing for the use of a smaller sample size.

The second type of limitation is related to organizational and managerial support for work analysis and validation processes. Many recommendations provided here rely on support from constituents outside of BHP (e.g., management astronauts). Cooperation from various constituents in the synthetic validation process might be challenging for no other reason than many of these individuals have inordinate demands on their time that might inhibit them from participating in these procedures. Additionally, as some managers are not necessarily astronauts themselves, the question remains as to the extent to which these individuals fully comprehend and can effectively evaluate various dimensions of astronaut performance and/or the relative importance of various competencies. Performance rater training is advisable to attain more accurate quantitative performance ratings.

The third type of limitation is related to potential moderators of relationships between psychological predictors, competencies, and ultimately astronaut performance (e.g., experience and technology). For instance, the use of management astronauts' perceptions of competency importance when establishing competency weights might be moderated by the individual's experience. Management astronauts who only served on shuttle missions might have different perceptions of what competencies are important compared to others who only served on ISS missions. At this point in time, it is unclear how these differences might impact individual perceptions of competency performance for Mars missions.

Future Considerations

Implementing synthetic validation processes for astronaut selection require additional considerations. First, once a synthetic validation process is fully developed and conducted, data should be maintained (and continually collected) so that the process can be periodically reviewed to examine its continued reliability and how it is impacted by the addition of newly selected astronauts. This repetition is particularly important until a more traditional validation approach is feasible. Second, the organization should examine the impact of statistical artifacts (e.g., range restriction and small sample sizes) on validity results. Increasing the amount of data collected from applicants as the selection process continues could mitigate these artifacts. Additionally, evaluation of psychological characteristics could be compared between current astronauts and those individuals not selected (i.e., those who did not qualify for the final stage of the selection process but who did complete psychological screenings) to determine group differences. However, these analyses are likely impacted by a lack of power due to small sample sizes.

The astronaut selection process is an important process that potentially influences the extent to which missions succeed. It is imperative that the process be valid, reputable, legally defensible, and correctly identifies the desired psychological characteristics of individuals who are likely to succeed as astronauts. Synthetic validation approaches help identify which individuals are potentially ready for specific mission types, and identify gaps in selection process that should be addressed in future selection cycles. As NASA continues to explore the universe and the unique, sometimes unknown features it presents, the astronaut selection process must be as consistent and sound as possible. This process must be validated not only for the expected impact on future missions, but for the safety and concern of astronauts as those missions continue to evolve.

Case Study #2 focused on alternative validation methods by examining potential ways to apply the synthetic validity approach in the context of an EEP such as the astronaut job. The recommendations, limitations, and caveats presented for Case Study #2 assume a strong linkage between the work analysis and the alternative validation approach. The alternative validation approach of synthetic validity rests on the evidence collected through a comprehensive work analysis, the focus of Case Study #3, and additional work analysis efforts conducted in the future as the astronaut job continues to develop and change.

CASE STUDY #3: ASTRONAUT JOB ANALYSIS PROJECT (2013–2014)

Case Study #3 sought to strengthen the work analysis-alternative validation linkage and builds upon the synthetic validity approach by describing how NASA conducted a comprehensive job analysis to identify the non-technical competencies needed for long-duration spaceflight. The most comprehensive astronaut job analysis to date was conducted from 2013 to 2014 (see Barrett, Holland, & Vessey, 2015). At the time of the job analysis, missions were increasing in length, multiple exploration missions were being considered, and a Mars mission was a future goal. Because of this, it became apparent that a better understanding of astronaut characteristics and associated job demands was needed. Astronaut training takes several years, so the job analysis aimed to inform the selection and training of astronauts for years to come. In this job analysis, psychological and behavioral competencies required for US astronauts were identified and prioritized to determine which competencies would be needed at the time of selection versus those that could be trained once astronaut candidates were identified. Additionally, the job analysis sought to identify psychological and behavioral competencies needed for different mission types, resulting in the exclusion of technical aspects of selection.

Industrial/Organizational (I/O) Psychologists at Johnson Space Center conducted research in addition to two external I/O psychologists who provided additional expertise throughout the process. One challenge during the project was that the previous work analysis effort (Case Study #1) was conducted before three of four mission types had taken place, meaning a pool of veteran ISS astronauts was not yet available. Given the lack of job analysis data based on experienced ISS astronauts, BHP decided that the 2013–2014 job analysis effort would draw primarily from the experiences of 3–6 month ISS flyers, shuttle astronauts, and BHP Operations Specialists. The aim of this project was to determine what competencies were needed to perform existing and future missions and to collect information that would strengthen alternative validation methods.

WORK ANALYSIS METHODOLOGY

Selection of Subject Matter Experts

SMEs consisted of a total of 23 veteran long-duration ISS astronauts, two shuttle astronauts, and three BHP Operations Specialists with extensive experience supporting long-duration spaceflight. Astronauts were recruited in stages, beginning with a Core Panel. The first astronaut who agreed to be the main project contact recruited five other astronauts to serve on the core panel.

Mission Types

Mission types to include in the job analysis were determined by reviewing mission specifications for current, near future, and future potential missions, primarily from Design Reference Mission (DRM) documents. Because several types of future exploration missions existed, missions were sorted into categories for use in the job analysis using mission specification documents available at the time, resulting in four mission types (referred to as A, B, C, and D). A-type missions involved specifications related to 6-month missions to the ISS that were ongoing at the time. Characteristics of A-type missions involved real-time communication and low net habitable volume. B-type missions referred to ISS missions that lasted for 12 months. Although similar to A-type missions in many regards, the extended duration of B-type missions would likely cause additional or more critical psychological and behavioral challenges to astronauts. Many potential exploration missions were considered (e.g., Asteroid missions), which made the task of identifying one key mission profile difficult. A careful review of the DRMs of the most likely exploration missions identified similarities in key mission specifications that were used to characterize C-type missions. C-type missions were similar to B-type missions only in duration (up to 12 months). C-type missions introduced key mission factors intended for Mars missions, such as use of a smaller vehicle and communication delays (5–10 minutes one-way). Considerations of these factors are important in terms of long-term goals for space exploration missions, namely those lasting longer than 12 months and involving another planetary surface (e.g., Mars). These distinctions in mission type were quite significant, and resulted in mission category D. This mission type included exploration missions up to 36 months, a 20-30 minute one-way communication delay, and possible surface operations. Although D-type missions were considered to be unique and did not yet exist, SMEs recruited for the job analysis were the most qualified to determine mission challenges and necessary considerations for selecting and training astronauts for these missions.

General Method

The job analysis activities took place in the following order: (1) first core panel meeting, (2) core panel individual interviews, (3) remaining SME interviews, (4) second core panel meeting, (5) survey, (6) third and final core panel meeting. After each activity, the qualitative data obtained by the team of researchers was analyzed and organized into KSAOs.

Core Panel (CP) Meetings

The first step in the job analysis was introducing the core panel to the project, identifying mission types, and having them generate an initial list of statements and descriptions that would eventually become KSAOs for each mission type. These lists were reviewed and sorted into categories by I/O Psychologists. The revised lists of mission-specific KSAOs were then presented to individual core panel members initially, and then to the rest of the participants in interviews for further clarification (see the next section titled "Interviews"). After the interviews, the CP again reviewed the competencies, provided feedback, and gave final approval of the list to be used in a subsequent survey. Once survey data was collected, a third CP meeting was held to review results, provide feedback, answer questions, and offer final approval of the job analysis findings before steps were taken to incorporate the competencies into the selection process.

Interviews

As mentioned previously, KSAO lists generated in the first CP meeting and revised by I/O Psychologists were further reviewed in interviews. First, members of the CP were interviewed individually so that their expert judgements could be recorded in addition to inputs provided in the panel meeting. In total, 21 long-duration astronauts, 2 shuttle astronauts, and 3 BHP Operations Specialists were interviewed. After the interviews, the KSAO lists were again revisited by the researchers to incorporate the new information for each mission type. This process then informed the development of astronaut competencies for Mars missions.

Competency Development

The next phase of the project involved a series of meetings to develop competencies based on previously identified KSAOs. Through this process it was determined that the KSAOs identified for each mission type were relevant across all mission types, thus a single list of KSAOs was developed for all four missions. Next, the I/O Psychologists worked through each category and sub-category in the single list of KSAOs to extract the overarching principle described in each category, which was used to identify a job competency. From this list, 18 job competencies were identified that suited all mission types.

Survey

To determine which competencies were the most critical, a web-based survey was sent via email. Survey respondents had flown a range of 0–3 shuttle flights and 1–2 ISS flights, with the total analog experience ranging from 0 to 18 weeks, and the maximum duration of the analog lasting 12 weeks.

After a brief demographics section, participants were asked to rate the importance of each competency for each mission type on a scale of 0 (Unimportant) to 100 (Essential). Ratings yielded an inter-rater agreement average r_{wg} of 80. After each competency rating, participants were then asked to indicate whether the competency was needed at the time a person was selected or if it could be trained on the job by selecting "Yes" or "No" or an "At Hire" option. SME participants then were asked to rank competencies in order of importance for each mission type by dragging and placing competencies into the order they thought fit.

Data Analysis and Results

Due to the small sample size, statistical analyses were limited. Therefore, only basic descriptive statistics were calculated for the ratings, at hire, and rankings. Due to the low response rate for the rankings ($N = 12$), little agreement was found across rankings. Therefore, further analysis of the rankings was not pursued. The low response rate was likely due to the high number of competencies that participants were asked to rank.

Research described in this case study example indicated an overall increase in the importance of all competencies as you increase the length of the mission and add a delay in real-time communication with Earth. This research also highlights similarities in competencies across specific mission types. Competencies identified as top competencies for all four mission types included teamwork, communication, self-care, and judgment. Importance ratings of some competencies varied with mission length. For example, the importance ratings for the Small Group Living competency were found to increase for mission types longer than 6 months. Generally speaking, a pattern seems to emerge in the ratings across the four missions, with one cluster of competencies being rated the highest and another, smaller cluster being rated the lowest. Further, competency ratings for A- and B-type missions were quite similar, with a small increase in importance ratings from A- to B-type missions, and competencies for C- and D-type missions were also quite similar, again with a small increase in importance ratings from C- to D-type missions. A major change in competency ratings seemed to occur between mission types B and C, with not only an overall increase in importance ratings, but different competencies emerging as the most important for those missions. This shift in importance lends support to the identification of two mission type themes based on interviews: an AB mission type, and a CD mission type.

For the "At Hire" question, a 70% agreement cutoff was used to indicate competencies more relevant for selection than for training. Using this standard, results indicated that 10 of 18 competencies should be assessed during the selection process. In general, these findings are not surprising, with the exception of Teamwork, which fell into the "At Hire" group, and Autonomous Worker and Learner/Teacher, which were not considered by the SMEs to be needed at the time of selection.

RECOMMENDATIONS

Case Study #3 described the methodology and main results of a comprehensive work analysis of the astronaut job. This type of information is needed for the development and validation of selection, training, and performance management tools and measures. What follows are recommendations for future work based on the research described in Case Study #3.

Recommendation 1

Replicate and expand upon the work analysis to identify additional information about technical job components associated with developing astronaut job. This research would strengthen the work analysis-alternative validation linkage by enhancing the use of a chosen alternative validity approach (e.g., synthetic validity approach or other approaches) in ways that increase the data upon which conclusions using these strategies are based.

Recommendation 2

Identify technical job elements and competencies specific to various types of astronauts or EEP missions. The current effort focused on the team and social competencies needed for current and future astronauts, however, the technical aspects of the job have yet to be fully addressed for training and selection. In doing so, similarly consider combining mission types when results indicate similarities or maintain separate job information for mission types that appear different based on ratings or other analyses.

Recommendation 3

Continue collecting information from knowledgeable, experienced SMEs regarding the specific mission competencies. For example, in Case Study #3 NASA was able to collect information from SMEs that had flown ISS missions. SMEs should be asked to identify competencies that can be developed versus those required upon entry (when hired for a new position). This information will help an organization make decisions regarding competencies to assess during the selection process versus those competencies that can be developed through training or other programs (e.g., identification of support countermeasures).

Recommendation 4

Use updated job analysis information as a basis to further develop, update, and validate selection measures and training programs. This information might also be used to identify and assess psychosocial risks and performance decrement risks in EEPs.

LIMITATIONS AND PRACTICAL IMPLICATIONS

Job analysis conclusions were intended to be applied during the selection and training of astronauts. Findings related to A- and B-type missions were relevant for current missions and could be used in current training and selection cycles. Because much was still unknown about C- and D-type missions, these findings should be considered preliminary. More research is needed to better understand the psychological and social challenges of longer-duration exploration missions and the competencies needed to successfully perform those missions.

Additional findings from the job analysis were applied to the development of training activities. While the job analysis was conducted, the 2013 class of astronauts were just beginning their training at the Johnson Space Center in Houston, TX. A requirement of this training is for Astronaut Candidates to complete Expeditionary Skills Training, or team and psychological skills training (Barrett, Slack, Holland, & Sipes, 2014). Job analysis results were used to develop the 2013 Expeditionary Skills and the associated training activities. Results were also used as part of an analysis of risk of performance and behavioral decrements related to competencies identified in the job analysis (Landon, Vessey, & Barrett, 2015).

CONCLUSION

Throughout this chapter we discussed the challenges faced by traditional approaches to work analysis methods, particularly those encountered by organizations with EEPs. Three case studies described alternative work analysis and validation methods explored by NASA to evaluate the astronaut job and illustrate how to address challenges associated with traditional work analysis approaches. The case studies presented here led to identified recommendations that could prove useful to organizations with EEPs or facing similar challenges to those faced by NASA, whether they include designing new jobs for which job requirements have yet to be identified, measured, or performance predicted or for analyzing the work of the future.

REFERENCES

American Educational Research Association, American Psychological Association, & National Council on Measurement in Education. (2014). *Standards for educational and psychological testing*. American Educational Research Association.

Barrett, J. D., Holland, A. W., & Vessey, W. B. (2015). *Identifying the "Right Stuff": An exploration focused astronaut job analysis.* Presented at the 30th Annual Conference of the Society for Industrial and Organizational Psychology, Philadelphia, PA.

Barrett, J. D., Slack, K., Holland, A. W., & Sipes, W. (2014, August). *Training the 8-balls: Psychological readiness preparation for the newest astronaut class.* Symposium at the annual convention of the American Psychological Association. Washington, DC.

Bessone, L., Coffey, E., Filippova, N., Greenberg, E., Inoue, N., & Shevchenko, O. (2008). *International space station human behavior & performance competency model Volume II mission operations directorate* (NASA STI Report Series). Washington, DC.

Campion, M. A., Fink, A. A., Ruggeberg, B. J., Carr, L., Phillips, G. M., & Odman, R. B. (2011). Doing competencies well: Best practices in competency modeling. *Personnel Psychology, 64,* 225–262.

Cascio, W. F., & Aguinis, H. (2018). *Applied psychology in talent management* (8th edition). Thousand Oaks, CA: Sage.

Equal Employment Opportunity Commission, Civil Service Commission, Department of Labor, & Department of Justice. (1978). *Uniform guidelines on employment selection procedures. Federal Register, 43*(166), 38294–38309.

Galarza, L., & Holland, A. (1999a). *Critical astronaut proficiencies required for long-duration space flight* SAE Technical Paper Series 1999-01-2096, SAE International. doi: 10.4271/1999-01-2096.

Galarza, L., & Holland, A. (1999b). *Selecting astronauts for long-duration space missions* SAE Technical Paper Series 1999-01-2097, SAE International. doi: 10.4271/1999-01-2097.

Gatewood, R. D., Feild, H. S., & Barrick, M. (2016). *Human resource selection* (8th edition). Mason: OH, Thomson.

Gibson, W. M., & Capliner, J. A. (2007). The transportation of validation results. In S. M. McPhail's. *Alternative validation strategies: Developing new and leveraging existing validity evidence.* San Francisco: Jossey-Bass.

Goffin, R. D., Rothstein, M. G., Rieder, M. J., Poole, A., Krajewski, H. T., Powell, D. M., … Mestdagh, T. (2011). Choosing job-related personality traits: Developing valid personality-oriented job analysis. *Personality and Individual Differences, 51*(5), 646–651. doi:10.1016/j.paid.2011.06.001

Griggs v. Duke Power Co., 401 US 424 (1971).

Hanges, P. J., Salmon, E. D., & Aiken, J. R. (2013). Legal issues in industrial testing and assessment. (Chapter 38). In K. F. Geisinger, B. A. Bracken, J. F. Carlson, J. C. Hansen, N. R. Kuncel, S. P. Reise, M. C. Rodriguez (Eds.), *APA handbook of testing and assessment in psychology. Vol 1: Test theory and testing and assessment in industrial-organizational psychology.* Washington, DC: American Psychological Association.

Hoffman, C. C., & McPhail, S. M. (1998). Exploring options for supporting test use in situations precluding local validation. *Personnel Psychology, 51,* 987–1003.

Hoffman, C. C., Rashkovsky, B., & D'Egidio, E., (2007). Job component validity: Background, current research, and applications (Chapter 3). In S. M. McPhail (Ed.),. *Alternative validation strategies: Developing new and leveraging existing validity evidence* (pp. 82–121). San Francisco: Jossey-Bass.

Hunter, J. E., & Hunter, R. F. (1984). Validity and utility of alternative predictors of job performance. *Psychological Bulletin, 96,* 72–98.

Hunter, J. E., & Schmidt, F. L. (2004). *Methods of meta-analysis: Correcting error and bias in research findings* (2nd edition). Newbury Park, CA: Sage.

Hysong, S., Galarza, L., & Holland, A. (2007). *A review of training methods and instructional techniques: Implications for behavioral skills training in US astronauts* (NASA Technical Publication # NASA/TP-2007-213726). Houston, TX: National Aeronautics and Space Administration.

Jeanneret, P. R. (1988). *Position Requirements for Space Station Personnel and Linkages to Portable Microcomputer Performance Assessment* (Technical Report to the National Aeronautics and Space Administration). Houston, TX: Jeanneret & Associates, Inc.

Johnson, J. W. (2007). Synthetic validity: A technique of use (finally). In S. M. McPhail (Ed.), *Alternative validation strategies: Developing new and leveraging existing validity evidence* (pp. 122–158). San Francisco: Jossey-Bass.

Landon, L. B., Vessey, W. B., & Barrett, J. D. (2015). *Evidence report: Risk of performance and behavioral health decrements due to inadequate cooperation, coordination, communication, and psychosocial adaptation within a team* (NASA Human Research Program). http://humanresearchroadmap.nasa.gov/evidence/

Lievens, F., Sanchez, J. I., & De Corte, W. (2004). Easing the inferential leap in competency modeling: The effects of task-related information and subject matter expertise. *Personnel Psychology*, 57(4), 881–904.

McCormick, E. J. (1959). Application of job analysis to indirect validity. *Personnel Psychology*, 12(3), 365–534.

McCormick, E. J., DeNisi, A. S., & Shaw, J. B. (1979). Use of the position analysis questionnaire for establishing the job component validity of tests. *Journal of Applied Psychology*, 64(1), 51–56.

McDaniel, M. A. (2007). Validity generalization as a test validation approach (Chapter 5). In S. M. McPhail (Ed.), *Alternative validation strategies: Developing new and leveraging existing validity evidence*. San Francisco: Jossey-Bass. pp. 159–180.

McPhail, S. M. (2007). Development of validation evidence (Chapter 1). In S. M. McPhail, *Alternative validation strategies: Developing new and leveraging existing validity evidence* (pp. 1–25). San Francisco, CA: Jossey-Bass.

McPhail, S. M., Blakley, B. R., Strong, M. H., Collings, T. J., Jeanneret, P. R., & Galarza, L. (1995). Work context. In N. G. Peterson, M. D. Mumford, W. C. Borman, & P. R. Jeanneret (Eds.), *Development of Prototype Occupational Information Network (O*NET) content model. Volume I: Report*. Washington, DC: American Institutes for Research.

Morgeson, F. P. & Dierdorff, E. C. (2010). Work analysis: From technique to theory (Chapter 1). In S. Zedeck (Ed.), *APA handbook of industrial and organizational psychology. Volume 2: Selecting and developing members of the organization* (pp 3–41). Washington, DC: American Psychological Association.

Mossholder, K. W., & Arvey, R. D. (1984). Synthetic validity: A conceptual and comparative review. *Journal of Applied Psychology*, 69, 322–333.

Mumford, M. D., & Owens, W. A. (1987). Methodology review: Principles, procedures, and findings in the application of background data measures. *Applied Psychological Measurement, 11*, 1–31.

National Aeronautics and Space Administration (2015, Feburary 12). *Expedition 1*. Retrieved from https://www.nasa.gov/mission_pages/station/expeditions/expedition01/index.html

Paquet, V. L., Mathiassen, S. E., & Dempsey, P. G. (2006, November). Video-based Ergonomic Job Analysis: A practitioner's guide. *Professional Safety*, 27–35.

Peterson, N. G., & Bownas, D. A. (1982). Skill, task structure and performance acquisition. In M. D., Dunnette & E. A. Fleishman, (Eds.), *Human performance and productivity: Human capability assessment*. Hillsdale, NJ: Lawrence Erlbaum.

Primoff, E. S. (1957). The J-coefficient approach to jobs and tests. *Personnel Psychology*, 10, 34–40.

Primoff, E. S. (1959). Empirical validations of the J-coefficient. *Personnel Psychology, 12*(4), 13–18.

Reilly, R. R., & Chao, G. T. (1982). Validity and fairness of some alternative employee selection procedures. *Personnel Psychology, 35*, 1–62.

Sackett, P. R., Walmsley, P. T., & Laczo, R. M. (2012). Job and work analysis: Industrial and organizational psychology. In N. Schmitt, & S. Highhouse (Eds.), *Comprehensive handbook of psychology, Volume 12: Industrial and organizational psychology* (Vol. 12, pp. 48–87). New York, NY: John Wiley & Sons.

Sanchez, J. I., & Levine, E. L. (2013). Work analysis for assessment (Chapter 23). In Geisinger, K. F., Bracken, B. A., Carlson, J. F., Hansen, J. C., Kuncel, N. R., Reise, S. P., & Rodriguez, M. C. (Eds), *APA handbook of testing and assessment in psychology. Volume 1: Test theory and testing and assessment in industrial-organizational psychology*. Washington, DC: American Psychological Association.

4 Applying Research-Based Training Principles
Toward Crew-Centered, Mission-Oriented Space Flight Training

Donna L. Dempsey
NASA's Lyndon B. Johnson Space Center

Immanuel Barshi
NASA's Ames Research Center

CONTENTS

A Brief History of Space Flight Training 64
Crew-Centered, Mission-Oriented Space Flight Training 68
Training for Mars 70
    Applied Training Principle: Contextual Reinstatement 71
    Applied Training Principle: Procedural Reinstatement....................................... 72
    Applied Training Principle: Easy to Difficult Ordering....................................... 72
    Applied Training Principle: Strategic Use of Knowledge................................... 74
    Applied Training Principle: Spacing... 74
    Applied Training Principle: Variability of Practice 75
    Applied Training Principle: Rehearsal 75
    Applied Training Principle: Focus of Attention 77
    Applied Training Principle: Deliberate Practice 77
    Applied Training Principle: Feedback 78
Conclusion 78
References.. 79

NASA's future deep space, exploration missions to Mars will be, by definition, space flight missions that require the onboard crew of astronauts to operate semi-autonomously to autonomously from the Mission Control Center (MCC) on the ground during periods of long communication delays and possible communication blackouts. Astronauts on these missions will be required to work together as a team to respond to high-risk, critical situations; to command, operate, and maintain their spacecraft; and to conduct scientific research in support of mission objectives. Such missions will require a small, well-trained crew ready to perform critical tasks across a wide range of disciplines and make challenging decisions necessary to achieve mission success, all without real-time ground support. While NASA has a long history of successfully training astronauts for low Earth orbit and lunar missions, it has never provided astronauts with the training necessary to operate at the level of autonomy that future deep space, exploration missions will require.

To provide our astronauts with the training they will require for their missions to Mars, we agree with Salas, Tannenbaum, Kraiger, and Smith-Jentsch (2012) that the design of a training program "should be informed by the best information science has to offer" (p. 74). As discussed by Salas, Cannon-Bowers, and Blickensderfer (1999), one of the challenges in designing an effective training program lies in how best to integrate training research into training practice. Based on the work of Salas et al. (1999), Bourne and Healy (2012) offered that training could be "optimized by the implementation of empirically valid training principles" (p. 7), where a training principle is defined as, "an underlying truth or fact about human behavior" (p. 7). Principles are then integrated into a training program via guidelines (i.e., "how to" or "what to do" statements) and training specifications or requirements (i.e., "shall" statements). Applying these concepts to the design of training for pilots at the airline level, Barshi (2015) offered a training design approach, including guidelines and specifications based on training principles offered by Healy and her colleagues (e.g., Healy, Kole, & Bourne, 2014; Healy, Schneider, & Bourne, 2012). His approach structured all airline pilot training as "line-oriented" flight training, where the "line" referred to is the air-line drawn on a map between a departure airport and a destination airport. That approach leads to a training design in which the acquisition of new knowledge and skills and the opportunities to use them are completely embedded within the context of a realistic flight timeline.

Our goal in this chapter is to take an approach similar to Barshi (2015) and offer a design approach for space flight training, including training guidelines and specifications, based on empirically valid principles of training reviewed in the companion volume by Kole, Healy, Schneider and Barshi (2019), as well as by other training science researchers (e.g., Ericsson, Krampe, & Tesch-Römer, 1993; Healy et al., 2012; Salas, Wilson, Priest, & Guthrie, 2006), thereby providing NASA with a design for training astronauts for deep space, exploration missions to Mars based on the best information that science has to offer.

A BRIEF HISTORY OF SPACE FLIGHT TRAINING

As the design of NASA's human space flight missions has changed over the decades, so has NASA's space flight training design. For Apollo-era and Space Shuttle missions, astronauts were provided extensive practice for mission operations as an intact team training to detailed flight plans with a well-defined set of duties or tasks for their assigned mission roles (Weaver, Weaver, & Weaver, 2015; Woodling et al., 1973). For current International Space Station (ISS) Expeditions, astronauts are provided generic-task training to support the flexibility to perform across a wide range of tasks that may occur throughout a long ISS Expedition (National Research

Council, 2011). What has not changed since the beginning of space flight is that each of NASA's space flight training programs has been primarily designed based on what we term a "system-siloed" training approach. That is, an approach in which training begins with vehicle system flows (e.g., an electrical power system training flow, a thermal control system training flow) and discipline flows (e.g., a robotics training flow, an inventory and stowage training flow), with training for mission operations being provided only after extensive training on vehicle systems and disciplines is completed. Additionally, the operational concepts for each of these programs have assumed that real-time expertise needed to respond to unplanned, complex technical problems or unforeseen medical issues would be provided by the flight control personnel in MCC, and a return to Earth within hours, or at most days, would always be an option.

In the early days of space flight, during the Mercury, Gemini, and Apollo programs, astronauts spent years learning the vehicle systems as they worked collaboratively with systems engineers on the vehicle designs. In fact, the selection criteria for the Mercury Seven included requiring candidates for NASA's first group of astronauts to have an engineering background along with test pilot experience (Weaver et al., 2015). Mission objectives for these early space flights were clearly defined (e.g., placing a manned spacecraft into orbit around the Earth, demonstrating the rendezvous and docking capability needed for lunar missions, landing men on the moon and returning them safely back to Earth). According to Woodling et al. (1973), the mission-specific training requirements were that the astronauts could practice and demonstrate proficiency in the critical aspects of their mission. To support this training, NASA made tremendous engineering advancements in designing simulators that could mimic the various space flight environments the crew would encounter (e.g., neutral buoyancy simulators for extravehicular activities (EVAs, aka spacewalks), motion-based simulators for ascent and entry, and reduced gravity simulators for lunar surface operations) allowing the astronauts to practice critical tasks planned for their missions (Weaver et al., 2015; Woodling, et al., 1973). Astronauts were assigned specific roles (e.g., commander, command module pilot) with unique job duties and provided numerous hours of individual and team training. Training took place in part-task trainers as well as in high-fidelity, full-task, fixed- and motion-based simulators. Astronauts practiced well-defined tasks based on detailed flight plans with MCC, averaging almost 1,000 hour of simulator time per crewman per mission during the Apollo program (Woodling et al., 1973). Skylab missions flown at the end of this era were longer in duration, but the pre-flight training remained the same in that the crew were provided extensive training for planned tasks (Schneider, 1976).

Much like astronauts in NASA's earlier programs, the first Space Shuttle astronauts learned the vehicle systems as they were being built. As the Space Shuttle program progressed, space flight training was formalized into lessons, where sets of lessons were designed into training flows, and training culminated in a series of simulations that provided crewmembers practice or rehearsal of critical tasks in their mission timelines. While lessons and flows were sequenced to ensure prerequisites from one flow were trained prior to being needed in a different flow, the fundamental design approach was based on distinct vehicle system and discipline flows.

The most influential factor in NASA's design was simple logistics – the instructors were grouped by system or discipline.

Newly hired Space Shuttle astronaut candidates (ASCANs) were provided 2 years of initial training, focused extensively on the vehicle's systems, prior to being designated as "astronauts" qualified for flight assignment and ready for flight-specific training. Between the end of ASCAN training and being flight-assigned, astronauts had additional training opportunities. Space Shuttle mission objectives were clearly defined (e.g., servicing the Hubble Space Telescope, installing the Joint Airlock to the ISS), and detailed flight plans were built for missions lasting up to 17 days. Flight-specific training for Shuttle missions was typically 1 year long, although flight delays often extended this training time. Crewmembers were assigned roles (e.g., commander, pilot, mission specialist) with unique job duties, and provided intensive training focused on ensuring they could perform their assigned duties and tasks as per their mission timeline. The commander and pilot were required to demonstrate proficiency in piloting the vehicle for ascent, entry, and rendezvous, as well as in docking and vehicle operations. They were provided training on these tasks in training facilities ranging from part-task trainers to high-fidelity, full-task, motion-based simulators, as well as training in the Shuttle Training Aircraft, an aircraft modified to duplicate the handling of a Space Shuttle during approach and landing. Mission specialists were required to demonstrate proficiency in performing EVAs, robotics operations, and scientific operations and were provided training on these tasks in mock-ups and simulators of varying fidelity, including EVA training in a neutral buoyancy simulator. Although much of this flight-assigned training was provided to individual or pairs of crewmembers within system or discipline training flows, flight-specific simulations allowed the entire crew to practice ascent and entry, as well as practice challenging longer mission flight plan sequences such as satellite deployments or EVA tasks, integrated as a team with MCC. Space Shuttle astronauts averaged about 120–160 hours of flight-specific integrated simulation time with MCC per crewmember in fixed- and motion-based simulators.

Unlike Space Shuttle missions, ISS missions differ significantly from NASA's previous missions in several important ways that impact the design of training. The ISS is a large, permanently-orbiting laboratory consisting of modules and elements provided by five international partners (NASA, Russia, the European Space Agency (ESA), the Japanese Aerospace Exploration Agency (JAXA), and the Canadian Space Agency (CSA)). The ISS was designed and built with the objective of supporting ongoing scientific research across a range of disciplines. Currently, astronauts travel to and from the ISS on the Russian three-person Soyuz spacecraft, and six crewmembers (two three-person Soyuz crews) are in space together for 6 months as an ISS Expedition crew. ISS operations are ongoing, and detailed flight plans, or timelines, are developed real-time based on long-range plans. Although astronauts are assigned roles (e.g., commander, flight engineer), because of the nature of ISS missions and the need for flexibility in assigning tasks throughout the mission, they are all required to have the skills necessary to perform tasks across a wide range of job duties including EVA, robotics, scientific research, repair and maintenance, and responding to potential malfunctions and emergency situations (National Research Council, 2011). During training, each NASA astronaut is required to demonstrate these skills for tasks conducted in NASA modules, as well as demonstrate the skills needed to perform in each international partner module. They must also meet Russian language proficiency requirements, and Russian Soyuz training requirements. (International partner astronauts and cosmonauts have similar training requirements, including training on tasks in their modules.)

ISS training for NASA astronauts again begins with 2 years of ASCAN training, including extensive systems training on NASA modules, as well as initial discipline training for EVAs, robotics operations, medical operations, and science operations. While flight assignments can occur immediately after ASCAN training is completed, typically an astronaut is assigned office or mission support duties while waiting for a flight assignment. Pre-assignment training opportunities during this period may include some refresher training on ASCAN skills (e.g., ASCANs assigned as capsule communicators (CAPCOMs) receive refresher training on ISS emergency response), additional training on robotics operations in Canada, and training on new skills as part of assignments (including CAPCOM certification). There are also opportunities for team training in analog missions such as the NASA Extreme Environment Mission Operations project (NEEMO) conducted in the underwater Aquarius habitat operated by Florida International University (Landon, Slack, & Barrett, 2018), and such as the European Space Agency's (ESA) Cooperative Adventure for Valuing and Exercising (CAVES) human behavior and performance skills course conducted in deep underground caves.

Flight-assigned training for ISS missions is approximately 2 years, and astronauts are provided portions of their training by each of the ISS international partners, requiring extensive international travel. NASA astronauts spend about one-third of their assigned training at NASA's Lyndon B. Johnson Space Center (JSC), about one-third at Roscosmos in Russia, much of which is training for ascent and entry on the three-person Russian Soyuz vehicle, and the remaining one-third either at ESA, JAXA, on holiday and vacation, and traveling between the international partner centers. Flight-assigned training at JSC builds on ASCAN training and covers a wide range of vehicle system's training, medical operations, robotics, EVA, in-flight maintenance and scientific research training, and also includes ongoing spaceflight readiness training in T-38N aircraft, Russian language training, team skills training, and physical training. Much of this flight-assigned training is provided to individual or pairs of crewmembers within vehicle system or discipline training flows, including generic two-person EVA training (mission-specific EVAs are not usually known prior to launch). Astronauts are also provided training as an intact three-person crew by Russia during Soyuz training, and by NASA during several operations simulations. Crews then practice typical tasks in a mission setting, as well as vehicle malfunction scenarios in which they practice responding to off-nominal conditions per published procedures. The only training astronauts are provided as a six-person ISS Expedition crew is for integrated emergency response. Because ISS timelines are developed real-time, very little training is to an actual timeline – the notable exception is Soyuz ascent and entry training.

Decades of successes in human space flight in low-Earth orbit and lunar missions have shown the effectiveness of NASA's space flight training programs for these missions. However, to date, the flight control team in MCC has always been able to provide real-time expertise to the onboard crew as needed, and a return to Earth has always been an option in response to any unforeseen event. Now there is Mars. Earth's closest planetary neighbor, but still up to 24 light-minutes away, and at times completely blocked by the Sun. A quick return to Earth will not be possible, and real-time expertise from MCC will no longer be available. The current "system-siloed" approach to the design of space flight training may not be able to adequately prepare future astronauts for their missions to Mars.

CREW-CENTERED, MISSION-ORIENTED SPACE FLIGHT TRAINING

While the detailed parameters for NASA's future deep space missions are not yet fully known, in NASA's design reference architecture for missions to Mars, Drake and Watts (2014) stated that flights will be either 2- or 3-year long missions to the Martian surface, with a surface stay of either 30 days for a conjunction-class mission, or almost 500 days for an opposition-class mission. Conjunction and opposition refer to the planetary alignments of Earth and Mars. The crew will consist of four to six astronauts, each of whom will be trained for multiple primary roles as well as trained as backup for critical mission operations and major mission objectives. Stuster, Adolf, Byrne, and Greene (2018) identified eight primary crew roles that must be divided among the crewmembers: leader, biologist, geologist, physician, mechanic, electrician, pilot/navigator, and computer specialist, as well as four additional ancillary roles: crew medical officer, botanist, astrophysicist, and equipment officer. Within these roles, the pilot/navigator is trained for robotics and surface rover operations, and all crewmembers are trained for EVAs. MCC is expected to provide the crew with a timeline of daily activities and to provide command and control of the vehicle for normal operations (e.g., course corrections, antenna pointing, software upgrades). However, given the communication delays, astronauts on a mission to Mars will be required to execute complex semi-autonomous and autonomous mission operations, such as responding to unanticipated medical and vehicle emergencies or major system malfunctions, including working outside the scope of published procedures, without real-time support from MCC. They will, therefore, require training to a level of autonomy that has never been needed before.

Training for Mars will be hard. Space flight incidents provide evidence that the current training design of system and discipline flows coupled with rehearsal or practice (though rarely any other training methodology) does not produce the level of autonomy astronauts will require for the challenges of future deep space, exploration missions (Barshi & Dempsey, 2016). While ISS astronauts demonstrate proficiency in pre-mission training (that is, acquisition does not seem to be an issue), Barshi and Dempsey (2016) documented that real-time ground support for ISS Expedition crewmembers is used to mitigate training retention and transfer issues. Additionally, crewmembers are not trained to the level of expertise needed for autonomous missions; such expertise is provided real-time by MCC (for challenges in providing this level of training, see e.g., Strauch, 2017). Because of the short duration of the early Mercury, Gemini, Apollo, and Space Shuttle missions, in-flight training retention was rarely an issue. Instructors from this era describe "hammering in" the training content. However, even on such short duration missions, astronauts acknowledged challenges in recalling details of complex technical tasks. Even if we shifted back to Space Shuttle-style task-based training to attempt to address retention issues, the length of the training would be impractical. If a 6-month ISS mission timeline could be developed and trained to, the ratio of Space Shuttle training duration to mission duration (one year of training to a twelve-day mission) would imply a 180-month (15 year) training flow for ISS missions. Missions to Mars may be up to six times longer than ISS missions. That won't work. NASA needs a training design that produces the needed skill durability and transferability within a reasonable pre-mission training template.

We propose that the level of autonomy needed for future missions could be achieved by relying on research results from the past two decades that support a training design in which systems knowledge is introduced in the operational context (Barshi, 2015), specific training methodologies that support skill acquisition and retention are implemented (Healy et al., 2012), and the intact team training that is critical to developing skills necessary for mission success is integrated throughout the entire training program (Landon et al., 2018). In this chapter, we offer a new design approach for space flight training based on empirically derived principles of training, inspired by the approach offered by Barshi (2015) for training airline pilots. This approach is very different from the "system-siloed" approach that has dominated space flight training for decades. "Crew-centered, mission-oriented" design is a training approach in which operational content is introduced to a crew in the context of use. Astronauts learn vehicle systems and procedures in an integrated fashion, as they would interact with them during a mission, rather than abstractly and independently learning this content from a system design or engineering perspective. The entire flow is structured based on the mission timeline, and team skills are learned and practiced in the operational context, rather than in some abstract or generic setting (Barshi, 2015). For example, in current ISS training, the communication and tracking system training flow begins with an introduction to the entire system and then progresses to detailed training on each component in each subsystem, one of which is the audio terminal unit, a component of the audio subsystem used for space-to-ground communications. In contrast, in a space flight training program based on the mission context, an astronaut might be introduced to the audio terminal unit in a training simulation early in their training program while practicing an Earth ascent timeline, but he or she would not be trained on the details of the audio subsystem, nor on other components of the communication and tracking system, until later in training when learning to respond to a loss of communication with the ground.

If the goal of NASA's space flight training program is to train astronauts to work together as a team to meet NASA's mission goals for space flight exploration, to respond to high-risk, critical situations, to command, operate, and maintain the spacecraft, and to conduct scientific research, shouldn't all astronaut training be designed to focus on these mission goals rather than on vehicle systems and engineering disciplines? A "crew-centered, mission-oriented" training design provides such a focus.

TRAINING FOR MARS

In this section, we imagine how such a "crew-centered, mission-oriented" training program might be designed. It is not our intention to provide a complete training syllabus but rather to demonstrate the application in developing such a training program for a mission to Mars of some of the training principles reviewed by Kole et al. (2019) in the companion volume, as well as by other researchers in training science. We provide three vignettes of training for Mars: Earth ascent, Saturday operations, and critical operations, and we follow each with the principles of training that support such a training design.

VIGNETTE 1:   Earth Ascent: Monitoring Orion

With such a training design in mind, instead of starting Day 1 with detailed training on one of the many vehicle's systems, a crew of newly hired ASCANs begins its training with an overview of a Mars mission and overall training objectives. The first mission phase trained is the Earth ascent, and the instructors provide a detailed review of the launch day timeline and nominal trajectory of the Orion spacecraft from the launch pad to rendezvous and docking with their on-orbit Mars Transfer vehicle (MTV), followed immediately by the ASCAN's first training simulation, their launch into space in their Orion vehicle.

In this first simulation, the instructor is assigned the role of commander, and the ASCANs are assigned the simplest of duties, monitoring the Orion vehicle displays during a nominal Earth ascent. As the instructor and ASCANs are strapped into their seats, the instructor begins familiarizing the ASCANs with the interior layout of Orion, such as showing the ASCANs where to stow equipment before launch. Rather than requiring the ASCANs to spend hours of classroom training on display navigation before using these skills in a mission context, the instructor shows the ASCANs how to access the mission timeline on their tablets or displays. As the instructor explains the features of and information contained in the timeline interface, such as the ability to view each scheduled activity in the launch sequence, the ASCANs practice navigating the timeline interface. The instructor shows the ASCANs how to access procedures for executing activities and how to navigate the vehicle system displays that the ASCANs must monitor during this first simulation.

Throughout the simulation, the instructor explains the roles and responsibilities of each of the teams involved in the launch (Launch Control Center, MCC, Crew, etc.) and demonstrates how to work and communicate with each, integrating teamwork and system training within the overall training flow. For example, as the instructor and ASCANs review the launch day timeline and execute the pre-flight checklist with the Launch Control Center (LCC), the instructor discusses the role of LCC with the ASCANs. The instructor demonstrates, and the ASCANs practice performing, the various call outs between the crew and LCC as they confirm readiness for launch. Just after Orion leaves the launch pad, the instructor explains that clearing the launch tower is the indication that communication switches from LCC to the Mission Control Center (MCC), and the instructor discusses the role of MCC with the ASCANs.

Launch is followed by a nominal rendezvous and docking. The ASCANs learn how to confirm docking on their displays, while the instructor confirms the data with a space-to-ground call with MCC. The instructor shows, and the ASCANs practice, how to confirm equalized pressure between the Orion spacecraft and the MTV, and how to open the Orion and MTV hatches to ingress the MTV, all within the context of the launch day timeline. After confirming MTV ingress with MCC, their first simulation ends with a facilitated debrief that includes a discussion of the purpose of and protocols used for crew-led debriefing.

Once a first Earth-ascent simulation is completed, training on subsequent simulations allows the instructors to review and reinforce all that the ASCANs learned in the first simulations, building on that knowledge, and, at the same time, starting to add complexity. For example, in their second simulation, as they continue to learn the procedures to monitor vehicle data on their Orion displays, the ASCANs practice using the audio equipment to make their space-to-ground calls. In so doing, they continue their training on communication equipment and protocols. In their third simulation, MCC directs the ASCANs to execute a procedure to configure to the backup communication system. The instructor uses the ASCAN's knowledge of the audio system gained in earlier simulations along with this direction from MCC to start teaching the ASCANs the information that is relevant to their job on the design of the communication system, including the system's redundancies.

Subsequent simulations add yet more complexity. They provide the ASCANs with additional training on Orion's vehicle systems, command and control interfaces, as well as procedures and protocols for executing a nominal launch, rendezvous, and docking. (Note, ASCANs will learn skills for piloting the Orion spacecraft and responding to vehicle emergencies and malfunctions later in the training flow.) It may take several weeks to train the entire timeline from launch to rendezvous to docking, with the knowledge required to understand all the relevant procedures and protocols that come into play in the course of a nominal ascent. Each simulation allows the ASCANs to acquire and practice new skills in the operational context, while also reviewing and reinforcing previously acquired skills.

In the training guidelines described above, the entire focus of the training is centered on the ASCAN's operational, or mission, perspective, and all of the training is presented within the context of the mission. There are three principles of training that motivate the overall design of such a "crew-centered, mission-oriented" space flight training program:

APPLIED TRAINING PRINCIPLE: CONTEXTUAL REINSTATEMENT

Kole et al. (2019) state that, "both retention and transfer are enhanced when context is reinstated." Specifically, training new information in the context in which it will be used supports retrieval of both declarative and procedural knowledge. Context primarily refers to the physical environment, but also includes "emotional factors" and "non-essential perceptual features of the task." The entire structure of the program of training described in this chapter is designed to provide training in the context in which the trained knowledge and skills will be used. This context includes the order and sequence of tasks as they will be performed in a mission (e.g., executing a launch day timeline), training as a team (e.g., flying the mission as an intact team, interacting with LCC and MCC), and training in the physical environment in which tasks will be performed (in mockups and simulators, noting the limitations of providing 1-g training for a reduced-g and μ-g missions).

APPLIED TRAINING PRINCIPLE: PROCEDURAL REINSTATEMENT

Kole et al. (2019) state that, "To maximize performance at test, the procedures required during training should be reinstated at test." For space flight training, the application of this principle goes the other way around; that is, the procedures required at "test," during the mission, are the procedures that should be used during training. The procedural reinstatement principle is similar to the contextual reinstatement principle; however, as Kole et al. (2019) explain, while the context relates to factors that are external to the task, the procedural reinstatement principle relates to procedural knowledge within a task. Applying the procedural reinstatement principle means basing the content of the training not on an engineering perspective, not on how a system or vehicle is designed or built, but rather – on what the ASCANs need to know and what they must be able to do to execute nominal and off-nominal procedures during their mission (e.g., making space-to-ground calls to MCC using correct communication protocols, opening hatches between vehicles, configuring to the backup communication system). The design approach of "crew-centered, mission-oriented" training is an application of the procedural reinstatement principle.

APPLIED TRAINING PRINCIPLE: EASY TO DIFFICULT ORDERING

In discussing the different views on the easy to difficult ordering principle, Healy and Bourne (2012) suggested, "Whether or not training should begin with the easiest or most difficult components of a fractionated task depends on task characteristics" (p. 20). They continued to recommend, "trainers need to be sensitive to these characteristics before deciding on the order of the subtasks" (p. 20). While the easy to difficult ordering principle informs the design of task training, Barshi (2015) suggested that this principle can motivate the design of the entire training flow, supporting a training design approach that structures the entire flow starting from the simplest of activities and gradually building to more challenging tasks. The easy to difficult ordering can be seen here in the progression from a nominal Orion flight in which the ASCANs simply monitor vehicle data to more demanding flights in which they execute procedures to configure vehicle systems. Further complexity is added later in the training flow when the ASCANs learn to pilot the Orion vehicle and respond to vehicle malfunctions and emergencies.

VIGNETTE 2: Cruise to Mars: Saturday Operations

As ASCANs continue to train on the skills necessary to monitor and operate the Orion vehicle during an Earth ascent, instructors start training ASCANs in the MTV for the cruise-to-Mars phase of their mission. Training continues to be provided within the context of the mission rather than structured by vehicle system or engineering discipline. Given the long duration of the cruise-to-Mars, instructors provide ASCAN training on several cruise-to-Mars timelines each covering a segment of this mission phase. On the first day of their cruise-to-Mars training, instructors begin training a crew of ASCANs with the simplest of these timelines – "Saturday operations."

The ASCANs' first MTV mission simulation begins with the instructors training the ASCANs how to prepare breakfast, and the ASCANs practice rehydrating and heating dehydrated meal and drink packets using the galley's potable water dispenser and food warmer. Training includes resupplying the food packets stowed near the galley, and as the ASCANs restock the food pantry, the instructors explains how the MTV inventory system automatically records food usage via the radio-frequency identification (RFID)-based inventory and management system. As the ASCANs continue learning their Saturday timeline, the instructors train them how to conduct their scheduled housekeeping activities. The ASCANs locate and use the vacuum cleaner to clean air vents, bacteria filters, and smoke detectors, and they properly dispose of wet cleaning wipes after cleaning the galley, table, and toilet. Instructors build on the ASCANs' knowledge of their timeline interface learned in their initial Orion training. The instructors describe the details in the stowage notes accessed via the timeline interface, as the ASCANs use the stowage notes to determine where needed equipment is stowed. The instructors train the ASCANs how to self-schedule "to-do list" activities in their timeline. As the ASCANs rearrange their daily schedule, instructors discuss the operational guidelines and constraints for doing so. Instructors continue to train activities typically scheduled on Saturdays, having the ASCANs practice making video calls to their family for private family conferences, logging their exercise bicycle workout data, and using the still and video cameras for Earth observations and public affairs events.

Again, it may take several weeks to train the entire "Saturday operations" timeline from breakfast, through morning housekeeping, to afternoon exercise and personal activities, including all the procedures and protocols associated with a typical Saturday. Each simulation concludes with a facilitated debrief of team and technical skills to ensure ASCANs stay focused on the training objectives (see more on feedback below).

As they gain competency in their trained skills, ASCANs practice the skills and tasks they have learned in a full-day training simulation independently from instructors. In their first instructor-independent "Saturday operations" simulation, the ASCANs might decide to work their housekeeping activities together, and then they might practice their newly learned galley skills by dividing the meal preparation duties for lunch. They might decide to rearrange their afternoon schedule by switching exercise and private family conference times with each other to accommodate a spouse's availability for the family conference. In the late afternoon, they might decide to conduct a team-building exercise such as the NASA-developed Moon Base simulation, a low-fidelity paper and pencil simulation designed to exercise important team skills such as leadership and communication.

In addition to the contextual reinstatement and procedural reinstatement principles that are carried throughout the flow, the easy to difficult ordering principle can be seen in the training specifications above that suggest beginning the cruise-to-Mars phase of training with the simplest of timelines and tasks (e.g., Saturday operations of housekeeping, food preparation, exercising on a bicycle) building to more complex operations that will be trained in subsequent cruise-to-Mars timelines later in the training flow (e.g., vehicle commanding, payloads operations, malfunction response). The easy to difficult ordering principle also enables the strategic use of knowledge, described next.

APPLIED TRAINING PRINCIPLE: STRATEGIC USE OF KNOWLEDGE

Kole et al. (2019) state that, "When acquiring new information, learners should attempt to relate that information to prior knowledge, regardless of whether or not that prior knowledge is related or conceptually similar to the new information." They go on to explain how to best support retention of new knowledge, "When committing new information to long-term memory, that information becomes associated with retrieval cues. ... By increasing the number of retrieval cues, the chance of successful retrieval [of new information] in the future increases". By starting cruise-to-Mars phase training with the simplest of tasks for which ASCANs should already have some familiarity (e.g., protocols for trash, constraints associated with galley operations, procedures for logging exercise data), ASCANs can begin to relate the new information to preexisting knowledge, that in this case is conceptually similar, and also related to their mission. As ASCANs build their knowledge of the vehicle layout, equipment, and interfaces, and as training explicitly expands into new areas (e.g., conducting research, piloting spacecraft, diagnosing and troubleshooting health and vehicle issues), training on subsequent mission timelines is designed to include a review of previous material learned, using the prior knowledge to build retrieval cues for more challenging information, iterating this process throughout the entire training flow.

APPLIED TRAINING PRINCIPLE: SPACING

Like each of the training principles discussed above, the spacing principle is also integrated throughout this "crew-centered, mission-oriented" training approach. Healy and Bourne (2012) described several studies supporting the advantage of spaced, or distributed, practice over massed practice for skills training and recommended that "for optimal benefits from training, repeated practice on particular items or responses should be spaced in time" (p. 21). Spacing can be seen throughout this training design in the way in which previously trained tasks and skills are reintroduced in different contexts during subsequent learning opportunities. For example, from the beginning of their Orion training, astronauts practice all aspects involved in their launch and ascent from Earth. They learn their preflight checklist along with the various call outs and other nominal procedures that they will execute during the flight and then a few days later practice executing these procedures in their first Earth ascent simulation. Each subsequent simulation involves practicing some aspect of the checklist and other nominal ascent procedures. Later training in MTV and Mars Surface Habitat simulations follow the same pattern of providing the astronauts with training on frequently used procedures such as galley operations, exercise protocols, and nominal maintenance tasks followed later still with practice of the same, or similar, MTV or Mars Surface Habitat procedures in subsequent simulations. Not only is training designed with spaces between practice, training is also designed to provide variability of practice throughout the training flow.

APPLIED TRAINING PRINCIPLE: VARIABILITY OF PRACTICE

Variability of practice refers to a training design that provides varying conditions under which a task is practiced so that the task is not always practiced in the same manner (Kole et al., 2019). Although variability of practice slows the acquisition process, according to Kole et al. (2019) it is a "particularly powerful" training principle in that it applies to both procedural and declarative memory tasks and supports both retention and transfer. Variable practice conditions include variations in the task itself, variations in the conditions under which the task is trained such as the sequencing of the task with other tasks, or even variations in similar but different tasks (Barshi, 2015; Healy & Bourne, 2012; Kole et al., 2019). All of these variable conditions are integral parts of the training approach described here and are present throughout the entire training flow. An example is a simple maintenance task, which is first learned in its most basic form under ideal conditions and is reintroduced in later simulations with significant variability. Part of the variability might come from executing a more complicated version of the trained maintenance task; another part of the variability might come from executing a repair task on the same equipment using an untrained procedure.

APPLIED TRAINING PRINCIPLE: REHEARSAL

Providing ASCANs with the opportunity to practice their skills is an important component of the training design (Salas et al., 2006), and each simulation is an opportunity to provide the ASCANs with variable and spaced rehearsal of their training. Because the entire training flow is structured to follow segments of the mission, everything is a rehearsal of the mission whether it is a short Orion ascent simulation, a full-day Saturday housekeeping simulation, or a full-mission, multi-day simulation. Since ASCANs are trained as a crew, along with LCC and MCC, from the very beginning of their training and throughout, they are also able to rehearse team skills that are critical to mission success.

VIGNETTE 3: Critical Operations: Piloting Orion, Performing Robotics Operations, and Executing EVAs

With a clear context of an overall mission, an understanding of their vehicle's hardware, software, systems, and equipment, and an understanding of the importance of working as a team, the ASCANs are ready to be trained for some of the most complex, high-risk tasks they will perform during their mission: piloting spacecraft, performing robotics operations, and conducting on-orbit and planetary surface EVAs. Skills associated with these tasks are among the most difficult to train and will require many hours of dedicated practice in laboratory or part-task trainers. While the overall design of the training in the context of mission operations remains, one way of structuring training for these tasks is to select a subset of skills, or even a single skill, to focus on. Classroom training and self-study provide any necessary background and knowledge for skill acquisition, and these sessions are paired with part-task or laboratory training allowing for instructor-led, dedicated practice. Training continues to include mission simulations during which the ASCANs practice their newly acquired skills as individuals and as a team in a mission-oriented context, unaided by their instructors, along with ongoing practice and training of nominal mission operations.

For example, although it is expected that the Orion vehicle will be fully automated and that astronauts will only be required to monitor the vehicle systems and issue nominal commands, there are scenarios in which they may be required to fly the vehicle, and therefore they will need training on the piloting skills necessary to do so. Because ASCANs have been provided training to monitor and command the vehicle from the start of their training, at this point in the training flow, they are familiar with the layout of the vehicle interior, the interfaces and displays for monitoring and commanding the vehicle, and the vehicle systems. All of that knowledge is used and built upon as they are trained to pilot the vehicle. For example, ASCANs will require training on flying a rendezvous and docking in their Orion vehicle in the event that the automated rendezvous and docking software fails. ASCANs practice this task in a part-task trainer with their instructor until they can perform the simplest version of the task. As soon as they have achieved a level of proficiency, the training is transitioned to a mission simulation environment.

Relocating a robotic arm to a new attachment point on the same vehicle requires astronauts to use a rotational hand controller and a separate translational hand controller along with video displays and data overlays to maneuver (or "fly") the free end of the robotic arm to a new attachment point and then release the fixed end of the arm. This task is among the easier to learn tasks because there is no relative motion between the end of the robotic arm being "flown" and an attachment point on the same vehicle. ASCANs are provided instructor-led training, with repeated practice, on this task to a measured proficiency level in a robotic part-task trainer. After demonstrating proficiency relocating the robotic arm in a part-task trainer, ASCANs are provided scenarios to use this skill in their MTV or Mars Surface Habitat simulation training as they continue to learn more challenging robotics tasks such as capturing a moving object.

EVA training is also designed to train skills to a proficiency level before moving into a mission timeline simulation. Hours of dedicated practice in the simulated μ-gravity environment of the Neutral Buoyancy Laboratory is provided to allow the ASCANs to develop the skills to maneuver in their spacesuits to locations outside the vehicle and to operate EVA equipment. Instructors provide feedback on the ASCANs' skill development, and provide progressively more challenging tasks as the training continues. Additionally, rather than training EVA tasks and skills separately from other systems, EVA training is integrated with other vehicle systems and payloads training, such as training vehicle external repairs, or conducting geological surveys, providing ASCANs with practice in the context of the mission.

Each of the three tasks described above (piloting, performing robotics operations, and conducting EVAs) require unique perceptual-motor skills, and there are specific training principles that inform the design of training to support the acquisition, retention, and transfer of such skills.

APPLIED TRAINING PRINCIPLE: FOCUS OF ATTENTION

While there is some research that supports that novices should maintain an internal focus of attention by focusing on their body movements when first learning a motor skill, Kole et al. (2019) state that once individuals have had at least some practice with learning a motor skill, they should maintain an external focus of attention in performing the task, focusing on the outcome of their actions rather than their body movements. This shift in focus of attention supports both retention and transfer of the trained tasks. Starting robotics training with the easiest to learn task is not only consistent with the easy-to-difficult ordering principle (see above), it is also consistent with the focus of attention principle in that it provides the ASCANs with the opportunity to focus initially on how their hand movements on the hand controllers affect the movement of the robotic arm. As they develop competency in robotics operations, instructors can shift training to have the ASCANs focus on the trajectory of the robotic arm rather than on their body movements.

APPLIED TRAINING PRINCIPLE: DELIBERATE PRACTICE

While researchers may debate the importance of innate factors such as general intelligence and working memory capacity in achieving expertise (e.g., Campitelli & Gobet, 2011; Macnamara, Hambrick, & Oswald, 2014), they do agree that deliberate practice over a prolonged period of time is important for expert performance (Ericsson et al., 1993). As stated by Ericsson et al. (1993), "The level of performance an individual attains is directly related to the amount of deliberate practice" (p. 370). Deliberate practice is more than simple repetition; it is highly effortful, focused practice relevant to the skill being trained and requires motivation to engage in. "In contrast to play, deliberate practice is a highly structured activity, the explicit goal of which is to improve performance" (p. 368). ASCANs' training is such a deliberate practice. For example, if an ASCAN is having difficulty with a high yaw rate in controlling the robotic arm, an instructor (or an adaptive simulator) can adjust the yaw rate until the ASCAN can successfully maneuver the arm. ASCANs are motivated to improve their performance knowing the skills they are learning are necessary for their missions. Furthermore, the instructors provide them with practice that is both spaced and variable (see above) on skills, or subsets of skills, designed to be both relevant and challenging, requiring focus and effort, namely – engaging the ASCANS in deliberate practice.

Applied Training Principle: Feedback

Because effective feedback is necessary for acquisition and retention of trained skills (see e.g., Healy et al., 2014; Schmidt & Bjork, 1992), ASCANs are provided extensive feedback on their performance throughout their training. Salas et al. (2006) provided criteria for effective individual and team feedback that included ensuring feedback is constructive (i.e., focused on the individual or team performance in training but not critical of the person or people), is focused on the desired outcome of the training, and is actionable and task focused ("should provide trainees with the necessary knowledge that allows them to adjust their learning strategies to meet the expected performance levels" (p. 482).) (see also, Salas et al. (2012). Timing of feedback is also critical, and is dependent both on the skill or task being trained and on the level of skill development in the learner (e.g., novice versus expert). For novices, frequent, trial-by-trial feedback can support efficient skill acquisition (Healy & Bourne, 2012), and instructors can transition to more challenging tasks as the learner's performance improves (Ericsson et al., 1993). For proficient and competent learners, less frequent summary feedback is more effective than continuous feedback at supporting retention and transfer (Healy & Bourne, 2012). Healy and Bourne (2012) hypothesize that delayed feedback may be preferable to immediate feedback due to the spacing effect (see above). Delayed feedback may be very effective especially following exhausting training such as Neutral Buoyancy Laboratory EVA training runs.

As ASCANs master their piloting, robotics, and EVA skills, instructors shift the training fully back to the mission simulation environment. The most time-critical events that ASCANs must be trained for are the skills necessary to respond to medical emergencies, vehicle emergencies (fire, rapid depressurization, and toxic atmosphere), EVA emergencies (incapacitated crewmember, suit failure), and major vehicle or system failures. Instructors again provide ASCANs training on this content in the mission simulation environment, training the correct procedures and protocols, including the very challenging decision-making that is needed to work outside published procedures to respond to unanticipated problems.

CONCLUSION

Training for a mission to Mars is a formidable challenge. For deep space missions, astronauts will require training to operate at a level of autonomy that has never been needed before, and they will need initial and refresher training to retain those skills for missions longer than have ever been flown before. Training for medical emergency, vehicle emergency, and major system malfunction will need to be provided premission and continually maintained and refreshed throughout the mission. Training for complex skills for activities such as EVAs, robotics operations, complicated repair and maintenance, and scientific research will need to be provided premission and refreshed prior to task execution or trained initially in-mission. And, training to live and work together as a team to accomplish mission objectives will be critical for mission success. We provide here three vignettes of a "crew-centered, mission-oriented" design approach based on empirically derived principles of training that could provide astronauts with the training needed to meet the challenges of NASA's future deep space, exploration missions to Mars. To turn the description of this training approach into a sustainable curriculum change, NASA's Spaceflight Training organization, instructors, and instructional designers will have to engage in its development and implementation.

REFERENCES

Barshi, I. (2015). From Healy's training principles to training specifications: The case of the comprehensive LOFT. *The American Journal of Psychology, 128*(2), 219–227. doi: 10.5406/amerjpsyc.128.2.0219.

Barshi, I., & Dempsey, D. L. (2016). *Evidence report: Risk of performance errors due to training deficiencies* (NASA Human Research Program). Retrieved from: https://humanresearchroadmap.nasa.gov/Evidence/reports/TRAIN.pdf

Bourne, L. E., Jr., & Healy, A. F. (2012). Training and Its cognitive underpinnings. In A. F. Healy & L. E. Bourne, Jr. (Eds.), *Training cognition: Optimizing efficiency, durability, and generalizability* (pp. 1–12). New York, NY: Psychology Press.

Campitelli, G., & Gobet, F. (2011). Deliberate practice: necessary but not sufficient. *Current Directions in Psychological Science, 20*(5), 280–285. doi:10.1177/0963721411421922

Drake, B. G., & Watts, K. D. (Eds.) (2014). *Human exploration of Mars design reference architecture addendum #2.* (NASA Center for AeroSpace Information. NASA/SP-2009-566-ADD2). Hanover, MD.

Ericsson, K. A., Krampe, R. T., & Tesch-Römer, C. (1993). The role of deliberate practice in the acquisition of expert performance. *Psychological Review, 100*(3), 363–406. doi:10.1037/0033-295X.100.3.363

Healy, A. F., & Bourne, L. E., Jr. (2012). Basic research on training principles. In A. F. Healy & L. E. Bourne, Jr. (Eds.), *Training cognition: Optimizing efficiency, durability, and generalizability* (pp. 40–66). New York, NY: Psychology Press.

Healy, A. F., Kole, J. A., & Bourne, L. E. Jr. (2014). Training principles to advance expertise. *Frontiers in Psychology, 5*(131). doi:10.3389/fpsyg.2014.00131

Healy, A. F., Schneider, V. I., & Bourne, L. E., Jr. (2012). Empirically valid principles of training. In A. F. Healy & L. E. Bourne, Jr. (Eds.), *Training cognition: Optimizing efficiency, durability, and generalizability* (pp. 13–39). New York, NY: Psychology Press.

Kole, J. A., Healy, A. F., Schneider, V. I., & Barshi, I. (2019). Training principles for declarative and procedural tasks. In Landon, L. B., Slack, K. J., and Salas, E. (Eds.), *Psychology and human performance in space programs.* Abingdon, UK: Taylor & Francis.

Landon, L. B., Slack, K. J., & Barrett, J. D. (2018). Teamwork and collaboration in long-duration space missions: Going to extremes. *American Psychologist, 73*(4), 563–575. doi:10.1037/amp0000260

Macnamara, B. N., Hambrick, D. Z., & Oswald, F. L. (2014). Deliberate practice and performance in music, games, sports, education, and professions: A meta-analysis. *Psychological Science*, 1–11. doi:10.1177/0956797614535810

National Research Council. (2011). *Preparing for the high Frontier: The role and training of NASA astronauts in the post-space shuttle era*. Washington, DC: The National Academies Press. doi:10.17226/13227

Salas, E., Cannon-Bowers, J. A., & Blickensderfer, E. L. (1999). Enhancing reciprocity between training theory and practice: Principles, guidelines, and specifications. In G. R. Ferris (Ed.), *Research in personnel and human resources management* (Vol. 17, pp. 291–321). Stamford, CT: JAI Press.

Salas, E., Tannenbaum, S. I., Kraiger, K., & Smith-Jentsch, K. A. (2012). The science of training and development in organizations: What matters in practice. *Psychological Science in the Public Interest, 13*(2), 74–101. doi:10.1177/1529100612436661

Salas, E., Wilson, K. A., Priest, H. A., & Guthrie, J. W. (2006). Design, delivery, and evaluation of training systems. In G. Salvendy (Ed.), *Handbook of human factors and ergonomics* (3rd edition, pp. 472–512). Hoboken, NJ: John Wiley & Sons, Inc.

Schmidt, R. A., & Bjork, R. A. (1992). New conceptualizations of practice: Common principles in three paradigms suggest new concepts for training. *Psychological Science, 3*, 207–217. doi:10.1111/j.1467-9280.1992.tb00029.x

Schneider, W. C. (1976). *Skylab lessons learned as applicable to a large space station* (NASA/TM-X-73073). Washington, D.C.: NASA. Retrieved from https://ntrs.nasa.gov/search.jsp?R=19760022256

Strauch, B. (2017). The automation-by-expertise-by-training interaction: Why automation-related accidents continue to occur in sociotechnical systems. *Human Factors, 59*(2), 204–228. doi:10.1177/0018720816665459

Stuster, J., Adolf, J. A., Byrne, V. E., & Greene, M. (2018). *Human exploration of Mars: Preliminary lists of crew tasks* (NASA/CR-2018-220043). Houston, TX: NASA. Retrieved from https://ntrs.nasa.gov/archive/nasa/casi.ntrs.nasa.gov/20190001401.pdf.

Weaver, C. (Executive Producer), Weaver, E. (Producer, Director), & Weaver, Z. (Producer, Director). (2015). *Apollo astronauts: Training NASA's moon men [Motion Picture]*. United States: Jansen Media.

Woodling, C. H., Faber, S., Van Bockel, J. J., Olasky, C. C., Williams, W. K., Mire, J. L. C., & Homer, J. R. (1973). *Apollo experience report – Simulation of manned space flight for crew training* (NASA Technical Note NASA-TN-D-7112). Houston, TX: NASA. Retrieved from https://www.hq.nasa.gov/alsj/NASATND7112.pdf

5 Team Training for Long-Duration Space Exploration
A Look Ahead at the Coming Challenges

Natalie Croitoru
University of North Carolina at Chapel Hill

Tiffany M. Bisbey and Eduardo Salas
Rice University

CONTENTS

An Overview of Team Training 82
    Training Content 84
    Delivery Methods 84
    Tools 85
    Summary 86
Team Training in Space 86
    The State of LDSE Teams Research 87
    Challenges to the Traditional Team Training Paradigm 88
        Implications for Training Content 89
        Implications for Delivery 90
        Implications for Tools 91
Conclusion 92
Acknowledgments 95
References 96

The field of team training research emerged from a need to safeguard against human error in high-stakes contexts, such as hospitals, flight decks, and military command centers (Bisbey, Reyes, Traylor, & Salas, 2019). In the context of spaceflight, fatal teamwork mistakes in decision-making and poor communication had disastrous consequences for manned shuttle missions – *Columbia* in 2003 and *Challenger* in 1986 (Columbia Accident Investigation Board, 2003; House Committee on Science and Technology, 1986). These tragedies provided an impetus for NASA to prioritize team training, and effectively positioned NASA as a leader in efforts to further team science. Today, as the demands of space exploration are becoming increasingly complex, the current paradigm for turning a team of experts into an expert team must shift to confront anticipated challenges. The purpose of this chapter is to take a futuristic look at team training by leveraging the science built over the past few decades to address the needs of long-duration space exploration (LDSE) and reveal gaps to drive future research.

The conveniences of low Earth orbit that we have enjoyed during International Space Station (ISS) missions will be lost when NASA sets its sight on Mars (Landon, Slack, & Barrett, 2018). Among other unique challenges, there will be no instructor, no formal setting to conduct training, and minimal oversight for an expected two and a half years. The benefits of pre-flight training may diminish throughout the long and arduous journey, so we can safely assume a need for continual refresher courses to attenuate the risk of teamwork breakdowns. This means that astronauts must also learn how to self-manage their development and have the tools for doing so, underlining the importance of broadening our focus on teamwork skills to include those that support teamwork and motivate engagement in skill development throughout the mission. In all, LDSE will require an evolved rendition of traditional team training that is adaptive, self-sufficient, and capable of real-time diagnosis. What will these systems look like? How will we continually assess training needs, ensure team learning, or deliver feedback in the absence of a facilitator or coach? Researchers must meet these challenges with new tools and methods to assess and detect deficiencies in core team processes and dynamics in this isolated environment.

There is a foundation for the science of team training (see Salas, 2015) – and space exploration offers new challenges to the effective design, delivery, and implementation of team training. In this chapter, we aim to contribute to our understanding of the advancements required to get effective teams to Mars. We begin with an overview of what we have learned, what we have accomplished, and the problems team training research has addressed throughout history. We consider the anatomy of team training, including its content, tools, and delivery methods. Then we extend the current framework of team training on Earth by considering the contextual constraints of LDSE and the scientific progress needed in order to adapt team training models for missions to Mars. Specifically, we consider the ways in which the fundamentals of team training – in particular, its measurement tools and delivery methods – may fall short of serving LDSE teams, and how the science must advance for team training to remain effective in this new frontier.

AN OVERVIEW OF TEAM TRAINING

A team is a "distinguishable set of two or more people who interact dynamically, interdependently, and adaptively toward a common and valued goal/objective/ mission, who have been assigned specific roles or functions to perform, and have a limited life-span of mentorship" (Salas, Dickinson, Converse, & Tannenbaum, 1992, p. 4). A key component of this definition is that teams possess task interdependence, meaning that team members must interact effectively in order to achieve their objectives. Advantages of teams are that they create synergy, learning opportunities, novel ways of doing things, foster flexibility and responsiveness, encourage multidisciplinary thinking, create efficacy, and provide a structured way to manage people. As a result, teams are leveraged for their potential to innovate and problem-solve in high-stakes conditions. However, the benefits of teams are only as strong as the team itself and how well team members work together.

Effective teamwork requires a group of individuals to harness their interrelated knowledge, skills, and attitudes (KSAs) to function as a single unit to solve problems and achieve goals (Baker, Day, & Salas, 2006). Initiatives to improve teamwork are referred to as *team training*. Team training consists of a systematic set of learning initiatives that target and build the KSAs relevant to effective teamwork (Salas, DiazGranados, Weaver, & King, 2008). As stated, the science underlying team training began and evolved with the investigation of fatal errors in flight decks, command centers, operating rooms, nuclear power plants, and spaceflight caused by failures in teamwork. The consequences of these failures mobilized industry leaders to collaborate with scientists across disciplines with the goal of eliminating team failures and improving safety. For decades, they worked to better understand teamwork and developed tools and methods for effectively delivering teamwork KSAs in training interventions (Bisbey et al., 2019).

Team training has been a massive success, with meta-analyses supporting its applications to improve team effectiveness (LePine, Piccolo, Jackson, Mathieu, & Saul, 2008), task and teamwork skills (Delise, Gorman, Brooks, Rentsch, & Steele-Johnson, 2010), and even to help save lives in healthcare (Hughes et al., 2016). Teamwork competencies are also transportable, meaning they are similarly useful across industries, teams, and tasks. In aviation, implementing team training in the form of Crew Resource Management improved teamwork behaviors as much as 20% (Salas, Fowlkes, Stout, Milanovich, & Prince, 1999). In the military, Team Dimensional Training stimulated effective teamwork processes and outcomes, and created more accurate and shared mental-models (Smith-Jentsch, Cannon-Bowers, Tannenbaum, & Salas, 2008). The TeamSTEPPS program has become the national standard for team training in healthcare (King et al., 2008). Research by Neily et al. (2010) shows an almost 50% greater decrease of annual patient-mortality rates in groups receiving team training compared to untrained groups in a control condition.

It is without question – team training works. A great deal of recent research is focusing efforts on new frontiers in team training, such as LDSE (Bisbey et al., 2019). Informing this work is a strong foundation of research that has been done in analogous environments, such as deployed military teams and healthcare. In the past 15 years, the healthcare industry has increasingly relied on training interventions to optimize teamwork (Weaver, Dy, & Rosen, 2014). A meta-analysis by Hughes and colleagues was able to quantify the effectiveness of healthcare team training and conclude that training is effective at improving reactions, learning, and transfer (Arthur, Bennett, Edens, & Bell, 2003; Hughes et al., 2016). A meta-analysis by Salas and colleagues more broadly examined relationships between team training interventions and team functioning through several meta-analytic integrations (Salas et al., 2008). Results further substantiated team training interventions as an effective means to the improvement of team outcomes, specifically cognitive outcomes, affective outcomes, teamwork processes, and performance outcomes.

In order to address the unique challenges astronaut teams will face, we must adapt all that we have learned to provide tailored solutions that consider crew capabilities and limitations in the LDSE context while remaining effective at improving teamwork. At the core of every effective team training program is the consideration of three key components: (1) the teamwork content to be learned, (2) the methods used to deliver it, and (3) the tools used in execution (Salas & Cannon-Bowers, 2000). These three components provide a lens for us to visualize a framework for team training and to later assess what is needed to extend training to LDSE astronaut teams.

Training Content

The basis of any training program is its learning objectives, which direct the content that should be trained. For team training, the learning objectives revolve around teamwork and the competencies that allow for it to emerge. One of the first major accomplishments of team training research was delineating the competencies required for successful teamwork across contexts, lending guidance to those looking to improve teamwork by shedding light on the content to target (Bisbey et al., 2019). The specific team competencies required for optimal performance may vary slightly based on the relevant needs and context of each team, but researchers have elucidated several foundational factors that drive effective teamwork across contexts (for discussion of those specific to astronaut teams in LDSE, see chapters elsewhere in this two volume set).

Kraiger, Ford, and Salas (1993) proposed a heuristic of the attitudes, behaviors, and cognitions (i.e., the "ABCs" of teamwork) that affect teamwork and are impacted by team training. Attitudes, or affect-based constructs, include what teams feel; such as trust, cohesion, psychological safety, and collective efficacy. Behaviors include skills related to communication, coordination, decision-making, planning, monitoring, and backup behavior (Salas et al., 2008; Smith-Jentsch et al., 2008). Cognitions include perceptual and knowledge-based competencies such as shared mental models, transactive memory systems, and teamwork knowledge. In sum, all teams need these ABCs to varying degrees in order to function effectively. The delivery of this content to learners is another core component of team training.

Delivery Methods

Whether or not content is successfully transferred or understood by trainees is contingent upon the way it is delivered, or the instructional model. Any effective instructional model involves giving the learner the information, demonstrating it in action, and allowing opportunities to practice applying content with feedback (Cannon-Bowers, Salas, Tannenbaum, & Mathieu, 1995; Salas, Tannenbaum, Kraiger, & Smith-Jentsch, 2012). When delivering information to the trainee, it is important to not only relay descriptive facts and definitions of a teamwork competency, but also to provide evidence of its importance and effectiveness at improving outcomes relevant to the learner. Supplementary information showing relevance to the learner can help boost engagement and motivation (Mento, Locke, & Klein, 1992). For example, if an astronaut team is participating in a training module to improve team debriefing, they not only need to know what exactly a debrief is, but also how doing it effectively can improve team performance or safety (see e.g., Tannenbaum, Mathieu, Alliger, Cerasoli, & Donsbach, 2015).

The provision of information should be followed by a demonstration of its application in action. This might include a facilitator demonstration, watching video clips, or observing a role-playing activity. Continuing with our debriefing example, a demonstration might involve a video clip of an astronaut team participating in an effective debrief contrasted with an example of an ineffective debrief. Demonstrations allow learners to visualize how learned content might be used on the job effectively and ineffectively. Demonstrations should be followed by opportunities for trainees to practice themselves while it is safe to make mistakes and feedback to improve can be provided. Opportunities for practice in a safe environment prior to using learned skills on the job are an essential part of learning (Salas et al., 2008). Instructors (or *facilitators*) are instrumental to this process, as they are able to monitor and correct team behaviors in real time. Facilitators are a major resource for learners by answering their questions, modeling good form, and providing immediate feedback to correct errors during practice. Methods that incorporate feedback can increase the transfer of trained content to the real-world scenarios teams encounter (Goldstein, 1993). In summary, the methods of delivery represent the structure of a team training initiative and provide different avenues for learners to receive training content. Enabling this process are the various tools leveraged throughout an initiative that make it possible to deliver content, assess performance, and achieve the goals of team training.

Tools

Tools and methods go hand-in-hand, as they are the means by which the delivery of content can be achieved. For example, through demonstration videos, simulations, exercises, or any materials used to illustrate learned content being applied in action. Arguably the most critical tools of team training are those used to measure learning and performance. Measurement is paramount to learning because it allows people to gauge how well they are performing, thus providing grounds for improvement. Measurement is the basis for assessment, analysis, and remediation of team performance (Cannon-Bowers & Salas, 1997; Marlow, Bisbey, Lacerenza, & Salas, 2018). Researchers cannot determine when or if learning has taken place without diagnostic tools that measure team performance before and after training. Therefore, team performance measurement must be as accurate as possible to provide the most effective assessments of learning.

The principles of learning and teamwork are also tools that can be leveraged in the design and delivery of effective team training (Salas & Cannon-Bowers, 2000). For instance, seminal work by McIntyre and Salas (1995) with US Navy tactical teams identified five principles to turn a team of experts into an expert team: (1) teamwork implies an openness to feedback, (2) teamwork implies the willingness, preparedness, and proclivity to back up fellow teammates during operations, (3) teamwork requires members to collectively view themselves as an interdependent group whose success depends on their interactions, (4) effective teamwork fosters within-team interdependence as essential, meaning the team adopts the value of depending on one another regardless of status, and (5) team leaders model effective teamwork to other members, making them more likely to follow suit. Evidence-based principles, such as these, guide a training schema (e.g., the content to deliver, order of events, optimal measurement points etc.) and provide a foundation to support the effectiveness of a team training design.

Summary

Research demonstrating the value of team training across industries is compelling; however, the current framework for team training and its proven outcomes only exist on Earth, and has only begun to extend to the unfamiliar context of LDSE. What is true for team training effectiveness on Earth may or may not translate to LDSE. Certain aspects of the typical design and delivery of team training will need to be adapted to the new paradigm of LDSE, and significant scientific advancement is required to support team learning so that the benefits of team training on Earth can also be achieved in the isolated context of outer space. In the next section, we examine the unique characteristics of LDSE that will augment our approach to team training and provide the basis for identifying considerations critical to team training for these missions.

TEAM TRAINING IN SPACE

We know that teamwork plays a critical role in safe and effective performance in high-risk, interdependent situations (Baker & Salas, 1992; Cannon-Bowers, et al., 1995; Flin & Slaven, 1995; Hughes et al., 2016). Thus, LDSE team development must be a priority. Research has clarified the teamwork requirements for effective astronaut teams (see Landon et al., 2018), but the next step needed is a way to ensure those competencies transfer to the team in-practice.

In light of the significant contributions of team training to high-stakes industries, NASA has recently integrated team science into their primary research objectives and incorporated team scientists into the LDSE design and astronaut selection and development processes. They have funded projects to create a standard set of measures for the International Space Station and in ground-based analogs targeted to assess psychological and team phenomena (Roma, Schneiderman, & Landon, 2019). NASA has also expanded its selection process by adding a series of experiential team exercises (Slack, 2016). Although much progress has been made to incorporate teamwork considerations into space exploration efforts, the LDSE context is difficult to replicate because of limited potential sample sizes and few generalizable research environments. Most of what we know about spaceflight team dynamics comes from analog environments (Landon et al., 2018). From these analog studies and the science of team training, we can anticipate how several situational characteristics might create barriers to training effectiveness in LDSE.

THE STATE OF LDSE TEAMS RESEARCH

Studies of teamwork and team training in extreme environments can inform the design of team training for LDSE, as some of the most salient contextual components are able to be replicated. Extreme environments are defined as "settings in which there are significant task, social, or environmental demands that entail high levels of risk and increased consequences for poor performance" (Driskell, Salas, & Driskell, 2018, p. 435). An extreme environment may be signaled by the presence of (1) hostile environmental demands, (2) danger and physical risk to the self or others, (3) restricted living or working conditions, and (4) social demands that may include isolation from outsiders, and close confinement with those inside (Harrison & Connors, 1984). A more recent definition put forth by Bell, Fisher, Brown, and Mann (2016) identifies extreme environments as those possessing a distinct level or type of demands where ineffective performance can result in severe consequences. Understanding how teams operate effectively in extreme contexts is critical, as high-stress situations are common in these environments and working as a team amplifies the intensity of shared experiences (Boothby, Clark, & Bargh, 2014).

Context matters greatly in teams, but sometimes teams performing in different contexts are more similar than they are different (Salas, Reyes, & McDaniel, 2018). This point is especially relevant to LDSE research, as teams scientists study space analogs or other isolated, confined, and extreme (ICE) contexts to inform training and procedures for space exploration. For example, astronaut Don Pettit confirmed that although the "physics" of Antarctica might be wrong, the psychological "mindset" is true to that of space (Pettit, 2007). Hence while the environment may differ, if certain fundamental characteristics are shared, such as psychosocial adaptation, findings can still be generalizable.

To meet the challenge of understanding what is needed for teams in space, researchers have made progress studying ICE environments to make projections about team phenomena in LDSE. For instance, Golden, Chang, and Kozlowski (2018) suggest a social support in an ICE context is more complex than simply giving and receiving support, as requests for support may strain interpersonal relationships and decrease well-being. Social support might be difficult to maintain over the course of an LDSE mission as negative emotions, avoidance, and tension prevail while cohesion diminishes (Golden et al., 2018). This has important implications for team training, as a supportive work climate promotes transfer of training to on-the-job performance (Richman-Hirsch, 2001). Given the importance of social support for team functioning, future research should establish the boundary conditions for social support. Specifically, a next step for LDSE research is to uncover moderators that reveal the conditions under which team members need and should request social support (Golden et al., 2018). Future research should also consider the concept of "matching" between the type of support, the source of support, and the type of stressor, and whether congruence matters (e.g., the source of support, like a teammate, is matched to the source of the stressor, a team-related issue) (Cohen & Willis, 1985; see also Jackson, 1992).

In addition to the use of environmental analogs of LDSE, team scientists also utilize similar populations, such as members of elite military, aviation, healthcare, and Antarctic exploration (Landon et al., 2018). Research topics cover a range of themes related to team effectiveness. Through observational studies of spaceflight crews, and testing teams in space analogs (e.g., ICE environments), researchers have advanced several indicators of the most critical team compositional factors needed for LDSE (Landon et al., 2018). Mathieu, Tannenbaum, Kukenberger, Donsbach, & Alliger (2014) have worked to clarify the social roles (e.g., "coordinator") crewmembers must play in order to fulfill their formal roles (e.g., pilot). In the Mars 500 simulation, researchers found that greater anxiety was related to more negative interactions among team members (Tafforin, Vinokhodova, Chekalina, & Gushin, 2015). Yet, in a study of teams in Antarctic conditions, individuals with greater levels of resiliency, adaptability, and team orientation were found to use appropriate stress- and problem-coping strategies, enabling them to better adapt to changing events, integrate into a group, and function effectively as a team (Bishop et al., 2006; Kanas et al., 2009; Vanhove, Herian, Harms, & Luthans, 2015).

Individual differences like these have significant implications for teams, as researchers must first consider how a team is composed before engaging in efforts to develop it. A 3-year study of teams in isolated Antarctic conditions found that personality traits influenced perceptions of team processes; specifically, those higher in conscientiousness were perceived as better performers (Webb, Olenick, Ayton, Chang, & Kozlowski, 2017). Recent work proposes a complete personality profile for team members that would likely work together effectively for LDSE missions (Landon, Rokholt, Slack, & Pecena, 2017; see also Bell, Brown, Abben, & Outland, 2015). Studies of teams in NASA's HERA (Human Exploration Research Analog) underline the importance of deep-level characteristics related to values and knowledge and their impact on mission success (Antone, Contractor, Bell, & DeChurch, 2017).

While the body of research on teams in LDSE-similar contexts is significant and growing, there remain questions unanswered and gaps unaddressed. Noe and colleagues' (2011) literature review of the state of this research outlined several specific needs, including expanding shared teamwork and taskwork models, identifying what combinations of converging models result in the best performance and which roles require greater convergence of knowledge, and a task analysis to identify the requirements unique to space. The complexities exhibited in these issues permeate to the study of team training for LDSE and add an additional layer of difficulty to addressing the challenges of LDSE team development.

CHALLENGES TO THE TRADITIONAL TEAM TRAINING PARADIGM

Research findings in ICE environments have helped inform and guide research for space teams, but similar environments still do not capture many LDSE characteristics, and the majority of current research uses static and cross-sectional data (Salas et al., 2015). To deploy team training ready for LDSE, we need extensive longitudinal research that continues to refine team training models. Most relevant is the need to design team training for maximum accessibility, usability, and learnability (Salas et al., 2015). We must create a system for enduring and sustaining teamwork in practice, as well as the means to evaluate the effectiveness of this system, including advanced measurement tools.

As stated, best practices for effective training involve a variety of instructional strategies to deliver teamwork content to learners that incorporate (1) relaying information, (2) demonstrating its application, and (3) providing opportunities to practice with feedback (Cannon-Bowers et al., 1995; Salas et al., 2012). The contextual components of LDSE have potential implications for several points in this framework. Unfortunately, these implications are currently difficult to investigate due to data limitations. Given what we know about team training, we can synthesize this knowledge with our findings from ICE environments to design training systems appropriate for LDSE. In the following sections, we explore the implications of these challenges as they relate to the content trained, the methods used to deliver training content, and the tools that enable training effectiveness (Figure 5.1).

Implications for Training Content

Although the study of teams in LDSE likely will not lead to the discovery of novel teamwork KSAs, the core competencies of effective teams may have additional considerations in light of the challenging contextual variables of space (Salas, Shuffler, Thayer, Bedwell, & Lazzara, 2015). For example, the remote location and high-stress tasking of LDSE may negatively impact the degree of collective orientation in the team, which has been shown to decrease one's consideration for others and hinder the supportive behaviors needed to establish and maintain cooperation (Smith-Jentsch et al., 2015). Conflict management is also complicated in LDSE, where different strategies employed by teammates might clash or interact to produce unexpected outcomes. Salas et al. (2015) suggest that it is important to avoid the path of least resistance and instead apply healthy strategies like team debriefs. Additionally, communication must be founded on the context-specific norms, and debrief protocols centered around these needs have proved effective in analog ICE environments (Tannenbaum et al., 2015).

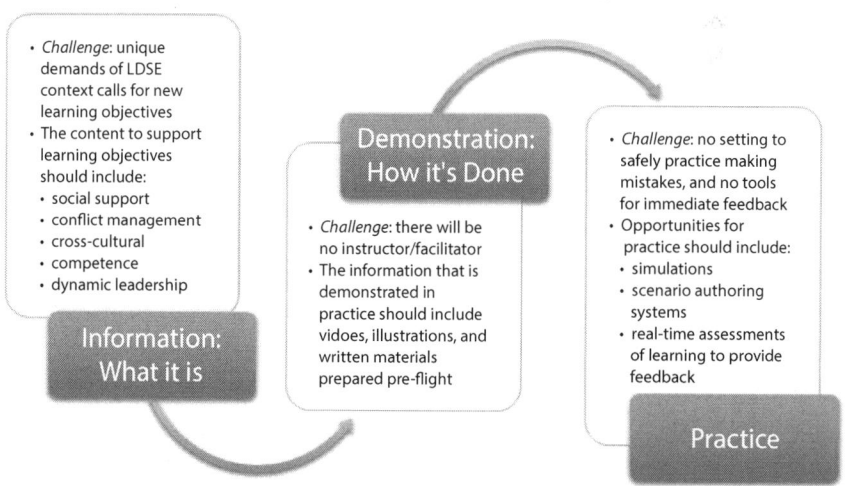

FIGURE 5.1 The structure of team training for long-duration space exploration (LDSE).

Given the multinational and multicultural composition of astronaut teams, researchers should be sensitive to differences in cultural power distance, which may result in individuals of a particular background to be more likely to assume a position of followership, even when the situation is better equipped for their leadership. Training should pay special attention to managing diversity and training teammates to take advantage of the multiple perspectives provided by a multinational team to avoid faultlines that divide the group. Coaching for effective leadership and followership is especially challenging for space because training programs are most effective when they provide opportunities to practice skills and receive feedback, but those opportunities are limited in the isolated context of LDSE. Because LDSE requires a high degree of role switching, training should focus on developing a shared knowledge of task and team KSAs, allowing for effective coordination at the team level. As proposed by Salas et al. (2015), leadership training for LDSE should incorporate modules of different leadership types to account for the dynamic leadership required of unexpected situations – be it collective, dyadically oriented, socio-emotional, or crisis-response leadership styles.

In order to engage in back-up behaviors, members should possess competencies in the taskwork of other team members with whom they directly interact, such that members can jump in and help when needed. Successful astronaut teams should have a high team orientation and recognize that their individual effectiveness *is* the team's effectiveness. Moreover, the leader must model the aforementioned behaviors in order to establish a norm of engaging in supportive behavior. We refer the reader to other chapters in this two volume work for a more comprehensive overview of the essential teamwork competencies for successful LDSE, and dedicate the remainder of our discussion to how this critical content might be delivered in team training and the tools needed to do so.

Implications for Delivery

The isolated space context poses unique challenges to the creation of a positive team training climate, to providing opportunities for demonstration, and to practice new skills and enable transfer of learning. To begin with, team training and related countermeasures for LDSE will need to be self-sufficient. As flight teams travel further away from Earth, communication delays with MCC increase (Noe, Dachner, Saxton, & Keeton, 2011). By the time the team reaches Mars, the communication delay could be as long as 45 minutes one-way. This makes it extremely difficult, if not impossible, to rely on an external teamwork-expert who can fill the role of training instructor. Knowledge cannot be relayed through real-time didactic formats in LDSE; thus, trainees may need to rely on written information or videos to receive information, as well as to experience an applied demonstration of its relevance.

Practicing teamwork skills learned in training will also be a challenge for LDSE teams. The lines between living and working together will be understandably blurred for these teams, so almost everything will require a certain level of interdependence. This could mean that there are many opportunities to apply new skills organically in their work, but it is also essential to practice them in an environment where it is safe to make errors from which to learn (Prince & Salas, 1999; Salas et al., 2012).

One potential avenue might be through a scenario authoring system that links realistic situations with learning objectives.

The isolation of LDSE teams requires a great degree of self-maintenance, meaning that it will be up to them to uphold habits that foster teamwork and recognize when it can be improved. Accordingly, they must also be open to receiving feedback, which will require astronauts to engage in tasks with an awareness of their strengths and weaknesses, be open to criticism, and foster a group climate that is receptive to critiques. In order to be aware of breakdowns in teamwork before a disaster occurs, teams should regularly assess what is working and what can be improved. Performance debriefs help team members make sense of what occurred in a performance episode, allow them to process their thoughts and feelings, and elicit problem-solving behaviors that aid in adapting their current strategies (Tannenbaum & Cerasoli, 2013; Tannenbaum et al., 2015).

Tannenbaum et al. (2015) found debriefing to be an effective method to improve teamwork and team performance in simulated space missions. Debriefing keeps team members intentional about their efforts to perform well together, but significant improvement may require precise, real-time performance feedback. Advancements in intelligent measurement and unobtrusive sensors would inform these efforts. In order to make the leap to extend team training to space, teams researchers must collaborate with leaders in other disciplines to develop and refine technology that is capable of overcoming the barriers to delivery posed by distance and isolation.

Implications for Tools

Arguably, the area most in need of scientific advancement is the development of training tools for delivery and assessment. Developing such a system would require collaboration across multiple disciplines such as cognitive, human-factors, learning, and organizational psychologists, as well as neuroscientists, mathematicians, and computer scientists. Once we validate the relevant team-based KSAs that matter most (see Fiore, Wiltshire, Sanz, & Pajank, 2015), we will have a framework for developing a robust measurement system to monitor and assess salient team states and processes. Team state classification measures could include semantic analysis, detection of voice levels and inflection, content analysis of learner speech or text, or understanding behaviors. This information might then inform trigger phrases or patterns (see Johnson, Johnson, & Stanne, 2000) for launching an automated instruction program, such as the generalized intelligent framework for tutoring (GIFT) tool (Sottilare et al., 2017) or other agent-based training tools.

Trainees could also view virtual demonstrations, respond to critical incident prompts, and review scenarios to identify key stress-points. This would provide multiple opportunities to exhibit learned content, and combining intelligent assessment technology could facilitate measurement. Intelligent assessment technology would have to be adaptive, as training instructors typically have the opportunity to be dynamic in their interaction styles by adapting when a particular tactic fails to effectively convey information or learners become disengaged. Perhaps the most critical implication of not having a training facilitator is the inability to receive feedback, which is especially problematic when ground support is inaccessible. Team science needs intelligent instructional systems that can recognize decrements in learner engagement and can motivate learning with adaptive delivery methods so that LDSE teams know what ineffective teamwork looks like and how it is affecting their performance. In short, we need robust measurement systems that can provide dynamic assessment, are developmental, and are unobtrusive to mission-critical team performance.

The criticality of teamwork in high-risk interdependent contexts makes team training and development a priority for LDSE teams, but training cannot be so obtrusive that it becomes inhibiting or negatively impacts motivation to participate. It is paramount for research to investigate the creation of a team training system that allows teams to continually improve while being adaptive to their development over time and preventing the breakdowns over the course of a mission to Mars. Flight crews will be balancing multiple goals to achieve mission success, so it is conceivable for needed refresher courses to slip through the cracks. We need to ensure buy-in from the team and understand what they need to remain dedicated to the role of team training in mission success. Future research should investigate how multiple goals are prioritized in the LDSE context and how self-managed teams can support shared-goal dedication.

Perhaps a system that integrates intelligent tools and tracks a trend in the proficiency of teamwork KSAs over time might alert the team of concerning patterns and support the decision to deploy a remedial team training module. Kozlowski and Chao (2018) suggest that we can better understand the dynamics behind team cohesion and cognition with unobtrusive team interaction sensors and process-oriented research methods like computational modeling. Researchers are also beginning to consider neurophysiological indicators and real-time communication pattern analysis to inform the design of training for LDSE. These advancements encourage more nuanced measurements of team dynamics, allow for automated scoring of these dynamics during task performance, and enable the precise targeting of countermeasures (Salas et al., 2015). Until these innovative methods are incorporated into training systems and further refined, understanding the dynamics underlying motivation of training engagement and learning for LDSE teams will be paramount.

CONCLUSION

Teams have been an enduring theme throughout the history of studying organizations on Earth, and will be an essential part of venturing to other planets and beyond. Teams are a central point of human social organization; as even before "teams" were formally conceptualized, humans were collaborating as hunter-gatherers and defenders, and forming communities to act as interdependent teams. In the modern workforce, organizations are harnessing the power of teams to produce novel ideas and drive innovation and agility (Pulakos, Kantrowitz, & Schneider, 2019). The history of team training should continue to inform future work, as principles and methods with an established track record can provide the basis for the design and implementation of a training program for LDSE.

The science of team training has advanced significantly over the past several years, shifting away from cause-effect models toward a more co-evolutionary systems-approach that recognizes the reciprocal influences between various internal and external components (Tannenbaum, Mathieu, Salas, & Cohen, 2012). The significant change themes true for space are also relevant for modern organizational teams (e.g., dynamic composition, advanced measurement), meaning that a framework for team training for LDSE would also have significant implications for modern teams on Earth that span geographic, cultural, and temporal boundaries. Looking ahead, teams will be expected to operate under unprecedented levels of efficacy and independence, for LDSE contexts and otherwise.

Spaceflight teams represent an apex of the trend of harnessing the power of teams in dynamic and demanding environments; yet the benefits of teams hinge on their ability to effectively work interdependently, and the fatal mistakes of our past in team decision-making and communication have proven that effective team behaviors are not guaranteed. Team training protects against such errors and avoids the often-tragic consequences that follow. Our understanding of the principles of team training in these settings combined with studies in space analog environments provide a working understanding of the future for team training for LDSE. We urge fellow researchers to further the understanding of what is needed for team training in LDSE put forth in this chapter, and to work to develop the tools and methods required to successfully implement an effective team training program in the prolonged isolation and confinement of extended missions in space (Table 5.1).

TABLE 5.1
Implications for the Design of Team Training for Long-Duration Space Exploration (LDSE)

Component	LDSE Issue	Implications	References
Content	**Social support** will be difficult to maintain in light of the mission's long duration, remote location, and high-stress tasking	Future work must establish the boundary conditions for social support – when should members request it?	Golden et al. (2018) and Salas et al. (2015)
	Conflict management strategies can clash to produce unexpected outcomes	Team debriefs are essential in order to avoid building tension	Salas et al. (2015)
	Communication must be a shared language related to the context-specific characteristics of LDSE	Debrief protocols must be founded on the context-specific norms unique to spaceflight	Tannenbaum et al. (2015)
	Leadership training must be sensitive to diversity and differences in cultural power distance	Astronauts must be trained to assume a position of leadership or followership based on the context of the problem rather than an individual's tendency to assume leadership	Salas et al. (2015)
	Coaching for leadership will require opportunities to practice skills and receive feedback, which will be difficult to identify during LDSE	Traditional coaching practices will have to be amended to accommodate the isolated space environment	Salas et al. (2015)

(Continued)

TABLE 5.1 (*Continued*)
Implications for the Design of Team Training for Long-Duration Space Exploration (LDSE)

Component	LDSE Issue	Implications	References
	Coordination behaviors will require a high degree of role switching demanded in LDSE	Training for coordinating behaviors will require the development of a shared knowledge of team KSAs	Salas et al. (2015)
	Leadership training must produce the dynamic leadership required for the various demands of LDSE	Leadership training must incorporate different leadership styles (e.g., collective, dyadic-oriented, socio-emotional, crisis-response)	Salas et al. (2015)
Delivery	**Opportunities for practice** will have to be reimagined, as astronauts cohabitating with their teammates have few opportunities to practice skills and make mistakes safely	Researchers must design multiple opportunities to exhibit learned content, and combining intelligent assessment technology could facilitate measurement	Salas et al. (2012)
	Self-sufficient measures and countermeasures will be paramount as astronauts will not have access to an external teamwork-expert to fill the traditional role of instructor. There will be no real-time instructor to provide real-time coaching and feedback and adapt to trainee needs	Measures and countermeasures will have to be identified and accounted for preflight, as well as once the team has launched for continual assessment and improvement of teamwork states	Noe et al. (2011)
	Self-maintenance behaviors will need to become the norm in order to prevent the breakdown of cooperative and supportive behaviors, or the emergence of faultlines	There must be an openness to feedback and performance debriefs to allow teammates to process a performance episode and adapt their behaviors	Tannenbaum et al. (2015)
Tools	**Robust measurement systems** can help monitor and assess salient team states and processes	Future work must validate the team-based KSAs most relevant to LDSE	Fiore et al. (2015)
	Updated team training models are required in order to design training for maximum accessibility, usability, and learnability for LDSE	Theory-building longitudinal research must update old team training models	Salas et al. (2015)

(*Continued*)

TABLE 5.1 (*Continued*)
Implications for the Design of Team Training for Long-Duration Space Exploration (LDSE)

Component	LDSE Issue	Implications	References
	Team state classification measures need to be updated to reflect and diagnose team states during LDSE	Future work must update team state classification measures for key teamwork competencies as antecedents for outcomes of interest, such as learning, performance, satisfaction, and viability	Sottilare, Burke, Salas, Sinatra, Johnston, and Gilbert (2017)
	Intelligent assessment technology will have to be exceptionally adaptive, as they will compensate for the lack of an external instructor or training facilitator	Researchers must collaborate to develop systems that can provide dynamic assessment, be developmental, and be unobtrusive	Kozlowski and Chao (2018) and Salas et al. (2015)
Other Factors to Consider	**Individual differences** are an essential consideration to compose a team that is fixed and can adapt to challenges and use appropriate stress- and problem-coping strategies	Most relevant to mission success is that individuals have a high team orientation and possess deep-level characteristics related to values and knowledge, namely resiliency, adaptability, and team orientation	Antone et al. (2017), Bishop et al. (2006), Kanas et al. (2009) and Vanhove et al. (2015)

Team science has provided much insight to how teams think, feel, and behave, but researchers are only beginning to advance methods of unobtrusive, real-time assessment. Effective team training for LDSE requires robust diagnostics in order to understand the attitudes, behaviors, cognition, and emergent states of flight crews and answer important questions such as *when is team training needed, how much is enough,* and *is learning actually occurring.* If learners feel training is irrelevant or redundant, they could be less motivated to learn or refresh their skills (Morrell & Korsgaard, 2011). In the same regard, research suggests understanding the outcomes, importance, and personal relevance of training content increases engagement (Mento et al., 1992). Without informed answers to these questions, it is difficult to know how team members might experience the training initiative. These questions should be the primary focus of team training as we explore new frontiers. It is time for the next great leap in team science – one that will take effective teamwork far beyond our history and into our future.

ACKNOWLEDGMENTS

We would like to thank the editors for their helpful feedback on previous versions of this chapter. This material is based upon work supported in part by grants NNX16AP96G and NNX16AB08G from the National Aeronautics and Space

Administration (NASA) to Rice University, as well as grant NNX17AB55G from NASA to Rice University via Johns Hopkins University (PI: Michael Rosen).

REFERENCES

Antone, W. B., Contractor, N. S., Bell, S. T., & DeChurch, L. A. (2017, January). *Faulty analysis: Analyzing the validity of different faultline measurement algorithms for long-duration space exploration*. Presented at the NASA Human Research Program Investigators' Workshop, Galveston, TX.

Arthur, W., Jr., Bennett, W., Jr., Edens, P. S., & Bell, S. T. (2003). Effectiveness of training in organizations: A meta-analysis of design and evaluation features. *Journal of Applied Psychology, 88*, 234–245.

Baker, D. P., Day, R., & Salas, E. (2006). Teamwork as an essential component of high-reliability organizations. *Health Services Research, 41*(4), 1576–1598.

Baker, D. P., & Salas, E. (1992). Principles for measuring teamwork skills. *Human Factors: The Journal of the Human Factors and Ergonomics Society, 34*(4), 469–475.

Bell, S. T., Brown, S. G., Abben, D. R., & Outland, N. B. (2015). Team composition issues for future space exploration: A review and directions for future research. *Aerospace Medicine and Human Performance, 86*, 548–556. doi:10.3357/AMHP.4195.2015

Bell, S. T., Fisher, D. M., Brown, S. G., & Mann, K. E. (2016). An approach for conducting actionable research with extreme teams. *Journal of Management, 20*, 1–26.

Bisbey, T. M., Reyes, D. L., Traylor, A. M., & Salas, E. (2019). Teams of psychologists helping teams: The evolution of the science of team training. *American Psychologist, 74*, 278–289.

Bishop, S. L., Dawson, S., Rawat, N., Reynolds, K., Eggins, R., & Bunzelek, K. (2006). Assessing teams in Mars simulation habitats. In J. D. Clarke (Ed.), *American Astronautical Society science and technology series* (pp. 177–196). San Diego, CA: Univelt.

Boothby, E. J., Clark, M. S., & Bargh, J. A. (2014). Shared experiences are amplified. *Psychological Science, 25*(12), 2209–2216.

Cannon-Bowers, J. A., & Salas, E. (1997). A framework for developing team performance measures in training. In M. T. Brannick, E. Salas, & C. Prince (Eds.), *Team performance assessment and measurement: Theory, methods, and applications* (pp. 45–62). Hillsdale, NJ: Erlbaum.

Cannon-Bowers, J. A., Salas, E., Tannenbaum, S. I., & Mathieu, J. E. (1995). Toward theoretically based principles of training effectiveness: A model and initial empirical investigation. *Military Psychology, 7*(3), 141–164.

Cohen, S., & Willis, T. A. (1985). Stress, social support, and the buffering hypothesis. *Psychological Bulletin, 98*(2), 310–357.

Columbia Accident Investigation Board. (2003). *Report of the Columbia accident investigation board*. Washington, DC: Government Printing Office and National Aeronautics and Space Administration.

Delise, L. A., Gorman, A., Brooks, A. M., Rentsch, J. R., & Steele-Johnson, D. (2010). The effects of team training on team outcomes: A meta-analysis. *Performance Improvement Quarterly, 22*(4), 53–80.

Driskell, T., Salas, E., & Driskell, J. E. (2018). Teams in extreme environments: Alterations in team development and teamwork. *Human Resource Management Review, 28*, 434–449.

Fiore, S. M., Wiltshire, T. J., Sanz, E. J., & Pajank, M. E. (2015). *Critical Team Cognitive Processes for Long-Duration Exploration Missions* (Report No. TM-2015-218583). Houston TX: NASA.

Flin, R. H., & Slaven, G. M. (1995). *Identifying the right stuff: Selecting and training on-scene*. Houston, TX: National Aeronautics and Space Administration.

Golden, S. J., Chang, C.-H., & Kozlowski, S. W. J. (2018). Teams in isolated, confined, and extreme (ICE) environments: Review and integration. *Journal of Organizational Behavior, 39*(6), 701–715.

Goldstein, I. L. (1993). *Cypress series in work and science. Training in organizations: Needs assessment, development, and evaluation* (3rd edition). Belmont, CA, US: Thomson Brooks/Cole Publishing Co.

Harrison, A. A., & Connors, M. M. (1984). Groups in exotic environments. In L. Berkowitz (Ed.), *Advances in experimental social psychology* (Vol 17, pp. 49–87). New York, NY: Academic Press.

House Committee on Science and Technology. (1986). *Investigation of the challenger accident* (House Report No. 99-1016). Retrieved from https://www.gpo.gov/fdsys/pkg/GPO-CRPT-99hrpt1016/pdf/GPO-CRPT-99hrpt1016.pdf

Hughes, A. M., Gregory, M. E., Joseph, D. L., Sonesh, S. C., Marlow, S. L., Lacerenza, C. N., & Salas, E. (2016). Saving lives: A meta-analysis of team training in healthcare. *Journal of Applied Psychology, 101*(9), 1266–1304. doi:10.1037/apl0000120

Jackson, P. B. (1992). Specifying the buffering hypothesis: Support, strain, and depression. *Social Psychology Quarterly, 55*(4), 363–378. doi:10.2307/2786953

Johnson, D. W., Johnson, R. T., & Stanne, M. B. (2000). *Cooperative learning methods: A meta-analysis*. Minneapolis: University of Minnesota.

Kanas, N., Sandal, G., Boyd, J., Gushin, V., Manzey, D., North, R., & Wang, J. (2009). Psychology & culture during LDSMs. *Acta Astronautica, 64*, 659–677.

King, H. B., Battles. J., Baker, D. P., Alonso, A., Salas, E., Webster, J., … Salisbury, M. (2008). TeamSTEPPS™: team strategies and tools to enhance performance and patient safety. In K. Henriksen, J. B. Battles, M. A. Keyes, &, M. L. Grady, (Eds.), *Advances in patient safety: New directions and alternative approaches* (Vol. 3: Performance and Tools). Rockville, MD: Agency for Healthcare Research and Quality. Available from https://www.ncbi.nlm.nih.gov/books/NBK43686/.

Kozlowski, S. W. J., & Chao, G. T. (2018). Unpacking team process dynamics and emergent phenomena: Challenges, conceptual advances, and innovative methods. *American Psychologist, 73*, 576–592. doi:10.1037/amp0000245

Kraiger, K., Ford, J. K., & Salas, E. (1993). Application of cognitive, skill-based, and affective theories of learning outcomes to new methods of training evaluation. *Journal of Applied Psychology, 78*(2), 311–328. doi:10.1037/0021-9010.78.2.311

Landon, L. B., Rokholt, C., Slack, K. J., & Pecena, Y. (2017). Selecting astronauts for long-duration exploration missions: Considerations for team performance and functioning. *REACH—Reviews in Human Space Exploration, 5*, 33–56.

Landon, L. B., Slack, K. J., & Barrett, J. D. (2018). Teamwork and collaboration in long-duration space missions: Going to extremes. *American Psychologist, 73*, 563–575. doi:10.1037/amp0000260

LePine, J. A., Piccolo, R. F., Jackson, C. L., Mathieu, J. E., & Saul, J. R. (2008). A meta-analysis of teamwork processes: Tests of a multidimensional model and relationships with team effectiveness criteria. *Personnel Psychology, 61*(2), 273–307.

Marlow, S., Bisbey, T., Lacerenza, C., & Salas, E. (2018). Performance measures for health care teams: A review. *Small Group Research, 49*(3), 306–356.

Mathieu, J. E., Tannenbaum, S. I., Kukenberger, M. R., Donsbach, J. S., & Alliger, G. M. (2014). Team role experience and orientation: A measure and tests of construct validity. *Group & Organization Management, 40*(1), 6–34.

McIntyre, R. M., & Salas, E. (1995). Measuring and managing for team performance: Emerging principles form complex environments. In R. Guzzo & E. Salas (Eds.), *Team effectiveness and decision making in organizations* (pp. 149–203). San Francisco, CA: Jossey-Bass.

Mento, A. J., Locke, E. A., & Klein, H. J. (1992). Relationship of goal level to valence and instrumentality. *Journal of Applied Psychology, 77,* 395–405. doi:10.1037/0021-9010.77.4.395

Morrell, D. L., & Korsgaard, M. A. (2011) Training in context: Toward a person-by-situation view of voluntary training. *Human Resource Development Quarterly, 22,* 323–342.

Neily, J., Mills, P. D., Young-Xu, Y., Carney, B. T., West, P., Berger, D. H., ... Bagian, J.P. (2010). Association between implementation of a medical team training program and surgical mortality. *Journal of the American Medical Association, 304*(15), 1693–1700. doi:10.1001/jama.2010.1506

Noe, R. A., Dachner, A.M., Saxton, B., & Keeton, K. E. (2011). *Team training for long-duration missions in isolated and confined environments: A literature review, an operational assessment, and recommendations for practice and research* (NASA/TM-2011-216162). Houston TX: NASA. Available from https://ston.jsc.nasa.gov/collections/TRS/_techrep/TM-2011-216162.pdf

Pettit, D. R. (2007). *Presentation on Antarctic expedition for meteorites.* Houston, TX: NASA Johnson Space Center.

Prince, C., & Salas, E. (1999). Team processes and their training in aviation. In D. Garland, J. Wise, & D. Hopkins (Eds.), *Handbook of aviation human factors* (pp. 193–213). Mahwah, NJ: Lawrence Erlbaum Associates.

Pulakos, E. D., Kantrowitz, T., & Schneider, B. (2019). What leads to organizational agility: It's not what you think. *Consulting Psychology Journal: Practice and Research, 71,* 305–320.

Richman-Hirsch, W. L. (2001). Posttraining interventions to enhance transfer: The moderating effects of work environments. *Human Resource Development Quarterly, 12*(2), 105–120.

Roma, P. G., Schneiderman, J. S., & Landon, L. B. (2019, January). *Overview of NASA behavioral health & performance standard measures.* Presented at NASA Human Research Program's Investigators' Workshop, Galveston, TX.

Salas, E. (2015). *Team training essentials: A research-based guide.* New York, NY: Routledge.

Salas, E., & Cannon-Bowers, J. A. (2000). The anatomy of team training. In S. Tobias & J. D. Fletcher (Eds.), *Training and retraining: A handbook for business, industry, government, and the military* (pp. 312–335). New York, NY: Macmillan Reference USA.

Salas, E., DiazGranados, D., Klein, C., Burke, S.C., Stagl, K.C., Goodwin, G.F., & Halpin, S.M. (2008). Does team training improve team performance? A meta-analysis. *Human Factors, 50*(6), 903–933. doi: 10.1518/001872008X375009

Salas, E., DiazGranados, D., Weaver, S. J., & King, H. (2008). Does team training work? Principles for health care. *Academic Emergency Medicine, 15*(11), 1002–1009.

Salas, E., Dickinson, T. L., Converse, S. A., & Tannenbaum, S. I., (1992). Toward an understanding of team performance and training. In R. W. Swezey & E. Salas (Eds.), *Teams: Their training and performance* (pp. 3–29). Wesport, CT: Apex Publishing.

Salas, E., Fowlkes, J. E., Stout, R. J., Milanovich, D., & Prince, C. (1999). Does CRM training improve teamwork skills in the cockpit? Two evaluation studies. *Human Factors, 41,* 326–343.

Salas, E., Reyes, D. L., & McDaniel, S. H. (2018). The science of teamwork: Progress, reflections, and the road ahead. *American Psychologist, 73*(4), 593–600. doi:10.1037/amp0000334

Salas, E., Shuffler, M. L., Thayer, A. L., Bedwell, W. L., & Lazzara, E. H. (2015). Understanding and improving teamwork in organizations: A scientifically based practical guide. *Human Resource Management, 54*(4), 599–622.

Salas, E., Tannenbaum, S. I., Kozlowski, S. W., Miller, C. A., Mathieu, J. E., & Vessey, W. B. (2015). Teams in space exploration: A new frontier for the science of team effectiveness. *Current Directions in Psychological Science, 24,* 200–207.

Salas, E., Tannenbaum, S. I., Kraiger, K., & Smith-Jentsch, K. A. (2012). The science of training and development in organizations: What matters in practice. *Psychological Science in the Public Interest, 13*(2), 74–101.

Slack, K. J. (2016, April). *Selecting astronauts and composing crews: Lessons applicable to earth-bound organizations*. Presented at the 31st Annual Conference of the Society of Industrial/Organizational Psychology, Anaheim, CA.

Smith-Jentsch, K. A., Cannon-Bowers, J. A., Tannenbaum, S. I., & Salas, E. (2008). Guided team self-correction: Impacts on team mental models, processes, and effectiveness. *Small Group Research, 39*(3), 303–327.

Smith-Jentsch, K. A., Sierra, M. J., Weaver, S. J., Bedwell, W. L., Dietz, A. S., Carter-Berenson, D., ... Salas, E. (2015). *Training "The Right Stuff": An assessment of team training needs for long-duration spaceflight crews* (Report No. TM/2015-218589).

Sottilare, R.A., Burke, S.C., Salas, E., Sinatra, A.M., Johnston, J.H., & Gilbert, S.B. (2017). Designing adaptive instruction for teams: A meta-analysis. *International Journal of Artificial Intelligence in Education, 28*, 225–264. doi: 10.1007/s40593-017-0146-z

Tafforin, C. & Vinokhodova, A. & Chekalina, A. & Gushin, V. (2015). Correlation of ethosocial and psycho-social data from "Mars-500" interplanetary simulation. *Acta Astronautica*, 111. doi:10.1016/j.actaastro.2015.02.005

Tannenbaum, S. I., & Cerasoli, C. P. (2013). Do team and individual debriefs enhance performance? A meta-analysis. *Human Factors, 55*, 231–245.

Tannenbaum, S. I., Mathieu, J. E., Alliger, G. M., Cerasoli, C. P., & Donsbach, J. S. (2015). *Using progressively realistic analog environments to test team self-debriefing for astronauts*. Presented at the Annual Conference for the Society for Industrial/Organizational Psychologists, Philadelphia, PA.

Tannenbaum, S. I., Mathieu, J. E., Salas, E., & Cohen, D. (2012). Teams are changing: Are research and practice evolving fast enough? *Industrial and Organizational Psychology, 5*(1), 2–24. doi:10.1111/j.1754-9434.2011.01396.x

Vanhove, A. J., Herian, M. N., Harms, P. D., & Luthans, F. (2015). *Resilience and growth in long-duration isolated, confined and extreme (ICE) missions* (NASA/TM-2015-218566). Retrieved from https://ston.jsc.nasa.gov/collections/TRS/_techrep/TM-2015-218566.pdf

Weaver, S. J., Dy, S. M., & Rosen, M. A. (2014). Team-training in healthcare: A narrative synthesis of the literature. *British Medical Journal Quality & Safety, 23*, 359–372.

Webb, J. M., Olenick, J., Ayton, J., Chang, C-H., & Kozlowski, S. W. J. (2017, January). *An examination of the relationships between the Big Five personality factors and team processes*. Poster to be presented at the NASA Human Research Program Investigator Workshop, Galveston, TX.

6 Mitigating the Impact of Communication Delay

Ute Fischer
Georgia Institute of Technology

Kathleen Mosier
San Francisco State University

CONTENTS

The Challenges of Communication Delay 102
Supporting Space/Ground Communication During Asynchronous Conditions 105
Acknowledgments 113
References 113

> We looked at the voice loops, we looked at the text loops that occurred during these scenarios, and we saw afterwards that it was broken ten ways to Sunday. We were talking past each other; we were taking one response to mean, to be a response to a totally different question, you know, it was incredibly broken, and you could only see it when you took the time to really analyze it afterwards (Astronaut reflecting on the impact of communication delay on crew/MCC collaboration during a space analog simulation, quoted by Vessey, Palinkas, & Leveton, 2013)

Space-ground communication will present a significant challenge for future exploration missions to destinations beyond low Earth orbit. As missions travel further from Earth, the communication between space crewmembers and ground support will be significantly delayed; for a mission to Mars the time lag can be up to 20 minutes one way. The presence of communication delays will require that crewmembers be given more autonomy in these missions than they have in current operations. However, the requirement for space-ground collaboration will remain. Crewmembers and ground support personnel will need to communicate mission-critical information to ensure that they have shared task and situation models as the mission progresses. Additionally, unforeseen problems for which crews will need assistance from ground, such as system failures or medical issues may arise as examples from Apollo missions to the present day illustrate. Communication delays will also pose a formidable challenge to the collaboration between crewmembers and ground support because they may degrade team members' communication efficiency and ultimately hinder their joint task success (Krauss & Bricker, 1967; Kraut, Fussell, Brennan, & Siegel, 2002). For instance, in an experiment on the ISS, Kintz and colleagues (Kintz, Chou, Vessey, Leveton & Palinkas, 2016) noted that even a delay as short as 50 seconds significantly decreased crew and flight controllers' perceptions of their communication quality. As the transmission delay is fixed by the laws of physics, it is therefore essential to explore solutions that focus on the communication process itself rather than transmission speed to help crew and ground support communicate effectively and efficiently under time delayed conditions. In this chapter we describe one such approach. Specifically, we developed a communication protocol to facilitate space-ground collaboration under time-delayed conditions, and assessed its effectiveness during several simulated missions in different space-analog environments.

THE CHALLENGES OF COMMUNICATION DELAY

Communication delay can have a substantial impact on the efficiency and success of distributed team collaborations (Krauss & Bricker, 1967; Kraut et al., 2002), especially those that are complex and time intensive (Olson & Olson, 2000). Research examining asynchronous communication in the laboratory and in space analogs showed that transmission delays of 50 seconds and 5 minutes impeded collaboration in distributed teams, irrespective of the communication medium (voice or text) used (Fischer & Mosier, 2014; Fischer, Mosier, & Orasanu, 2013). An obvious threat associated with communication delay stems from the fact that team members have to wait for responses to potentially time-critical communications; less evident may be threats to message management and comprehension inherent in two additional features of communication delay described below.

When audio-based communications involve a delay, message management will be difficult and simultaneous speech is likely to occur; that is, as a team member – for example, a space crewmember – is speaking, a communication from CAPCOM that had been transmitted some time earlier is received. These so-called *step-ons* may compromise mutual understanding insofar as parts of a received message could not be heard. Additional communications by the team members will be necessary to ensure comprehension; an effort which, given the transmission delay, is likely associated with considerable costs both in terms of time and workload as partners have to wait for critical information and keep track of concurrent tasks. The second challenging feature of communication delay is present in both audio- and text-based communications and has to do with the temporal order of related messages, such as a question posed by a team member and its answer provided by his/her remote partner. Specifically, because there is a lag between the time a message is transmitted and the time it is received, related messages by different team members may not necessarily follow each other (as they would in synchronous communication); rather, messages passed on during the lag, such as updates on an evolving situation, can intervene. As an illustration of this issue, consider the following excerpt from an interaction between team members (called the Pioneer crew and the Flight Systems Engineer) who collaborated remotely with a 5 minute (one way) communication delay during a computer-based task (Fischer & Mosier, 2014). The task required the Pioneer crewmembers to monitor the (simulated) life support system of their space ship, to report critical system parameters to the Fight Systems Engineer, and to request assistance in case of a system error. The Flight Systems Engineer, as the team member with the prerequisite system training and knowledge, was responsible for helping the Pioneer

Mitigating the Impact of Communication Delay

crew with the diagnosis and repair of any system issue. The excerpt begins with the Pioneer crew informing the Fight Systems Engineer that their life support system shows an error with the Oxygen valve (Figure 6.1).

Speaker	TURN SEQUENCE FROM THE PERSPECTIVE OF THE PIONEER CREW (P)	Speaker	TURN SEQUENCE FROM THE PERSPECTIVE OF THE FLIGHT SYSTEMS ENGINEER (FSE)
P-1	5 min check: CO₂ .2, O₂ 19.7, pressure 1012, temp 20.4, humidity 39. And we have an error on the O₂ valve is stuck open, time since it occurred 22 sec. And we received your initial transmission.	FSE-1	*Whenever you guys get this message, let me know what your primary readings for your CO2, O2, etc.*
P-2	Error O2 valve stuck open, time since it occurred 48 sec	P-1	5 min check: CO₂ .2, O₂ 19.7, pressure 1012, temp 20.4, humidity 39. And we have an error on the O₂ valve is stuck open, time since it occurred 22 sec. And we received your initial transmission.
P-3	Error O2 valve stuck open. Time since error occurred 92 seconds	FSE-2	*Can you repeat the temp reading as well as the problem (with your system)?*
P-4	O2 tank at 7055, first valve 10, after the mixer valve 10.	P-2	Error O2 valve stuck open], time since it occurred 48 sec
P-5	Error O2 valve stuck open. Time since error occurred 203 sec. O2 tank at 26353, ohm first level 8, and two tank at 28112, first level 0, and the mixed is at 8	FSE-3	*What are the readings for the O2, the O2 valve and the tanks?*
P-6	10 min check: CO2 .2, O2 26.5, pressure 1013, temp. 19.29, humidity 41.2. Just to clarify pressure is one thousand thirteen. And error O2 valve stuck open, time since error occurred 332 sec. The O2 tank is at 25211, the first tank is at 8, the N2 tank is at 28112, the first tank is at 0, the mixed tank is at 9.	P-3	Error O2 valve stuck open. Time since error occurred 92 seconds
FSE-1	*Whenever you guys get this message, let me know what your primary readings for your CO2, O2, etc.*	P-2	O2 tank at 7055, first valve 10, after the mixer valve 10.
P-7	15 min check: CO2 .4%, O2 30.9%, pressure 1008, temp 19.9, humidity 38.6, and we still have an error O2 valve stuck open time since error occurred 640 sec.	FSE-4	*Is your N2 tank flowing?*
FSE-2	*Can you repeat the temp reading as well as the problem with your system?*	P-5	Error O2 valve stuck open. Time since error occurred 203 sec. O2 tank at 26353, ohm first level 8, and two tanks at 28112, first level 0, and the mixed is at 8
P-8	We just received your first inquiry. Right now the error O2 valve stuck open since error occurred 660 sec. The temp reading is 21.6.	FSE-5	*Ok. What I want you to do is check the graph for the N2 levels, and if it's at the top in range, then it's going to be a valve stuck open.*
FSE-3	*What are the readings for the O2, the O2 valve and the tanks?*	FSE-6	*If that is the case then what you want to do is go to the O2 to the top right corner, click that and press, flow off, click repair, choose O2 valve stuck open, and hit repair again.*
P-9	The O2 tank is at two thousand 22 thousand 20, the O2 valve is at 9 and the mixer is at 9.	P-6	10 min check: CO2 .2, O2 26.5, pressure 1013, temp. 19.29, humidity 41.2. Just to clarify pressure is one thousand thirteen. And error O2 valve stuck open, time since error occurred 332 sec. The O2 tank is at 25211, the first tank is at 8, the N2 tank is at 28112, the first tank is at 0, the mixed tank is at 9.
FSE-4	*Is your N2 tank flowing?*	FSE-7	*If you can give me the first reading for the temp, the first 5 min, one more time, also let me know if that repair was successful.*
P-10	The N2 tank is at 28 thousand 109 and 12, the valve is at 0, the, the mixer is at 9. Error O2 valve stuck open time since error occurred 809 sec.	P-7	15 min check: CO2 .4%, O2 30.9%, pressure 1008, temp 19.9, humidity 38.6, and we still have an error O2 valve stuck open time since error occurred 630 sec.
FSE-5	*Ok. What I want you to do is check the graph for the N2 levels, and if it's at the top in range, then it's going to be a valve stuck open.*	P-8	We just received your first inquiry. Right now the error O2 valve stuck open time since error occurred 660 sec. The temp reading is 21.6
FSE-6	*If that is the case then what you want to do is go to the O2 to the top right corner, click that and press, flow off, click repair, choose O2 valve stuck open, and hit repair again.*	P-9	The O2 tank is at two thousand 22 thousand 20, the O2 valve is at 9 and the mixer is at 9.
P-11	20 min update: CO2 at .2, O2 is at 33.9, pressure is at one thousand thirteen, temp is at 21.4, humidity is at 41.9.	P-10	The N2 tank is at 28 thousand 109 and 12, the valve is at 0, the, the mixer is at 9. Error O2 valve stuck open time since error occurred 896 sec.
P-12	Error O2 valve stuck open time since error occurred 986 sec. O2 tank at 19 thousand 607, O2 valve at 8, and N2 tank 28 thousand 100 and 12, N2 valve at 0, mixer at 8. Please advise.	FSE-8	*Ok. What I want you to do is check if the O2 valve has a constant flow, if the N2 tank in the flow meters, N2, if the N2 tank is not flowing, and the pressure graph for N2 is remaining at the top then it is a valve stuck open, what you gonna do is click O2 on the right, top right corner, click flow off, click repair, choose O2 valve stuck open, click repair, and report to me and let me if that fixed it.*
FSE-7	*If you can give me the first reading for the temp, the first 5 min, one more time, also let me know if that repair was successful.*	P-11	20 min update: CO2 at .2, O2 is at 33.9, pressure is at one thousand thirteen, temp is at 21.4, humidity is at 41.9.
P-13	Time 23 min. First reading on temp 20.4 degrees. And oh we haven't tried to fix it. Could you repeat instructions.	P-12	Error O2 valve stuck open time since error occurred 986 sec. O2 tank at 19 thousand 607, O2 valve at 8, and N2 tank 28 thousand 100 and 12, N2 valve at 0, mixer at 8. Please advise.
P-14	24 min 40 sec. Attempted repair O2 valve stuck open. Waiting for results	P-13	Time 23 min First reading on temp 20.4 degrees. And oh we haven't tried to fix it. Could you repeat instructions.
P-15	25 min 50 sec. Error successfully repaired.	FSE-9	*The instructions for O2 valve stuck open are: click O2 at the top right, click flow off, click repair, then choose O2 valve stuck open, click repair. If the dot in the right side turns green, then it was successful. Let me know if that worked.*
P-16	25 min check: CO2 .2, O2 33.7, Pressure 1015, Temp 20.9, humidity 39.3. And no error messages	P-14	24 min 40 sec. Attempted repair O2 valve stuck open. Waiting for results
P-17	29 min 20 sec. Error O2 valve leak, time since error occurred 27 sec. This is a new error.	P-15	25 min 50 sec. Error successfully repaired.
FSE-8	*Ok. What I want you to do is check if the O2 valve has a constant flow, if the N2 tank in the flow meters, N2, if the N2 tank is not flowing, and the pressure graph for N2 is remaining at the top then it is a valve stuck open, what you gonna do is click O2 on the right, top right corner, click flow off, click repair, choose O2 valve stuck open, click repair, and report to me and let me if that fixed it.*	P-16	25 min check: CO2 .2, O2 33.7, Pressure 1015, Temp 20.9, humidity 39.3. And no error messages
P-18	30 min 30 sec error O2 valve leak, time since error occurred 95 sec, O2 tank eighteen thousand thirty five, O2 valve 0, N2 tank twenty two thousand nine hundred seventy six, N2 valve 17, and the mixer is at 18. So it looks like there is no flow through the O2 tank right now and the error message is error O2 valve leak, time since error occurred 105 sec.	P-17	29 min 20 sec. Error O2 valve leak, time since error occurred 27 sec. This is a new error.
P-19	32 min, current O2 level is at 10.7%, at and it's in the red zone. Ah, error O2 valve leak, time since error occurred 205 sec, the O2 tank is at eighteen thousand, the O2 valve is at 0, the N2 tank is at twenty one thousand two hundred fifty, the N2 valve is at 22 sec, the mixer is, at 22, the mixer is at 22. So it appears there is no flow in the O2 tank,	P-18	30 min 30 sec error O2 valve leak, time since error occurred 95 sec, O2 tank eighteen thousand thirty five, O2 valve 0, N2 tank twenty two thousand nine hundred seventy six, N2 valve 17, and the mixer is at 18. So it looks like there is no flow through the O2 tank right now and the error message is error O2 valve leak, time since error occurred 105 sec.
FSE-9	*The instructions for O2 valve stuck open are click O2 at the top right, click flow off, click repair, then choose O2 valve stuck open, click repair. If the dot in the right side turns green, then it was successful. Let me know if that worked.*	P-19	32 min, current O2 level is at 10.7%, at and it's in the red zone. Ah, error O2 valve leak, time since error occurred 205 sec, the O2 tank is at eighteen thousand, the O2 valve is at 0, the N2 tank is at twenty one thousand two hundred fifty, the N2 valve is at 22 sec, the mixer is, at 22, the mixer is at 22. So it appears there is no flow in the O2 tank,
P-20	33 min 54 sec. Error O2 valve leak, time since it occurred 300 sec. Attempting fix O2 valve stuck open, attempting repair.	P-20	33 min 54 sec. Error O2 valve leak, time since it occurred 300 sec. Attempting fix O2 valve stuck open, attempting repair.

FIGURE 6.1 Representation of the same conversation under time-delayed conditions as perceived by different team members, Pioneer Crew (P) and Flight Systems Engineer (FSE).

Note: Each row is a different turn in the conversation. Turns are numbered as P-1…. P-20 and FSE-1 … FSE-9, dependent on speaker, and topics are identified by shades of grey. Additionally, turns by FSE and P's responses to them are italicized and in the same typeface to highlight their relationship.

As can be seen, the turn sequence – that is, the serial order of messages – unfolded differently for the Pioneer crew and the Flight Systems Engineer. Because of the time lag, messages that were consecutive for one party (e.g., the Flight Systems Engineer) did not occur in the same order for remote partners. For instance, the second message by the Flight Systems Engineer, FSE-2, was in response to (and thus followed) the Pioneers' first message, P-1. However, the Pioneer crew provided further updates before receiving a reply, and from their perspective, FSE-2 followed P-7 rather than P-1. The fact that remote team members do not necessarily share the same perspective on their evolving discourse may not be readily apparent to conversational partners and thus hamper mutual understanding. This sentiment is succinctly expressed in the quotation at the beginning of this chapter after a space-mission simulation in the NASA Extreme Environment Mission Operations (NEEMO) facility, an undersea research station off Key Largo.

Disruptions in the turn sequence that are associated with communication delay come with a considerable cognitive cost as remote team members need to keep track which of their messages go together. Team members were found to exacerbate this situation by misapplying assumptions and conventions of synchronous discourse to asynchronous conditions, behavior that resulted in unnecessary conversational turns, or worse, in misunderstandings (Fischer & Mosier, 2016). For instance, team members frequently used anaphoric expressions, such as pronouns, when they responded to a message by a remote partner, apparently because they believed that the correct referent of the anaphora could be easily identified. This assumption is viable in synchronous communication where the message sequence is identical for conversational partners and related messages are consecutive from everybody's perspective. However, in asynchronous communication, as discussed above, related contributions may be temporally adjacent (i.e., directly following) only for the responding partner while for the other participant unrelated contributions may intervene. Consequently, establishing the correct referent for an anaphoric expression such as "that repair didn't work," or "got it" may be cognitively taxing, if not impossible.

A related issue identified by Fischer and Mosier (2016) stemmed from team members' tendencies to break up complex information into small portions and to include these in separate turns. When communication is synchronous an efficient strategy is to present information, especially if it is complex, in small units and wait for a partner's feedback. Communication problems can thus be detected early and resolved quickly. In asynchronous communication, in contrast, information splitting may impede comprehension insofar as related content may be separated by several turns, requiring partners to keep in mind individual pieces of information for an extended period of time before a coherent representation is achieved. For example, the Flight Systems Engineer in the excerpt above requests diagnostic information in separate messages (FSE-3, -4, and -5) rather than in one message; thus making it difficult for himself to keep track of and synthesize critical diagnostic cues.

A third problem detected in this research was proximity bias; that is, the inclination of team members to interpret a communication by a remote partner that immediately followed their own contribution to be their partner's response to it. While this is a feature of synchronous discourse it may not necessarily be true under asynchronous conditions. When team members misalign contributions, serious misunderstandings can arise. This problem happened in the crew whose discourse is depicted in Figure 6.1. The Pioneer crew erroneously assumed that the repair instruction provided by the Flight Systems Engineer in FSE-8 was a response to their failure announcement in P-17. However, the Flight Systems Engineer's instruction was in response to previous requests by the Pioneer crew (P-9 and P-10) to repeat the repair instructions for the initial failure and was incompatible with their current malfunction. During the remaining 70 minutes of the simulation, the team never recovered from this misunderstanding and failed to repair their second system failure.

A final problem was the result of participants' insensitivity to time constraints insofar as they repeated information or requested feedback before their remote partner could have responded to their original message. This behavior is displayed in the preceding excerpt by Flight Systems Engineer who in FSE-7, probes the crew to give him feedback on the repair (he transmitted in FSE-6) without allowing sufficient time for the crew to perform the repair and report back on their efforts.

These findings highlight three aspects of the communication process that need support when team members communicate under asynchronous conditions:

- Time – how to track the timing of individual messages; how to know when to expect a response from a remote partner.
- Thread – how to keep track of conversational threads to ensure that messages by conversational partners are aligned correctly.
- Transmission efficiency – how to ensure shared situation understanding between remote partners in as few messages as possible.

Our solution was to design a communication protocol that specifically focused on the three T's – Time, Thread, and Transmission efficiency – to facilitate time-delayed space/ground communication.

SUPPORTING SPACE/GROUND COMMUNICATION DURING ASYNCHRONOUS CONDITIONS

The communication protocol we created is a structured template. Its content not only addresses the problems with asynchronous communication that we identified in our research, but also incorporates recommendations put forth by Love and Reagan (2013). Its structural characteristics are informed by schema-based approaches to instruction design (Morrow & Rogers, 2008; Morrow, Leirer, Andrassy, Decker Tanke, & Stine-Morrow, 1996; Morrow, Leirer, Andrassy, Hier, & Menard, 1998; Morrow et al., 2005) (Figures 6.2 and 6.3).

We developed two protocol versions – one for voice-only communication, and one for text-based communication – to account for medium-specific affordances and constraints. As shown in Figures 6.2 and 6.3, a protocol consists of four segments and several communication conventions that tackle the major challenges of asynchronous communication – Time, Conversational Thread, and Transmission

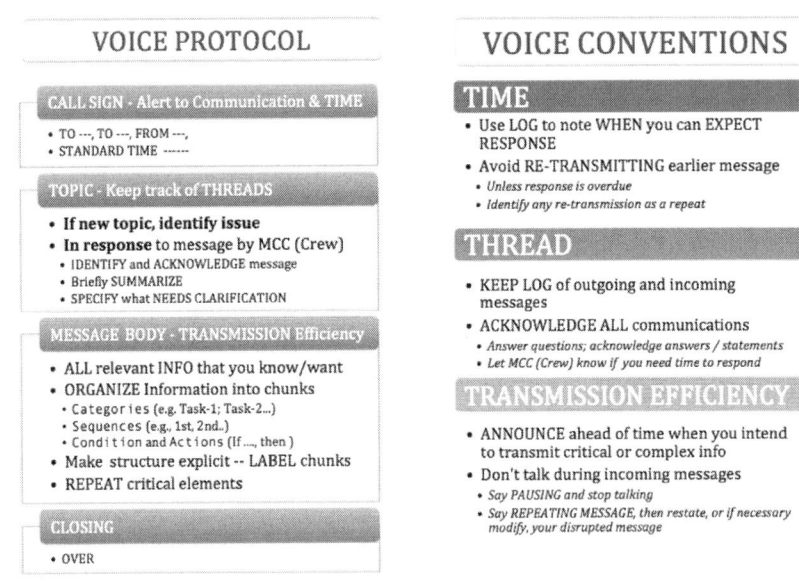

FIGURE 6.2 Protocol template for voice communication.

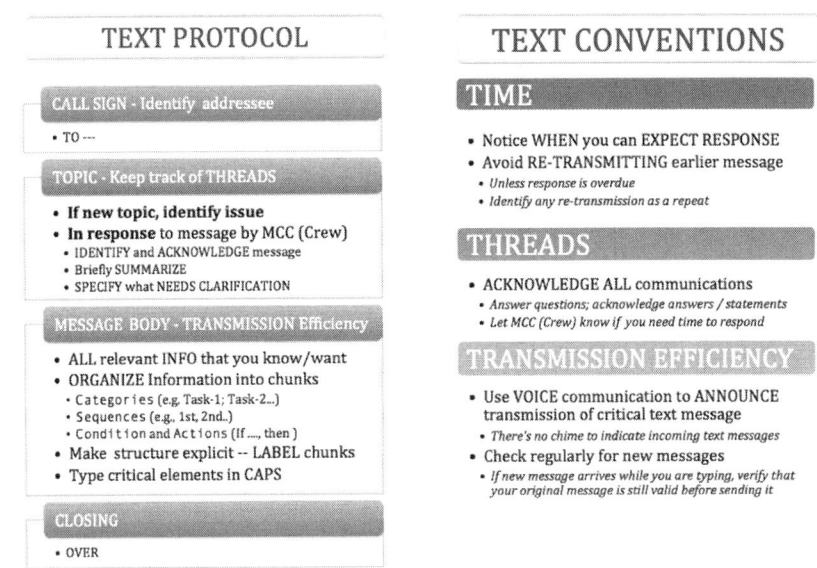

FIGURE 6.3 Protocol template for text communication.

Efficiency. Medium-specific instructions concern aspects of the call sign and conventions that follow from characteristics (or limitations) of audio or text communication. The call sign during voice communication for instance needs to do more than identify who is talking to whom. It also needs to catch remote partners' attention because they may be engaged in some other task and the communication may come as a surprise. Thus to ensure attention capture, an addressee's name should be called out twice, as in the following example from HERA: *MCC, MCC, Graphos. Time is 11:03.* The call sign, moreover, needs to anchor a message in time to highlight the temporal sequence of participants' contributions and thus safeguard against proximity bias. All references to time need to be independent of a partner's perspective and should be linked to an objective time, such as standard time. As text messages typically include time stamps and the identity of the sender, call signs need to identify only the addressee. On the other hand, because the texting tool may not have an attention-getting feature such as announcing incoming messages with a chime, protocol conventions direct partners communicating via text to note the time of both their transmission and the expected response and to check for new messages accordingly. Text communication provides a written record of partners' contributions; thus no record keeping is required. In contrast, when distributed team members communicate by voice, protocols require them to maintain a log of their ongoing discourse to keep track of conversational threads.

Medium-independent instructions concern the topic section of a message, the message body and the final – closing – section as well as several conventions designed to support conversational coherence, message comprehension and shared task understanding, as well as communication efficiency. To this end, team members should preface their messages with a topic, or make explicit the relationship of their message to a preceding one from their partner (e.g., response to a specific question, information requested, etc.). This behavior is evident in the message by the HERA crewmember quoted above as it continues with: *This is CDR with a System Update. I have three numbers. They are: 106, 107 122. Again the numbers are 106, 107, and 122 Over.* Likewise, MCC explicitly links her response to the commander's message: *Graphos, Graphos, MCC for Commander. System Update received. I have the following numbers: 106, 107, and 122.* Providing and referencing a topic enables partners to keep track of conversational threads and avoid proximity bias. Team members are also instructed to transmit all relevant information in one turn, to present it in a clearly structured fashion, to repeat critical items, and to postpone transmission of non-time-critical information while they await crucial input from their partner. These elements are meant to facilitate comprehension and maintain communication efficiency as related information is kept together. Mutual understanding is further enhanced when team members explicitly acknowledge and paraphrase or "readback" a partner's messages instead of providing generic feedback, such as "copy all." Moreover, by indicating their understanding of a partner's message, team members can preclude unnecessary communication. Appropriate feedback is essential; if no feedback is given, partners may repeat their message or ask for verification. Likewise, team members are told to note when they should receive a response to discourage unwarranted repetition that could potentially confuse their partner. Lastly, team members are instructed to announce when they plan to transmit important information to cue their remote partner to attend to it, and to mark the end of a transmission to let partners know that their message is complete.

The communication protocol was implemented in several space-analog simulations to assess their usability for space exploration missions. One set of studies was conducted at NASA's NEEMO facility, an undersea research station 62 ft below sea level off Key Largo. In NEEMO, as Herve Stevenin, a crewmember of mission 19, recounts

> we simulate a mission to Mars and its moons. Not the way to fly to it, but our simulation started around Mars. Here we are, with 5 minutes delay in all our communications with Mission Control. If we have a question, we can only get the answer at the earliest 10 minutes later. It requires to be clear and concise in our communications and we test different operational modes and tools to assess the best set-up for such a mission to Mars. Aquarius is our "spaceship". We all feel, that we are part of it. (Stevenin, 2014)

Crewmembers of two missions, NEEMO-18 and NEEMO-19, agreed to use the medium-appropriate communication protocol during space-ground interactions on days with a communication delay. Each mission involved four crewmembers from the astronaut corps of NASA and its international partners (CSA; ESA; JAXA).

The second set of simulations took place in NASA's Human Exploration Research Analog (HERA), a space-analog habitat located at Johnson Space Center. Four missions were dedicated to the study of the impact of space stressors (confinement, isolation, communication delay) and of countermeasures on crewmembers' physiological and psychological well-being. Each mission included four crewmembers who were astronaut-like research volunteers; that is, individuals comparable to astronauts in terms of education, physical fitness, personality, and age.

Crew and mission control personnel of the NEEMO missions and of the last two of the HERA simulations received 30 minutes of communication training during the pre-mission phase. Communication training identified the challenges of asynchronous communication and explained the elements of the communication protocols and conventions. There was one joint training session for participants in the NEEMO missions, 5 weeks prior to NEEMO-18 and 13 weeks prior to NEEMO-19. The NEEMO-19 participants received a refresher training 3 weeks before their mission started. HERA crewmembers and HabComs (i.e., personnel of the Flight Analogs group at JSC acting as HERA mission control) of missions 3 and 4 received training during the week preceding their mission; participants of missions 1 and 2 served as control and thus did not participate in any communication training.

NEEMO-18 was a 9-day mission with 4 days of communication delay. Two days involved a delay of 5 minutes one way, the other 2 days presented a 10-minute delay. Communication medium (voice vs. text) was crossed with communication delay. NEEMO-19 lasted for 7 days. On 4 days, communication between the crew and mission control was delayed by 5 minutes one way, and remote partners could choose which medium (voice or text) to use during a given interaction.

HERA missions were 7 days long and included 2 days during which communication was delayed by 10 minutes one way. On the first of these days, communication between the crew and mission control was voice-only; on the second day participants were given a choice of communication medium (voice or text).

In all NEEMO and HERA missions communication delay occurred on consecutive mission days. Copies of the communication protocols were given to trained participants at the start of a mission to serve as a reference aid on days with a transmission delay.

A daily survey administered to NEEMO-18 crewmembers included one question that asked participants to rate the effectiveness of their communications with mission control. In addition, a separate survey was given on the days on which communication with mission control was delayed. In this survey crewmembers were asked to evaluate the extent to which the communication protocol and conventions were effective in supporting communication with mission control during important events of the day. On the mission day immediately following the days with communication delay, crewmembers received a survey in which they were asked to rate how critical each of the elements of the protocol and individual conventions was in facilitating asynchronous communication. In NEEMO-19 only the communication-specific and final surveys were included due to mission constraints.

HERA crewmembers were given daily communication surveys assessing the effectiveness of their interactions with mission control during assigned tasks. HERA crewmembers who had communication training also completed a final survey at the end of their mission evaluating protocol elements and communication conventions.

Given the small sample size, only descriptive statistics were conducted on participants' ratings. This analysis is summarized in Table 6.1 and indicates that trained participants considered the protocol to be effective in supporting crew/MCC communication when there was a transmission delay. Astronauts in the NEEMO missions as well as trained volunteers in the HERA simulations gave effectiveness ratings >4 (out of 5). Moreover, participants' ratings of crew/MCC communication suggest that the protocol "normalized" interactions on days with communication delay. As can be gleaned from Table 6.1, trained crewmembers perceived that the effectiveness of their interactions with mission control did not suffer when communication was delayed. In contrast, untrained HERA crewmembers gave considerably lower effectiveness ratings on time-delay days compared to days with synchronous communication. Untrained HERA participants also commented that they were less willing to contact mission control for guidance on tasks when their communication

TABLE 6.1
Crewmembers' Mean Effectiveness Ratings of Their Communications with Mission Control (MCC)

	Effectiveness of Crew/MCC Communication		
	No Comm Delay	Comm Delay	Effectiveness of Protocols
NEEMO-18	4.46 (0.69)	4.31 (0.48)	4.69 (0.52)
NEEMO-19	N/A	N/A	4.14 (0.35)
HERA (*trained crews*)	3.93 (0.89)	3.87 (1.14)	4.25 (0.46)
HERA (*untrained crews*)	4.07 (1.09)	2.95 (1.68)	N/A

Notes: Numbers reflect mean ratings across days (days with communication delay vs. no delay); standard deviations are in parentheses. Maximum rating was 5.

was delayed. As a result, as mission control noted, they performed the tasks improperly and required time-consuming additional assistance from ground.

Crewmembers generally rated protocol elements and conventions as fairly critical to ensuring effective communication with MCC during asynchronous conditions, and tended to follow the protocol as the exchange between the NEEMO-18 crew and MCC shown below illustrates (Fischer & Mosier, 2016). However, this example also indicates that some protocol elements were not consistently applied. Both crews and MCC failed to repeat the initial call sign or dropped the closing in some of their voice messages. While a falling intonation may suffice to signal the end of a message, there is no comparable way to signal a message beginning and its target. Failure of MCC to state the initial call sign twice in MCC-1 may have contributed to the crew's partial understanding of that message as expressed in their third call to MCC. The exchange also highlights the importance of message timing – to specify for partners and take into account for oneself the time a message was transmitted. As can be seen, both the crew and MCC transmitted messages at 8:04. The message from MCC (MCC-3) was an answer to the crew's initial request (Crew-2), but it also, fortuitously, addressed their second (repeat) request in Crew-3. MCC, on the other, faced a more confusing turn sequence. Five minutes after they had transmitted the heading information to the crew, they received the crew's request to repeat this information. MCC apparently did not take into account the time of the crew's latest message; if they had, they would have realized that the crew by now would have received the required heading information and that no additional response was necessary. Instead, MCC repeated their instructions; however, this time they tied their feedback explicitly to the crew's preceding messages and thus established that the heading information was now knowledge shared by crew and MCC.

Crew-1: MCC, Aquarius on space-to-ground 2, we have some question for you regarding the EPR. We will transmit in a minute. Then it will be 7:50 am.

Crew-2: MCC, MCC this is Aquarius on space to ground 2 regards the EPR. We do not have the headings for the EVA activities. We have some maps and the distance but we do not have the bearings for each site. If you can inform us about the headings for each site before the EVA starts we would appreciate it. And that's it from Aquarius. Have a great day.

MCC-1: *Aquarius, MCC. We just received your message concerning the bearings for the EVA. We will work on that, and we think we will provide you a file with the updated distances and bearings and ahm in a little bit. We will let you know as soon as we send them.*

Crew-3: MCC, MCC, Aquarius. It is 8:04 am. And we heard a call regarding the heading for the mission today. The crew has a distance but they do not have a heading. So please repeat the heading for the crew. Again. MCC, MCC, this is Aquarius. End of transmission.

MCC-2: *Aquarius, Aquarius, MCC at 8:04 on the <> loop. We do have a new picture showing the distances and heading, and we send them up to you via the mission log. Repeat. We have a picture with distance and heading for the EVA, and we're sending it up on the mission log. Out.*

MCC-3: *Aquarius, Aquarius, MCC on 2 for EVA message. We will give you 15 seconds and then we go with the message.*

MCC-4: *Aquarius, Aquarius, MCC for the EVA. We heard your messages requesting headings for the EVA. We have now posted a file, a picture on the mission log with the distances and headings, approximate headings. They are not absolutely precise, approximate headings. That should answer your questions.*

Table 6.2 presents NEEMO and HERA crewmembers' criticality ratings of protocol elements and communication conventions. As can be seen, the majority of the items received a criticality rating of at least 3.5. Very high ratings across crews for several items – providing a topic, using a log to track related messages, and announcing complex or critical messages – reflect the value of protocols for keeping track of message threads. However, ratings by NEEMO crewmembers for some items – most notably, pushing and chunking information and tracking time – were surprisingly low. This finding may indicate that crewmembers underappreciated the importance of these elements and point to specific training needs and technological improvements.

The importance of technological improvements to facilitate communication is apparent in NEEMO 19. During this mission the crew opted to use exclusively text as their communication medium on time-delayed days. Their choice may reflect the implementation in this mission of a new text tool (VOXER) whose features seem better suited to meet the demands of asynchronous communication than the text tool that was available in NEEMO-18 and HERA. For instance, with VOXER the time a message was sent was prominently displayed and messages included a time stamp that indicated the earliest time a response could be received (Figure 6.4).

TABLE 6.2
Crewmembers' Mean Criticality Ratings of Individual Protocol Elements and Conventions

	NEEMO-18	NEEMO-19	HERA (Trained)
Repeat addressee (voice)	3.75 (1.26)	N/A	2.75 (1.28)
Include time (voice)	3.50 (1.73)	N/A	4.25 (1.04)
Provide topic	4.75 (0.50)	4.88 (0.35)	4.63 (0.52)
Acknowledge communications	4.00 (0.82)	4.25 (0.89)	3.75 (1.04)
Push information	3.25 (0.50)	3.33 (1.53)	4.63 (0.74)
Chunk information	3.50 (0.56)	3.33 (0.58)	4.25 (0.71)
Repeat critical Info (voice)	4.25 (0.50)	N/A	4.50 (0.76)
Type critical info in caps (text)	2.50 (0.56)	3.50 (1.29)	3.00 (1.07)
Note earliest time to expect response	3.00 (1.41)	3.75 (1.23)	4.25 (0.71)
Use log to track related messages	4.75 (0.50)	4.75 (0.50)	4.00 (1.60)
Announce complex or critical messages	4.50 (1.00)	4.25 (0.96)	4.75 (0.46)
Postpone non time-critical message to wait for critical info	4.00 (0.82)	3.50 (0.58)	3.63 (1.19)

Notes: Standard deviations are in parentheses. Maximum rating was 5. NEEMO-19 crew used text communication only.

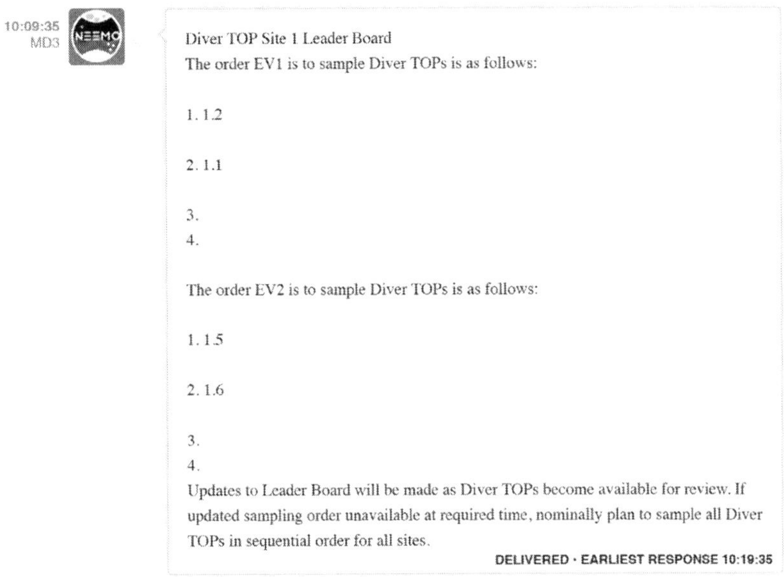

FIGURE 6.4 Text communication in NEEMO-19 with tool indicating earliest time to expect response to message.

Overall findings suggest that the communication protocol approach holds promise for helping space crewmembers and MCC communicate and collaborate effectively and successfully even when their communication is delayed. In reflecting on his experience with living in Aquarius and working under communication delay, Randy Bresnik, the commander in NEEMO-19 writes:

> This past week of living aboard Aquarius as saturated divers has been filled with awe and wonder. The majesty of this beautiful undersea world was a beauty to behold. The dangers are self-evident and ever present, but so were the amazing opportunities to train in such a unique and hostile environment. Overcoming these challenges made the results of our work seem all that more rewarding. Evaluating equipment, developing procedures, and researching operations in an environment with a delay in communications was our mission. Thanks to the hard work and dedication of the entire team of NEEMO 19, we were wildly successful.
>
> The critical element evaluated during the mission was the element of time. A 10 minute round-trip communications delay was implemented to determine how operations between Spacewalking crew and MCC could function. This has a direct application to possible future human exploration of other planets or asteroids. (Bresnik, 2014)

Based on our research in NEEMO and HERA we strengthened the communication training. We added examples that illustrate how easy it is for remote team members to misapply well-rehearsed habits of synchronous communication to asynchronous conditions, and used these examples to emphasize the importance of protocol elements that NEEMO and HERA crews undervalued. We also converted the communication training into a stand-alone training module that can be used to prepare crewmembers and flight controllers for the challenges of communication delay.

Notably, the communication protocols not only target how to speak or write during asynchronous conditions, but also point to technological solutions. In fact, some technological changes have already been implemented in response to our early findings. One example is the text tool that was adopted in NEEMO-19 and assisted the crew with the temporal aspects of communication. Further improvements might be a less chat- and more email-like text tool that includes a subject header and establishes links between related messages to make it easier for conversational partners to follow a conversational thread. A text tool could also provide a template that gives structure to a message and highlights its components. Likewise, voice communication could be facilitated if recordings of messages were available to both sender and receiver, and if the recordings indicated when a message was transmitted. And lastly, it is conceivable that the recording tool would include prompts for specific message components (e.g., This message is in regard to…. The time is….). Ultimately, technological implementation of protocol elements can reduce cognitive workload for both the crew and MCC, and can provide viable communication support for long-duration exploration missions.

ACKNOWLEDGMENTS

Funding for our research on communication protocols was provided by NASA grant NNX12AR19G to the Georgia Institute of Technology and San Francisco State University. We are grateful to our colleagues Laura Bollweg, Sarah Huppman, Barbara Janoiko, Lauren Landon, Lauren Leveton, Yvonne Parsons, Holly Patterson, Marcum Reagan, Andy Self, and Brandon Vessey at NASA Johnson for their support and their flexibility in accommodating our research in their overall mission design. Funding for the preparation of this chapter was provided by NASA grant NNX16AM16G to the Georgia Institute of Technology.

REFERENCES

Bresnik, R. (2014). *NEEMO 19 crew shares undersea experiences: Randy's Journal.* Retrieved from https://www.nasa.gov/content/neemo-19-crew-shares-undersea-experiences

Fischer, U., & Mosier, K. (2014). The impact of communication delay and medium on team performance and communication in distributed teams. In *Proceedings of the Human Factors and Ergonomics Society 58th Annual Meeting* (pp. 115–119). Santa Monica, CA: HFES.

Fischer, U., & Mosier, K. (2016). *Protocols for asynchronous communication in space operations: Communication analyses and experimental studies* (Final Report on NASA Grant NNX12AR19G). Atlanta, GA: Georgia Institute of Technology.

Fischer, U., Mosier, K., & Orasanu, J. (2013). The impact of transmission delays on Mission Control – Space Crew communication. In *Proceedings of the Human Factors and Ergonomics Society 57th annual meeting* (pp. 1372–1376). Santa Monica, CA: HFES.

Kintz, N. M., Chou, C-P., Vessey, W. B., Leveton, L. B., & Palinkas, L. A. (2016). Impact of communication delays to and from the International Space Station on self-reported individual and team behavior and performance: A mixed-methods study. *Acta Astronautica*, 129, 193–200.

Krauss, R., & Bricker, P. (1967). Effects of transmission delay and access delay on the efficiency of verbal communication. *Journal of the Acoustical Society of America, 41,* 286–292.

Kraut, R. E., Fussell, S., R., Brennan, S. E., & Siegel, J. (2002). Understanding the effects of proximity on collaboration: Implications for technologies to support remote collaborative work. In P. Hinds & S. Kiesler (eds.), *Distributed work* (pp. 137–162). Cambridge, MA: MIT Press.

Love, S. G., & Reagan, M. L. (2013). Delayed voice communication. *Acta Astronautica, 91,* 89–95.

Morrow, D. G., Leirer, V. O., Andrassy, J. M., Decker Tanke, E., & Stine-Morrow, E. (1996). Medication instruction design: Younger and older adult schemas for taking medication. *Human Factors, 38*(4), 556–573.

Morrow, D. G., Leirer, V. O., Andrassy, J. M., Hier, C. M., & Menard, W. E., (1998). The influence of list format and category headers on age differences in understanding medication instructions. *Experimental Aging Research, 24,* 231–256.

Morrow, D. G., & Rogers, W. A. (2008). Environmental support: An integrative framework. *Human Factors, 50*(4), 589–613.

Morrow, D. G., Weiner, M., Young, J., Steinley, D., Deer, M., & Murray, M. D. (2005). Improving medication knowledge among older adults with heart failure: A patient-centered approach to instruction design. *The Gerontologist, 45*(4), 545–552.

Olson, G. M., & Olson, J. (2000). Distance matters. *Human-Computer Interaction, 15,* 139–178.

Stevenin, H. (2014). *NEEMO 19 crew shares undersea experiences: Herve's Journal.* Retrieved from https://www.nasa.gov/content/neemo-19-crew-shares-undersea-experiences

Vessey, W. B., Palinkas, L., & Leveton, L. B. (2013, May). *Supporting teams under conditions of communication delay: Lessons learned from NEEMO 16.* Symposium presented at the Aerospace Medical Association 84th Annual Meeting, Chicago, IL.

7 Behavioral Health Adaptation in ICE Environments
Process and Countermeasures for NASA Astronauts

Walter E. Sipes
Aerospace Psychology Consultants

Kelley J. Slack
Birkman International/Minerva Work Solutions PLLC

Gary E. Beven
NASA's Lyndon B. Johnson Space Center

CONTENTS

Factors Affecting Behavioral Health Adaptation 117
Behavioral Health Outcomes 119
Spaceflight Adaptations 120
Inter- and Intra-Agency Coordination of BHP Support 122
History and Evolution of Behavioral Health Support 123
    Designed for Longer-Duration Missions 123
    Emerging Need for BHP Support 124
Fundamentals of Behavioral Health Support 125
    Behavioral Medicine 125
    Behavioral Health Training 127
The Future – Exploration and Earth-Bound Concerns 128
References 129

All one needs to effect a murder is lock two men into a cabin, 18 feet by 20 feet, and keep them there for two months.

Valery Ryumin
Cosmonaut, Salyut 6 (Mundell, 1963, p. 34)

Viewing our planet was so compelling. Words like beautiful and awesome don't do it justice. I felt I was looking at paradise. I was looking at heaven. I can't imagine any place more beautiful than our planet and how lucky we are to be able to live here.

Mike Massimino
NASA Astronaut, STS-125 (Massimino, 2016)

The concept of behavioral health adaptation, as defined here for the US space program, is an overall encompassing term that includes aerospace medicine, behavioral medicine, operational psychology, family support, and psychosocial disciplines to train astronauts to adapt to spaceflight. The areas of operational psychology and the Johnson Space Center's Family Support Office are discussed in detail in another chapter. This chapter discusses the process of behavioral health adaptation to isolated, confined, and extreme (ICE) environments, with primary focus on National Aeronautics and Space Administration (NASA) astronauts and countermeasures provided to those astronauts by the Behavioral Health and Performance group at NASA's Lyndon B. Johnson Space Center (JSC). Behavioral health adaptation requires that US astronauts adapt to the space environment and therefore draw upon closely related/overlapping disciplines (or multidisciplinary effort) of medicine, psychiatry, psychology, and physiology. Gazenko (1989), the father of Soviet space medicine, concluded that the limitations of living in space are not only medical, but also psychological. The required adaptation areas for astronauts and cosmonauts include physiological, psychological, and psychosocial. As summarized by Flynn (2005) the role of the astronaut's flight surgeon is to maximize the astronaut's health throughout all phases of the LDM: preflight, in flight, and postflight. In support of the flight surgeon, BHP has focused on four key factors that impact the astronaut's behavioral health and performance. These factors are defined as sleep and circadian factors; behavioral health factors; psychological adaptation factors; and human-to-system interface (the interface between the astronaut and the mission workplace) factors.

Both the flight surgeon and BHP providers must earn the crewmember's trust preflight to encourage problem identification and problem solving in these four areas. Once on orbit, the crew medical officer (the crewmember tasked with the health of fellow crewmembers) becomes a valuable extension of the crew surgeon and BHP on the ground due to the crew medical officer's constant interaction with crewmembers and pre-flight training in these four factors. However, the flight surgeon, BHP, and the crew medical officer need tools that will help predict, prevent, monitor, and respond to developing problems. The Behavioral Medicine section of the Behavioral Health and Performance group primarily focuses on the prediction, diagnosis, monitoring, and treatment of biological, physiological, and neurocognitive behavioral processes with the goal of preventing a decrement in functioning that may lead to the development of a mental disorder. The reasoning of this focus remains the more traditional practice of medicine and psychiatry reliance on the illness model. In the US space program, this model still maintains its place due to the fact that a serious behavioral health decrement or disorder during spaceflight would cause an adverse mission impact. However, the primary means of ensuring mission

Behavioral Health Adaptation in ICE Environments

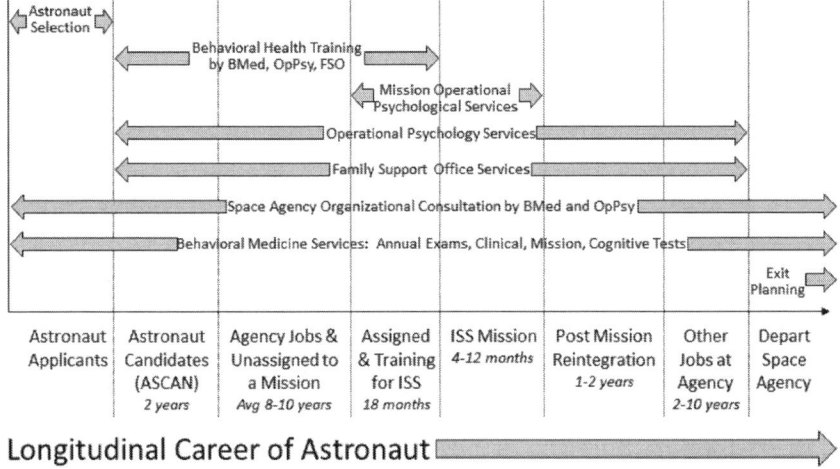

FIGURE 7.1 Behavioral Health and Performance services over a typical NASA astronaut career.

success and preventing a decrement in behavioral health and performance is a proactive focus on training astronauts how to adapt to spaceflight, maintaining healthy lifestyles and practices, and enhancing performance from all of their training and during operational space missions.

Professional disciplines in the Behavioral Health and Performance Group include aerospace psychiatrists, operational psychologists, clinical psychologists, industrial/organizational psychologists, research psychologists, behavioral specialists, and family support specialists. These personnel have roles in the selection, training, support, evaluation, and provision of behavioral health services during the astronauts' careers. A best practice chronological approach includes professional involvement with astronaut applicants at the time of selection, as those selected undergo training as Astronaut Candidates (ASCANs), perform assigned jobs within the space agency as active astronauts, are selected for a specific space mission, train for that mission, fly that mission, undergo multiple debriefings after the mission, and then continue a career as an active astronaut or leave the space agency. Figure 7.1 shows the chronological progression of an astronaut and the involvement of BHP in providing behavioral health services during their career.

FACTORS AFFECTING BEHAVIORAL HEALTH ADAPTATION

Spaceflight is relatively dangerous. In the 59 years since Yuri Gagarin's first human spaceflight, 18 reported crew deaths have occurred during spaceflight with other astronauts and cosmonauts dying during training. These include two events in Russian spacecraft (1967 Soyuz 1; 1971 Soyuz 11) and two in American (1986 Space Shuttle Challenger; 2003 Space Shuttle Columbia). A smaller number of other astronauts and cosmonauts have died during training (Burgess et al., 2003). The physical dangers associated with spaceflight do not end with a return to Earth. Crews are exposed to higher amounts of radiation as the ISS is in orbit beyond the Van Allen Belt, which may increase their chances of different types of cancer (Cucinotta, 2014) and other long-term health effects such as cataracts (Cucinotta et al., 2001).

In addition to these threats, the work performed during spaceflight missions can be physically and emotionally exhausting. Crewmembers have had injuries to their fingernails, hands, shoulders, and feet from extra-vehicular activities (EVA or spacewalk) (Gernhardt, 2009). These stressors, while primarily physical, may have an impact on psychological well-being. Kanas and Manzey (2008) summarize that astronauts encounter four types of stressors during space flight: physical, habitability, psychological, and interpersonal. They list examples of *physical* stressors as acceleration, microgravity, ionizing radiation, meteoroid impacts, and light/dark cycles. Under *habitability* are vibration, ambient noise, temperature, lighting, and air quality. The *psychological* stressors include isolation, confinement, danger, monotony, and workload. Finally, the *interpersonal* stressors are gender issues, cultural effects, personality conflicts, crew size, and leadership issues. Furthermore, long-duration spaceflight is qualitatively and quantitatively different from short-duration flights simply because of the increased mission length. The stressors of long-duration missions can be acute, but more frequently they are gradual, chronically wearing over time. Chronic irritants, daily hassles, and annoyances have contributed to the development of depression, anxiety, or other significant behavioral health symptoms in first responders (Larsson, Berglund, & Ohlsson, 2016). As these stressors can be directly and indirectly psychologically harmful, support and countermeasures must address all aspects. Table 7.1 lists events occurring during spaceflight that have had an acute or chronic impact on astronauts.

TABLE 7.1
Sample Events That Have Occurred During Long-Duration Space Missions (Russian and USA)

- Death of family members and friends
- Excessive sleep shifting
- Hot or noisy cabins
- Mixed/same gender crews
- Dark and crowded station
- Work underload/overload
- Anger with ground team
- Periods of low motivation
- Delayed return to Earth
- Onboard fire (Mir)
- Depressurization (Mir & ISS)

- Crew friction
- Overscheduling
- Insufficient timeline control
- Conflict with ground control
- Foreign language difficulties
- Isolation
- Cultural misunderstandings
- Persistent system and communication failures
- Terrorist activities (e.g., 9/11)
- Aged and frail parents, near death

Source: Beven (2012).

BEHAVIORAL HEALTH OUTCOMES

Behavioral events have manifested during long-duration spaceflight. Adverse outcomes include physical reactions to stress, depressed mood, and team-level conflicts (Clark, 2007). One significant source of stressors is not directly related to the mission. On Mir 18, a crewmember's mother died. This and other family member illnesses and deaths have placed additional burdens on crewmembers (Dunn, 2001). Incidences of minor depression were experienced by crewmembers of Shuttle-Mir 3 and Salyut 7 missions (Carpenter, 1997) and by a US astronaut on Mir (Schneider, 1997). Signs of mission-related stress during Salyut 7 provided further evidence that even carefully selected and highly trained individuals require some compassion, empathy, and support in order to thrive in the hostile environment of space. The Soyuz T-10 crew on Salyut 7 in 1985 reported possible visual hallucinations to mission control. The cosmonauts reported an orange cloud enveloping the station followed by a flash of light and the appearance of seven angelic-looking figures (Troitsyna, 2011). On three occasions, early Russian Salyut flights were curtailed with psychological issues (e.g., psychosomatic illness) being cited as part of the cause (Cooper, 1976; Clark, 2007). The 1976 Soyuz-21 crew to Russian space station Salyut-5 returned to Earth early due to crew complaints of an unknown odor that no other crew detected. In the latter part of 1985, the Soyuz T-14 mission to Salyut 7 was terminated early, after a record setting 237 days in space. Official reports state the early return of the crew was due to Commander Vasyutin falling ill. However, the premature return has also been attributed to mood and performance issues in the crew (Buckey, 2006; Burrough, 1998). A decade later, the Soyuz TM-2 mission was also cut short for unspecified psychosocial reasons.

Multiple team-level conflicts also have been seen in crews. Soyuz 21, Soyuz T14, and Soyuz TM 2 all experienced significant crew-crew interpersonal conflicts. In all three of these cases, the missions were ended early for psychologically based reasons (Clark, 2007). Team-level conflict has also occurred between the flight crew and ground control, as was the case for Skylab 4 and Shuttle-Mir 4. In 1974, the crew of Skylab 4 took an unscheduled day off citing being overworked and not being listened to by ground control (Eschner, 2017).

Anecdotally, astronauts have reported subjectively experienced cognitive decrements during both short- and long-duration spaceflight (Kanas & Manzey, 2008). A minority of short- and long-duration crew members have reported a sense of feeling "foggy" (Kanas, 2015). This may be related to elevated CO_2 levels on the space vehicles (James, 2013) or brain changes due to spaceflight (Talan, 2017). This space fog has not yet been objectively measured and no clear operational impacts have been noted or measured. A similar condition is reported in other ICE environments, including crewmembers wintering-over in Antarctica (Gunderson, 1974). Space fog has been reported during the period astronauts are adjusting to life in microgravity, but other astronauts have reported the feeling throughout their entire short- or long-duration mission. A period of adjustment to microgravity typically lasts 4–6 weeks. Self-reported symptoms included problems with concentration, short-term memory, multitasking abilities, and organizational skills and force the need for determined concentration and deliberate performance of tasks. A comprehensive neurocognitive inflight study is underway that might provide answers about this phenomenon (Basner et al., 2015; NASA, 2019).

Additionally, the Russians have identified a behavioral syndrome afflicting cosmonauts during previous long-duration missions called spaceflight asthenia (Kanas & Mazey, 2008). Asthenia is characterized by physical and emotional fatigue or weakness; hypoactivity; irritability and tension; emotional lability; appetite and sleeping problems; attention and memory deficits; and withdrawal from others and territorial behavior. Spaceflight asthenia has not thus far been objectively identified in US crewmembers. The question remains open as to whether spaceflight asthenia occurs and if so whether its manifestations are affected by cultural factors or expectations.

SPACEFLIGHT ADAPTATIONS

Adaptation is defined as an "adjustment to environmental conditions" (Merriam-Webster). The term *adaptation* traditionally refers to biological processes. Adaptation is a process occurring continually in every walk of life. The vast majority of adaptations are minute in scale and require virtually no discernable changes in our behavior or thought paradigm. Occasionally, however, an event will occur requiring greater adaptation: a child's first day of school, the aftermath of a hurricane, exchange of marriage vows, and a new career as an astronaut. Like events, environments also can lead to a need for adaptation. For those in an isolated, confined, extreme (ICE) environment, the adaptation required is compounded by the environment itself. Astronauts on the International Space Station (ISS) must adapt physiologically to microgravity with the fluid shift within their bodies; in addition, there are space motion sickness, cardiovascular, neurovestibular, musculoskeletal, and immune/hematologic issues as well (Scheuring & Jones, 2007). Others, such as scientists wintering-over in Antarctica, deployed military forces, ultra-long distance runners, and mountain climbers likewise must adapt to their environments. Additionally, astronauts must adapt psychosocially to spaceflight. Psychosocial denotes the mental and the social factors in a person's life, for instance, relationships, education, age, and employment that pertain to a person's life history (Pugh, 2002). It is the accommodation of a person to a life-altering event or transition (Anderson, Keith, & Novak, 2002). Psychosocial adjustment acknowledges the interrelatedness of our internal selves with our external world.

Our thoughts, emotions, and behaviors interact with our culture, traditions, and relationships (INEE, 2018). Londono and McMillan (2015) have identified five attributes characterizing psychosocial adaptation. These are change, process, continuity, interaction, and influence. These attributes are also experienced by astronauts. *Change* allows people to adjust to disequilibrium in their lives and can be emotional, behavioral, or cognitive in nature as an astronaut seeks equilibrium with a new career. *Process* reflects the time component inherent in psychosocial adaptation as astronauts first go through up to 2 years of training as astronaut candidates and then many years of various jobs and training for a specific mission. *Continuity* indicates that psychosocial adaptation does not always have an endpoint. Adjusting to the new life condition can take years. *Interaction* is the exchange between the individual and his/her environment and suggests a dynamic component to psychosocial adaptation. It can occur within the individual through self-reflection as we see with Stuster's astronaut journals projects (2010, 2016) and with myriad astronaut autobiographical books. Interaction also can occur externally when the individual is forced to interact with his/her environment. During a mission, astronauts must contend with the pleasures and frustrations of living, working, and sleeping in microgravity. At times, individuals *influence* the psychosocial adaptation process because of factors such as their personality, social support, values, and beliefs. Astronaut biographies and autobiographies again provide evidence of how uniquely each astronaut experienced every aspect of life as an astronaut. Taken together, psychosocial adaptation can be defined as a dynamic process of change over time requiring ongoing adjustments, which is affected by the actions and behaviors of the individual.

An event or situation acts as the catalyst necessitating psychosocial adaptation. For astronauts, the first event is becoming an astronaut with its rigorous life and at a later point the event of their initial spaceflight mission and the concomitant ICE environment of a space vehicle. An astronaut's psychosocial adaptation to a mission ensues long before the spaceflight and continues through to the end of the mission and resumption of life on Earth. NASA's Behavioral Health and Performance group is tasked with supporting astronauts during their flight assignments and aiding in the psychosocial adaptation process. Successful psychosocial adaptation is key to mission safety and mission goals. Individuals who have adapted well psychosocially demonstrate stronger psychological well-being, which is linked with being team players and higher performers (Schmidt, 2015).

As important as what has been reported to occur during spaceflight is what has *not* occurred. What has not been reported as occurring during space flight is physical confrontation or aggression; major depression or suicidality; mania; delusions; delirium induced by anoxia, head injury, or illness; panic attacks; or any other major psychiatric disorders (Kanas, 2002). Medical kits on US and Russian crewed space missions have included a variety of psychoactive medications, including anxiolytics such as diazepam, sleeping pills such as zolpidem, antipsychotics such as haloperidol, and intramuscular promethazine for space motion sickness. Astronauts on the ISS have used medication for space motion sickness and to aid sleep. There has been no known or reported need for the antipsychotics and antidepressants during space missions (Friedman & Bui, 2017; Pavy-Le Traon et al., 1997).

Not all stressor responses during human space missions, however, are negative and indeed, most are positive (Slack et al., 2016). Astronauts and cosmonauts report feelings of excitement, contentment, exhilaration, fulfillment, and transcendence (Connors et al., 1985; Ihle et al., 2006; Kanas, 1990; Slack et al., 2016; Stuster, 2010; 2016; Suedfeld & Weiszbeck, 2004; Yaden et al., 2016). The term salutogenic is often used to describe experiences that promote a sense of health (Antonovsky, 1979; Harrop, Addis, Elliott, & Williams, 2006) and is an important component in successful psychosocial adaptation. Salutogenic experiences in spaceflight can be differentiated into positive environmental aspects and positive personal and social aspects of being in space (Suedfeld, 2005). The mystery and beauty of space and views of Earth comprise external environment aspects with the internal aspects of the environment including the safe haven and familiarity of the spacecraft. Personal and social salutogenic aspects of spaceflight involve astronaut group dynamics (e.g., superordinate goals and membership in an elite group) and post-mission consequences (e.g., new skills and values, overview effect of Earth, self-confidence).

INTER- AND INTRA-AGENCY COORDINATION OF BHP SUPPORT

Organizations with employees who live and work in an ICE environment because of their job have a responsibility to support those employees in order to maximize successful psychosocial adaptation and job performance. For astronauts, NASA has mandated the operational arm of the Behavioral Health and Performance group at Johnson Space Center to ensure ISS crewmembers adapt to spaceflight and are otherwise psychologically prepared for the rigors of long-duration spaceflight missions. A component of NASA's Human Research Program, the Human Factors and Behavioral Performance (HFBP) Research Element is tasked to provide and coordinate academic, laboratory, and operational research to fill the gaps and needs of BHP Operations. Examples of the research topics include sleep, lighting, crew coordination, and cognition. Details of the HFBP Research Element can be explored in detail in Volume 1 of this book set.

The operations arm of BHP (BHP Operations) delivers individualized behavioral health and psychological support services directly to ISS crewmembers and their families before, during, and after each space mission. The mission of BHP Operations is to provide a safe, productive, and enjoyable spaceflight experience and ideally a peak life event. The basic underlying model BHP employs is one of prevention, mitigation, and treatment. The first goal is to prevent the occurrence of any negative behavioral health outcome through training, modification of the environment, and support. If prevention is not possible, then the second goal is to mitigate the impact of stressors. BHP Operations accomplishes this through the application of countermeasures – systems and products designed to minimize the negative impact of stressors and to maximize, as mentioned previously, any potential salutogenic benefits of life in the ICE environment of space. If prevention and mitigation are not successful, then treatment options are available.

Many ICE environments, such as foreign peacekeeping and space missions, involve more than one nationality. Deployed military service members and astronauts often work closely with people from other nations. As part of a crew of six on the International Space Station (ISS), NASA astronauts share a mission expedition with Russians and typically one or two astronauts from Canada, Japan, or Europe (David et al., 2010; Kanas et al., 2009; Tomi et al., 2008). Preparing astronauts for their future work with their counterparts from other space agencies begins early with astronaut candidates receiving cross-cultural training sponsored by the BHP group (Slack et al., 2016) that is specifically focused on both the national and space agency cultures of NASA's international partners (Sandal & Manzey, 2009).

The Spaceflight Human Behavior and Performance Working Group (SHBPWG), established in 1998, allows for coordination among the five ISS space agencies and consists of BHP providers from Canada, Europe, Japan, Russia, and the US. The primary function of SHBPWG is to coordinate international partner input in the areas critical to human performance in spaceflight. Specifically, SHBPWG focuses on psychological adaptation and support; behavioral health; sleep and circadian health and fatigue monitoring; and human-system interface issues. It makes recommendations to the ISS Program's Multilateral Medical Operations Panel on standards for psychological and psychiatric aspects of selection; prevention and care for psychological and psychiatric health of crewmembers; content of psychological training for crewmembers; psychological monitoring, support, and countermeasures; and emergency support for those experiencing performance or behavioral difficulties (Duncan et al., 2008). The working group, with its representatives from each agency, meets annually to discuss and implement a common behavioral monitoring and countermeasures program for all ISS crewmembers. The resulting operational model for behavioral health and performance and its associated set of competencies required for successful psychosocial adaptation and performance are based on collective experience gained through decades of human spaceflight. The shared model allows research and experiential knowledge to be disseminated more easily across agencies. Consensus across space agencies will become of even greater importance if future long-duration exploration missions are indeed international as expected. Even with the shared model, cultural differences affect how each space agency defines and supports behavioral health. The Russians, for example, diagnose and treat space asthenia. While the symptomology of space asthenia is recognized by NASA, the aggregation of these symptoms into the condition space asthenia is not (Slack et al., 2016). Further, while the Russian space program monitors the voices of their cosmonauts for stress, the other space agencies do not. Other differences exist such as each space agency having their own approved list of medications their astronauts or cosmonauts may take.

HISTORY AND EVOLUTION OF BEHAVIORAL HEALTH SUPPORT

With the close of the Apollo moon missions, NASA turned to low Earth orbit and space stations, giving rise to the era of the Shuttle. Missions on the new Space Transportation System were not significantly longer than Apollo moon missions. The level of support offered to shuttle astronauts largely remained the same as that offered to earlier astronauts. It was not until the advent of NASA's participation in space stations that the agency began to realize that longer missions required a different level of support.

Designed for Longer-Duration Missions

Space stations have no major propulsion system, no landing system, are typically flown from mission control on the ground, and rely on other space vehicles for transport to and from the station. The earliest space stations were monolithic, constructed and launched in one piece, and later manned by crew (Teitel, 2016). Russia (then the USSR) launched the first of these monolithic stations, Salyut 1, in April of 1971 followed by the United States 2 years later with Skylab. Over its life, Skylab hosted three crews with missions of 28, 56, and 84 days, respectively (NASA, 2017). The Salyut space stations, over their collective 20 years of life, were home to 38 Russian crews, 13 of which were considered long-duration. In February 1986, the USSR launched the first modular space station, Mir. Until its deactivation in early 2001, Mir hosted 39 mission crews, 28 of which were long-duration, and was home to astronauts from 12 other countries (NASA, 2007). Amid increasing issues with the aging Mir space station, the International Space Station was built. The first expedition crew, consisting of two Russians and one American, arrived on November 2, 2000 and marked the beginning of the longest consistent human presence in space. Over the past 48 years of space station operations dating to Salyut 1 in 1971, and approximately 100 long-duration missions, NASA and its international partner space agencies have gained considerable experience regarding psychosocial adaptation to space.

EMERGING NEED FOR BHP SUPPORT

Until the advent of space stations, missions lasted from hours to a couple of weeks. A space station, designed to orbit the earth for an extended period, afforded the opportunity for longer-duration missions. As space station crew members began living and working in the ICE environment of space for weeks and then months, this produced greater stressors on the human body, both physical and psychological.

The first 6-month space station mission occurred on Salyut 6 in 1980. Coinciding with missions of increasing duration, signs of stress among cosmonauts were noted. The Russian space agency responded by creating a psychological support program dedicated to addressing this concern. NASA's BHP group was created later in the same decade when the Shuttle-Mir missions commenced. The in-flight psychological support activities of the United States are modeled after those first pioneered by the Russian system (Kanas, 1991) and included surprise presents and favorite foods sent up on resupply vehicles; two-way communication with family and friends on the ground via audio-video links, e-mail, ham radio; and on-board recreational software and videos for leisure time use.

Multiple factors influence the degree of stress felt by crews in ICE environments. For those in space, the habitable volume of the station, station amenities, crew size, crew interpersonal dynamics, and the change in the mission from primarily exploration to that of science all contribute to the amount of stress a crew perceives (Kanas & Manzey, 2008). Arguably, the single greatest contributor to psychological stress, however, is mission duration. As the mission length increased from 2 weeks on the space shuttle orbiter to months on Mir and the ISS, the mindset of the crew and those on the ground supporting the crew likewise had to shift from viewing the mission as a sprint to a marathon. Early astronauts and cosmonauts were more likely able to handle space mission-related stress through compartmentalization, usually an effective method of coping for the short-term. As missions grew longer, compartmentalizing stressors is less effective and no longer adequate if it is the primary coping mechanism used. Astronauts and cosmonauts required additional methods of effectively addressing the psychosocial stressors of an extended period living and working in space. In response, NASA BHP developed a more robust repertoire of countermeasures supporting astronauts and their families. Over time, the tools and countermeasures developed and delivered by BHP have included astronaut and spouse briefings on expectations of long-duration missions, video-conferencing in the astronaut's home for weekly Private Family Conferences, Internet Protocol phone on the ISS to allow the astronaut to easily make calls to Earth, first DVD movies and later digitized videos uploaded to the ISS and stored for later use.

FUNDAMENTALS OF BEHAVIORAL HEALTH SUPPORT

BEHAVIORAL MEDICINE

Operational components of BHP services consist of three primary elements – behavioral medicine (BMed) services, behavioral support services (also called operational psychology), and the family support office. The latter two are delineated in other chapters in this volume. The behavioral medicine services conduct annual behavioral and pre-flight assessments, performs behavioral health evaluations pre-flight, performs neurocognitive assessment prior to and during missions, conducts private psychological conferences during missions, and conducts post-flight behavioral medicine assessments and neurocognitive testing. The BMed providers also offer clinical (psychiatric and psychological) services to the astronauts and their family members during their career as astronauts on an elective basis. BMed services follow a prevention, mitigation, treatment model and, to be fully prepared, has contingency plans for worst-case scenarios such as severe illness or death of an astronaut's family member during a mission.

BMed performs annual behavioral health evaluations on active astronauts which follow a semi-structured interview format. Included in the evaluation are the current NASA career status; professional training and workload; sleep and fatigue issues; peer and management relationships; social and family life; greatest professional and personal challenges; primary goals for the coming year; and brief mental status examination and conclusions of the evaluation. This evaluation allows the active astronaut and NASA clinician to develop trust and rapport that is later utilized during space mission operations, as well as gauge overall psychological fitness and well-being in order to ensure optimal performance and mission safety. BMed providers also offer fatigue management services and education in order to optimize alertness and performance during international travel as well as during space missions.

Once an astronaut is assigned to a spaceflight, BMed providers conduct pre-flight behavioral assessments at intervals of 1 year, 180 days, and 60 days prior to launch. Pre-flight evaluation topics include : pre-flight training including perception of mission readiness; training workload and fatigue; family and personal relationships; crew training interactions, familiarity, and concerns; NASA management support; mood and anxiety; mission goals, desires, challenges, and risks; and post-mission rehabilitation or family concerns.

The astronaut assigned to a mission as the crew medical officer (CMO) receives training in behavioral medicine prior to flight. This training highlights the possible worst-case scenarios such as delirium due to injury or illness and complicated bereavement. CMOs are taught to recognize common symptoms of major mood and anxiety disorders, and familiarized with the treatment options on the ISS. Current options on the ISS include aripiprazole (PO), ziprasidone (IM), sertraline, venlafaxine, diazepam (IM), lorazepam (PO), Ambien, Sonata, and Provigil. No psychotropic medicines have been required on the ISS (Friedman & Bui, 2017).

Neurocognitive assessment is another aspect of BMed that occurs once an astronaut is assigned to a spaceflight. The Spaceflight Cognitive Assessment Tool for Windows (WinSCAT) is the current medical standard use by NASA as well as by the European and Japanese space agencies (Seaton, Slack, Sipes, & Bowie, 2009). WinSCAT is a brief neurocognitive test that provides a baseline level of cognition. This baseline can be used to assess an astronaut after a neurological injury (head trauma, exposure to toxins, medication side effects, etc.) on the ISS to judge severity and gauge recovery. The subtests of WinSCAT are adapted from the Automated Neurological Assessment Metrics (ANAM) and similar to the pre-deployment neuropsychological screen given to military service members. ANAM has been used extensively in neuropsychological research and is the result of over 30 years of psychological test development by the US Department of Defense. In 11–15 minutes, WinSCAT assesses response time, sustained attention/concentration, visual working memory, and verbal working memory. Administration of WinSCAT begins 13 months prior to launch, continues through the flight, and is concluded 30 days postflight (Seaton, Kane, & Sipes, 2010).

During flight, astronauts receive support from all areas within BHP to ensure that psychosocial adaptation to the ISS is successful. The support services provided specifically by the BMed component of BHP include regular WinSCAT assessments and biweekly Private Psychological Conferences (PPCs). PPCs are a critical component of assessing the well-being of astronauts and fellow crewmembers. The Russians developed the PPC as a standard psychological countermeasure beginning with Salyut 6 and continued to use them on Salyut 7 and Mir (Beven, 2012). NASA followed suit and began using PPCs during Shuttle-Mir in 1995 (Beven, 2012). All crewmembers on board the ISS have individual PPCs with their assigned aerospace psychiatrist and operational psychologist who work together as a team. NASA PPCs with ISS crew members are held via private video conference. They are not recorded and are confidential medical events that typically last 15–20 minutes depending on the subject matter discussed and the mission phase. Each PPC covers a set of topics that reflect the main clinical and operational concerns of BHP (Beven, Vander Ark, & Holland, 2015). PPC topics are: sleep (duration and quality) and sleep shift issues; fatigue level; workload and pace of work; individual and crew morale; crew relationships; crew-ground relationships; mood; cognition; family and personal relationships; environment and habitability issues, including food; operational psychology issues or requests; and preparation for important tasks, such as space walks. The PPCs are discussed with the mission-assigned flight surgeons who then consider and act upon any recommendations. BMed support services are also available upon request by the astronaut and as needed following unexpected or critical events.

In addition to post-flight WinSCAT assessment, BMed clinicians perform post-flight assessments at 3, 14, and 30–60 days after landing. Topics covered during post-flight evaluations include: mission in retrospect and the astronaut's level of personal satisfaction; greatest challenges, frustrations, and joys during the mission; retrospective review of fatigue level prior to critical events; family reintegration; post-flight mood, anxiety, and cognition; short- and long-term career plans; a review of all BHP services provided; and recommendations for BHP service improvement. Data gained from the latter two points is used to improve BHP services for future spaceflight crews.

BEHAVIORAL HEALTH TRAINING

BHP provides training classes and briefings to aid in the behavioral health adaptation to space flight. The focus of the classes and class names have evolved over the years. The following represents classes typically provided.

Behavioral Health and Performance Overview is an astronaut candidate's (ASCAN's) first introduction to the services BHP provides to astronauts. Included is a description of clinical services, preparation for flight, and support while in flight. The overview also provides an introduction to the BHP training astronauts will receive once they are assigned to a flight.

Conflict Management is a discussion-oriented training lesson that introduces a three-point cycle that drives, escalates, and de-escalates conflict. The course reviews methods for breaking the cycle at each of the three points so that conflicts are resolved in ways that preserve relationships with colleagues, friends, and family. Techniques include "rules" for fair fighting, checking the accuracy of interpreted meanings, and recognizing and managing emotions that can perpetuate conflict.

Stress Management as a class has morphed over the years from its original focus on traditional stress management techniques. The training now also covers the fundamentals and methods of psychosocial adaptation – becoming accustomed to the stressors inherent in living and working in the spaceflight environment for months on end. As part of this, self-care/self-management, which refers to keeping oneself satisfied and productive under demanding circumstances and managing one's own stress, is covered. This class teaches ASCANs to apply strategies of self-care/self-management as they encounter the stressors that are common to being astronauts, both on the ground and during an expedition.

Cross-Cultural Training exposes US astronauts to special circumstances that can arise from working with crew members and ground control personnel from the International Partners of NASA. The course addresses cultural factors, communication and negotiation styles, and work and social factors. Potential positive and negative effects of cultural differences are identified. Methods, strategies, and resources that can be used to handle cross-cultural challenges are described and practiced within the context of case-situations that occurred previously. This course was devised in answer to the interview requests of astronauts who flew on the ISS and Mir for more and better cross-cultural training.

Expeditionary Workshop is structured on the primary BHP competencies (e.g., teamwork and self-care/self-management) used during selection. The workshop, facilitated by BHP operational psychologists, is conducted by experienced long-duration astronauts. The ASCANs hear stories and lessons learned from astronauts who have already been through the rigors of life on the ISS and review ISS critical incidents, experiences, and effective behaviors and coping strategies for living on the ISS.

National Outdoor Leadership School (NOLS) is time in the wilderness practicing those skills covered in the expeditionary workshop. NOLS is designed to develop leadership and followership skills in particular and also provides opportunities to practice teamwork and self-care skills in a field setting.

ISS Behavioral Medicine Training is provided to astronauts assigned as crew medical officers and also to flight surgeons. This training provides an overview of the potential psychiatric symptoms and disorders that might be seen in a worst-case scenario during a mission. Discussion includes the therapeutic clinical response and resources that are available on the ISS should a crew member exhibit seriously disordered behavior. The focus of this training is on serious psychiatric symptoms or illness as opposed to behaviors that fall within the norm for persons who are living in stressful circumstances.

THE FUTURE – EXPLORATION AND EARTH-BOUND CONCERNS

A human mission to Mars will cover approximately 250 million miles and last approximately 3 years, depending on propulsion and time on the Martian surface (NASA, 2012). The nature of a Mars mission, more so than any other exploration mission beyond low Earth orbit, has extensive ramifications for the type and quantity of support BHP currently offers. BHP is familiar with the risks and uncertainties associated with low Earth orbit for mixed sex multinational crews of 2–6 up to 12 months in duration. Current knowledge gaps include the provision of optimal behavioral health and performance services for interplanetary missions, all missions with a duration significantly greater than 1 year, and missions with a significant communication delay, no possibility of resupply, limited to no escape options, and little to no view of Earth. Astronaut Michael Lopez-Alegria stressed the importance of seeing Earth, "Looking out the window and seeing the Earth below and seeing places you recognize and where you grew up and places you visited has a lot to do with keeping sane, so to speak." (Greenfieldboyce, 2010). Adding further complexity to ultra-long duration and deep space missions include the insidious neurocognitive response to microgravity, confinement, isolation and certainly prolonged, and increased, space radiation (Basner et al., 2015). However, one may use the analogy of past explorers who left their home on sailing ships, out of sight of their homeland, even out of sight of land because of the draw of exploration. So, to compare astronauts to these past explorers, the astronauts' land are planets and moons and space is their high seas.

BHP services will require adjustment to meet the parameters and challenges of exploration missions. Private psychological conferences (PPC) with the crew, for example, will need to be conducted in a manner compatible with communication limitations. The communication delay of up to 20 minutes one-way to Mars will preclude real-time video conferencing. Dyssynchronous communications will require the crew to operate with greater autonomy. With respect to behavioral health, this increase in autonomy will require crew medical officers (CMO) to receive advanced training in behavioral health diagnosis and treatment. No longer would the CMO provide any routine or urgent care under real time guidance by the flight surgeon or aerospace psychiatrist as is the current practice on the ISS. Compounding this burden on the CMO, the odds of an adverse behavioral event increase significantly in response to longer, more isolated missions (Slack et al., 2016). In response, software designed to support the CMO in diagnosis and treatment could mitigate the loss of real-time interaction with an aerospace psychiatrist or psychologist on the ground. Other crewmembers would also be able to utilize similar software to self-monitor their own behavioral health or as a form of asynchronous therapy. Also, relying more heavily on software programs and nonobtrusive measurement such as sociometric badges is expected to allow the early detection of, and intervention in, crew conflict or a crewmember choosing isolation.

BHP Operations works closely with NASA's Human Research Program to determine and meet needs and fill the gaps for future long-duration exploration missions. When humans eventually depart Earth for Mars, those astronauts will have a full complement of countermeasures to ensure that psychosocial adaptation on long-duration exploration missions is as seamless as it is on the ISS.

REFERENCES

Allan, B. A., Batz-Barbarich, C., Sterling, H. M., & Tay, L. (2019). Outcomes of meaningful work: A meta-analysis. *Journal of Management Studies, 56*(3), 500–528.

Anderson, D. M., Keith, J., & Novak, P. D. (Eds.), (2002). *Mosby's medical dictionary* (6th edition). St. Louis, MO: Mosby, A Harcourt Health Science Company.

Antonovsky, A. (1979). *Health, stress, and coping.* San Francisco, CA: Josey-Bass.

Barshi, I., & Dempsey, D. L. (2016). *Evidence report: Risk of performance errors due to training deficiencies.* Houston, TX: NASA. Retrieved from https://humanresearchroadmap.nasa.gov/evidence/reports/TRAIN.pdf

Basner, M., Savitt, A., Moore, T. M., Port, A. M., McGuire, S., Ecker, A. J., ... Dinges, D. F. (2015). Development and validation of the cognition test battery for spaceflight. *Aerospace Medicine and Human Performance, 86*(11), 942–952.

Beven, G. (2012). NASA's behavioral health support for International Space Station (ISS) missions. *Cleveland Clinic Department of Psychiatry and Psychology Grand Rounds.* Retrieved September 13, 2012, from https://ntrs.nasa.gov/archive/nasa/casi.ntrs.nasa.gov/20120014571.pdf

Beven, G., Vander Ark, S. T., & Holland, A. W. (2015). *Psychological support operations and the ISS one-year mission.* Houston, TX: NASA. Retrieved from https://ntrs.nasa.gov/archive/nasa/casi.ntrs.nasa.gov/20150020947.pdf

Buckey, J. C., Jr. (2006). *Space physiology.* Oxford, England: Oxford University Press.

Burgess, C., Doolan, K., & Vis, B. (2003). *Fallen astronauts: Heroes who died reaching for the Moon.* Lincoln, NE: University of Nebraska Press.

Burrough, B. (1998). *Dragonfly: NASA and the Crisis Aboard Mir.* New York, NY: HarperCollins.

Carpenter, D. (1997, July 18). Are blunders on Mir signs the stress is too great? *San Francisco Examiner*, A1.

Clark J. (2007, September). *A flight surgeon's perspective on crew behavior and performance.* Presented at the Workshop for Space Radiation Collaboration with BHP, Center for Advanced Space Studies, Houston, TX.

Connors, M. M., Harrison, A. A., & Akins, F. R. (1985). *Living aloft: Human requirements for extended spaceflight.* Washington, DC: NASA.

Cooper, H. F. S. (1976). *A house in space.* Austin, TX: Holt, Rinehart and Winston.

Cucinotta, F. A. (2014). Space radiation risks for astronauts on multiple International Space Station missions. *PLoS One, 9*(4): e96099. doi:10.1371/journal.pone.0096099

Cucinotta, F. A., Manuel, F. K., Jones, J., Iszard, G., Murrey, J., Djojonegro, B., & Wear, M. (2001). Space radiation and cataracts in astronauts. *Radiation Research, 156*(5), 460–466.

David, E. M., Rubino, C., Keeton, K. E., Miller, C. A., & Patterson, H. N. (2010). *An examination of cross-cultural interactions aboard the International Space Station* (NASA/TM-2011-217351). Houston TX: NASA. Retrieved from https://ston.jsc.nasa.gov/collections/TRS/_techrep/TM-2011-217351.pdf

Duncan, J. M., Bogomolov, V. V., Castrucci, F., Koike, Y., Comtois, J. M., & Sargsyan, A. E. (2008). Organization and management of the International Space Station (ISS) multilateral medical operations. *Acta Astronautica, 63*(7–10), 1137–1147.

Dunn, M. (2001, August 26). Bad news an extra burden in space. *The washington post*. Retrieved from https://www.washingtonpost.com/archive/politics/2001/08/26/bad-news-an-extra-burden-in-space/1e46ca62-654f-4115--9c813189d27f9dc9/

Eschner, K. (2017, February 8). Mutiny in space. *Smithsonian*. Retrieved from https://www.smithsonianmag.com/smart-news/mutiny-space-why-these-skylab-astronauts-never-flew-again-180962023/

Fairlie, P. (2011). Meaningful work, employee engagement, and other key employee outcomes: Implications for human resource development. *Advances in Developing Human Resources, 13*(4), 508–525.

Flynn, C. F. (2005). An operational approach to long-duration mission behavioral health and performance factors. *Aviation, Space and Environmental Medicine, 76*(Supplement 1), B42–B51.

Fynn-Evans, E., Gregory, K., Arsintescu, L., & Whitmire, A. (2016). *Evidence report: Risk of performance decrements and adverse health outcomes resulting from sleep loss, circadian desynchronization, and work overload*. Houston, TX: NASA. Retrieved from https://humanresearchroadmap.nasa.gov/evidence/reports/Sleep.pdf

Friedman, E., & Bui, B. (2017). A psychiatric formulary for long-duration spaceflight. *Aerospace Medicine and Human Performance, 88*(11), 1024–1033.

Gagarin, Y. (1961, April 21). From out of this world. *Life, 50*(16), 20–25.

Gazenko, O. G. (1989). Man in space. Bioastronautics: Yesterday, today, tomorrow. *Space Science Reviews, 50*(3–4), 500–502.

Gernhardt, M. L., Jones, J. A., Scheuring, R. A., Abercromby, A., Tuxhorn, J. A., & Norcross, J. R. (2009). Risk of compromised EVA performance and crew health due to inadequate EVA suit systems. In J. C. McPhee & J. B. Charles (Eds.), *Human health and performance risks of space exploration missions* (NASA SP-2009–3405). Houston, TX: NASA—Johnson Space Center.

Greenfieldboyce, N. (2010). Fake Mars mission: 'Real world' meets space travel. *NPR morning edition*. Retrieved from https://www.npr.org/templates/story/story.php?storyId=127368225

Gunderson, E. E. (1966). *Selection for Antarctic* (service report #66-15). San Diego, CA: United States Navy Medical Neuropsychiatric Research Unit. Retrieved from https://apps.dtic.mil/dtic/tr/fulltext/u2/632497.pdf.

Gunderson, E. E. (1974). *Psychological studies in Antarctica. Human adaptability in Antarctic conditions* (Antarctic research series, Vol. 22, pp. 115–131). Washington, DC: American Geophysical Union.

Harrop, E., Addis, S., Elliott, E., & Williams, G. (2006). *Resilience, coping and salutogenic approaches to maintaining and generating health: A review*. Cardiff, Wales: Cardiff University.

Holland, A. W., Miller, C., & Johnson, J. C. (2000). Predictors of behavior and performance in extreme environments: The Antarctic space analogue program. *Aviation, Space, and Environmental Medicine, 71*(6), 619–625.

Ihle, E. C., Ritsher, J. B., & Kanas, N. (2006). Positive psychological outcomes of spaceflight: An empirical study. *Aviation, Space, and Environmental Medicine, 77*(2), 93–101.

INEE. (2018). *Guidance note: Psychosocial support: Facilitating psychosocial well-being and social and emotional learning*. New York, NY: INEE. Retrieved from http://s3.amazonaws.com/inee-assets/page-images/INEE_Guidance_Note_on_Psychosocial_ Support_ENG.pdf.

James, J. T. (2013). Surprising effects of CO_2 exposure on decision making. In *43rd international conference on environmental systems* (p. 3463). Reston, VA: American Institute of Aeronautics and Astronautics. Retrieved from https://arc.aiaa.org/doi/10.2514/6.2013-3463

Kanas, N. (1990). Psychological, psychiatric, and interpersonal aspects of long-duration space missions. *Journal of Spacecraft and Rockets, 27*(5), 457–463.

Kanas, N. (1991). Psychological support for cosmonauts. *Aviation, Space, and Environmental Medicine, 62*, 353–355.

Kanas, N. (2002). Psychological and psychiatric issues in space. *Journal of Gravitational Physiology: A Journal of the International Society for Gravitational Physiology, 9*(1), P307–P310.

Kanas, N. (2015). *Humans in space: The psychological hurdles*. New York, NY: Springer.

Kanas, N., & Manzey, D. (2008). *Space psychology and psychiatry* (2nd edition). El Segundo, CA: Microcosm Press & Kluwer Academic Publishers.

Kanas, N., Sandal, G., Boyd, J. E., Gushin, V. I., Manzey, D., North, R.,… Inoue, N. (2009). Psychology and culture during long-duration space missions. *Acta Astronautica, 64*(7–8), 659–677.

Landon, L. B., Vessey, W. B., & Barrett, J. (2016). *Evidence report: Risk of performance and behavioral health decrements due to inadequate cooperation, coordination, communication, and psychosocial adaptation within a team*. Houston, TX: NASA. Retrieved from https://humanresearchroadmap.nasa.gov/evidence/reports/Team.pdf

Larsson, G., Berglund, A. K., & Ohlsson, A. (2016). Daily hassles, their antecedents and outcomes among professional first responders: A systematic literature review. *Scandinavian Journal of Psychology, 57*(4), 359–367. doi:10.1111/sjop.12303

Londono, Y., & McMillan, D. E. (2015). Psychosocial adaptation: An evolutionary concept analysis exploring a common multidisciplinary language. *Journal of Advanced Nursing, 71*(11), 2504–2519.

Massimino, M. (2016). *Spaceman: An astronaut's unlikely journey to unlock the secrets of the universe*. New York, NY: Three Rivers Press.

McPhee, J. C., & Charles, J.B. (Eds.). (2009). *Human health and performance risks of space exploration missions*. Houston, TX: NASA. Retrieved from https://humanresearchroadmap.nasa.gov/Evidence/reports/EvidenceBook.pdf

Mundell, I. (1963). Stop the rocket, I want to get off. *New Scientist, 138*(1869), 34.

NASA. (2007). *Shuttle-Mir*. Retrieved from https://www.nasa.gov/mission_pages/ shuttle-mir/

NASA. (2012). *Mars Program Planning group frequently asked questions*. Retrieved from https://www.nasa.gov/offices/marsplanning/faqs/

NASA. (2017). *Skylab*. Retrieved from https://www.nasa.gov/mission_pages/skylab

NASA. (2019). *Individualized real-time neurocognitive assessment toolkit for space flight fatigue*. Retrieved from https://www.nasa.gov/mission_pages/station/research/experiments/explorer/Investigation.html?#id=1125

Palinkas, L. A., Gunderson, E., Tomi, L. M., Rossokha, K., & Hosein, J. (2002). The role of cross-cultural factors in long-duration international space missions: Lessons from the SFINCSS-99 study. *Space Technology, 22*(3–4), 137–144.

Pavy-Le Traon, A., Saivin, S., Soulez-LaRiviere, C., Pujos, M., Guell, A., & Houin, G. (1997). Pharmacology in space: Pharmacotherapy. *Advances in Space Biology and Medicine, 6*, 107–121.

Pugh, M. B. (Ed.). (2002). *Stedman's medical dictionary* (27th edition). New York, NY: Lippincott, Williams, & Wilkins.

Sandal, G. M., & Manzey, D. (2009). Cross-cultural issues in space operations: A survey study among ground personnel of the European Space Agency. *Acta Astronautica, 65*(11–12), 1520–1529.

Santy, P. A. (1994). *Choosing the right stuff: The psychological selection of astronauts and cosmonauts.* Westport, CT: Praeger.

Scheuring, R., & Jones, J. (2007, June). *Space medicine issues and healthcare systems for space exploration medicine.* Presentation to the Korean Aerospace Medicine Association meeting. Retrieved from https://ntrs.nasa.gov:archive:nasa:casi.ntrs.nasa.gov:20070029270.pdf

Schneider, M. (1997, January 24). Astronaut says he was feeling low. Associated Press. *San francisco chronicle*, A6. Retrieved from https://www.pressreader.com/; Alternative version available at http://www.nbcnews.com/id/17300028/ns/technology_and_science-space/t/star-crazy-plans-deal-breakdowns-space/#.XWQoU-hKiUk.

Seaton, K. A., Kane, R. L., & Sipes, W. (2010). *Cognitive assessment during long-duration space flight.* Presented at the 82nd Annual Scientific Meeting of the Aerospace Medical Association, Anchorage, AK.

Seaton, K. A., Slack, K. J., Sipes, W. A., & Bowie, K. (2009). Cognitive functioning in long duration head-down bed rest. *Aviation, Space, & Environmental Medicine, 80*(5 Suppl), A62–A65.

Schmidt, L. A. (2015). *A model of psychosocial factors for long-duration spaceflight exploration missions* (NASA TM-2015-218582). Houston, TX: NASA.

Setlow, R. B. (2003). The hazards of space travel. *European Molecular Biology Organization Reports, 4*(11), 1013–1016. Retrieved from https://www.ncbi.nlm.nih.gov/pmc/articles/PMC1326386/pdf/4-embor7400016.pdf

Slack, K. J., Williams, T. J., Schneiderman, J. S., Whitmire, A. M., & Picano, J. J. (2016). *Evidence report: Risk of adverse cognitive or behavioral conditions and psychiatric disorders.* Houston, TX: NASA. Retrieved from https://humanresearchroadmap.nasa.gov/evidence/reports/BMed.pdf.

Stuster J. (2010) *Behavioral issues associated with long-duration space expeditions: Review and analysis of astronaut journals* (NASA/TM-2010-216130). Houston, TX: NASA.

Stuster, J. (2016). *Behavioral issues associated with long-duration space expeditions: Review and analysis of astronaut journals experiment phase 2* (NASA/TM-2016–218603). Houston, TX: NASA.

Suedfeld, P. (2005). Invulnerability, coping, salutogenesis, integration: Four phases of spaceflight psychology. *Aviation, Space, and Environmental Medicine, 76*(6), B61–66.

Suedfeld, P., & Weiszbeck, T. (2004). The impact of outer space on inner space. *Aviation, Space, and Environmental Medicine, 75*(7), C6–C9.

Talan, J. (2017). Brains in space: MRI shows the impact of flight on astronauts. *Neurology Today, 17*(7), 37–38.

Teitel, A. S. (2016). What was the Mir space station? *Popular science.* Retrieved from https://www.popsci.com/what-was-mir-space-station/.

Tomi, L., Kealey, D., Lange, M., Stefanowska, P., & Doyle, V. (2008). Cross-cultural training requirements for long-duration space missions: Results of a survey of International Space Station astronauts and ground support personnel. *Proceedings of the International Symposium on Space technology and Science*, 1–10.

Troitsyna, M. (2011, June 14). Angels in space nothing but top secret hallucinations. *Pravda.* Retrieved from http://www.pravdareport.com/society/anomal/14-06-2011/118195-angels-0/

Yaden, D. B., Iwry, J., Slack, K. J., Eichstaedt, J. C., Zhao, Y., Vaillant, G. E., & Newberg, A. B. (2016). The overview effect: Awe and self-transcendent experience in space flight. *Psychology of Consciousness: Theory, Research, and Practice, 3*(1), 1–11.

8 Space Flight Operational Psychological Support for Astronauts and Their Families

Jessica L. Hughlett and Elizabeth T. Turner
KBR/NASA's Lyndon B. Johnson Space Center

Kelley J. Slack
Birkman International/Minerva Work Solutions PLLC

Walter E. Sipes
Aerospace Psychology Consultants

CONTENTS

Space Flight Operational Psychological Support for Astronauts and Their Families....134
Brief Overview of Operational Psychology (OpPsy) and Family Support
Office (FSO)..134
Operational Psychology at NASA 135
    History of Operational Psychological Support in Space Flight 136
    Early Operational Psychology Support for the ISS..137
    Current Operational Psychology Support 139
    Psychological Support for the Families 144
Family Support Office...145
    History of the FSO 145
    Support for Astronaut Spouses Group...145
    Liaison for Astronaut Office..146
    Preflight and Launch Support...146
    Landing Support..147
Evidence Supporting Efficacy of Psychology Support at NASA 148
    Psychological Support during Off-Nominal Events..148
Considerations for the Future...150
    Conclusion..152
References...152

SPACE FLIGHT OPERATIONAL PSYCHOLOGICAL SUPPORT FOR ASTRONAUTS AND THEIR FAMILIES

The purpose of work-related psychological support is to maximize employee safety and performance by protecting the physical and mental well-being of those individuals and groups. When individuals are placed in extreme environments, such as low Earth orbit, Antarctica, or combat zones, their safety and well-being become of paramount importance. Organizations operating in isolated, confined, extreme (ICE) environments actively provide psychological support to their employees. National Aeronautical and Space Administration (NASA) recognizes that astronauts working and living in the hostile ICE environment of space require specialized psychological support. The Behavioral Health and Performance (BHP) Operations group at NASA's Lyndon B. Johnson Space Center (JSC) was created to provide such support to astronauts and their families. BHP, as the group is colloquially known at NASA, helps astronauts acclimate to space with the overarching purpose of ensuring no loss of mission goals occurring due to deterioration in crewmember or family functioning (Beven, 2012). Psychological support for ICE environments typically supports the person in that extreme environment, but often, some support is provided to the family as well. Additionally, a subtle distinction can be made between support focused on directly helping the person through more traditional, clinical means versus less traditional support, which is focused on more indirectly helping the person by creating a supportive environment for that person. Figure 8.1 illustrates the types of psychological support created by this distinction and found in BHP. Direct support of the astronaut with a more clinical focus is termed Behavioral Medicine and is discussed more fully in another chapter in this volume. The current chapter focuses on how and what is provided to the astronauts and their families to create a supportive environment. At NASA, the non-clinical support offered to astronauts is termed Operational Psychology (OpPsy), and the non-clinical support offered to families and in coordination with the NASA-JSC is termed the Family Support Office (FSO).

BRIEF OVERVIEW OF OPERATIONAL PSYCHOLOGY (OpPSy) AND FAMILY SUPPORT OFFICE (FSO)

The role of OpPsy within BHP is to assist and support astronauts and their families once an astronaut is assigned to a mission. Support provided by OpPsy at NASA follows the medical care guidelines, flight rules, and evidence-based medical requirements governed by the International Space Station (ISS) Program and the Human Health and Performance Medical community. As another part of BHP, FSO provides psychological support primarily to the families of all active astronauts. A primary goal for FSO is to provide a sense of comfort to astronauts through the knowledge that their family is secure and aware of the space flight processes, allowing astronauts to focus on what is happening at work, while at work (Curtis, Beven, Holland, Sipes, & Vander Ark, 2014).

FSO and OpPsy primarily work in coordinated independence of one another, with related, yet separate goals. OpPsy focuses on preparing mission-assigned astronauts

Space Flight Operational Psychological Support

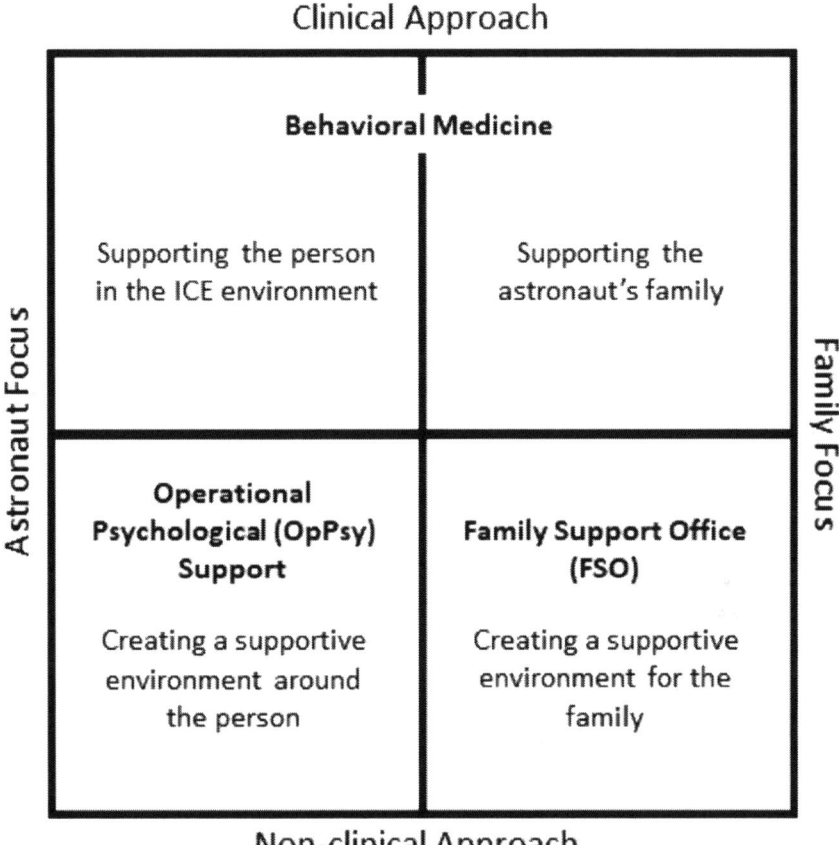

FIGURE 8.1 NASA Behavioral Health and Performance (BHP) Operations group's distinction between focus of psychological support and distinction between clinical and non-clinical psychological support.

and their families for the astronaut's specific mission and then supporting them throughout the entire process from preflight to postflight. FSO focuses on the family regardless of whether an astronaut is assigned to a mission. Table 8.1 provides an overview of how the purposes and approaches of OpPsy and FSO align and differ.

OPERATIONAL PSYCHOLOGY AT NASA

OpPsy within BHP at the Johnson Space Center is a part of operations and also works closely with NASA behavioral health and psychological researchers. Projects with an operational psychology focus that are under the purview of BHP research are explored in the Research volume of this series. This chapter focuses on what has been and what is provided to astronauts and their families to aid them in their adaptation to space flight stressors and separation from family and friends.

TABLE 8.1
Key Features of Operational Psychology and Family Support Office

	Behavioral Health and Performance (BHP) Operations Group	
	Operational Psychology (OpPsy)	Family Support Office (FSO)
Mission	Mission preparation and psychological services for astronauts and their families from assignment to a mission through post-flight reintegration	Assure no loss of mission goals due to deterioration in family functioning
Customer Focus	Astronaut with tangential support to immediate family	Astronaut and family
Timing of Support	While assigned to a mission	Tenure as an astronaut
Founded	1994	1998
Organizational Structure	OpPsy is in BHP under the Space Operations and Clinical Division	Joint effort between Astronaut Office and BHP
Roles and Responsibilities	Training, support offered preflight, on-orbit, postflight; Outreach to family and friends	Family briefings including planning for flight, contingency, postflight; Support for the Astronaut Spouse Group

HISTORY OF OPERATIONAL PSYCHOLOGICAL SUPPORT IN SPACE FLIGHT

Early space missions were short, lasting from a few hours for the earliest missions to a couple of weeks for Shuttle missions. Given the restricted mission length, crewmembers' timelines on orbit were tightly scheduled, allowing for little off-duty time. Today, leisure time during missions that last for months to one year is necessary for the continued well-being of astronauts. Even though these early astronauts had little leisure time, the short duration of their missions offset the relative lack of leisure time and psychological support experienced by early astronauts.

Still, some aspects of psychological support emerged. For example, the tradition of waking astronauts with music began with the Gemini program in the mid-1960s. During the Space Transportation System (Space Shuttle) program, astronauts were awakened with meaningful songs chosen by their families. Astronauts were also allotted one private family video conference per mission, with the families of Shuttle astronauts receiving a video copy of the conference. Technology at the time required each family to come to Johnson Space Center to conduct the short conference.

After the Apollo moon missions, our focus began to shift to living, working, and conducting science in microgravity. The Shuttle was developed both to carry large payloads and to conduct science experiments in microgravity. In the 1970s, NASA experimented with its first space station, Skylab. While NASA turned its focus on the Shuttle program during the 1980s, Russia invested more completely in space stations with their Salyut program and later space station *Mir*. With the advent of space stations came longer duration missions, and the stress that those longer missions created for both astronauts and their families (Kanas, 1990; Palinkas, 2007).

NASA learned inconveniences and annoyances associated with space flight could largely be ignored or psychologically minimized for the duration of short missions, such as those of the Shuttle era. Astronauts reported being able to "just deal with it" (e.g., Whitmire et al., 2013). This strategy did not hold once mission lengths began to increase. For example, the crew of Skylab 4 took an unscheduled day off when they felt overwhelmed by the schedule set by Mission Control (Eschner, 2017). While the reactions of this Skylab crew were unusual, their actions spotlighted the need for additional and different support. What NASA was doing for short duration astronauts was not sufficient to support the well-being of long-duration astronauts. As the duration of the mission increased, the small inconveniences and annoyances began to accumulate, potentially reaching a mission-impacting level. This is a lesson that those in the Russian space program, with their earlier emphasis on space stations, learned two decades earlier than NASA (Harrison & Fiedler, 2013).

In March 1995, Norm Thagard arrived at *Mir* for a 115-day mission. At that point, NASA had limited practical knowledge regarding how to best provide psychological support to astronauts on longer duration missions. BHP, newly formed in reaction to lessons learned from Skylab, drew on what Russia (then the USSR or Soviet Union) knew about providing psychological support. The psychological support received by NASA astronauts on *Mir* was limited by a lack of experience, the technology available in the mid-1990s, and the fact that NASA was essentially a guest on a Russian space station. Shuttle-*Mir* program manager Frank Culbertson remarked on the challenges Thagard experienced in 1995 as the first NASA astronaut on *Mir* (Morgan, 2001). Jerry Linenger, who in 1997 followed the path Thagard blazed, candidly wrote in his memoir about some of the challenges he faced on *Mir* such as the emergency fire that erupted early in his mission. He recounted two types of challenges – the first related to the space station itself; and second related to the difficulty of living and working in a confined, isolated, and dangerous environment with limited social interaction (Linenger, 2000). Knowledge accumulated over the lifetime of the Shuttle-*Mir* program was vital in preparing for the coming truly international space station.

Early Operational Psychology Support for the ISS

On October 31, 2000, a Soyuz spacecraft lifted off from the Baikonur Cosmodrome at 10:53 a.m. Kazakhstan time. Onboard were ISS Expedition One Commander William M. (Bill) Shepherd of NASA and cosmonauts Sergei Krikalev and Yuri Gidzenko of Roscosmos (Russia's space agency). The trio arrived at the International Space Station (ISS) on November 2, marking the start of an uninterrupted human presence on the orbiting laboratory. At that time, the station was a modest pair of modules, one Russian and the other from the United States. The crew stayed on the ISS for 136 days. Being the first to live on the ISS, they overcame many complications related to setting up the outpost. Commander Shepherd, while commending the STS-97 Shuttle crew, discussed Expedition One, stating, "I can't think of a mission that we've flown in a long time that's been a bigger challenge" (Associated Press, 2000).

During the early stages of Expedition One, the crew activated critical life-support systems, unpacked supplies and equipment, and set up multiple areas including the galley, crew quarters, and exercise equipment (NASA, 2017a). There were times the crew requested permission to set up items earlier than scheduled in order to better meet their needs. Sometimes the crew would be asked to stand down due to the incomplete procedures or when ground-based experts for a particular system were unavailable during the requested time. Delays in requests can lead to frustration on both the crewmembers' and the ground support's sides. If not managed or mitigated, minimal group effect (Tajfel, 1970) can easily create an "us versus them" scenario and adversely affect both crew and ground support's psychological well-being.

Psychological support during the earliest long-duration ISS expeditions was still in its infancy. BHP group began to develop countermeasures, such as opportunities to talk with family, to offset the stressors of living and working in space for extended periods of time. Technology available in the early 2000s did not allow much flexibility. For example, family members were required to come into Mission Control Center at Johnson Space Center, Houston, TX, to participate in Private Family Conferences with their astronaut. This gave the astronaut no control over initiating contact with his/her family. A lack of control can negatively impact an individual (Goemaere, Van Caelenberg, Beyers, Binsted, & Vansteenkiste, 2019; Spector, 1986). On the early ISS missions, few leisure activities were available. Viewing Earth through the ISS windows was (and continues to be) a favorite activity, even more so later with the addition of the multi-windowed cupola in 2010. The limited number of movies on the ISS were on hardcopy DVDs (which required valuable volume onboard vehicles launched to ISS) and watched on a shared laptop computer. Exercise, a preferred leisure activity for many astronauts (in addition to being a medical requirement), was limited to a treadmill.

The US crewmember of Expedition One arrived back at Ellington Field, near Johnson Space Center, in late March, 2001. There was much we, in OpPsy and FSO, did not yet know about living and working in space for extended periods of time. It was immediately apparent when Shepherd, newly returned from Expedition One, walked cautiously and unsteadily crossed the Ellington Field tarmac to address the waiting crowd (authors' personal observation). His uncharacteristic physical movements spoke to the need for better countermeasures to prevent physical deterioration in microgravity. BHP also recognized a potential knowledge gap related to the need to develop more psychological support and countermeasures such as briefings, access to news, access to the internet, and better access to family to ensure the well-being of our astronauts, and their families, before, during, and after their missions.

In the early years of the ISS, the Shuttle Program was the workhorse for the assembly of the space station. The Shuttle provided needed resupplies and hardware for the growing ISS as well as fresh faces of the Shuttle crews with whom the ISS crewmembers could interact. Both the delivery of new supplies and seeing new faces were psychological boosters in and of themselves. The resupplies offered increased variety to a monotonous environment (e.g., the arrival of fresh food) and the visiting crew offered a larger social network, while the Shuttle was docked to the ISS for up to 2 weeks.

The Shuttle became a regular visitor to the ISS until the loss of Space Shuttle Columbia (STS-107) and her crew during reentry on February 1, 2003, which caused the Space Agencies to depend on the Russian Soyuz and Progress missions for ISS crew rotations and resupply. Two and a half years would pass before the Shuttle

Program would launch another Shuttle vehicle to the ISS (STS-114, July 26, 2005). The continuation of Shuttle missions to the ISS had a positive impact on the psychological well-being of current and future ISS crews until the Shuttles were retired in the Summer of 2011 (NASA, 2011). During the Shuttle-ISS period, psychological support continued to improve due to advances in technology, which allowed internet protocol (IP) phone, internet, and streaming digital videos to be added to the list of countermeasures.

CURRENT OPERATIONAL PSYCHOLOGY SUPPORT

Astronauts eligible for flight are classified as unassigned or assigned depending on whether they are on the schedule for a specific expedition to the ISS. For those who are assigned to a mission, NASA distinguishes between three primary mission phases: preflight, in-flight, and postflight. Launch and landing events mark the transition to the next phase. As the needs of astronauts and their families vary during the different mission phases, so does the support offered by BHP OpPsy and FSO. Operational psychology support provided to crewmembers and families has evolved as technology and mission profiles have evolved and lessons learned have accumulated. The support currently offered by OpPsy is described below.

Preflight Phase

Anecdotal reports along with some empirical evidence indicate the preflight phase to be more stressful for astronauts than the mission itself or post-flight phase (Dinges et al., 2014). One potential factor may be that crewmembers are required to split their attention between their upcoming mission and their family during preflight training, and are able to focus more on the work while in flight. Another contributing factor is that during the preflight training, astronauts are required to regularly travel and train for two to four weeks at a time between Houston, Russia, Canada, and Europe. These trainings may take place for up to 30 months with many family separations.

Two members of the OpPsy team are assigned to each NASA or Canadian astronaut, one as lead and the other as back-up. These OpPsy members are critical to the psychological care of crewmembers and families. Part of preparing an astronaut and the family for an upcoming mission involves educating them on the services that are available and what to expect during the mission phases. The primary purpose of BHP-related trainings, at times called briefings, is to prepare astronauts for the unique behavioral health and psychological demands of space flight. While OpPsy is involved in initial trainings provided to ASCANs (astronaut candidates or new astronauts), the bulk of trainings and briefings led by OpPsy occur in the assigned preflight phase. In-flight Resource Planning (IRP) I and II are both the first opportunity and the last scheduled opportunity upcoming crewmembers have to meet with OpPsy members prior to flight. At IRP I, crewmembers learn about general in-flight resources available to them and identify any personal items, such as pictures drawn by their children or mementos they wish to take onboard their launch vehicle or on subsequent re-supply vehicles in their Crew Care Packages (CCP), as long as the items meet certain restrictions such as weight and volume. During this time, OpPsy personnel also summarize the timeline of significant events (e.g., delivery dates for family photo albums, birthdays, anniversaries) and review the preliminary plan for in-flight psychological support. IRP II is the final formal meeting between the OpPsy lead and the crewmember. Crewmembers are afforded the opportunity to review and finalize their individualized in-flight resource plan. As necessary and available, crewmembers will also have opportunity for a demonstration of resources, such as viewing a sample crew webpage, with their individualized requests and also their Family and Friends outreach that OpPsy manages for them in-flight.

In-Flight Phase

Once aboard the ISS, crewmembers have access to a plethora of options provided to promote their continued psychological well-being. Astronauts are often interested in music, as is evidenced by US astronaut bands that have existed on Earth over the years, and at times crewmembers conduct ad hoc performances on the ISS. Over the years, various crewmembers have requested OpPsy provide an electronic keyboard and acoustic guitars. These now reside permanently on the station and are available to astronauts and cosmonauts alike. Others, such as Frank Culbertson and Cady Coleman, have chosen to fly their own instruments (trumpet and flutes, respectively) (Figure 8.2).

Food is known to have a positive psychological effect on individuals and on group cohesion (Clay, 2017; Kniffin, Wansink, Devine, & Sobal, 2015; Stuster, 2010). Unmanned resupply space vehicles bring food not normally stowed on the ISS, such as fresh fruit, as well as CCPs containing items sent by their families. Crewmembers often create special meals to share with their fellow crewmembers and regularly make time to visit with each other during group meals.

A large library of movies and music has been placed on the ISS over the life of the station. The movies began as actual DVD videos flown to the ISS, but now have evolved into an electronic movie and television show library. Crewmembers have the flexibility to watch a movie or listen to music or a podcast within the privacy of

FIGURE 8.2 Expedition 30 commander Dan Burbank and flight engineer Anton Shkaplerov playing music in the Unity node of the ISS.

their crew quarters, while exercising, or as a social activity with other crewmembers. Some crews have designated a weekend movie night, where crewmembers share newly arrived edible items while watching a movie together.

Likewise, holidays play an important role in maintaining crew cohesion and individual well-being. Over the years, decorations for different holidays have accumulated. There are, for example, a Christmas tree banner and individual crewmember stockings for Christmas.

Staying connected as a crew is critical for mission success. Also critical is maintaining crewmembers' connections to their families and friends on the ground. During the early years of the ISS, families came into the Mission Control Center (MCC) and had a video conference at a designated time for a designated number of minutes. The video was recorded on a VHS tape for each crewmember and family to have as a keepsake, and as technology advanced, videoconference equipment was provided and set up at the family's home. Today, families are no longer confined to the MCC or one room in their home. Families are now given an electronic tablet with conferencing software to conduct their private family conferences (PFCs) with the Space Station, allowing them to be mobile and conduct conferences anywhere there is signal reception. It also allows the crewmember and family to have a more interactive conference as the tablet can be moved throughout an area (in the home, backyard, a park, etc.) to show different places or things as desired. For example, families have chosen to show their astronaut Texas bluebonnets blooming in the Spring or "take" the crewmember along to a dinner with friends. This technology also allows for multipoint conferences, so that if primary family members are in multiple locations, the crewmember can visit with them all during a single scheduled conference. A critical task of OpPsy is to coordinate the weekly PFCs between crewmembers and their families. Since 2003, astronauts have been able to supplement the weekly private family conferences, with an internet protocol (IP) phone. Crewmember can call their family as the Station digital bandwidth allows, although the phone on the ISS cannot receive calls from Earth.

Items arriving in a CCP are always a welcome sight for the crew aboard the ISS. The package can contain greeting cards, gifts for significant events such as birthdays or holidays, a child's drawings, photos, chocolates, other candies, meats, some cheese as well as other items the crewmember may have requested. The OpPsy personnel are critical in obtaining the proper process of approvals and clearances for the CCP items from various Space Agency offices due to expiration dates (food), off-gassing (i.e., release smells and other chemicals), and size and volume restrictions.

Additional resources are provided to crewmembers to help them stay connected with what is occurring on the ground. Each crewmember has a private webpage onboard the ISS. Personal selections of movies, news, music, family photos, and videos are posted there for their use during crew downtime and exercise activities. A second webpage, the ground-based family and friends webpage, allows crewmembers to send down videos and photos of their experiences on the ISS. This by-invitation-only webpage also provides family and friends with one location for all NASA and mission-related links. This eliminates the burden for crew and family to provide the same information multiple times and allows family and friends to easily follow the mission (Figure 8.3).

FIGURES 8.3 Screen shots of sample main Crew Personal Support Webpage and Ground Based Family and Friends Webpage.

Crewmembers are offered Crew Discretionary Events (CDE), such as a videoconference with a favorite author or professor. These are private events for the psychological well-being of the crewmember and thus never publicized. These CDEs are a tremendous morale booster for the crewmembers. Occasionally, astronauts mention them in their journals, kept as a part of a study conducted by Jack Stuster (2010; 2016). For example, one crewmember mentioned talking with a favorite chef, Giada De Laurentiis, while another wrote about Norm Abram, from "This Old House" (Stuster, 2016, p. 31), and a third astronaut journaled about being able to talk with a life-long hero:

> Last night I had a once-in-a-lifetime experience, and I must admit, it was one that I hoped to have some time in my life, but never really expected it to happen. I spoke directly to the most famous spaceship commander of all time. It was awesome.
>
> *Stuster (2010, p. 16)*

There are also crew choice and education events. During these events, the crew interacts with school children, celebrities, college alma maters, or other groups. These public events have the benefit of creating interest in science and space as well as building crew morale. Expedition 14 Navy Captain Michael Lopez-Alegria and Navy Commander Suni Williams re-enlisted sailors onboard the USS Eisenhower while the ship was deployed at sea. During Expedition 12, William McArthur joined a Paul McCartney concert in Houston. Cornhusker astronaut Clay Anderson participated in a Nebraska football game via a pre-recorded downlink message played during half-time. NASA crewmembers can also participate in other events on the ground via their life-sized picture cut-out (known affectionately within OpPsy as "flat astronauts"). These flat astronauts make appearances at schools and events such as the one celebrating the 100th day of that crewmember's expedition (Figure 8.4).

FIGURE 8.4 During a visit to JSC in 2017, Garth Brooks enjoyed himself alongside a flat cutout of astronaut Jack Fischer (NASA, 2017b).

Post-flight Phase

Once a NASA, JAXA, or CSA astronaut is back at the Johnson Space Center, OpPsy specialists conduct a debriefing with the astronaut for lessons learned to help future crews, astronauts, and families. OpPsy also provides electronic keepsakes of family conferences, special conferences, and outreach forums, if desired to be given to the astronaut after they have completed their mission.

PSYCHOLOGICAL SUPPORT FOR THE FAMILIES

Two "missions" begin when astronauts are assigned to a flight: the astronaut's mission and the astronaut's family mission. Preparations for a six-month mission (i.e., the current average mission length) start approximately 18 months prior to launch. The long training flow and the international nature of the ISS require assigned crewmembers to spend about a third to half of this time training outside of the United States (it varies with left or right seat assignment on the Soyuz). Crewmembers face a heavy, sometimes remotely located, training schedule, which introduces a potential source of stress to the crewmember and family. Conversely, these early, shorter separation periods have the benefit of allowing the family to explore different separation techniques (e.g., communication via an online video chat platform or a recorded video of the astronaut reading a favorite bedtime story) to discover those that will work best for the family's situation. The time spent training outside of the United States also provides an opportunity for the astronaut and family to deal with situations similar to those that might occur during a flight (e.g., a broken washing machine or even the family evacuating their Houston home due to an approaching hurricane when the astronaut is on another continent).

Even though there is 20 years of NASA experience in long-duration missions on the ISS, challenges remain. The isolation and confinement of long-duration operations creates an environment with unique and powerful stressors that must be managed for astronauts, their families, and the ground crews (Flynn, 2005). During the mission, astronauts are separated from their families by approximately 230 nautical miles (370 km) above the Earth (NASA, 2016). The support that families provide to their astronaut family members is an important component to maintaining crewmember resilience (Vanhove et al., 2015). Equally important is the impact the expedition has on the family.

A primary mission of OpPsy is to provide and encourage engagement in activities to connect crewmembers with their families and families with their crewmembers. Some of the services OpPsy provides primarily for the benefit of the astronaut, such as videoconferencing, crewmember website, and CCPs, also offer families a means of maintaining that connection and actively support their astronaut. Other special events, such as sharing the first photos of his newly born child during a special private family conference conducted at the hospital when Mike Finke was on the ISS, can be photographed and shared with the crewmember. Technology today allows real-time uplink of events such as a high school or college graduation and affords crewmembers an opportunity to be a part of the event for their children.

FAMILY SUPPORT OFFICE

Maintaining connections with their families is of high priority to astronauts on a mission (Johnson, 2010). Complementing OpPsy's approach, the Family Support Office's (FSO) actions make staying connected easier for astronaut and family. Creating a sense of community between the family members of the astronauts provides a source of support for astronaut families, in particular for spouses. A major part of the FSO's mission is to encourage that sense of community.

HISTORY OF THE FSO

Family separations have a long history of having negative impacts on those separated from their families and on the families themselves (Blaydes & Paik, 2016; Eaton et al., 2008; MacDermid Wadsworth, 2010; Mansfield et al., 2010; Palmer, 2008). Significant others left at home have increased responsibility for their family's daily life, from making sure the grass is mowed to shuttling children between after school events, all without their partner to share the load. On top of the additional stressors put on the deployed individual's spouse, children with a deployed parent are more likely to experience psychological distress resulting in lowered academic success and behavioral problems, according to research on military deployments (Cederbaum et al., 2014; Chandra et al., 2011), especially when the parent at home is also experiencing increased behavioral symptoms (Flake, Davis, Johnson, & Middleton, 2009; Lester et al., 2010).

As deployments get longer, the distress and adjustment difficulties felt by the families also increase (Chandra, Martin, Hawkins, & Richardson, 2010; Chartrand, Frank, White, & Shope, 2008; Mansfield et al., 2010; Wiens & Boss, 2006). Fortunately, children and families tend to be resilient, with family members typically recovering from the stress of being separated, especially when the family is prepared for the challenges of deployment (Meadows et al., 2016; Wiens & Boss, 2006). The Department of Defense also has established Family Support Offices for deployed members of the military.

The astronaut Family Support Office at NASA was created in August of 2000. The need for an astronaut FSO arose with the advent of the ISS and longer missions when NASA recognized that astronaut families, and thus the astronaut, would benefit from additional support. The FSO at NASA's Lyndon B. Johnson Space Center is a collaborative effort between Behavioral Health and Performance Operations group and the Astronaut Office. The FSO acts as a liaison between itself, Astronaut Spouses Group (ASG), Astronaut Office, Flight Medicine operations group, and other sections within BHP. Some of its work as a liaison occurs with all astronauts; whether they are unassigned, assigned or veteran fliers.

SUPPORT FOR ASTRONAUT SPOUSES GROUP

The ASG, whether formally chartered or not, has been in existence since the beginning of the space program. It is a volunteer-run organization that offers support for

NASA and International Partner astronaut families. Most astronaut families do not have extended family in the Houston area. As such, many partners of astronauts rely on local friends to provide daily support. The ASG is comprised of astronaut spouses and significant others uniquely qualified to empathize with and support the significant other of an assigned astronaut. The veteran spouses who have experienced a long-duration mission separation can share their experiences and pass on their lessons learned. Being able to talk with someone who has gone through a mission offers comfort to newer spouses.

The ASG also serves other critical functions. It acts as both advocate and liaison between families and NASA and serves as a common means of communicating with astronaut families. The group also interprets changes to NASA/Astronaut Office policies and relays how these might impact the families.

One of the FSO's roles is to provide support to the ASG. Much of this support is administrative in nature, such as maintaining their membership roster and acting as a centralized clearinghouse of information helpful to astronaut families. The FSO also coordinates and sponsors educational events for issues regarding long-duration space missions. It is an essential link in communication between NASA and the ASG. The FSO regularly sends notices and space-related news to families and provides contingency notification and support.

Liaison for Astronaut Office

As a liaison with the Astronaut Office, the FSO assists families with crewmember travel, aids in preparing contingency action plans for launch and landing and expeditionary (analog) training. Expeditionary training may occur in such locations as NASA Extreme Environment Mission Operations (NEEMO) in the Aquarius undersea research station in the Florida Keys, the European Space Agency's Cooperative Adventure for Valuing and Exercising human behavior and performance Skills (CAVES) course in an Italian cave, or the National Outdoor Leadership School (NOLS) customized for astronauts. In addition to NASA astronauts, the FSO also provides support for International Partner crewmembers (e.g., crewmembers from the European Space Agency, the Japanese Space Exploration Agency, the Canadian Space Agency) and their families in the US. This can be invaluable when navigating NASA bureaucracy and connecting with local services, especially when there is a language or cultural barrier.

Once assigned to a mission, astronauts and their families receive additional, specialized support from the FSO. The bulk of this support, in the form of briefings and coordination, occurs at launch and landing.

Preflight and Launch Support

Upon assignment, crewmembers and their immediate family members attend a training class in Practical Planning for Long-Duration Missions. This training encompasses information given to the crewmembers such as key contacts in the community, assistance in personal and disaster readiness, foreign travel resources, and example forms of emergency data. Before the mission, the FSO assists in developing and maintaining Family Support Itineraries, outlining what the family and crew can expect as far as travel, support, and visits prior to launch. The FSO also assists in managing individual Contingency Action Plans. These plans encompass both events occurring on the ground that are of particular relevance to the crewmember and mission-related events directly involving the crewmember. In the former case, the plan outlines how and by whom the crewmember wants to be notified of the contingency. For the latter, the plan details how families want to be notified and by whom if the contingency involves the crew. The FSO provides contingency action plan information to Crew Support Astronauts and Casualty Assistance Calls Officers (CACOs) who will assist the next of kin in working with NASA.

Leading up to launch, the FSO briefs the crewmember and immediate family about launch protocols. This briefing is also provided to the Astronaut Office escorts assigned to family members to ensure the escorts understand their responsibilities. Typically, these escorts are astronauts the family selects to help. As needed, the FSO also works with International Partner family or crew support representatives to coordinate events and transportation schedules.

In essentials, family support has not varied much regardless of whether provided for Shuttle astronauts or ISS astronauts launching or landing via shuttle or Soyuz. The events supported by the FSO are the same; for Soyuz launches and landings, the location is different. With the advent of the Commercial Crew Program with its commercially made spacecraft flown by NASA astronauts, the sheer number of people the families will need be surrounded by at a launch goes from 15 guests in Russia to possibly 1,000 as was the case for Shuttle. For Soyuz and commercial landings, families await their crewmember's return in Houston.

LANDING SUPPORT

All ISS crewmembers currently launch and return to Earth on the Russian Soyuz. Manned Soyuz landings occur in the steppes of Kazakhstan. Crewmembers receive a brief medical exam and are then transported via Russian helicopter to the airport at Karaganda or Kustanai, where they have their first "welcome home" ceremony. Under NASA's Direct Return protocol, NASA astronauts, along with any Japanese or Canadian crewmembers, are flown directly from Kazakhstan to Houston on NASA aircraft. They arrive at Ellington Field, TX, to a second "welcome home" ceremony. About 24 hours after landing, crewmembers are reunited with their families and begin post-flight medical tests.

As was provided prior to launch, the FSO Coordinator briefs family on Soyuz landing and direct return procedures and provides updates to the family regarding the arrival of their astronaut at Ellington Field in Houston. The FSO also develops Family Support Plans for landing and direct return as well as implementing other logistics such as family access to Astronaut Crew Quarters on campus at the Johnson Space Center, coordination with the JSC Food Laboratory to stock breakfast and lunch foods in the JSC Crew Quarters for returning crewmembers, and transportation for crewmember and immediate family to Crew Quarters at NASA. The FSO also coordinates with their European, Canadian, and Japanese Space Agency counterparts as needed.

As for launches, FSO support for landings was similar for Shuttle astronauts and for ISS astronauts landing via Shuttle. Shuttle families met their returning astronauts at Kennedy Space Center. Whether return is via Soyuz landing in Kazakhstan or a commercial vehicle, families await the return of their ISS crewmembers in Houston.

EVIDENCE SUPPORTING EFFICACY OF PSYCHOLOGY SUPPORT AT NASA

Over the years, the anecdotal evidence of the efficacy of psychological support has accumulated to the point that it can be examined more empirically. Stuster (2010) reported psychological support as the fourth most common topic of outside communication for astronauts on the ISS to report in the astronaut journals. Notably, the efforts of OpPsy routinely receive special recognition by crewmembers. Long-duration astronauts like Clay Anderson and Scott Kelly mention the importance of the support they received from OpPsy personnel, frequently mentioning the OpPsy coordinator assigned to their mission and other members of BHP by name (Anderson, 2015; Giffords, Kelly, & Zaslow, 2011). Astronauts often choose to bestow a coveted Silver Snoopy award on their OpPsy lead. The Silver Snoopy is the highest award an astronaut can give to those who have supported a mission or the space program.

For years, NASA has had Jack Stuster (2010; 2016) collect journals from astronauts willing to participate. A sizable proportion of these entries involve astronauts recognizing the psychological support they receive. Almost always these mentions are very positive, with negative reports of support largely related to issues with technology such as loss of connection during a phone call (a harbinger for Mars missions). "Outstanding" and "amazing" are typical terms used by astronauts to describe the psychological support they receive (Stuster, 2016).

Psychological Support during Off-Nominal Events

Unexpected events, called off-nominal events at NASA, provide additional evidence of the efficacy of psychological support provided to crewmembers and families. During off-nominal events, the standard multi-pronged approach BHP has in place for supporting crewmembers is augmented for astronauts and their families.

In 2003, as the Columbia Space Shuttle tragedy was unfolding, two astronauts and one cosmonaut remained at work on the International Space Station (ISS) 250 miles above Earth. They were Americans Ken Bowersox and Donald Pettit and Russian cosmonaut Nikolai Budarin. The onboard crew was notified by General Jefferson Howell, the then director of the Johnson Space Center.

Bowersox stated:

> They came in and told us that we lost a vehicle on entry. My first reaction was pure shock, I was numb and it was hard to believe that what we were experiencing was really happening. And then as the reality wore on, we were able to feel some sadness. It's the classic grieving responses that our psychologists have warned us about, you feel sad, you feel angry, all those things. And now as time goes on, we're able to put those aside

and focus a lot better on our work, although we will be going through the process [of grieving] for probably until we get home or much after.

CNN (2003)

Science officer Don Pettit stated:

> When I first heard, at that point it was not known what or the condition of the crew were in and so we were hoping that there were going to be survivors. And then as it unwound, we learned that there were no survivors and that's when the magnitude of the event really hit me.
>
> *CNN (2003)*

Pettit was on his first trip to space. Pettit had played chess via radio and e-mail with Columbia pilot Willie McCool during the Columbia STS-107 science flight (Stenger, 2003). As Ken Bowersox, the American commander of the Expedition Six crew commented,

> The whole situation was very personal for us because we knew those guys who were on [Columbia mission] STS-107 very well.
>
> They were good friends. We had contact with them here and we shared a mission – a mission to explore and a mission to do science in space. So, it was very painful.
>
> *(NPR, 2003)*

For events like this, contact is increased onboard the ISS with crewmembers to more closely monitor crew morale. Pettit and the others reported they did not feel isolated because they could contact family and friends whenever they wish via e-mail.

Pettit stated:

> Now, in terms of family, I could not be here if it wasn't for the support I get from my wife. And we communicate as often as we can via e-mail and through the NASA-arranged family conferences. And the support you get with this kind of contact is the—gives me the fundamental strength I need in order to stay up here and continue on with the work for our mission.
>
> *NASA (2003)*

In response to the tragedy, as with other contingency plans developed by BHP and OpPsy, the ground team reduced the crewmember's schedules to allow for the onboard crewmembers to grieve.

Bowersox stated:

> That was very important. When you're up here this long, you can't just bottle up your emotions and focus all the time. I mean, it's important for us to acknowledge that the people on [Columbia] STS-107 were our friends and we had a connection with them and that we feel their loss, and each of us had a chance to shed some tears. But now it's time to move forward and we're doing that slowly. This press conference today is a huge step that's helping us move along towards our normal objectives and fulfilling our mission here
>
> *NASA (2003)*

Pettit remarked, "The way you grieve is sort of a personal thing, and myself, I like the privacy to grieve in the quiet surroundings here that we have on the Space Station" (NASA, 2003).

Unfortunately, other tragedies have occurred while crewmembers were living on the ISS. The ISS flies in an ever-changing orbit around the Earth. For example, some days the crew can view their home on the Texas Gulf Coast, some days they cannot. On September 11, 2001, the orbit took the crew over New York City. Frank Culbertson remembers the day vividly writing, "Well, obviously the world changed today" (Culbertson, 2011). When astronaut Dan Tani was stationed aboard the ISS in 2007, he received the tragic news that his mother was killed in an automobile accident. A NASA flight surgeon along with Tani's wife contacted him while he was serving aboard the ISS. A private two-way conference was established for him to "attend" a portion of the funeral service.

In advance of their mission, crewmembers meet with astronaut office management to discuss individual preferences regarding notification of emergencies, such as these in the Contingency Action Plan (CAP). When the worst does occur, multiple groups within NASA rally to provide support. The NASA flight surgeon, psychological services, and family support services are all available, among other groups. Even when the tragedy is personal, such as Tani's experience or the death of astronaut Patricia Hilliard Robertson in a small airplane crash, the close-knit nature of the astronaut corps means that what affects crewmembers also affects other astronauts and their families. In such cases, NASA and BHP provide psychological support for all astronauts, not just those in space. Positive comments about the psychological support they receive (e.g., Stuster, 2010, 2016) speak to the importance of that support and the resilience of the astronaut corps.

CONSIDERATIONS FOR THE FUTURE

NASA is adept at 6-month missions in low Earth orbit. Over the past 20 or so years, astronauts have shown themselves to be able to adapt to the physiological and psychological demands of the ISS. Ground support in all its variety has likewise demonstrated their abilities to sustain the crew. Mission Control operates on a 24-hour day with 3 shifts, watching and protecting the systems keeping the ISS aloft and functioning. The food lab prepares food able to stay shelf-stable without losing nutritional value. BHP provides support in the forms of behavioral health, operational psychology, and family support. But, when humans leave low Earth orbit and venture to Mars, every system and every person will need to adapt. No system will be untouched.

The physical constraints will create new and greater psychological challenges. Mission Control and the astronaut crew will need to account for a Mars day that is 39 minutes longer, a seemingly insignificant amount of time with grave consequences for circadian rhythm over a longer period (DeRoshia, Colletti, & Mallis, 2008). The food lab is currently working to create foods with lower mass and longer nutritional and palatability shelf lives (Sirmons et al., 2018). BHP is studying methods to support crewmembers individually and as a team under conditions arising from a mission to Mars, particularly under conditions of communication delays of up to 22 minutes each way between Mars and Earth. In the words of one ISS astronaut,

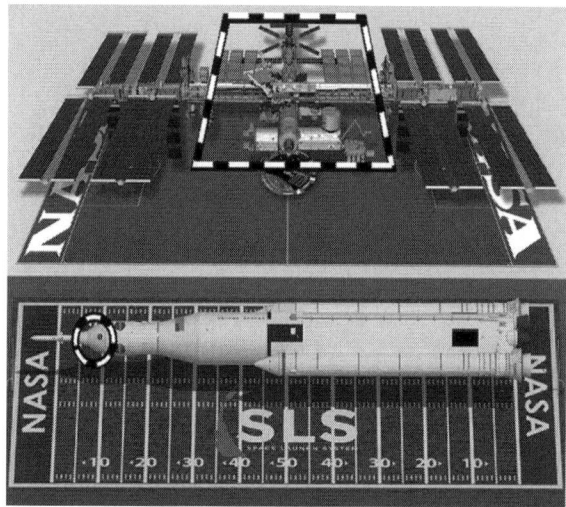

FIGURE 8.5 Relative sizes of the habitable volumes of the ISS and the Orion crew capsule marked with a dashed line. A trip to Mars will include a habitat module, which will more than double the total habitable volume, yet still leave the spacecraft far smaller than the ISS. (Reference: nasa.gov)

"It is going to be a much, much, much different crew experience when you don't have a spaceship sufficiently large to ever get away from each other during the day" (Stuster, 2016, p. 15). The smaller vehicle size (Figure 8.5) is only one of many obstacles to be addressed prior to beginning a mission to Mars.

OpPsy Support is concerned with providing services that will be as effective as the ones they currently provide. A significant change will be a lack of resupply vehicles. This not only affects inventory, stowage, and personal items a crewmember will be able to bring and receive, but also means there will be not visiting crewmembers to relieve the social monotony. No resupply vehicles mean no surprise crew care packages, a morale booster. All special items meant to mark special occasions will need to be on the spacecraft at launch. There will be no fresh foods except that which crews can grow themselves. A significantly smaller vehicle will also limit available options for leisure activities. The favorite leisure activity of looking at and photographing Earth will transform into watching their home fading into nothingness. We do not yet know the impact losing sight of Earth will have on crewmember well-being. With no resupply vehicles and with the communication delays that will occur as the crew moves away from Earth, crewmembers' world will increasingly narrow down to what and who is on their spacecraft. As the distance from Earth increases, so will the lag between sending and receiving communication. This will prevent real-time interactions including calls, emails, and videos to Earth. Staying connected to family, friends, and colleagues will become more difficult and could negatively impact a crewmember's family structure. Challenges due to the delay in communication cannot be addressed in PPCs as they too will be impacted.

Conclusion

Operational Psychological Support and Family Support Office both provide services critical to maintaining the psychological health of astronauts and their families. The FSO supports astronauts and families throughout the astronaut's tenure, while OpPsy targets assigned astronauts and their families. The countermeasures provided by OpPsy and the FSO have been proven to be effective for low Earth orbit 6–12 months missions. There is much we still need to learn about the impact a mission to Mars will have on astronauts and families. We are working with psychological researchers at NASA, universities, and other space agencies to study methods for ensuring crews and families continue to thrive in deep space.

REFERENCES

Anderson, C. C. (2015). *The ordinary spaceman: From boyhood dreams to astronaut.* Lincoln, NE: University of Nebraska Press.

Associated Press. (2000, December 9). Endeavour's astronauts go aboard space station. *New haven register.* Retrieved from https://www.nhregister.com/news/article/Endeavour-s-astronauts-go-aboard-space-station-11716476.php

Beven, G. (2012). *NASA's behavioral health support for International Space Station (ISS) missions.* Presentation to the cleveland clinic Department of Psychiatry and Psychology Grand Rounds, September 13, 2012. https://ntrs.nasa.gov/archive/nasa/casi.ntrs.nasa.gov/20120014571.pdf

Blaydes, L., & Paik, C. (2016). The impact of Holy Land Crusades on state formation: war mobilization, trade integration, and political development in medieval Europe. *International Organization, 70*(3), 551–586.

Cederbaum, J. A., Gilreath, T. D., Benbenishty, R., Astor, R. A., Pineda, D., DePedro, K. T., … Atuel, H. (2014). Well-being and suicidal ideation of secondary school students from military families. *Journal of Adolescent Health, 54*(6), 672–677.

Chandra, A., Lara-Cinisomo, S., Jaycox, L. H., Tanielian, T., Han, B., Burns, R. M., & Ruder, T. (2011). Views from the homefront: The experiences of youth and spouses from military families. *Rand Health Quarterly, 1*(1) 12. Retrieved from https://www.ncbi.nlm.nih.gov/pmc/articles/PMC4945219/

Chandra, A., Martin, L. T., Hawkins, S. A., & Richardson, A. (2010). The impact of parental deployment on child social and emotional functioning: Perspectives of school staff. *Journal of Adolescent Health, 46*(3), 218–223.

Chartrand, M. M., Frank, D. A., White, L. F., & Shope, T. R. (2008). Effect of parents' wartime deployment on the behavior of young children in military families. *Archives of Pediatrics & Adolescent Medicine, 162*(11), 1009–1014.

Clay, R. A. (2017). The link between food and mental health. *APA Monitor on Psychology, 48*(8), 26.

CNN. (2003, February 11). *Transcript: Eyes on space.* Retrieved from http://transcripts.cnn.com/TRANSCRIPTS/0302/11/se.02.html

Culbertson, F. L. (2011). *Letter from September 1, 2001.* Retrieved from https://www.nasa.gov/topics/nasalife/features/sept11_culbertson.html

Curtis, K., Beven, G., Holland, A., Sipes, W., & Vander Ark, S. (2014, May 13). *Astronaut family support office.* Symposium presented at the 85th Annual Scientific Meeting of the Aerospace Medicine Association, San Diego, CA.

DeRoshia, C. W., Colletti, L. C., & Mallis, M. M. (2008). *The effects of the Mars Exploration Rovers (MER) work schedule regime on locomotor activity circadian rhythms, sleep and fatigue* (NASA/TM-2008-214560). Moffett Field, CA: NASA, Ames.

Dinges, D. F., Basner, M., Mollicone, D. J., Jones, C. W., Ecker, A. J., & Bartels, R. (2014, February). Effects of time in mission: ISS astronaut's ratings of stress. Presented at the NASA Human Research Program Investigators' Workshop (HRP 2014), Galveston, TX.

Eaton, K. M., Hoge, C. W., Messer, S. C., Whitt, A. A., Cabrera, O. A., McGurk, D., ... Castro, C. A. (2008). Prevalence of mental health problems, treatment need, and barriers to care among primary care-seeking spouses of military service members involved in Iraq and Afghanistan deployments. *Military Medicine, 173*(11), 1051–1056.

Eschner, K. (2017, February 8). Mutiny in space: Why these Skylab astronauts never flew again. *Smithsonian*. Retrieved from https://www.smithsonianmag.com/smart-news/mutiny-space-why-these-skylab-astronauts-never-flew-again-180962023/

Flake, E. M., Davis, B. E., Johnson, P. L., & Middleton, L. S. (2009). The psychosocial effects of deployment on military children. *Journal of Developmental & Behavioral Pediatrics, 30*(4), 271–278.

Flynn, C. (2005). An operational approach to long-duration behavioral health and performance factors. *Aviation, Space, and Environmental Medicine, 76*(6), Section II, B42–B51.

Giffords, G., Kelly, M., & Zaslow, J. (2011). *Gabby: A story of courage and hope*. New York, NY: Scribner.

Goemaere, S., Van Caelenberg, T., Beyers, W., Binsted, K., & Vansteenkiste, M. (2019). Life on Mars from a Self-Determination Theory perspective: How astronauts' needs for autonomy, competence and relatedness go hand in hand with crew health and mission success-Results from HI-SEAS IV. *Acta Astronautica, 159*, 273–285.

Harrison, A. A., & Fiedler, E. R. (2013). Behavioral health. In D. A. Vakoch (Ed.), *On orbit and beyond* (pp. 3–24). Berlin: Springer.

Johnson, P. J. (2010). The roles of NASA, US astronauts and their families in long-duration missions. *Acta Astronautica, 67*(5–6), 561–571.

Kanas, N. (1990). Psychological, psychiatric, and interpersonal aspects of long-duration space missions. *Journal of Spacecraft and Rockets, 27*(5), 457–463.

Kniffin, K. M., Wansink, B., Devine, C. M., & Sobal, J. (2015). Eating together at the firehouse: How workplace commensality relates to the performance of firefighters. *Human Performance, 28*(4), 281–306.

Lester, P., Peterson, K., Reeves, J., Knauss, L., Glover, D., Mogil, C., ... Beardslee, W. (2010). The long war and parental combat deployment: Effects on military children and at-home spouses. *Journal of the American Academy of Child & Adolescent Psychiatry, 49*(4), 310–320.

Linenger, J. M. (2000). *Off the planet: Surviving five perilous months aboard the space station Mir*. New York, NY: McGraw-Hill.

MacDermid Wadsworth, S. M. (2010). Family risk and resilience in the context of war and terrorism. *Journal of Marriage and Family, 72*(3), 537–556.

Mansfield, A. J., Kaufman, J. S., Marshall, S. W., Gaynes, B. N., Morrissey, J. P., & Engel, C. C. (2010). Deployment and the use of mental health services among US Army wives. *New England Journal of Medicine, 362*(2), 101–109.

Meadows, S. O., Beckett, M. K., Bowling, K., Golinelli, D., Fisher, M. P., Martin, L. T., ... Osilla, K. C. (2016). Family resilience in the military: Definitions, models, and policies. *RAND Health Quarterly, 5*(3).

Morgan, C. (2001). *Shuttle-Mir: The United States and Russia share history's highest stage* (NASA SP-2001-4225). Retrieved from https://history.nasa.gov/SP-4225/toc/toc-level1.htm

NASA. (2003, February 11). *Accident response briefing*. Retrieved from https://www.nasa.gov/columbia/media/021103_iss_brief.html

NASA. (2011). *NASA sets launch date for final space shuttle mission*. Houston, TX. Retrieved from https://www.nasa.gov/home/hqnews/2011/jun/HQ_11-193_Launch_Date.html

NASA. (2017a). *Expedition 1 status reports*. Houston, TX. Retrieved from https://www.nasa.gov/mission_pages/station/expeditions/expedition01/statusreports.html

NASA. (2017b, July 21). Friends in high places. *RoundUp* (Image Credit: NASA/Robert Markowitz). Retrieved from https://roundupreads.jsc.nasa.gov/mobi.aspx?pageid=678

NPR. (2003, February 22). *A chat with the space station crew: Astronauts share thoughts on Columbia tragedy*. Retrieved from https://www.npr.org/templates/story/story.php?storyId=1171198

Palinkas, L. A. (2007). Psychosocial issues in long-term space flight: overview. *Gravitational and Space Research*, 14(2), 25–33.

Palmer, C. (2008). A theory of risk and resilience factors in military families. *Military Psychology, 20*(3), 205–217.

Sirmons, T., Douglas, G., Schneiderman, J., Slack, K., Whitmire, A., Williams, T., & Young, M. (2018, January 22–25). *Meal replacement mass reduction integration and acceptability study*. Presented at the Human Research Program Investigator's Workshop (HRP IWS), Galveston, TX.

Spector, P. E. (1986). Perceived control by employees: A meta-analysis of studies concerning autonomy and participation at work. *Human Relations, 39*(11), 1005–1016.

Stenger, R. (2003, February 12). *Space station skipper on loss: 'I was numb'*. Retrieved from http://www.cnn.com/2003/TECH/space/02/11/sprj.colu.station.interview/index.html

Stuster, J. (2010). *Behavioral issues associated with long-duration space expeditions: Review and analysis of Astronaut Journals Experiment 01-E104 (Journals): Final report* (NASA/TM-2010-216130). Houston, TX: NASA—JSC.

Stuster, J. (2016). *Behavioral issues associated with long duration space expeditions: Review and analysis of astronaut journals experiment: Phase 2 final report* (NASA/TM-2016–218603). Houston, TX: NASA—JSC.

Tajfel, H. (1970). Experiments in intergroup discrimination. *Scientific American, 223*, 96–102.

Whitmire, A., Slack, K. J., Locke, J., Keeton, K. E., Patterson, H., Faulk, J., & Leveton, L. (2013). *Sleep quality questionnaire: Short-duration flyers* (NASA/TM-2013-217378). Houston, TX: NASA.

Vanhove, A. J., Herian, M. N., Harms, P. D., & Luthans, F. (2014). Resilience and Growth in Long-duration Isolated, Confined and Extreme (ICE) Missions: A Literature Review and Selection, Training and Countermeasure Recommendations (White paper). Prepared for NASA-Johnson Space Center. Houston, TX: Behavioral Health and Performance.

Wiens, T. W., & Boss, P. (2006). Maintaining family resiliency before, during, and after military separation. In C. A. Castro, A. B. Adler, & T. W. Britt (Eds.), *The Military Life. Military life: The psychology of serving in peace and combat: The military family* (pp. 13–38). Westport, CT: Praeger Security International.

9 Extremely Stressed and Extremely Bored
Team Self-Maintenance in Long-Duration Space Exploration

Deborah DiazGranados
Virginia Commonwealth University

Jessica L. Wildman
Florida Institute of Technology

Michael T. Curtis
Bonsai Institute, LLC

CONTENTS

LDSE and the Need for Self-Maintenance 157
Defining Team Self-Maintenance: What It Is, and What It Is Not......................... 158
    Self-Maintenance versus Resilience 159
    Self-Maintenance versus Adaptation.. 160
Previous Research on Self-Maintenance.. 161
Best Practices for Self-Maintenance in LDSE... 162
    Best Practices to Combat Boredom... 162
    Best Practices to Combat Interpersonal Conflicts.. 166
    Best Practices to Encourage Psychological Well-Being 168
Other Key Considerations for LDSE 171
Conclusion 173
Acknowledgements.. 173
References.. 173

> Things can go badly if the psychosocial elements aren't managed properly. When you talk about longer and longer missions with a small crew it becomes really critical to have that social aspect right.
>
> **Scott Kelly**
> *(Stirone, 2016)*

As exciting as it is, traveling to Mars has some level of monotony. There is no shortage of research that discusses the imminent danger lurking behind every systems failure, lost connection to Earth, and exciting extravehicular activity (EVA) excursions that comprise a mission to Mars. It is easy to understand the need for fielding a crew that is capable of performing at the highest level in these moments of extreme life or death risk. What is often buried in the discussion about a long trip into space is that between the bursts of high workload and danger, there will be a crew who is going to withstand stretches of mundanity. Automated systems of the spacecraft will relieve crew workload by navigating to and from the Earth's surface, day-to-day activities will begin to feel monotonous after weeks and months of repeating them, and the crew will find themselves anticipating any event that may break up their day-to-day activities. The simple fact is that long-duration space exploration (LDSE) crews will spend a sizable portion of their mission living, sleeping, exercising, and interacting with each other every moment of every day, celebrating milestones such as birthdays or anniversaries far from family and loved ones, and even addressing conflict that arises from work or leisure time. If left unaccounted for, these mundane parts of LDSE are likely to have a slow, acutely imperceptible effect on the spaceflight crew's well-being and performance.

The conditions surrounding LDSE are extreme, and to understand the psychosocial stressors that these extreme conditions can impose upon the crew, an empirical stream of research is needed. This research requires using artificial analogs created specifically to replicate and test flight conditions, or looking to research done in other similar extreme work environments. For example, research conducted on teams who function in the extreme cold of Antarctica and the silent isolation of a nuclear submarine has identified the external support systems that crews rely on to function (Palinkas, 1992; Suedfeld, 2001). The farther expeditionary teams get away from Earth, the more heavily those teams will have to rely upon themselves. In effect, once the "long-duration" part of LDSE sets in, teams will be forced to maintain from within. We label this phenomenon *team self-maintenance*, and define it as the constantly evolving process of monitoring, adjusting, and maintaining the psychological well-being and overall performance of a team in the absence of external support (DiazGranados, Curtis, & Wildman, 2016). It should be noted that because teams are comprised of individuals, and individuals are nested in the team context, this chapter is broadly concerned with self-maintenance at both levels, as they will relate to one another.

In order to systematically explore the concept of self-maintenance within LDSE contexts, we conducted an operational assessment in which we interviewed nine subject matter experts (e.g., astronaut, flight director, payload communicator or PayComm, crew support psychologist, analog research director, crewmember, mission operations planner) between April and July 2015 in order to determine the particular challenges that the crew faces during spaceflight and how these challenges relate to self-maintenance. All interviews were conducted via teleconference in conjunction with another research team, whose research question focused on resilience and adaptation. Interviews were 60 minutes long and followed a semi-structured protocol designed to foster discussion about the meaning of team self-maintenance, team self-maintenance issues experienced or observed as members of mission teams, and the extent to which countermeasures and training could resolve issues pertaining to team self-maintenance. This chapter provides an examination of the pressures of LDSE as well as proposed solutions. First, we outline the key issues that were highlighted as a result of our operational assessment that are expected to make team self-maintenance both challenging and important within the context of long-duration spaceflight. Second, we provide ten best practices for ensuring effective self-maintenance of individual crewmembers and the team as a whole.

LDSE AND THE NEED FOR SELF-MAINTENANCE

Given that other chapters in this volume provide an in-depth analysis of the challenges inherent in spaceflight contexts, we will not repeat that discussion. We will, however, highlight how our operational assessment uncovered particular aspects of long-duration spaceflight that are likely to create particularly challenging situations in terms of (1) boredom, (2) interpersonal issues, and (3) psychological well-being, and why we believe the process of self-maintenance will be so critical to overcoming these challenges.

One huge contextual factor inherent in LDSE that will make self-maintenance critical is the lengthy communication delays that will be experienced once the vehicle is far enough away from Earth. Current International Space Station (ISS) and other near-earth missions have had the benefit of near real-time communication with ground control, crewmember families, and the rest of the world. This includes voice, video, and internet connection. For more distant missions, the communication link to Earth will not be real-time (i.e., 3–20 minutes delay depending on orbit positions), and at times, crews may encounter completely "dark" periods with no communication for days or weeks at a time. This means that there will be times when external, real-time support cannot be provided to the team, making self-maintenance the only available alternative.

A related issue is what is known as "Earth-out-of-view" phenomenon (Manzey, 2004). Earth photography is one of the most enjoyed and meaningful parts of the job, and simply looking at the Earth, and identifying it as home, is a major sensory stimulator for crewmembers. Long-duration spaceflight will present the crew with unprecedented experiences in terms of social isolation and disconnection from Earth. For ISS crewmembers, a look out the window provides an often awe-inspiring vantage of our home planet – from Mars or other deep-space destinations, the earth will appear as little more than a distant spot of light in the Martian sky. As the crew approaches Mars, it will come into view and might be spectacular visually, but the view will not have a connection to our home Earth. Many experts believe that this phenomenon is likely to create an increased sense of isolation that has literally never been experienced by anyone alive today – and the repercussions will not be known until the first mission is launched. Depression, anxiety, fatigue, cognitive impairment, interpersonal conflict, and individual and team performance decline (Collins, 2003; Palinkas, 2007) are all risks inherent to ICE contexts that are likely to only be exacerbated under these yet-experienced extremes. In other words, the need to actively monitor and self-manage well-being will be essential in these contexts.

Confinement has always been an issue for spaceflight. Although the ISS is designed with a "roomy" 64.6 m^3 per person, the physical limitations of getting a crew to a distant location in deep space and back safely necessitate a much smaller 14.8 m^3 of space for surface habitats and 1.5 m^3 per person in the Orion transport module. For a Mars mission, which equates to six crewmembers sharing a space for roughly 12 months in the Orion module in transit to and from Mars and another 18 months in the slightly larger surface habitat, it is important to note that NASA is currently working through options to expand the space provided to the crewmembers. Current analog habitats on Earth have replicated similar confinement issues; however, there are still many unknowns associated with confinement without a safety net (i.e., knowledge of being in an analog environment and not in actual deep space). It is expected, however, that this confinement will increase the likelihood of interpersonal conflicts simply due to the forced proximity of the crewmembers to one another. Culturally diverse teams embarking on LDSE must not only work together as a team to complete task/mission-related goals, they must also live together and co-exist in all aspects of daily life.

The impact of sensory deprivation (e.g., exposure to nature, variation of food, lights, and sounds, and interaction with family members) on the well-being of crewmembers has received attention by researchers working with NASA (see Vessel & Russo, 2015). Scientific evidence shows that while spaceflight can be exhilarating, the sensory restriction in the setting impacts mood not only positively but also negatively. Suedfeld and Steel (2000) identified a negative impact on psychological well-being from the sensory restriction experienced in LDSE analogs. Vessel and Russo (2015) suggest countermeasures such as ensuring engagement in meaningful work, mindfulness practices, crew celebrations, and the use of music as countermeasures to the effects of sensory deprivation.

Finally, our operational assessment suggested that automation will be an unexpected challenge to the psychological well-being of the crew. The importance of LDSE missions means that the vast majority of systems onboard will be automated and backed up, at least ideally – as long as nothing goes wrong, the systems will require very little interaction from the crewmembers. This is obviously a good thing, and the safety of the crew is of paramount importance. However, high levels of automation mean that the crew will need other meaningful work to keep themselves engaged. In sum, the extreme context of LSDE is likely to exacerbate feelings of boredom and interpersonal frustration that could cause significant decrements in spaceflight crew performance and health, if not managed effectively.

DEFINING TEAM SELF-MAINTENANCE: WHAT IT IS, AND WHAT IT IS NOT

Based on an in-depth analysis of the literature and the operational assessment previously described, DiazGranados et al. (2016) put forth a framework for team self-maintenance built around several key mediating processes: information sharing, shared leadership, self-regulation, recovery, and emotional support. One of the main points of the framework is that effective self-maintenance requires that processes be managed within the team rather than externally. On one hand, this empowers the

TABLE 9.1

Defining and Distinguishing Self-Maintenance from Similar Constructs

	Ability	Focus on Process	Focus on Performance	Focus on Well-Being	Requires Trigger/Cue (e.g., Adversity)
Team Self-Maintenance: The process of monitoring, adjusting, and maintaining well-being and performance in the absence of external guidance		✓	✓	✓	
Team Resilience: The team's emergent ability to respond to adversity, absorb the stress that results from adversity, as well as recover to a normal level of functioning and learn from the challenge to emerge stronger than before	✓		✓		✓
Team Adaptation: The response to a salient trigger/cue that results in a positive outcome	✓	✓			✓

team – emphasizing the importance of developing trust and cohesion. On the other hand, it requires the team to address conflict and stress with minimal external intervention. Again, we define team self-maintenance as a process in which individuals and the team as a whole *monitor, adjust, and maintain* well-being and performance when there is no guidance from external resources. Understanding the process and the construct of team self-maintenance requires a discussion of how it is distinct from other constructs that may overlap with the meaning of self-maintenance. While literature from the research streams discussed below informed our understanding of self-maintenance, we highlight the differences between self-maintenance, resilience, and adaptation (see Table 9.1).

SELF-MAINTENANCE VERSUS RESILIENCE

Resilience has been defined as the ability to respond to adversity, absorb the stress that results from adversity, as well as recover to a normal level of functioning and learn from the challenge to emerge stronger than before (Sutcliffe & Vogus, 2003; Stephens, Heaphy, Carmeli, Spreitzer, & Dutton, 2013). Maynard and Kennedy (2016) clarify the construct of team resilience, in particular, within the context of space crews by detailing that team resilience is an emergent state (i.e., a property of a team that is dynamic and varies as a function of team context, inputs, processes, and outcomes; Marks, Mathieu, & Zaccaro, 2001).

The distinction between self-maintenance and resilience is focused on the fact that resilience is defined as a dynamic emergent state (Maynard & Kennedy, 2016) whereas we define self-maintenance as an unfolding behavioral process. However, also relevant to the distinction between these two constructs is that resilience is a product of the interaction between team members who have specifically faced some definable challenge, adversity, or difficult situation. We suggest that the process of self-maintenance is independent of the existence of a definable challenge or adversity. In other words, resilience is an ability that is developed in reaction to definable adverse events, whereas self-maintenance is a behavioral process that can be deliberately enacted at any time throughout a mission, regardless of whether or not a trigger event has occurred. It is likely that the process of self-maintenance and the emergency of resilience are related in a mutual feedback loop, with prior resilience acting to improve the team self-maintenance process, and engaging in self-maintenance helping the team to build and develop their resilience over time, but we posit they are separate constructs.

Self-Maintenance versus Adaptation

Space crews and ground control teams working on LDSE missions will be functioning in a context that is highly dynamic, and they are likely to experience frequent changes and interruptions in routines. These changes may be expected (e.g., the change in communication lag between space crew and mission control) and some changes may be unexpected (e.g., what will space crews encounter when they reach Mars). Regardless, change is a reality and an expectation that LDSE crews should prepare for. One of the many benefits that may result from organizing work in teams is how teams respond to situations where change is inevitable. Because teams have a broader capacity from which to draw resources (Zaccaro & Bader, 2003), as compared to a single individual, it is believed that teams are better able to respond, or adapt, to changes such as those that may be experienced in LDSE. Adaptation is defined as the response to a salient trigger/cue that results in a positive outcome for the entire team (Burke, Stagl, Salas, Pierce, & Kendall, 2006). Burke and colleagues highlight that team adaptation is manifested as an outcome via "the innovation of new or modification of existing structures, capacities, and/or behavioral or cognitive goal-directed actions" (p. 1190).

There are some similarities between adaptation and self-maintenance; however, there are also important distinctions between these constructs. One distinction is that team adaptation results from a *salient* trigger or cue. Teams who will be co-working and co-habiting on LDSE missions may not experience salient triggers and as previously stated, it is at times where work is monotonous and mundane that teams will need to engage in the process of team self-maintenance in order to maintain their skills and reduce the possibility of experiencing team skill decay (DiazGranados, Lazzara, Lyons, Wooten, & Salas, 2013). A second distinction is that team adaptation is focused on the outcomes of the team in terms of work products and outcomes, whereas self-maintenance is focused not only on team performance but also on the well-being of the team. In other words, self-maintenance is expected to contribute to the well-being and available resources within the spaceflight team, and therefore it will likely contribute to the ability to effectively adapt in response to salient trigger events, but self-maintenance and adaptation are still distinct constructs.

PREVIOUS RESEARCH ON SELF-MAINTENANCE

One of the primary areas of research that is directly relevant to the concept of self-maintenance is the study of autonomous teams – teams without any external management. Autonomous teams have the freedom to manage tasks, schedules, and roles within the team. Autonomy is not a new concept to workplace research. In fact, there is an extensive body of research that extols the virtues of adopting autonomy in a wide range of work environments, with individual and team outcomes of higher job satisfaction, commitment, trust, and better mental health (Kemp, Wall, Clegg, & Cordery, 1983). With autonomous teams, the onus of team effectiveness hinges on how well individuals coordinate, communicate, and execute tasks *within* the team. In autonomous teams, factors like verbal and nonverbal communication, accountability, shared knowledge, role assignment, and clear goal definitions influence individual performance (Eccles & Tenenbaum, 2004).

For LDSE, additional factors like the level of autonomy in the team and culture could impact team cohesiveness. Langfred (2000) found that autonomy enhances team effectiveness when task interdependence is high, but that high individual autonomy resulted in less cohesive teams. Conversely, individual autonomy and individual task demands were found to have a mediating effect on team autonomy in relation to emotional exhaustion and active learning (Mierlo, Rutte, Vermunt, Kompier, & Doorewaard, 2007). Taken together, these findings suggest a complex balance between team cohesiveness and individual well-being in autonomous teams.

Team self-managing (autonomous) behaviors have been found to have a positive relationship with team performance, viability, and team process improvement (Rousseau & Aube, 2010). Task routineness moderates the effect between self-managing behavior and team performance such that performance on ambiguous, complex, or new tasks improves with self-managing behavior. In LDSE, it is fair to assume that there will not only be a number of complex tasks to perform, but also a number of day-to-day maintenance tasks that quickly become routine. For these tasks, astronauts may become bored performing the same tasks repeatedly. In these instances, engaging in task-switching can alleviate negative effects on job satisfaction or low task identity, as long as the task is not hazardous or expertise-specific (Blumberg, 1980).

One of the most critical issues inherent in self-maintenance is the necessity for the team to be self-sufficient in terms of all necessary support functions, including leadership functions. There has always been a strong emphasis on leadership within spaceflight crews, but traditionally, that leadership has often resided within one particular individual crewmember, such as the flight commander. However, within the LDSE context, because there will be reduced opportunity for real-time support provided by ground control, the overall demands on the team will likely increase, including leadership demands. Thus, shared leadership will be essential, and it has been recognized as crucial for space flight. This increase in workload, and variation in how "connected" they are with mission control, may require that the team distribute and share leadership responsibilities. Understanding the antecedents, outcomes, and mediating mechanisms (i.e., the how) relating to shared leadership will be critical to the effective team self-maintenance of LDSE spaceflight crews.

Fortunately, there has been a recent explosion of research examining the concept of shared leadership in teams. In fact, enough research on shared leadership had accumulated to result in three meta-analytic summaries of the topic (D'Innocenzo, Mathieu, & Kukenberger, 2014; Nicolaides et al., 2014; Wang, Waldman, & Zhang, 2014). One clear finding that emerged from all three meta-analyses is that there is a positive relationship between the extent to which teams share leadership and team performance, and that shared leadership explains variance in performance above and beyond traditional vertical leadership. Teams with high levels of shared leadership are associated with higher levels of trust, which then results in crewmembers behaving in a way that benefits the crew – thus engaging in processes within the team that promote team self-maintenance.

BEST PRACTICES FOR SELF-MAINTENANCE IN LDSE

Because very little research has directly addressed the topic of self-maintenance in teams, especially teams in extreme environments such as LDSE, much of what we highlight as best practice is integrated from other related disciplines and areas of study, with the focus driven by the results of our operational assessment. In the following sections, we provide several recommendations regarding how to develop, encourage, and support effective self-maintenance of spaceflight crews during long-duration space exploration. In general, these recommendations correspond to the key challenges identified through the operational assessment: (1) combating boredom, (2) combating interpersonal issues, and (3) encouraging overall psychological well-being. Finally, we also outline (4) other key considerations in terms of how to enact these best practices.

BEST PRACTICES TO COMBAT BOREDOM

One of the key contextual features of long-duration spaceflight that poses a significant challenge to the performance and well-being of the crew is the high likelihood of experiencing stretches of monotony and isolation that can lead to feelings of boredom. As one of the SMEs interviewed in our operational assessment stated, "…the majority of the flight will be automated, which reduces task load for the teams, but that leaves nothing for them to do. And that's the worst thing that could happen." Key aspects of spaceflight missions that create a sense of boredom and frustration include repetitive and tedious task work, the repetitive nature of daily scheduling, and the bland and repetitive nature of meals. While boredom seems like a relatively benign concept at first glance, it is a form of stress that can have a negative impact on psychological health and overall crew performance. Therefore, the following best practices aim to improve crew performance in the face of boredom.

Best Practice 1: Select on Psychological Competencies That Support Self-Regulation, Not Just Technical Competencies

Members of a spaceflight crew will be responsible for a number of complex and critical technical and scientific activities during any long-duration spaceflight mission, and therefore it is of course critical to make sure that each individual selected is highly qualified in their particular area of technical expertise. However, selecting on technical proficiency alone will not be sufficient for optimal crew performance. In order to ensure that crewmembers fare well during missions that will include periods of routine maintenance, monotony, and boredom, members should also be assessed and selected based on competencies that will increase their ability to self-regulate their well-being in these conditions. For example, Prakash, Hussain, and Schirda (2015) found that individuals with a predisposition for mindfulness experience less stress. Furthermore, recent research suggests that boredom proneness and dispositional mindfulness are inversely related, and that mindfulness may mitigate the negative effects between boredom proneness and negative outcomes such as depression and anxiety (Lee, 2018). Therefore, assessing and selecting highly mindful individuals may help to buffer against the negative effects of boredom.

Relatedly, several SMEs interviewed during our operational assessment of challenges in spaceflight suggested that loners and introverts do better during spaceflight because they do not require much social interaction to maintain their well-being, which has been suggested by previous research (Francis, 1969). This particular competency presents a bit of a paradox, however: as will be discussed in a later section, the ideal candidates for spaceflight will need to be interpersonally skilled and able to handle spending a long-duration in close proximity of their teammates, but also need to be introverted enough to not mind feelings of social isolation. In other words, ideal spaceflight candidates may display a combination of personality traits (e.g., introversion, interpersonal skill) that are not commonly found together; individuals may be what are called ambiverts (i.e., a balance of extrovert and introvert features), a person who falls in the middle of the introversion/extraversion continuum but also demonstrates effective emotion regulation ability. Moreover, Vessel and Russo (2015) recommend the need to consider other individual difference variables such as coping strategy.

Best Practice 2: Develop Realistic Expectations of Spaceflight That Highlight the Likelihood of Boredom

A recurring theme emerging from interviews with spaceflight experts was that astronauts' expectations often are not aligned with the realities of spaceflight. Because individual crewmembers are generally selected to be highly skilled and achievement-oriented, they often experience more disappointment when research or other activities do not succeed as intended. Informally, a countermeasure currently in place for NASA spaceflight crews is to share lessons learned from past spaceflight experiences with trainees. One expert suggested that sharing small things like how there is a zipper at the bottom of the sleeping bag for cooling can help adjust expectations for the challenges of living in space. Another emphasized the importance of debunking the myths about what an astronaut does in space for new and in-training crews. It is important to note, that currently, NASA provides a series of behavioral health and performance trainings, which include stress management training, conflict management, cross-cultural, and team skills. This training is created with an operations psychologist and crewmember, such that the crewmember facilitates and shares stories providing trainees with a realistic job preview of the issues they may encounter. These training sessions are provided during ASCAN (astronaut candidate) training and reinforced throughout their career (Barrett, 2016).

Accordingly, we suggest that future spaceflight crews need to be provided with realistic job previews of spaceflight that ensure that expectations include not only the possibility of life-and-death high-stress situations, but also stretches of repetitiveness, unappealing routine maintenance tasks, and social isolation leading to boredom. One way to do this could be to have individuals with previous spaceflight experience describe their own struggles with repetitiveness and boredom. This could be done through live discussions, allowing for a more interactive question-and-answer dynamic, or through pre-recorded video or audio. Additionally, exposing crewmembers to simulated periods of monotony, boredom, and isolation before actually engaging in a long-duration spaceflight mission may be of use.

Best Practice 3: Train Spaceflight Crew to Recognize Well-Being and Performance Decrements Due to Boredom

One issue that was discussed in our operational assessment was the tendency for crewmembers to hide any negative feelings or issues they experience from their fellow crewmembers for fear that it might impact their likelihood of participating in future missions if they are seen as less than ideal. Furthermore, Rapp, Bachrach, Rapp, and Mullins (2014) examined performance monitoring in teams, arguing that too much efficacy (i.e., confidence in the team's ability to complete a task) can lead to overconfidence and complacency, and therefore regular performance monitoring is necessary to avoid this risk. In other words, it may be difficult to recognize when spaceflight crewmembers are suffering from well-being or performance decrements caused by the stresses of monotony and boredom, as highly skilled astronauts may be overconfident in their abilities to manage this stress while also having a tendency to hide any negative feelings that are being experienced.

Therefore, in future long-duration spaceflight missions, it will be important that crewmembers are trained to recognize and openly discuss decrements in crew functioning in response to periods of boredom and monotony. We recommend having spaceflight crewmembers discuss ahead of time how they plan to address boredom and how they plan to respond when they may experience boredom during their mission. Addressing the issue of boredom as a team would help for all members to understand how compatible they are in terms of their responses to boredom. Moreover, individuals should be encouraged to discuss any feelings of boredom experienced so that they understand that it is a natural reaction to the mission and not indicative of their commitment to the mission.

Best Practice 4: Train Spaceflight Crew in Boredom Management Techniques

The spaceflight crew team is one of several component teams involved with the execution of successful LDSE missions. A unique challenge that the spaceflight crew will endure is a changing presence of any external resources (e.g., mission control, psychologists, psychiatrists, etc.) that may provide support to the team because of the varied levels of connectivity the crew will experience. For current missions, it is typical for crewmembers to have weekly conferences with a psychologist or psychiatrist to discuss issues such as sleep, fatigue, crew dysfunction, family issues, mood, and interaction with the ground. A recurring theme from the operational assessments was that the external resources available to the space team were helpful in managing the stress they experienced during their missions. In the long-duration spaceflight context, however, the lack of real time connectivity with ground and the extreme duration of the mission will both make this approach less feasible and less effective. In other words, in order for LDSE crews to self-maintain their psychological well-being, it will be necessary for this support to be found within the spaceflight crew itself rather than via an external source. Given the need for the team to self-manage in long-duration spaceflight contexts, future spaceflight crews should be provided with training on boredom management techniques that they can use independently.

Physiologically, boredom manifests similarly to stress (Merrifield & Danckert, 2014), and therefore one type of training that may be useful for more effectively managing boredom is mindfulness training. There is a growing evidence base that links mindfulness training to reduced stress when treating medical conditions (e.g., chronic pains, substance abuse, depression, anxiety disorders; Astin, 1997; Kabat-Zinn, 1990; Kabat-Zinn, Lipworth, & Burney, 1985; Kabat-Zinn et al., 1992; Kristeller & Hallett, 1999; Marlatt & Kristeller, 1999; Speca, Carlson, Goodey, & Angen, 2000; Teasdale et al., 2000). Enhanced mindfulness generally has also been linked to increased interpersonal competence, situational awareness, adaptability, and performance (Glomb, Duffy, Bono, & Yang, 2011) and to increased ability to cope with and recover from stress in extreme environments (Jha, Stanley, Kiyonaga, Wong, & Gelfand, 2010). We posit that using established mindfulness training techniques will likely improve the crewmembers' ability to effectively cope with boredom.

Finally, research has also examined emotion regulation techniques, which may be of use in managing the negative emotions associated with experiencing boredom. The field of emotion regulation research is still rife with ambiguity, and "there exists no consensual and empirically validated taxonomy of emotion-regulation strategies" (Koole, 2009, p. 29). However, emotion regulation techniques can generally be categorized into three groups based on the target of the emotion regulation: attention (e.g., turning attention away from negative information), cognitive emotion-relevant knowledge (e.g., cognitive reappraisal), and bodily manifestations of emotion (e.g., progressive muscle relaxation). In general, cognitive strategies tend to be more effective than bodily strategies, but specific approaches have been found to provide benefits under different circumstances. For example, cognitive reappraisal, or changing the subjective evaluation of an event, can reduce the negative emotional impact of a particular emotional event. Another technique that has demonstrated benefits more broadly is progressive muscle relaxation, in which individuals successively tense and relax their muscle groups in different parts of the body. This technique has been shown to reduce heart rate, salivary cortisol, and stress-related disease (Koole, 2009), and may be a promising approach for reducing both the short-term and long-term negative outcomes of emotions in long-duration spaceflight. The science of emotion regulation should be used as a basis for providing spaceflight crews with training and support surrounding effective emotion regulation strategies.

Best Practice 5: Provide Spaceflight Crew with Technology-Based Boredom Management Support Systems

Despite boredom being a state that most people understand implicitly, research on it has only recently picked up momentum (e.g., Cummings, Gao, & Thornburg, 2016), and there is still notable controversy surrounding its definition and measurement. One recent study set out to more clearly identify the set of psychophysiological signals that make up the "signature" of boredom (Merrifield & Danckert, 2014). It was found that boredom was characterized by a rising heart rate, decreased skin conductance levels, and increased cortisol levels, as compared to experiencing a state of sadness. Furthermore, it was found that boredom may lead to difficulties with sustained attention (Hunter & Eastwood, 2018), further emphasizing the dangers of boredom for long-duration space exploration.

Spaceflight crews should be provided with technology-based boredom management support systems that are synced with physiological and psychological measurement tools such that these support systems are automatically triggered when crewmembers experience the psychophysiological signature associated with boredom. For example, crewmembers could be provided with wearable physiological monitors that track heart rate, blood pressure, and galvanic skin conductance, and these wearables could be used to notify the crewmembers if and when they experience high levels of boredom, especially if experienced during tasks that require sustained vigilance. Ideally, these wearables could be used to track the crewmembers' physiological signals for a significant period of time prior to the mission, in order to develop individualized baselines regarding what constitutes high or problematic levels of boredom. Ultimately, a technology-based system for monitoring and managing boredom will be most useful if paired with effective individualized boredom management techniques, as described in the previous best practice.

BEST PRACTICES TO COMBAT INTERPERSONAL CONFLICTS

When asked about the issues that often derail team performance and cause problems within spaceflight crews, the overwhelming consensus is that interpersonal issues between crewmembers, rather than anything task-related, are the most dangerous and problematic, but that positive relationships could also facilitate very effective teamwork. In past missions, interpersonal issues have been tolerated since the crewmembers knew they would only have to deal with the issues for a finite and manageable amount of time. However, in future long-duration space exploration, these same small issues are more likely to escalate into full-blown conflict because of the unprecedented length of the mission and isolation from other people. Therefore, the following best practices are aimed at reducing the likelihood of these interpersonal issues occurring, and in cases when they cannot be avoided, at reducing the negative impact of interpersonal issues on the crew's performance and functioning.

Best Practice 6: Select on Interpersonal Competencies That Support Effective Conflict Management, Not Just Technical Competencies

The first way to reduce the likelihood, severity, and potential impact of interpersonal conflict is to select crewmembers in such a way as to make conflict less likely.

Research and practice suggest that spaceflight crews are more successful when individuals are compatible not just based on technical competencies, but based on a combination of interpersonal skills that will increase the likelihood that crewmembers are interpersonally compatible. As one of the SMEs interviewed in our operational assessment stated,

> You'll certainly need crews that have interpersonal skills; you won't want to just pick the best five individuals. You'll need to pick people and train people to work well together. One of these interpersonal issues, if left unresolved, could be a real hazard.

Adopting an avoidance or "tolerate it because it is temporary" approach to interpersonal conflict can cause a build-up of stress until it becomes detrimental to team performance and psychological well-being. In terms of individual competencies, interpersonal skills are especially important for enabling positive team interactions while resilience and introversion are important to managing stress and psychological well-being within the socially isolated and confined environment. It is worth noting the juxtaposition in the coinciding need for interpersonal skills and introversion. Another competency that improves an individual's ability to maintain positive interpersonal interactions is emotion regulation. Jiang, Zhang, and Tjosvold (2013) found that individuals skilled in emotion regulation can take advantage of task conflict (i.e., disagreements over how to do the work) to perform effectively and can limit the negative impact of relationship conflict (i.e., clashes in personality). Overall, this study suggests that selecting team members to be effective at emotion regulation is beneficial for reaping the performance benefits of task conflict and avoiding the detrimental effects of relationship conflict on team performance.

Best Practice 7: Develop Realistic Expectations of Spaceflight That Highlight the Likelihood and Importance of Interpersonal Issues

Many of the issues likely to occur in long-duration spaceflight can be drawn from research in analogous extreme and confined contexts. For example, in Antarctic research stations, tension has been found to increase over time (Palinkas, Johnson, Boster, & Houseal, 1998; Wood, Lugg, Hysong, & Harm, 1999) due to issues of boredom and monotony, and the biggest contributor to tension is interpersonal conflict (Sandal, Leon, & Palinkas, 2006). When tension arises within the habitat, individuals typically turn to their external social support systems (e.g., family or friends). In another example, for submarine crews, communication from outside the environment is extremely limited. As a result, the crew is less able to rely on external social support systems. Kimhi (2011) found that shared purpose and high social cohesion helped offset some of the stress for submarine crews. Crewmembers engage in conflict avoidance behaviors and covert coping techniques such as using humor to vent and relying on mealtime and crew rituals as a source of support (Van Wijk & Cia, 2016). Finally, Rico, Molleman, Sánchez-Manzanares, and Van der Vegt (2007) found that high task autonomy can exacerbate the negative effects of interpersonal differences in teams, making this an even bigger risk for long-duration spaceflight contexts.

Similar to the recommendation in relation to boredom, we suggest that spaceflight crews be provided with realistic job previews that highlight the fact that interpersonal conflicts over day-to-day activities (e.g., meal times, cleaning tasks) are more common than interpersonal conflicts over more clearly mission-related tasks, and that the impact of these interpersonal conflicts can "spill over" and affect performance elsewhere. For example, interviews with spaceflight experts mentioned meal habits and cleanliness as cultural factors that could affect team self-maintenance. One expert, with ISS experience, mentioned that an unintended consequence of conflict caused by cultural differences is a tendency to try to just ignore the problem due to the relatively short time they are in space. This approach will be ineffective in LDSE contexts.

It should be emphasized that each team member will respond differently to each phase of flight (i.e., beginning, middle, end) and each unexpected event encountered during flight. Differences among crewmembers, especially those that are more difficult to identify with individuals who are not familiar with each other, could be highlighted. In sum, crewmembers should be made aware of one another's key differences in terms of personality, culture, and preferences, prior to mission start. One indirect way to enhance this awareness is to train the crew as an intact team as much as possible. Training crews as intact teams will allow them to gain more knowledge of each other's taskwork and teamwork capabilities. In addition, training as intact teams will allow them to build their team level interpersonal and psychological competencies.

Best Practices to Encourage Psychological Well-Being

The discussion of psychological well-being in the context of space travel has changed over the decades in which NASA has sent crews to explore our solar system. Initially, the concern was the emotional stability of the individuals who would volunteer to be propelled into outer space. Although the initial hunch of NASA scientists was that astronauts would be individuals who might suffer from psychopathology, in actuality, the contrary was found. The individuals selected as astronauts were exceptional human beings who could absorb extraordinary stresses. While current crews are comprised of equally exceptional people, the changes to the missions as have been discussed so far in this chapter and in more detail in other parts of this book are the concerns for the well-being of the crew. Therefore, the following best practices highlight a need to focus on the psychological well-being of the crew and how the team can encourage psychological well-being.

Best Practice 8: Train Team Members to Engage in Team Member Back-Up Behavior and Support, Including Support Directly Focused on Emotional and Psychological Well-Being

Task and interpersonal processes are critical components of the psychological well-being and performance of all teams that will work on the execution of LDSE missions. The uniqueness of the spaceflight teams who will be a part of the mission is that they function as isolated teams who must not only work together, but also live together, and serve as each other's social and emotional support. This is very different from current missions, where crewmembers have weekly conferences with a psychologist or psychiatrist to discuss issues such as sleep, fatigue, crew dysfunction, family issues, and mood with the ground. A reoccurring theme from the operational assessments was that these external resources available to the space team were helpful in managing the stress they experienced during their missions. Information can be found in the mental health or counseling literature to inform guided self-care (see Khan, Bower, & Rogers, 2007). Therefore, the crew may be in need of basic training regarding how they can act as mental health supporters for one another in the absence of this external support. Training should focus on the science of interpersonal processes and the emotional and social well-being of team members. Moreover, training should provide strategies to the team members for providing back-up behaviors.

Best Practice 9: Engage in Debrief Behaviors that Focus on Self-Management of Emotional and Psychological Well-Being

Debriefs are effective because they engage the individuals in a learning context. Having team members engage in reflection and future planning improves team performance. Team members who engage in self-discovery (Eddy, D'Abate, Tannenbaum, Givens-Skelton, & Robinson, 2006) and active learning techniques (Kolb, 1984) are pushed to experiment with ideas that challenge teams to continue to develop and improve (Tannenbaum & Cerasoli, 2013). Research on team debriefs (i.e., team reflexivity) has shown an impact on health-related outcomes, such as emotional exhaustion, cynicism, and inefficacy (Chen, Bamberger, Song, & Vashdi, 2018). Chen and colleagues explain their findings of decreased levels of emotional exhaustion, cynicism, and inefficacy because team debriefs increase a perception of social support from colleagues and control over taskwork. Job control is impacted by team debriefs because team members are able to systematically reflect and change behaviors that would improve taskwork and teamwork results (DeRue, Nahrgang, Hollenbeck, & Workman, 2012).

Since it is well established that debriefs focused on teamwork processes have been shown to improve performance, there is reason to believe that similar positive outcomes will result from team self-maintenance debriefs that expand their scope to include discussion of "new" functions and processes of LDSE teamwork-like processes related to psychological well-being and work recovery. Therefore, we suggest that spaceflight crew debriefs should be designed to focus on not only taskwork and teamwork, but also on the social, emotional, and psychological well-being of the crew. These debriefs could be structured to capitalize on the mental health concepts and techniques that the crew receives training on, as suggested in the previous best practice.

Best Practice 10: Train Team Members on Work Recovery Activities and Provide Opportunities for Effective Work Recovery Activities

Because LSDE contexts are stressful and challenging, the ability to recover cognitive and emotional resources and maintain motivation and energy over time will be critical to spaceflight crew success. Work recovery is the process through which individuals restore psychological and physical resources after engaging in work activities. Physiologically, during work recovery, arousal levels (e.g., heart rate) returns to a baseline (Zijlstra & Sonnentag, 2006) and psychologically, mental resources are disengaged and restored so as to be ready to deal with new demands and stressors later (Zijlstra & Sonnentag, 2006). According to Sonnentag and Fritz (2007), there are four core aspects of recovery: psychological detachment, relaxation, mastery experiences, and control during leisure time. Psychological detachment from work is the ability to disengage mentally, relaxation is a state of low activation and increased positive affect, mastery experiences refer to off-job activities that provide distraction from work and also provide challenge, and control during leisure time is the ability to decide what to do with one's off-work time.

Sonnentag, Binnewies, and Mojza (2008) studied the relationships between the four core recovery experiences, sleep quality, and affect, and found that a lack of psychological detachment increased negative affect and fatigue, experiencing relaxation, increased feelings of serenity, and mastery experiences increased positive affect. Siltaloppi, Kinnunen, Feldt, and Tolvanen (2011) suggest that high levels of all four recovery experiences are necessary to maintain long-term psychological well-being. In terms of contextual factors that impact the need for recovery, Sonnentag and Zijlstra (2006) found that high job demands, particularly situational constraints, increased the need for recovery whereas having high job control decreased the need for recovery. If people did not have job control, psychological detachment and mastery experiences were more important for recovery, and under high time demands, relaxation was especially necessary (Siltaloppi, Kinnunen, & Feldt, 2009).

The primary way to restore resources in the recovery process is engaging in off-job activities. The literature generally groups off-job activities into five categories: work-related, household, social, physical, and low-effort activities. Because work-related activities use up resources and effort, they result in poor recovery (Oerlemans, Bakker, & Demerouti, 2014). Household activities (e.g., grocery shopping and cooking) also lead to poor recovery because they are obligatory in nature and require physical effort, adding more fatigue. Social activities (e.g., spending time with family) generally provide recovery, as they are resources for social support (Oerlemans et al., 2014). However, they can also have negative outcomes if individuals have used up their social resources at the job, such as in customer service (Sonnentag & Natter, 2004). Physical activities (e.g., engaging in sports) enhance work recovery (Oerlemans et al., 2014). Research shows mixed results regarding low-effort activities (e.g., watching television) in that they do not require any resources, but they are also found to have no effect on recovery (Oerlemans et al., 2014). Finally, for all off-job activities, except low-effort activities, recovery was highest when happiness experienced during the activities was high.

It is important to note that there may be unique challenges to engaging in effective work recovery during LDSE. For example, psychological detachment can be facilitated by physical separation of work and non-work spaces, but this may be more difficult to do in the confined settings of LDSE. Furthermore, certain aspects of the job (e.g., the life-and-death nature of the job depending upon the equipment around you) by definition are always present, and therefore, psychologically detaching from them may be extremely difficult. Control during leisure time and mastery experiences are the two aspects of work recovery that may be of most utility in LDSE contexts, as it is feasible to give spaceflight crews complete control of their own leisure time, and to provide access to activities that provide mastery experiences (e.g., learning a new language, beating video games). However, the current research on work recovery is limited in terms of direct applicability to LDSE, which highlights the importance of future research examining the impact of various recovery activities on team self-maintenance.

OTHER KEY CONSIDERATIONS FOR LDSE

Combating failures in team dynamics through focusing on best practices in combating boredom, interpersonal conflicts, and psychological well-being would serve crews on LDSE missions well. However, as with any set of recommendations, there are other key considerations that must be kept in mind when preparing crews for these long and arduous missions. In particular, we briefly discuss important considerations in terms of technology and the relationship between the ground and crew.

Technology. There are personal limitations to an individual being able to detect and monitor their own psychological reactions. We are limited by our memory, ability to self-reflect, and biases. As such, the use of technology as a resource for LDSE teams would be extremely valuable. Wearable sensors, particularly in organizational research, have received much attention for investigating the social aspects of organizations, units, and teams. LDSE missions are no exception to the fact that organizations, or in this case – missions – are "relational arenas" (Matusik et al., 2019). Therefore, we suggest that spaceflight crew be provided with technology that assists them in monitoring and detecting the social, emotional and psychological well-being of the crew, in an effort to provide them with evidence to make data-driven decisions about their needs.

What current spaceflight informs us of is that during LDSE there will be many simultaneous demands on the spaceflight crews, especially in terms of technical and scientific expertise. If resources can be provided to the crew to "offload" or automate other responsibilities, this could benefit the crew and their effectiveness. Therefore, we suggest that technology-based systems to be used in LDSE should be designed to automatically track physiological and other bio-marker data and also provide feedback to the team and individuals that can be used to prompt and structure debriefs and work recovery activities. Particularly during times in which communication will be delayed, feedback that is easily understandable and actionable will be imperative so the crew can easily receive the information and act upon it. Moreover, the crew will need to understand what interventions or actions align with the feedback received, so the crew can autonomously choose the appropriate intervention.

With the use of technology, crewmembers will be relieved of the need to schedule activities and rather they would be reminders embedded within the technology. Similar to the use of reminders, feedback and achievements that are found in activity or break mobile applications or accessories (e.g., apple watch, standapp, move, etc.). As an example, one could imagine the crewmembers wearing devices or even having sensing platforms embedded within the technology (e.g., tablets or other portable computer devices) they interact with that might detect prolonged negative mood, which could indicate symptoms of depression (Zenonos et al., 2016). With the data collected by this technology, a debrief or well-being activity would be automatically added to the crews' schedule.

Ground-Space Crew Relations. The leadership requirements for LDSE are uncertain and unknown, which highlights the need for additional research in this area. However, the fact that crews on LDSE will have to adjust to having no contact with ground control will require them to expect shifts in their levels of autonomy. Therefore, this will require more flexible leadership structures and thus we recommend that crews (both in space and ground) be trained to be comfortable with and effective at sharing and transferring of leadership functions across crewmembers, especially under conditions of high autonomy (i.e., crewmembers should not be rigid in terms of hierarchy or team roles, as there will be a high likelihood that adaptation will be necessary).

In other words, the crew needs to be trained to step outside of rigid status-based hierarchies when necessary, and to engage in effective sharing of leadership. Moreover, this means all crewmembers need to be adept at not just providing leadership, but also accepting leadership and being a good follower as well. Additionally, the crew may need to think about how to transition leadership between team members without ineffective processes like power struggles or role confusion.

The majority of the best practices (see Table 9.2) highlighted in this chapter have focused on what can be provided to the crew to engage in team self-maintenance.

TABLE 9.2
Summary of Best Practices for Self-Maintenance in LDSE Contexts

Best Practice	Notes
1. Select on psychological competencies that support self-regulation, not just technical competencies.	• Consider self-regulation skills • Consider mindfulness
2. Develop realistic expectations of spaceflight that highlight the likelihood of boredom.	• Debunk common myths about living in space • Expose crewmembers to simulated monotony and boredom prior to missions
3. Train spaceflight crew to recognize well-being and performance decrements due to boredom.	• Make plans for how to address boredom • Ensure discussing boredom is seen as acceptable
4. Train spaceflight crew in boredom management techniques.	• Train mindfulness techniques • Train emotion regulation techniques
5. Provide spaceflight crew with technology-based boredom management support systems.	• Utilize wearables to capture physiological signals of boredom
6. Select on interpersonal competencies that support effective conflict management, not just technical.	• Consider the complementarity of crewmember personalities
7. Develop realistic expectations of spaceflight that highlight the likelihood and importance of interpersonal issues.	• Discuss crewmember differences prior to missions
8. Train team members to engage in team member back-up behavior and support, including support directly focused on emotional and psychological well-being.	• Train crewmembers to provide basic mental health support to one another
9. Engage in debrief behaviors that focus on self-management of emotional and psychological well-being.	• Design debriefs to focus on social, emotional, and psychological well-being
10. Train team members on "work recovery" activities and provided opportunities for effective work recovery activities.	• Enable the four aspects of recovery: psychological detachment, relaxation, mastery experiences, and control

While we mention the ground team in a few of the best practices, we feel it is important to note that the ground crew and the relationship it has with the spaceflight crew is important in the effectiveness of LDSE. As such, we recommend that the ground crew receive complimentary messaging and training to ensure that the two teams can work together effectively to ensure teams with adequate and high levels of well-being throughout the mission.

CONCLUSION

This chapter has introduced the term team self-maintenance with the intention of presenting research and best practices that can inform the selection and training of crews for LDSE missions. As mentioned in the beginning of the chapter, this chapter provides an examination of the pressures of LDSE as well as proposed solutions. It is our hope that the information reported here could be used to guide future research and to inform operational changes that will ensure a successful LDSE for spaceflight crews and ground crews.

ACKNOWLEDGEMENTS

This work was supported by NASA Contract NNJ15HK22P. The views expressed in this work are those of the authors and do not necessarily reflect the organizations with which they are affiliated or their sponsoring associations and agencies.

REFERENCES

Astin, J. A. (1997). Stress reduction through mindfulness meditation. *Psychotherapy and Psychosomatics*, *66*(2), 97–106.

Barrett, J. D. (2016, April). Team skills training: Evidence from spaceflight and ground teams. In L. Landon (chair), *Long-duration intact teams: Organizational lessons from spaceflight*. Presented at the 31th Annual Conference of the Society for Industrial and Organizational Psychology, Anaheim, CA.

Blumberg, M. (1980). Job switching in autonomous work groups: An exploratory study in a Pennsylvania coal mine. *Academy of Management Journal*, *23*(2), 287–306.

Burke, C. S., Stagl, K. C., Salas, E., Pierce, L., & Kendall, D. (2006). Understanding team adaptation: A conceptual analysis and model. *Journal of Applied Psychology*, *91*(6), 1189.

Chen, J., Bamberger, P. A., Song, Y., & Vashdi, D. R. (2018). The effects of team reflexivity on psychological well-being in manufacturing teams. *Journal of Applied Psychology*, *103*(4), 443–462.

Collins, D. L. (2003). Psychological issues relevant to astronaut selection for long-duration spaceflight: A review of the literature. *Journal of Human Performance in Extreme Environments*, *7*, 43–67.

Cummings, M. L., Gao, F., & Thornburg, K. M. (2016). Boredom in the workplace: A new look at an old problem. *Human Factors*, *58*(2), 279–300.

Derue, D. S., Nahrgang, J. D., Hollenbeck, J. R., & Workman, K. (2012). A quasi-experimental study of after-event reviews and leadership development. *Journal of Applied Psychology*, *97*, 997–1015.

DiazGranados, D., Curtis, M. T., & Wildman, J. L. (2016). *Team self-maintenance: A literature review, an operational assessment, and recommendations for practice and research.* Technical report prepared under contract NNJ15HK22P for the National Aeronautics and Space Administration (NASA): Lyndon B. Johnson Space Center, Houston, TX.

DiazGranados, D., Lazzara, E. H., Lyons, R., Wooten, S. R. II, & Salas, E. (2013). Team performance decay: Why does it happen and how to avoid it? In W. Arthur, Jr., E. A. Day, W. Bennett, Jr., & A. M. Portrey (Eds.), *Applied psychology series. Individual and team skill decay: The science and implications for practice* (pp. 364–402). New York, NY: Routledge/Taylor & Francis Group.

D'Innocenzo, L., Mathieu, J. E., & Kukenberger, M. R. (2014). A meta-analysis of different forms of shared leadership–team performance relations. *Journal of Management,* 47(7), 1964–1991.

Eccles, D. W., & Tenenbaum, G. (2004). Why an expert team is more than a team of experts: A social-cognitive conceptualization of team coordination and communication in sport. *Journal of Sport and Exercise Psychology,* 26(4), 542–560.

Eddy, E. R., D'Abate, C. P., Tannenbaum, S. I., Givens-Skeaton, S., & Robinson, G. (2006). Key characteristics of effective and ineffective developmental interactions. *Human Resource Development Quarterly,* 17, 59–84.

Evans, Jr, C. H., & Ball, J. R. (Eds.). (2001). *Safe passage: Astronaut care for exploration missions.* Washington, D.C.: National Academies Press.

Francis, R. D. (1969). Introversion and isolation tolerance. *Perceptual and Motor Skills,* 28(2), 534.

Glomb, T. M., Duffy, M. K., Bono, J. E., & Yang, T. (2011). Mindfulness at work. *Research in Personnel and Human Resources Management,* 30, 115.

Hunter, A., & Eastwood, J. D. (2018). Does state boredom cause failures of attention? Examining the relations between trait boredom, state boredom, and sustained attention. *Experimental Brain Research,* 236(9), 2483–2492.

Jha, A. P., Stanley, E. A., Kiyonaga, A., Wong, L., & Gelfand, L. (2010). Examining the protective effects of mindfulness training on working memory capacity and affective experience. *Emotion,* 10(1), 54.

Jiang, J. Y., Zhang, X., & Tjosvold, D. (2013). Emotion regulation as a boundary condition of the relationship between team conflict and performance: A multi-level examination. *Journal of Organizational Behavior,* 34(5), 714–734.

Kabat-Zinn, J. (1990). *Full catastrophe living: The program of the stress reduction clinic at the University of Massachusetts Medical Center.* New York, NY: Dell Publishing.

Kabat-Zinn, J., Lipworth, L., & Burney, R. (1985). The clinical use of mindfulness meditation for the self-regulation of chronic pain. *Journal of Behavioral Medicine,* 8(2), 163–190.

Kabat-Zinn, J., Massion, A. O., Kristeller, J., Peterson, L. G., Fletcher, K. E., Pbert, L.,… Santorelli, S. F. (1992). Effectiveness of a meditation-based stress reduction program in the treatment of anxiety disorders. *The American Journal of Psychiatry,* 149(7), 936–943.

Kemp, N. J., Wall, T. D., Clegg, C. W., & Cordery, J. L. (1983). Autonomous work groups in a greenfield site: A comparative study. *Journal of Occupational Psychology,* 56(4), 271–288.

Khan, N., Bower, P., & Rogers, A. (2007). Guided self-help in primary care mental health: Meta-synthesis of qualitative studies of patient experience. *The British Journal of Psychiatry,* 191(3), 206–211.

Kimhi, S. (2011). Understanding good coping: A submarine crew coping with extreme environmental conditions. *Psychology.* 2, 961–967. doi:10.4236/psych.2011.29145

Kolb, D. (1984). *Experiential learning: Experience as a source of learning.* Englewood Cliffs, NJ: Prentice Hall.

Koole, S. L. (2009). The psychology of emotion regulation: An integrative review. *Cognition and Emotion, 23*, 4–41. doi:10.1080/02699930802619031

Kristeller, J. L., & Hallett, C. B. (1999). An exploratory study of a meditation-based intervention for binge eating disorder. *Journal of Health Psychology, 4*(3), 357–363.

Langfred, C. W. (2000). Work-group design and autonomy A field study of the interaction between task interdependence and group autonomy. *Small Group Research, 31*(1), 54–70.

Lee, K. S. F. (2018). *Boredom proneness and symptoms of depression, anxiety and stress: The moderating effect of mindfulness* (Order No. AAI10616594). Available from PsycINFO. (1994020283; 2017-54456-112). Retrieved from https://search-proquest-com.portal.lib.fit.edu/docview/1994020283?accountid=27313.

Manzey, D. (2004). Human missions to Mars: New psychological challenges and research issues. *Acta Astronautica, 55*(3–9), 781–790.

Marks, M. A., Mathieu, J. E., & Zaccaro, S. J. (2001). A temporally based framework and taxonomy of team processes. *Academy of Management Review, 26*(3), 356–376.

Marlatt, G. A., & Kristeller, J. L. (1999). Mindfulness and meditation. In W. R. Miller (Ed.), *Integrating spirituality into treatment: Resources for practitioners* (pp. 67–84). Washington, DC: American Psychological Association.

Matusik, J. G., Heidl, R., Hollenbeck, J. R., Yu, A., Lee, H. W., & Howe, M. (2019). Wearable bluetooth sensors for capturing relational variables and temporal variability in relationships: A construct validation study. *Journal of Applied Psychology, 104*(3), 357–387.

Maynard, M. T., and Kennedy, D. M. (2016). *Team adaptation and resilience: What do we know and what can be applied to long-duration isolated, confined, and extreme contexts.* Houston, TX: National Aeronautics and Space Administration.

Merrifield, C., & Danckert, J. (2014). Characterizing the psychophysiological signature of boredom. *Experimental Brain Research, 232*(2), 481–491.

Mierlo, H. V., Rutte, C. G., Vermunt, J. K., Kompier, M. A. J., & Doorewaard, J. A. C. M. (2007). A multi-level mediation model of the relationships between team autonomy, individual task design and psychological well-being. *Journal of Occupational and Organizational Psychology, 80*(4), 647–664.

Nicolaides, V. C., LaPort, K. A., Chen, T. R., Tomassetti, A. J., Weis, E. J., Zaccaro, S. J., & Cortina, J. M. (2014). The shared leadership of teams: A meta-analysis of proximal, distal, and moderating relationships. *The Leadership Quarterly, 25*(5), 923–942.

Oerlemans, W. G., Bakker, A. B., & Demerouti, E. (2014). How feeling happy during off-job activities helps successful recovery from work: A day reconstruction study. *Work & Stress, 28*(2), 198–216.

Palinkas, L. A. (1992). Going to extremes: The cultural context of stress, illness and coping in Antarctica. *Social Science and Medicine, 35*, 651–664.

Palinkas, L. A. (2007). Psychosocial issues in long-term spaceflight: Overview. *Gravitational and Space Research, 14*, 25–33.

Palinkas, L. A., Johnson, J. C., Boster, J. S., & Houseal, M. (1998). Longitudinal studies of behavior and performance during a winter at the South Pole. *Aviation, Space and Environmental Medicine, 69*(1), 73–77.

Prakash, R. S., Hussain, M. A., & Schirda, B. (2015). The role of emotion regulation and cognitive control in the association between mindfulness disposition and stress. *Psychology and Aging, 30*(1), 160.

Rapp, T. L., Bachrach, D. G., Rapp, A. A., & Mullins, R. (2014). The role of team goal monitoring in the curvilinear relationship between team efficacy and team performance. *Journal of Applied Psychology, 99*(5), 976.

Rico, R., Molleman, E., Sánchez-Manzanares, M., & Van der Vegt, G. S. (2007). The effects of diversity faultlines and team task autonomy on decision quality and social integration. *Journal of Management, 33*(1), 111–132.

Rousseau, V., & Aubé, C. (2010). Team self-managing behaviors and team effectiveness: The moderating effect of task routineness. *Group & Organization Management, 35*(6), 751–781.

Ruff, G. E., & Levy, E. Z. (1959). Psychiatric evaluation of candidates for space flight. *American Journal of Psychiatry, 116* (389).

Sandal, G. M., Leon, G. R., & Palinkas, L. A. (2006). Human challenges in polar and space environments. *Reviews in Environmental Science and Bio/Technology, 5*, 281–296

Siltaloppi, M., Kinnunen, U., & Feldt, T. (2009). Recovery experiences as moderators between psychosocial work characteristics and occupational well-being. *Work & Stress, 23*(4), 330–348.

Siltaloppi, M., Kinnunen, U., Feldt, T., & Tolvanen, A. (2011). Identifying patterns of recovery experiences and their links to psychological outcomes across one year. *International Archives of Occupational and Environmental Health, 84*(8), 877–888.

Sonnentag, S., Binnewies, C., & Mojza, E. J. (2008). "Did you have a nice evening?" A day-level study on recovery experiences, sleep, and affect. *Journal of Applied Psychology, 93*(3), 674.

Sonnentag, S., & Fritz, C. (2007). The Recovery Experience Questionnaire: Development and validation of a measure for assessing recuperation and unwinding from work. *Journal of Occupational Health Psychology, 12*(3), 204.

Sonnentag, S., & Natter, E. (2004). Flight attendants' daily recovery from work: Is there no place like home? *International Journal of Stress Management, 11*(4), 366.

Sonnentag, S., & Zijlstra, F. R. (2006). Job characteristics and off-job activities as predictors of need for recovery, well-being, and fatigue. *Journal of Applied Psychology, 91*(2), 330.

Speca, M., Carlson, L. E., Goodey, E., & Angen, M. (2000). A randomized, wait-list controlled clinical trial: The effect of a mindfulness meditation-based stress reduction program on mood and symptoms of stress in cancer outpatients. *Psychosomatic Medicine, 62*(5), 613–622.

Stephens, J. P., Heaphy, E. D., Carmeli, A., Spreitzer, G. M., & Dutton, J. E. (2013). Relationship quality and virtuousness: Emotional carrying capacity as a source of individual and team resilience. *The Journal of Applied Behavioral Science, 49*(1), 13–41.

Stirone, S. (2016, August 4). *Can virtual reality help astronauts keep their cool?* [blog post]. Retrieved from http://blogs.discovermagazine.com/crux/2016/08/04/can-virtual-reality-help-astronauts-keep-their-cool/#.XURqwm9Kg2x.

Suedfeld, P. (2001). Applying positive psychology in the study of extreme environments. *Journal of Human Performance in Extreme Environments, 6*(1). doi: 10.7771/2327-2937.1020

Suedfeld, P., & Steel, G. D. (2000). The environmental psychology of capsule habitats. *Annual Review of Psychology, 51*, 227–253. doi:10.1146/Annurev.Psych.51.1.227

Sutcliffe, K. M., & Vogus, T. J. (2003). Organizing for resilience. In K. S. Cameron, J. E. Dutton & R. E. Quinn (Eds.), *Positive organizational scholarship: Foundations of a new discipline* (pp. 94–110). San Francisco, CA: Berrett-Koehler.

Tannenbaum, S. I., & Cerasoli, C. P. (2013). Do team and individual debriefs enhance performance? A meta-analysis. *Human Factors: The Journal of the Human Factors and Ergonomics Society, 55*(1), 231–245.

Teasdale, J. D., Segal, Z. V., Williams, J. M. G., Ridgeway, V. A., Soulsby, J. M., & Lau, M. A. (2000). Prevention of relapse/recurrence in major depression by mindfulness-based cognitive therapy. *Journal of consulting and clinical psychology, 68*(4), 615–623.

Van Wijk, C. H., & Cia, V. D. (2016). "Covert coping" in extreme environments: Insights from South African submarines. *Journal of Human Performance in Extreme Environments, 12*(2). doi: 10.7771/2327-2937.1083

Vessel, E. A., & Russo, S. (2015). *Effects of reduced sensory stimulation and assessment of countermeasures for sensory stimulation augmentation.* Technical report prepared under contract for the National Aeronautics and Space Administration (NASA). Houston, TX: Lyndon B. Johnson Space Center.

Wang, D., Waldman, D. A., & Zhang, Z. (2014). A meta-analysis of shared leadership and team effectiveness. *Journal of Applied Psychology, 99*(2), 181–198.

Webb, T. L., Miles, E., & Sheeran, P. (2012). Dealing with feeling: A meta-analysis of the effectiveness of strategies derived from the process model of emotion regulation. *Psychological Bulletin, 138*(4), 775–808.

Wood, J., Lugg, D. J., Hysong, S. J., & Harm, D. L. (1999). Psychological changes in hundred-day remote Antarctic field groups. *Environment and Behavior, 31*(3), 299–337.

Zaccaro, S. J., & Bader, P. (2003). E-Leadership and the challenges of leading E-teams: Minimizing the bad and maximizing the good. *Organizational Dynamics, 31*(4), 377–387.

Zenonos, A., Khan, A., Kalogridis, G., Vatsikas, S., Lewis, T., & Sooriyabandara, M. (2016, March). HealthyOffice: Mood recognition at work using smartphones and wearable sensors. In *2016 IEEE international conference on Pervasive Computing and Communication Workshops (PerCom Workshops)* (pp. 1–6). IEEE. Sydney, NSW, Australia.

Zijlstra, F. R., & Sonnentag, S. (2006). After work is done: Psychological perspectives on recovery from work. *European Journal of Work and Organizational Psychology, 15*(2), 129–138.

10 Working in Space
Managing Transitions between Tasks

Jessica Mesmer-Magnus
University of North Carolina Wilmington

Alina Lungeanu, Alexa Harris, Ashley Niler, Leslie A. DeChurch, and Noshir Contractor
Northwestern University

CONTENTS

Team Task Transitions 181
Part 1: Five Factors That Affect Work in Space 184
    Factor 1 – Task Characteristics 185
    Factor 2 – Social Factors 186
    Factor 3 – Technology Affordances 187
    Factor 4 – Situational Constraints 188
    Factor 5 – Individual Differences 188
Part 2: Perceptions of Working in Space 189
Part 3: Computational Modeling of Working in Space 192
Context: Project RED 193
The Model: CREST (Crew Recommender for Effectively Switching Tasks) 194
Conclusion 199
References 200

> Space sure is a busy place.
> I am sensing a common theme: non-stop days.
> There are only two days in a week on ISS: Monday and Friday, with a couple of hours in between.

These three reflections on work in space were captured in the diaries of astronauts living and working aboard the International Space Station (ISS; Stuster, 2010). Working in space has been characterized in many ways. One of the prevalent themes percolating in diaries and interviews with astronauts is the intense timeline where astronauts perform many tasks in a day, each with a small amount of time allocated to it, fueling a constant pressure to monitor the clock and stay on schedule. As one astronaut put it: "It's like a continuous battle against time up here. There is a lot of stress with that. It's just a continuous time battle (Stuster, 2010, p. 24)."

A second prevalent theme is the collaborative and interdependent nature of working in space. Collaboration sometimes describes the interactions within the crew, helping one another, or providing social support: "This is a really good crew to work together and it is more fun that way. I think we all enjoy doing stuff together (Stuster, 2010, p. 22)." At other times, collaboration refers to the crew working with mission control: "Ground has been a huge help, but they cannot win us back time and that is what we need now (Stuster, 2010, p. 24)."

A third prevalent theme is that not all work in space is equally engaging. In fact, many of the tasks that must get done for the station to function can be frustrating:

> This procedure was awful. Steps were missing, the stowage note was wrong in multiple places, nothing made sense. I remarked to X that if this is how things used to be every day on ISS, I can definitely understand why people get fed up with ops here. It was a disaster. And it went about 2 hours over the allocated time, which made it even worse.
>
> *Stuster (2010, p. 61)*

In a similar vein, work in space can be repetitive:

> Sometimes it's a little bit like Groundhog Day. You wake up at the same time every day. You look at the schedule and figure out what you're going to do. Even though the tasks are different, it feels like you're doing the same thing over and over again.
>
> *Stuster (2010, p. 19).*

Taken together, these themes about the nature of working in space provide a useful framework for shaping research and interventions around work design. The picture of work in space is a tight timeline: "your life is marked in 5-minute increments" (ISS astronaut, personal communication). The day is divided into many tasks assigned to tiny increments – 5 minutes to do this, 10 minutes to do that. In addition to the frenzied pace is a tacit collaborative aspect to the work. Indeed, two of this chapter's authors interviewed an ISS astronaut soon after she returned. When we asked her for an example of work tasks that she did alone, she paused. She said that everything in space requires teamwork. Even when a task is assigned to a single astronaut to complete, someone came before and someone will come after. Before, there were the individuals who wrote the procedure, and the astronaut is trying to figure out what they intended. After, there are those who will check on the work. Even when one is working alone in space, there is an imagined web of interdependence. From this we come to understand that not only are astronauts jumping from task to task, they are traversing social dynamics as well. They work with different people, in space and on Earth, from different educational and cultural backgrounds.

A final note about the themes associated with work in space is the constant mention of material artifacts that affect the nature and efficiency of collaboration: schedules, procedures, tools, supplies, computers, sensors. For example, the awareness of a sensor that allows the ground to know what an astronaut is doing: "The freezer cannot be open for more than 1 minute. The ground can see when I open the door and close it, so no cheating (Stuster, 2010, p. 38)." There are also entries that highlight how astronauts come to associate expertise with people in the course of doing their work: "It is a Russian system originally, so X has expertise, especially when it comes to those pesky Russian fluid connectors (Stuster, 2010, p. 38)." A simple email message shapes a crewmember's perception of what the ground is doing and why they are doing it:

> I received an email from X about the EVA. They were looking at changing the date... The more I am here I can see how much things are analyzed or over analyzed and how much they are trying to protect crew time.
>
> Stuster (2010, p. 30)

As such, working in space requires jumping from task to task, traversing social dynamics, and interacting with a variety of material artifacts that can meaningfully shape action and interaction.

Interviews with current and former astronauts as well as reports from astronauts on the International Space Station (ISS) highlight the potential for decrements in crew performance stemming from difficulties in shifting back and forth between independent work and highly interdependent work (Smith-Jentsch, 2015). Given the ebbs and flows of space work, focusing on work transitions allows one to understand the switching costs and flow advantages that come from the particular sequencing of tasks. We define this as a problem of team task transitions. The core idea of this chapter is that the scheduling and sequencing of work affects how easy or difficult it is for astronauts to complete it. In the next section, we elaborate on the factors that shape task transitions.

TEAM TASK TRANSITIONS

The nature of work in space involves completing a variety of tasks and interacting with a variety of technologies and tools. This work also varies in terms of how much interdependence and interaction crewmembers have with their fellow crewmembers, with their disciplinary teams on Earth, and/or with mission control during their work. Therefore, an astronaut's work involves transitioning among tasks, tools, technologies, and people/teams, which can place cognitive, motivational, and behavioral demands on crewmembers as they adjust to changes in tasks/tools/people. Further, the structure of NASA includes teams of teams working on all aspects of a mission, so the crew's interdependence with this system of teams often requires individuals to shift goal focus in response to dynamic situational requirements with very little warning. So while an astronaut may be working independently on a task, they could be interrupted to assist with an emergent condition and quickly come up to speed, working interdependently with fellow crewmembers as well as mission control. Their ability to juggle the implications of switching across tasks, tools, and teams ultimately affects performance.

In order to illustrate how the interdependence of work affects how easy or difficult it is to move from one task to another, we present survey data provided by six astronauts as they worked aboard the ISS. Each astronaut provided data on 14 occasions that were approximately evenly spaced across their time on the ISS. We asked these astronauts to rank a series of work transitions in order of how difficult they are, "How difficult is each type of transition for you (1 = least difficulty, 6 = most difficult)". First, we distinguished work tasks that a crewmember completes alone (e.g., stowage, running errands around the station), work tasks completed with the help of one or more crewmembers (e.g., research, airlock tasks), and work tasks requiring direct coordination with mission control (e.g., EVAs). When transitioning work tasks, each transition can involve an increase or decrease in autonomy. For example, when moving from a solo task to a task with Mission Control Center (MCC), the crewmember decreases autonomy and substantially increases the amount of interdependence or mutual reliance on others required by the work. We detailed six transitions. The first three transitions involve an increase in autonomy: moving from a crew task to a solo task (Crew to Solo), moving from a task completed with mission control to a solo task (MCC to Solo), and moving from a task completed with mission control to a task completed with the crew (MCC to crew). The second three transitions involve a decrease in autonomy: moving from a solo task to a crew task (Solo to Crew), moving from a task completed with the crew to one completed with mission control (Crew to MCC), and moving from a task completed alone to one completed with mission control (Solo to MCC).

Figure 10.1 presents the average ranked difficulty of these transitions reported by the six ISS astronauts who participated. The three shifts that involve increases in autonomy are presented on the left, and the three shifts that involve decreasing autonomy are on the right. Interestingly, work transitions that involve a gain in autonomy were reported as easier to make by astronauts. Work transitions that involve a loss in autonomy, or conversely, an increase in interdependence, were ranked as being more challenging to astronauts. The easiest transition to make is to go from working with

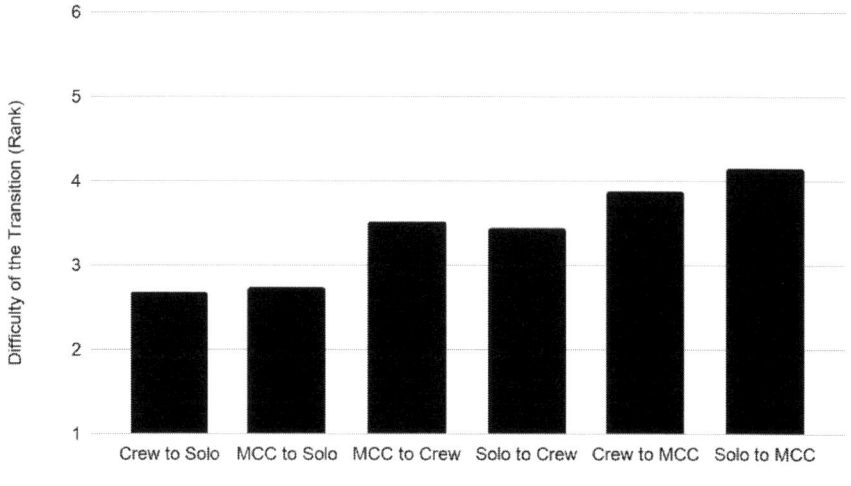

FIGURE 10.1 Astronaut rankings of the relative difficulty of task transitions made while working aboard the International Space Station ($N = 6$).

the crew on something to working on a task alone. In contrast, the most challenging transition is to go from a task an astronaut is completing alone to working on a task with mission control. A key message from this data is that the sequencing of work over the course of day matters.

In order to better understand the complete set of factors that may determine the ease or difficulty of making task transitions, we turned to two research literatures. The first is the literature on task switching within human factors in cognitive psychology (Allport & Wylie, 1999; Payne, Duggan, & Neth, 2007; Monk, Trafton, & Boehm-Davis, 2008; Wickens, Santamaria, & Sebok, 2013). The second is the literature on team effectiveness within social and industrial psychology as well as organizational behavior (DeShon, Kozlowski, Schmidt, Milner, & Wiechmann, 2004; Gersick & Hackman, 1990; McGrath, Arrow, & Berdahl, 2000; McGrath & Kelly, 1986). From a human factors and cognitive psychology perspective, the problem of task transitions has been examined in terms of how individuals allocate their time between an ongoing task and one or more alternative tasks. An operator's decision to remain on the ongoing task or move on to one of many alternative tasks is defined in terms of "choice probabilities" (Wickens et al., 2013). This probabilistic approach to task switching includes weighting factors that contribute to the "stickiness" of the ongoing task (i.e., switch avoidance, task inertia difficulty effect, priority, and interest), and the "attractiveness" of alternative tasks (i.e., alternative task difficulty effect, priority and interest; Wickens et al., 2013). The following quote by a former Skylab astronaut highlights how differences in alternative task attractiveness may have implications for decisions about task transitions:

> We literally pinned the [list of tasks to be done] up on the wall of the spacecraft and when we had a free minute we'd go down and pick a job we felt like doing on [the list], draw a line through it, then go do it.
>
> *Carr (1986, pp. 19–20, as cited in Wittenbaum, & Stasser, 1996, p. 80.)*

A cognitive perspective on task switching does not provide a complete picture of the predictors of adaptive task switching nor of the implications of maladaptive task switching, particularly within environments where individuals must switch among tasks that are independent as well as interdependent, and wherein interdependencies cross team and multi-team boundaries. In these work environments, task switching is also a social phenomenon. From a social/organizational psychology perspective, one reason crewmembers may experience difficulties when switching between work modes may stem from social entrainment to a particular working style (McGrath & Kelly, 1986). When an individual spends a great deal of time working in one task mode (e.g., on independent tasks or with a particular team), he or she may become entrained to a work mode (speed, efficiency, quality) that does not translate efficiently and effectively to a new task or team context, decrementing performance (McGrath et al., 2000). In space, crewmembers can be entrained to the rhythms of their own independent tasks, to the rhythms of other team members (e.g., during interdependent team tasks), to the rhythms of other teams (e.g., ground control), and/or to the rhythms of other external or internal pacers. A crewmember's difficulty in task switching may also stem from other social factors, like varying levels of trust, familiarity, similarity, or experience they have within the various social collectives within which they work (Mortensen, Woolley, & O'Leary, 2007).

Transition costs have a direct bearing on *performance adaptation,* which refers to the "cognitive, affective, motivational, and behavioral modifications made in response to the demands of new or changing situational demands" (Baard, Rench, & Kozlowski, 2014, p. 50). Pulakos, Arad, Donovan, and Plamondon (2000) defined adaptability as a set of behaviors "demonstrating the ability to cope with change and to transfer learning from one task to another as job demands vary" (Allworth & Hesketh, 1999, p. 98). Crewmembers' ability and motivation to switch efforts among different task-based work styles in response to changing environmental demands is an essential element of successful performance adaptation in LDSE.

Building on Baard and her colleagues' (2014) definition of performance adaptation, we define *adaptive team task switching as an individual's cognitive, affective, motivational, and behavioral modifications made in response to team task switches.* Some researchers define performance adaptation as "individuals' willingness to adapt (e.g., Cronshaw & Jethmalani, 2005)", others define it as the "ability to adapt (e.g., Allworth & Hesketh, 1999)," and still others as the "demonstration of effective adaptation (e.g., Pulakos, Schmitt, Dorsey, Arad, Borman, & Hedge, 2002)." We disentangle these in our model to identify the specific factors that lead to adaptive task switching. Doing so is critical to the design of effective countermeasures, as it is plausible that different levers can be used to target each of these important components of adaptive team task switching. For example, certain aspects of crew composition may affect the ability to switch, whereas other aspects of composition may affect the willingness to switch. Similarly, job design countermeasures are likely critical to the motivational aspects of task switching (Hackman & Oldham, 1976).

Astronaut crews must frequently, and sometimes spontaneously, engage in team task transitions, which requires them to shift between one or more core dimensions of their work – tasks, teams, and/or tools – to accomplish new work demands. NASA recognizes that task and team transitions com with switching costs in terms of depleted attentional, cognitive, and motivational resources, and these costs have implications for performance at individual, team, and multiteam levels. Next, we introduce a model that integrates the disparate cognitive and social perspectives on team task switching to highlight five key factors that affect work in space.

PART 1: FIVE FACTORS THAT AFFECT WORK IN SPACE

Task management refers to how individuals decide among the tasks they will execute when multiple tasks are available (Wickens, Gutzwiller, & Santamaria, 2015). There is a natural propensity to continue doing what one is already doing, due to the state of flow that develops as an individual continues to engage in a task (i.e., task inertia; e.g., Csikszentmihalyi, 1991). When one is engaged in an ongoing task, there are costs associated with changing tasks. Wickens and colleagues (2015) define "task stickiness" as the sum of the inertial forces acting upon an individual to remain on a given task. Not only do tasks vary in their level of stickiness, they also vary in terms of their level of "attractiveness" (Wickens et al., 2015). A task's "attractiveness" is defined as all attributes of a task that increase the likelihood that someone will switch

Working in Space

to that task given the opportunity (Wickens et al., 2015). Some tasks are inherently more interesting, fun, and engaging than others and therefore are more tempting to switch to despite the associated costs of switching. Other tasks are inherently more boring, repetitive, or time consuming, and therefore are less attractive in nature.

A review of the literature as well as interviews with astronauts and support personnel have revealed five core factors that affect task transitions in space: (1) task characteristics, (2) social factors, (3) technology affordances, (4) situational constraints, and (5) individual differences. In this section, we describe the literature on each factor and summarize how it is believed to shape the two critical components of task transitions: stickiness and attractiveness. These factors are visually depicted in Figure 10.2.

FACTOR 1 – TASK CHARACTERISTICS

The first factor that affects task stickiness and attractiveness relates to the attributes of the task. Research suggests perceptions regarding task (1) difficulty, (2) interest, (3) importance, and (4) salience, have implications for an individual's ability and willingness to switch tasks (Wickens et al., 2015). With regards to *task difficulty*, research has demonstrated that individuals are more likely to switch to an easy task than a difficult task (Wickens et al., 2013), since there is a natural tendency to avoid additional workload, particularly if it may affect their performance (i.e., par hypothesis; Helson, 1949). An exception is that an individual currently working on a difficult task tends to want to complete the difficult task before switching to a new

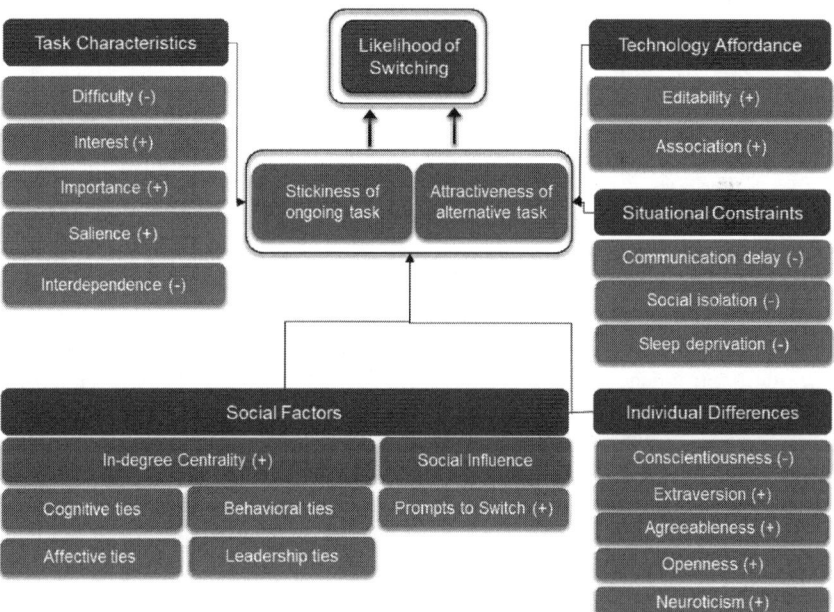

FIGURE 10.2 Conceptual integration of factors affecting task stickiness and attractiveness in space crews.

task (Wickens et al., 2013). Similarly, perceptions of *task interest* may contribute to the likelihood an individual will be inclined to switch tasks. Research supports this idea as individuals have been found to be more likely to switch to an interesting yet difficult task than a boring yet easy task (Wickens et al., 2013). With regards to *task importance*, individuals tend to prioritize tasks based upon their level of importance; alternative tasks perceived to be more important than the ongoing task may prompt a greater willingness to switch. Finally, with regards to *task salience*, some tasks possess characteristics that attract one's attention more than others. For example, a flashing alert on a display may demand an operator's attention away from an ongoing task.

FACTOR 2 – SOCIAL FACTORS

A second element of team task switching requires individuals to shift attention across teams. Crewmembers on the International Space Station and in long duration space exploration are concurrently members on multiple teams (MTM; O'Leary, Mortensen & Woolley, 2011). Hence they are responsible to all of these teams and likely face differing demands, expectations, and constraints within each team. The multi-teaming aspect of team task switching requires individuals to allocate time and effort across the goals, demands, and constraints of multiple teams. It also requires them to adjust to changes in who they work with on a given task. Even though the tasks performed by these teams are somewhat constant, the particular people they interface with to perform this task can change (e.g., mission control is comprised of functional groups who rotate on three 8-hour work shifts, so individuals within a ground control team may change even though the team itself has not changed). Multi-teaming affects individuals in two ways. First, the amount of time/energy they have to devote to any given team is diminished according to increasing demands of their other team memberships (Mortensen et al., 2007). Second, there is a switching cost associated with moving between teams that may have different behavioral norms, interaction dynamics, etc. Cognitive, affective, motivational, and team composition mechanisms affect both the ability and motivation to switch between teams.

Characteristics of the team may also affect the lateral inertia between the "stickiness of an ongoing team" and the "attractiveness of an alternative team", including (1) cognitive ties, (2) affective ties, (3) behavioral ties, and (4) leadership ties. With regards to *cognitive ties*, shared cognition helps teams cope with changing conditions (Mathieu, Heffner, Goodwin, Salas, & Cannon-Bowers, 2000). The cost of team switching is diminished if each team is structured such that there are standardized methods for accomplishing work (Zika-Viktorsson, Sundström, & Engwall, 2006), and predictable roles and responsibilities in each team context, thereby facilitating the development of compatible shared mental models within each team. When teams have a similar understanding of their environment, roles, and responsibilities, members are able to effectively function and adapt without explicit coordination (Cannon-Bowers & Salas, 2001). With regards to *affective ties*, team affective states – like familiarity, trust, and cohesion – set the stage for positive working relationships across multiple teams (Mortensen et al., 2007). Further, in MTM contexts where time and effort are limited, resources, familiarity, trust, and cohesion mitigate the risks associated with teamwork (e.g. teammates' failure to contribute to the team task; Hinds,

Carley, Krackhardt, & Wholey, 2000), and create a sense of collective efficacy and shared motivation (*behavioral ties*) among the team, likely improving the feasibility of team switching. Finally, *team leadership* factors, like the extent to which leadership is shared/dispersed across members of the team versus being centralized to a subset of team members may affect both the tendency and motivation to switch across tasks.

FACTOR 3 – TECHNOLOGY AFFORDANCES

Tools and technologies used in the workplace carry with them various attributes and affordances that may affect task transitions. Astronauts' work requires the use of a variety of technological tools. Often these tools have unique interfaces, learning curves, and best practices, placing unique cognitive and attentional demands on the user. Much of the extant literature on multi-tooling discusses the motivations for switching across technologies, e.g., boredom (e.g., Mark, Iqbal, Czerwinski, & Johns, 2014; Gergle & Tan, 2014). This literature explores the motives prompting individuals to freely choose to switch platforms. However, in a space flight context, astronauts have less volition and are often forced to make switches across tools in order to meet the demands of their scheduled work. When forced to switch technology platforms, individuals are likely to experience cognitive interference from differences in the interface characteristics or requirements of the ongoing versus alternative tools.

Characteristics of the tool also come into play in affecting perceptions of stickiness and attractiveness. Software collaboration tools vary by the extent to which they provide "affordances" that enable users to maintain a record of shared information, allow members to edit communications, and/or represent or replicate task/team relationships. Further, when users are accustomed to tool-specific techniques for accomplishing an ongoing task, switching tools may result in "tool interference" wherein techniques used in one tool may take time to drop below threshold and temporarily compete with activation of knowledge relevant to new tools used for an alternative task (Memory for Goals Model; Altmann & Trafton, 2002; Chung & Byrne, 2008; Mayr & Keele, 2000). Further, cognitive engineering models of attention allocation (e.g., the NSEEV Model; Wickens, Hooey, Gore, Sebok, & Koenicke, 2009) describe how individuals develop an expectation that particular pieces of information can be found within elements of a particular technology platform, or that they'll have to store certain information using an external tool (e.g., a post-it note; Zhang & Norman, 1994). When using highly automated systems, automation reliance (Lee & See, 2004) could factor in to one's ability to efficiently and effectively switch to a new technology platform.

Two technology affordances may be especially relevant to working in space: editability and association. Editability refers to the extent to which a tool allows users to modify or revise content they've created, allowing the creator to maintain some control over the information over time (Treem & Leonardi, 2012). Editability enables users additional time to craft content or to complete a task, which ultimately permits more purposeful information sharing across members of a team as well as a greater chance for quality, accuracy, and comprehension. Examples of features that afford editability include asynchronous entries, historical data on edits, and ability to revise/delete content. Association refers to the extent to which a tool establishes connections among individuals or between individuals and content (Treem & Leonardi, 2012). This affordance gives users data regarding the relation between users and content as well as among users. Examples of features that enable the association affordance include lists of editors for entries, indications of who has privileges/rights/contributions, links to related information contributed by others, and lists of others who viewed the same content. Editability and association may be particularly helpful in promoting efficient and effective work in space because they foster the (1) exchange and retention of information within and across teams both in space and on Earth, (2) development and maintenance of shared cognition among team members and within the multiteam system, (3) development and maintenance of transactive memory (e.g., who knows what and who did what) within and across teams, and (4) ease and efficiency by which astronauts can switch to/from various tasks/teams/tools. By seeing a record of who knows what and who contributed what, being able to add to and edit prior content, and being able to identify associations among people and content, more efficient communication and greater retention of information is facilitated. Further, individuals can more seamlessly shift into and out of various tasks/teams/tools as they have access to a "cheat sheet" of prior decisions/information, which will allow them to get up to speed more quickly and decrease instances of performance decrements as well as information loss.

Factor 4 – Situational Constraints

Long duration space exploration carries with it unique situational constraints not as frequently experienced by teams on Earth. The dynamics of space explorations require astronauts to work within the confines of lengthy *communication delays* between the astronauts and supporting teams on Earth. A mission to Mars, for example, may encumber a 42-minute round-trip communication delay between the astronauts on Mars and their ground control on Earth. Such delayed communication requires astronauts to be more self-sufficient than ever before and may have implications for task transitions. Space exploration also forces astronaut teams to live in close quarters and to be *socially isolated* from the outside world. Although they have limited opportunities for virtual interactions with colleagues, family, and friends, these interactions are often more sterile than would be the case if they were executed in person. The experience of social isolation may have consequences for task transitions in that astronauts may either have a tendency toward task entrainment, wherein they are less likely to want to switch tasks or they may be forced to engage in task transitions when there are constrained human resources. Finally, astronauts often work extended shifts, and must work through periods of *sleep deprivation*, which is known to affect mental (Lim & Dinges, 2008) and social processes (Driskell, Salas, & Driskell, 2018; Ellis, 2006; Marques-Quinteiro, Curral, Passos, & Lewis, 2013).

Factor 5 – Individual Differences

The contextual reality within which astronauts work suggests sets of personal characteristics may predict likelihood of switching tasks. These factors are particularly critical to crew composition, and so we focus on the personal characteristics needed to have both the ability and motivation to adaptively switch tasks. One's ability to successfully multitask (i.e., the extent to which an individual is capable of switching among tasks in contexts requiring multi-tasking without compromising performance; König, Buhner, & Murling, 2005; Morgan et al., 2012) is not reliably self-assessed by most individuals. Research suggests multi-tasking ability along with its related construct, polychronicity (i.e., an individual's preference for and comfort with multi-tasking and *motivation* to switch among tasks), have implications for work satisfaction, commitment, withdrawal, and turnover intentions (Fahr, 2011; Kaff, 2004; Mesmer-Magnus, Viswesvaran, Bruk-Lee, Sanderson, & Sinha, 2014), and are best predicted by personality characteristics, like emotional stability (e.g., Conte & Jacobs, 2003; Kantrowitz, Grelle, Beaty, & Wolf, 2012; König et al., 2005; Poposki, Oswald, & Chen., 2009), conscientiousness (Conte & Jacobs, 2003; Girgis, 2010; Kantrowitz et al., 2012; Stachowski, 2011), and extraversion (Sanderson, 2012). As such, our model includes the Big Five dimensions of personality as predictors of task transitions.

PART 2: PERCEPTIONS OF WORKING IN SPACE

In reviewing the task management literature, we identified five factors that affect task transitions. Three of these factors can be shaped in work design interventions such as scheduling: task characteristics, social factors, and technology affordances. One way to think about these three is that each places a set of constraints on the individual. The transitions can be easier or harder depending on the nature of the work (task), the interdependence of the work (social), and the technology affordances (tools).

Astronaut perceptions. In order to better understand the relative impact of each type of factor on work transitions, we asked six astronauts working aboard the International Space Station to rank the difficulty of the three factors: orienting to the task, orienting to the people, and orienting to the technologies or tools used to do the tasks. Since the most difficult transition was from solo work to work involving MCC, we then asked these astronauts to rank "How difficult is each factor when transitioning from a solo task to one involving mission control (1 = least difficult, 3 = most difficult)." Figure 10.3 presents the responses broken out by time in mission. Examining Figure 10.3 shows that overall, astronauts ranked "orienting to the people" as the most difficult, followed by "orienting to the tools," and then by "orienting to the tasks." Interestingly, the rankings change over time. "Orienting to the task" is ranked as "less difficult" relative to the other two as time progresses. "Orienting to the technologies or tools used to do the task" is ranked as "more difficult" relative to the other two as time progresses. "Orienting to the people" has the overall highest ranking, and generally maintains a similar ranking over time relative to tasks and technologies. The data reported by ISS astronauts provides some useful recommendations for designing work in space. The survey results gathered aboard the ISS suggest four observations and associated practical recommendations (Table 10.3, #s 1–4).

HERA analog perceptions. Next, in order to understand how these perceptions of work are affected by factors like communication delay that will be encountered on long distance missions, we conducted the survey in NASA's HERA (Human Exploration Research Analog) analog on crews living in the habitat for 45 days performing highly scheduled work under various communication delays. We report

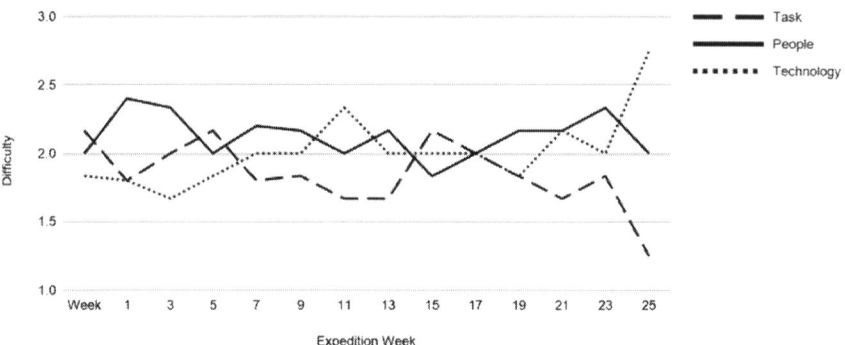

FIGURE 10.3 Astronaut rankings of the relative difficulty of orienting to tasks, people, and technologies when transitioning from solo to multiteam work aboard the International Space Station ($N = 6$).

data from Campaign 4 which included five, four-person crews ($N = 20$ individuals). Due to Hurricane Harvey's landfall in Houston, the second crew (Mission 2) was aborted after they completed four of the surveys. A second crew (Mission 3) experienced a scheduling issue and missed one of the survey administrations. All in all, we present 140 survey responses characterizing crewmembers' work perceptions over time. The task perception survey was administered to each analog participant a total of eight times, evenly spaced throughout the mission.

Each mission within the campaign followed the same mission arc, which entailed a simulated round-trip mission to an asteroid to obtain samples. As HERA moves far enough away from Earth, they begin to experience increasing times for their communications to reach Earth, and from Earth back to HERA. This communication delay begins with a 30 second delay on mission-day 15, reaches its peak of 300 seconds (5 minutes) when HERA reaches their destination on mission-days 20–24, then decreases back to no delay as they approach Earth on mission-days 29–45.

Examples of solo tasks completed in HERA include developing procedures for an onboard system, calculating thruster velocities for reentry, or completing physical fitness regimens. Examples of team **tasks** completed in HERA include the MMSEV task or the rover assembly. Examples of multiteam tasks in HERA include interfacing with mission control to conduct extravehicular activities or to make modifications to systems during a system failure.

HERA crewmembers ranked tasks completed alone (solo), with crewmembers (crew), and working with those outside the crew (MCC) in terms of relative difficulty. For comparison with the ISS data, we have labeled this category MCC though we note that there was not a MCC operating at HERA. In HERA there are two relevant groups outside the crew. The first is the HabCom, or habitat communicator, a person working on console 24 hours a day to ensure the health and safety of the crew. The second is an eight-member Mission Control located at a university that the crew works with on remote problem-solving tasks.

Figure 10.4 presents the average ranked difficulty of these transitions reported by the 20 HERA participants in Campaign 4. The three shifts that involve increases

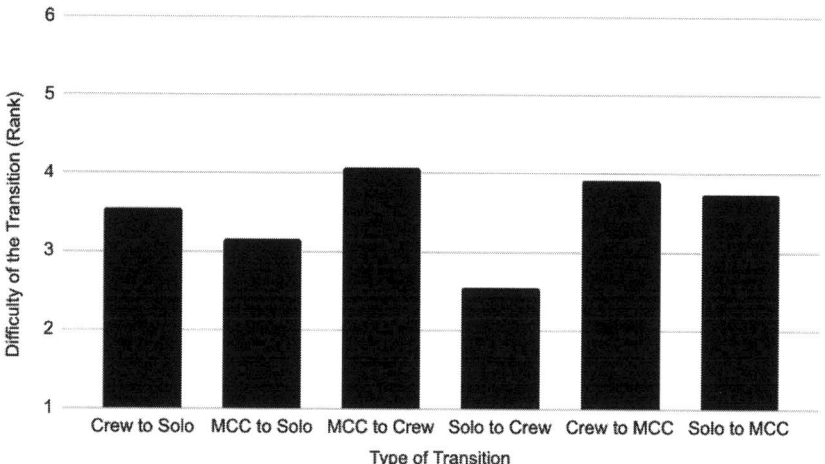

FIGURE 10.4 Analog participant rankings of the relative difficulty of task transitions made while working in HERA ($N = 20$).

in autonomy are presented on the left, and the three shifts that involve decreasing autonomy are on the right. The pattern for HERA participants differs from ISS astronauts. On the ISS, transition difficulty is affected by whether autonomy is being gained or lost. This was true of four of the six types of transitions made in HERA. There were two differences. First, "solo to crew" transitions involve a decrease in autonomy but were the easiest transition reported by HERA participants. Second, transitioning from an MCC task to a crew task, which increases autonomy, was the most difficult transition reported by HERA participants.

In order to understand the relative impact of each type of factor on work transitions, we asked the HERA participants to rank the difficulty of the three factors: orienting to the task, orienting to the people, and orienting to the technologies or tools used to do the tasks. Since the most difficult transition was from solo work to work involving MCC, we then asked these astronauts to rank "How difficult is each factor when transitioning from a solo task to one involving mission control (1 = least difficult, 3 = most difficult)." Figure 10.5 presents the responses broken out by time in mission. Examining Figure 10.5 shows that overall, HERA participants were similar to astronauts in their ranking of "orienting to the people" as the most difficult, followed by "orienting to the tools," and then by "orienting to the tasks." However, the change in rankings during the mission did not mirror that of the ISS astronauts. "Orienting to the people" was ranked as progressively less difficult whereas "orienting to the task" and "orienting to the technology" were both ranked as more difficult as the mission progressed.

The data reported by HERA participants also provides useful insight for designing work in space, particularly related to a high autonomy mission. The ISS astronauts work closely with mission control each relying on the other in crucial ways in order to accomplish work. In contrast, the HERA crew is largely autonomous as a crew. They experience extended periods of communication delay and must rely on

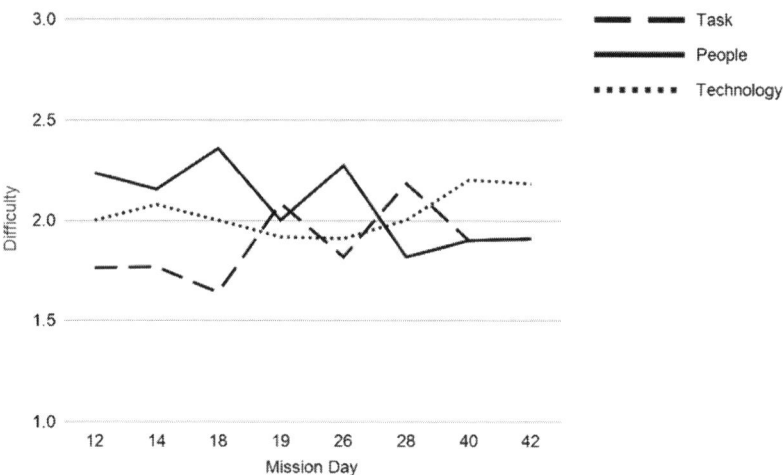

FIGURE 10.5 Analog participant rankings of the relative difficulty of orienting to tasks, people, and technologies when transitioning from solo to multiteam work in HERA ($N = 20$).

one another to answer questions and resolve issues that arise. This difference was born out in some of our survey data about the relative difficulty of task transitions. Overall, an additional preliminary recommendation for designing work for more autonomous missions follows (Table 10.3, # 5).

PART 3: COMPUTATIONAL MODELING OF WORKING IN SPACE

Whereas some work design recommendations can be usefully grounded in astronaut accounts of work, there are some additional considerations that require a different approach. Astronaut accounts are especially useful for designing work in space aboard the ISS or in work situations that will be similar to the work completed on the ISS. There are particular features of this situation that generalize well to planned missions to the moon (e.g., Artemis), but there are also particular aspects of this situation that may not generalize very well to missions beyond low Earth orbit (LEO) such as a mission to Mars. In this case, the aid of a computational model that can harness data gathered from analog recruits becomes a highly useful decision aid. Computational models afford insights into emergent behavior resulting from actions and interactions that occur within complex systems and are useful for understanding social context in the area of teams and multiteam systems (Harrison, Lin, Carroll, & Carley, 2007; Macy & Willer, 2002; Monge & Contractor, 2003; Sullivan, Lungeanu, DeChurch, & Contractor, 2015). Such a model allows us to do two things. First, we can use the model to conduct virtual "what if" experiments of conditions that would be prohibitively costly to conduct in a space environment. Second, we can extrapolate to conditions that may not be observable in current space missions. In this final section, we describe our efforts at building such a model that can be used to inform work design recommendations.

In this section of our chapter, we present the development of an agent-based model that estimates the stickiness of an ongoing task and the attractiveness of an alternative task to predict the probability that an individual will switch from an ongoing task to an alternative task. This model incorporates the task, social, technological, contextual, and individual factors that affect the perceived stickiness and attractiveness of ongoing versus alternative tasks. Then we parameterize the agent-based model using empirical data collected in HERA to better simulate and understand the context of work in space.

CONTEXT: PROJECT RED

The ABM was parameterized using data collected on analog participants as they participated in a complex problem-solving task. This period of observation had the analog crew working with a remote mission control on a series of tasks, some of which were completed alone, with the crew, with functional teams, and with the full group. The data reported here were collected as part of NASA's HERA space analog Campaign 3. The four-member crew in our study underwent a 30-day mission in which the goal was to journey to the asteroid "Geographos" and collect rock samples before returning home. In order to reach the surface of the asteroid, crewmembers participated in a variety of tasks, one of which is Project RED. Crewmembers spend the first half of the mission (days 1–15) in the outbound phase in which they simulate the trip to the asteroid. Crewmembers rendezvous with the asteroid on mission-day 16 and spend the next few days conducting operations on the asteroid. Crewmembers then leave the asteroid on mission-day 19 and are in the return phase of the mission from mission-days 19–30, returning to earth on day 30.

Multiteam task: Project RED. We conducted our experiment on mission-days 9, 16, and 28. On each of these days, the crew worked with a different eight-member mission control on Project RED, which is a 12-member online software platform that requires 12 specialized members to design a well on Mars. In order to represent the essential features of a multiteam system, or "team of teams", we designed the task so that individuals use specialized expertise to pursue team goals, but must collaborate across teams to attain the superordinate goal. The four teams were: Space Geology, Space Robotics, Extraterrestrial Engineering, and Space Human Factors. One HERA crewmember was trained in each of the four functions. The remaining two team members of each of the four functional teams were "back on Earth" in MCC.

Each team pursued a different goal. **Geology's** team goal was to find a location for the well that has the most water available for a future colony. **Robotics'** team goal was to develop a well construction plan that minimizes the total direct cost (i.e., the amount of money required to build the well using robots and rovers). **Engineering's** team goal was to design a well that maximizes total clean water output, determined by the total water output and the number of contaminants in the water. **Human Factors'** team goal was to minimize the terrain cost (i.e., the amount of money that will need to be spent constructing and utilizing the well). The superordinate goal of the multiteam system was to determine a plan for the location and design of the well that would support as large a colony on Mars as possible. All four teams' expertise was required to accomplish the MTS goal.

Each member of the MTS had a unique information database with role-relevant information and had an individualized view of the Martian landscape where he or she could look up information and run calculations related to their specific goals. Members discussed options and jointly negotiated the plan for the well for up to

30 minutes. After 30 minutes, the interface prompted members to input their final values and sign off. Sign off completed the task.

Experiment conditions. In order to understand the effects of mission phases on task transitions, we conducted Project RED sessions on mission days 9, 16, and 28. The early-misison data collection was conducted on mission-day 9. The HERA crew worked with an eight-member MCC on the Project RED task. The HERA crew was not experiencing communication delay on this day, and so all communication in and out of the habitat occurred in real time (i.e., normal conditions). The mid-mission data collection occurred on mission-day 16. The crew worked with a different eight-member MCC on the Project RED task. At this point in the mission, the crew was experiencing a 1-minute communication delay as they were farther from Earth (hypothetically). Thus, all communication in and out of the habitat was lagged by 1 minute each way. Finally, the late-mission data collection was conducted on mission-day 28. Although the crew was no longer experiencing communication delay at this point, as this was nearing the end of their mission, the crew was now in their 28th day of social isolation (i.e., extended isolation).

Collaborative behavior. As participants were interacting with the Project RED software, a server log was documenting their actions. As part of the design of the multiteam task, we developed a comprehensive list of required solo, team, and multiteam tasks. Every log entry for every individual was mapped onto a solo, team, or multiteam task. For example, a solo task would be using the decision calculator to examine role specific costs; a team task would be using the chat interface to communicate with one's teammates; and a multiteam task would be proposing a well location to a member of another functional team. Using these server logs, we classified the amount of time each person spent on solo, team, and multiteam tasks. We also created metrics reflecting the number of transitions each participant made during the task. By examining sequences of tasks, we computed the number of (1) vertical transitions (e.g., when an individual transitioned between a solo task to a team/MTS task or vice versa), and (2) lateral transitions (e.g., when an individual switched between tasks requiring the same degree of interdependence, such as moving from one team task to another team task).

THE MODEL: CREST (CREW RECOMMENDER FOR EFFECTIVELY SWITCHING TASKS)

We built an agent-based model of the Project RED task, and used a combination of survey, server, and ratings data to obtain empirical estimates of all variables thought to explain what work individuals choose to complete: solo, team, and/or multiteam tasks. We based our model on the conceptual model presented in Part 1 of this chapter, Figure 10.2.

Model development. The agent-based model (ABM) was used to explain and predict task transitions based on theories from human factors (e.g., Wickens et al., 2013), organizational psychology (e.g., McGrath & Kelly, 1986), and social networks (e.g., Hinds et al., 2000). The model estimates the stickiness of an ongoing task and the attractiveness of an alternative task to derive the probability that an individual will switch from one task to another task. The ABM consists of three steps.

In the first step, at each timestep (t) each individual (i) assesses his/her own likelihood of switching from an ongoing task (m) to an alternative task (n) at time $t + 1$. This likelihood is the difference between the attractiveness of the alternative task (*n*) at time (*t*) and the stickiness of the ongoing task (*m*) at time (*t*). Individual (*i*) assesses a total of (*T*) likelihood scores for all possible alternative tasks. $n \in T$ The perceived stickiness of the current task for an individual (*i*) is modeled as a function of task attributes, his/her social relations, tool affordances, situational constraints, and his/her individual attributes. Similarly, the perceived attractiveness of an alternative task is modeled as a function of the aforementioned factors that pertain to the alternative task being considered. We additionally estimate the effect of social influence that other individuals exert upon the focal individual in switching to a particular task. These likelihood scores are submitted to a logistic function to derive the binomial probability $Pr(i, m, n)_{t+1}$ of individual (*i*) switching from an ongoing task (*m*) to an alternative task (*n*) at time $t + 1$. That is:

$$Pr(i, m, n)_{t+1} = \frac{e^{\text{likelihood}(i, m, n)_{t+1}}}{1 + e^{\text{likelihood}(i, m, n)_{t+1}}}$$

In the second step, each individual decides whether to continue to work on the current ongoing task (*m*) or switch to another task (*n*) based on the maximum of the likelihoods that was assessed in the first step. This binary "stick vs. switch" decision is based on the probability of switching to the most attractive alternative task at that point in time (i.e., $\max(Pr(i, m, n)_{t+1})$). Hence, with $\max(Pr(i, m, n)_{t+1})$, an individual decides to switch to an alternative task (*n*) and with $1 - \max(Pr(i, m, n)_{t+1})$, the individual decides to continue to work on the current task (*m*). If the individual decides to continue to work, no further steps are taken and the model proceeds to the next iteration. On the other hand, if the individual decides to switch to another task, s/he goes through an additional procedure (third step) to decide which alternative task s/he will work on in the next time period. Again, the individual makes a probabilistic decision among the alternative tasks where the probabilities are proportional to the binomial probabilities of each alternative task. Once all individuals update their decisions, the simulation proceeds to the next iteration. The simulation ends when ProjectRED ends.

Model validation. The model was implemented in the NetLogo ABM platform (Wilensky, 1999) using the process described above. After the agent-based model was built, the parameters were fitted to the empirical data collected from the ProjectRED task. Specifically, model parameters were fitted using the BehaviorSearch tool (Stonedahl & Wilensky, 2010). BehaviorSearch is a calibration tool for models implemented in NetLogo (Thiele, Kurth, & Grimm, 2014). The aim of calibration is to find the parameter combination that best fits the observational data (Railsback & Grimm, 2012). Calibration describes the process of manipulating a model to get closer to a desired behavior. In this case, the desired behavior is matching the tasks performed by each individual at each time point in the ABM with the tasks performed in ProjectRED.

To investigate the space of parameters, we used the standard genetic algorithm search method with "GrayBinaryChromosome" representation. Genetic algorithms offer a flexible meta-heuristic search mechanism which has been successful in combinatorial optimization and search problems. Gray codes have generally been found to give better performance for search representations. The optimization function was measured as the minimum objective function over ten simulations. Each simulation contained 20,000 model runs with five replications of each previous best model obtained. The variables in the model were all weighted to fall between 0 and 1. Additionally, all parameters were specified to range between −1 and 1. We performed the validation separately for each condition: (1) early mission, normal conditions, no communication delay, (2) mid-mission, 1-minute communication delay, and (3) late mission, extended isolation, no communication delay.

Model results. Tables 10.1 and 10.2 present the values of the parameters estimated for ongoing task stickiness and alternative task attractiveness. Table 10.1 displays the parameters indicating the degree to which each factor affected task stickiness at each of the three mission phases. Table 10.2 displays the parameters reflecting the influence of each factor on task attractiveness. The results of the computational model generally show two things. First, the magnitude of these estimates is generally above/below zero indicating all five sets of factors are explaining stickiness and attractiveness. Second, there is substantial variation in the weights associated with each factor early-, mid-, and late-mission. A few effects are consistent across observed conditions. For example, individuals confined to the

TABLE 10.1
ABM Results: Parameters Estimated for Ongoing Tasks Stickiness

	Early Mission: Normal Conditions	Mid Mission: Communication Delay	Late Mission: Extended Isolation
	Task Characteristics		
Difficulty	−0.39	−0.98	−0.96
Importance	0.11	−0.34	−0.99
Interdependence	0.53	0.79	−0.18
	Social factors		
Leadership	0.51	0.20	−0.14
Behavioral ties	−0.51	0.50	−0.20
Affective ties	−0.86	0.06	0.57
Cognitive ties	0.61	−0.08	−0.27
Affect toward synchronous collaborators	0.77	−0.01	−0.19
	Technology Affordances		
Editability	0.67	0.35	−0.76
Association	0.06	−0.06	0.09
	Situational Constraints		
Confinement	0.65	0.06	0.91
	Individual differences		
Extraversion	−0.52	0.17	−0.37
Agreeableness	−0.20	−0.74	−0.93
Conscientiousness	0.21	−0.91	−0.93
Openness	0.90	−0.78	−0.52
Neuroticism	0.63	0.64	0.02

TABLE 10.2
ABM Results: Parameters Estimated for Alternative Task Attractiveness

	Early Mission: Normal Conditions	Mid Mission: Communication Delay	Late Mission: Extended Isolation
Task Characteristics			
Difficulty	−0.62	0.94	−0.82
Importance	−0.10	−0.78	0.70
Interdependence	−0.04	0.05	−0.45
Salience	−0.30	−0.37	−0.87
Social Factors			
Leadership	0.17	0.26	−0.47
Behavioral ties	0.93	−0.12	0.55
Affective ties	−0.48	0.56	−0.34
Cognitive ties	0.58	0.55	0.50
Social influence from close neighbors	−0.51	0.82	0.63
Social influence from far neighbors	0.88	−0.09	−0.16
Technology Affordances			
Editability	0.03	−0.08	0.67
Association	0.68	0.29	0.90
Situational Constraints			
Confinement	0.62	0.22	0.55
Individual Differences			
Extraversion	−0.15	−0.89	0.28
Agreeableness	−0.74	0.53	−0.25
Conscientiousness	−0.08	0.39	0.03
Openness	−0.35	−0.02	0.18
Neuroticism	0.94	−0.86	0.71

analog found all tasks to be stickier and more attractive than did the participants who were in the remote mission control. The confinement parameter was always positive. Difficult tasks were always less sticky, and salient ones more attractive. Personality variables also showed interesting patterns. Consider trait agreeableness. Agreeable individuals are described as being warm, cooperative, considerate, kind, and sympathetic to others. Agreeable individuals found all tasks to be less sticky across all conditions. They found all tasks to be less attractive as well, except under communication delay when agreeableness was positively associated with task attractiveness. The interpretation of each parameter is less important than the global observation that the most important factors, and the weights of these factors, differ across mission stages. This leads us to a final recommendation based on our computational model (Table 10.3, #6).

TABLE 10.3
Observations and Recommendations

#	Observation	Recommendation
1	*Gaining autonomy is easier than losing it.* Task transitions involving decreasing autonomy (increased interdependence) are reported to be more difficult than those that increase autonomy (Figure 10.1).	*Schedule interdependent work first.* Task transitions involving decreasing autonomy (increased interdependence) are reported to be more difficult than those that increase autonomy (Figure 10.1). Thus, it is preferable to schedule interdependent work first, followed by more independent work.
2	*Orienting to people is a challenging aspect of transitioning tasks.* Orienting to the people is rated as the most difficult aspect of work transitions (Figure 10.3) overall.	*Provide interventions that lessen the resources required to orient toward different groups of people.* Interventions that lessen the resources required to orient toward different groups of people will benefit collaboration between the crew and mission control. In addition, when designing work schedules there may be a benefit to grouping tasks that are completed with the same crewmembers or with the same mission control members/groups. By grouping tasks completed with the same individuals together, the cognitive resources needed to transition can be reduced fostering a smoother transition.
3	*Orienting to the task is a challenging aspect of task transitions at early mission stages.* Orienting to the tasks is rated as the most difficult aspect of work transitions early in the mission and decreases over the course of the mission (Figure 10.3). Conversations with astronauts confirm that interpreting procedures and initially adjusting to work in space can be challenging during the first few weeks of the mission.	*Provide interventions that make task instructions, procedures, and resources clear during early mission stages.* Interventions that make task instructions, procedures, and resources clear are most valuable at early mission stages as crewmembers are in their initial adjustment phase. Interventions to improve the clarity of procedures during this early period can make task transitions easier.
4	*Orienting to the technology is a challenging aspect of task transitions at late mission stages.* Orienting to technologies and tools needed to complete work is reported to be relatively more difficult as the mission progresses (Figure 10.3).	*Provide interventions that make technology easier to use during later mission stages.* Interventions that make technology easier to use may be especially valuable in later mission phases. It is also desirable to ensure that whenever possible, technology interfaces use similar user interfaces and social affordances in order to ease transitions lessening the cognitive demands placed on crewmembers as they interact with different onboard tools and interfaces.

(Continued)

TABLE 10.3 (Continued)
Observations and Recommendations

#	Observation	Recommendation
5	***Work transitions toward and away from mission control are the most challenging for autonomous crews.*** The most challenging task transitions reported by HERA crews involved moving into work tasks requiring interaction with mission control or moving from work with mission control to working with the crew (Figure 10.4).	***Schedule work with mission control early in the crew's work day.*** As with recommendation one, during periods of high autonomy, it would be desirable to schedule interactions with mission control at times most convenient to the crew in terms of their sleep-wake cycle. Given that crew and MCC days will not always overlap, scheduling work with mission control early in the crew's day will ensure the most difficult to handle work transitions occur first, followed by easier transitions as cognitive resources are depleted over the course of the day.
6	***The factors affecting work transitions change across mission stages.*** Whereas our model estimates sizeable effects of all five sets of factors on task stickiness and attractiveness, the relative importance of these characteristics changes over the mission (Tables 10.1 and 10.2).	***Work designs should be customized to the mission phase.*** Our genetic algorithm shows the most important factors that explain how long individuals persist on tasks, and how likely they are to start them, changes over time based on conditions like communication delay. This means that work design interventions should be developed based on computational models that account for these changing dynamics.

Computational models like this one can be used to design interventions by conducting synthetic or virtual experiments. Models with empirically validated parameters provide a powerful platform to conduct computational experiments (Monge & Contractor, 2003). In computational experiments, we create large numbers of virtual agents (in the computer) to mimic human participants. Conducting computational experiments with these virtual agents enables us to ask "what-if" questions to assess the impact of changing the value of certain variables on outcomes before conducting an actual experiment to collect data. Hence, they offer a low-cost strategy to assess if, and how, differences in the values of certain variables impact outcomes.

CONCLUSION

The nature of work in space is likely to undergo a transformation in the near future as space exploration traverses longer distances from Earth. Distance equals communication delays between the crew and mission control on Earth, and thus introduces the potential for greater crew autonomy and disengagement from counterparts on Earth. Space exploration crews will need to complete tasks that vary in terms of interdependence (solo, team, and multiteam tasks), though there will be greater potential for crewmember "choice" in when and how to execute tasks during longer duration and distance missions than has historically been the case.

Human factors research suggests perceptions of task difficulty, importance, and interest affect the likelihood an individual will want to stay with a current task or switch to an alternative task. We extend this work drawing on adjacent literatures and detailing four sets of factors that affect task stickiness and attractiveness. These include social factors like the quality of interpersonal relationships, technology affordances like the degree of editability, situational constraints like extended confinement, and individual differences like trait agreeableness.

Surveys administered on the ISS and in HERA suggest shifts in autonomy affect the ease of transitioning tasks, and that orienting to people is the most difficult aspect of transitioning into highly interdependent work like coordinating with mission control. We also illuminate how agent-based modeling can shed light on how a human crew may respond under a variety of circumstances so that mission control might know when support mechanisms and interventions are particularly important for crew and mission welfare. We highlight six observations suggesting recommendations for designing work in space.

In sum, interviews, diaries, and other accounts of work and life in space are remarkably consistent in their depiction of the importance of scheduling, collaboration, and engagement as central to the experience of work. By exploring how perceptions of independent and interdependent tasks change as a function of time in the mission and extent of communication delay using analog experimentation and agent-based modeling, we shed light on new and important implications for the timing and development of countermeasures that support and promote effective crew process and performance.

REFERENCES

Allport, A., & Wylie, G. (1999). Task-switching: Positive and negative priming of task-set. In G. W. Humphreys, J. Duncan, & A. Treisman (Eds.), *Attention, space, and action: Studies in cognitive neuroscience* (pp. 273–296). New York, NY: Oxford University Press.

Allworth, E., & Hesketh, B. (1999). Construct-oriented biodata: Capturing change-related and contextually relevant future performance. *International Journal of Selection and Assessment, 7*(2), 97–111. doi:10.1111/1468-2389.00110

Altmann, E. M., & Trafton, J. G. (2002). Memory for goals: An activation-based model. *Cognitive Science, 26*(1), 39–83.

Baard, S. K., Rench, T. A., & Kozlowski, S. W. (2014). Performance adaptation: A theoretical integration and review. *Journal of Management, 40*(1), 48–99.

Cannon-Bowers, J. A., & Salas, E. (2001). Reflections on team cognition. *Journal of Organizational Behavior, 22*, 195–202. doi:10.1002/job.82

Carr, M. H. (1986). Mars: A water-rich planet? *Icarus, 68*(2), 187–216.

Chung, P. H., & Byrne, M. D. (2008). Cue effectiveness in mitigating postcompletion errors in a routine procedural task. *International Journal of Human-Computer Studies, 66*(4), 217–232. doi:10.1016/j.ijhcs.2007.09.001

Conte, J. M., & Jacobs, R. R. (2003). Validity evidence linking polychronicity and big five personality dimensions to absence, lateness, and supervisory performance ratings. *Human Performance, 16*(2), 107–129. doi:10.1207/S15327043HUP1602_1

Cronshaw, S. F., & Jethmalani, S. (2005). The structure of workplace adaptive skill in a career inexperienced group. *Journal of Vocational Behavior, 66*(1), 45–65.

Csikszentmihalyi, M. (1991). *Flow: The psychology of optimal experience.* New York, NY: Harper Perennial.
DeShon, R. P., Kozlowski, S. W., Schmidt, A. M., Milner, K. R., & Wiechmann, D. (2004). A multiple-goal, multilevel model of feedback effects on the regulation of individual and team performance. *Journal of applied psychology, 89*(6), 1035–1056.
Driskell, T., Salas, E., & Driskell, J. E. (2018). Teams in extreme environments: Alterations in team development and teamwork. *Human Resource Management Review, 28*(4), 434–449. doi:10.1016/j.hrmr.2017.01.002
Ellis, A. P. (2006). System breakdown: The role of mental models and transactive memory in the relationship between acute stress and team performance. *Academy of Management Journal, 49*(3), 576–589. doi:10.5465/amj.2006.21794674
Fahr, R. (2011). Job design and job satisfaction – Empirical evidence for Germany? *Management Revue, 22,* 28–46.
Gergle, D., & Tan, D. S. (2014) Experimental research in HCI. In J. Olson, W. Kellogg (Eds.), *Ways of knowing in HCI.* New York, NY: Springer.
Gersick, C. J., & Hackman, J. R. (1990). Habitual routines in task-performing groups. *Organizational Behavior and Human Decision Processes, 47*(1), 65–97.
Girgis, Z. M. (2010). *Predicting multitasking performance and understanding the nomological network of polychronicity* (unpublished master's thesis). San Diego State University, San Diego, CA.
Hackman, J. R., & Oldham, G. R. (1976). Motivation through the design of work: Test of a theory. *Organizational Behavior and Human Performance, 16*(2), 250–279.
Harrison, J. R., Lin, Z., Carroll, G. R., & Carley, K. M. (2007). Simulation modeling in organizational and management research. *Academy of Management Review, 32*(4), 1229–1245. doi:10.5465/amr.2007.26586485
Helson, H. (1949). Design of equipment and optimal human operation. *The American Journal of Psychology, 62*(4), 473–497.
Hinds, P. J., Carley, K. M., Krackhardt, D., & Wholey, D. (2000). Choosing work group members: Balancing similarity, competence, and familiarity. *Organizational Behavior and Human Decision Processes, 81*(2), 226–251. doi:10.1006/obhd.1999.2875
Kaff, M. S. (2004). Multitasking is multitaxing: Why special educators are leaving the field. *Preventing School Failure, 48,* 10–17.
Kantrowitz, T. M., Grelle, D. M., Beaty, J. C., & Wolf, M. B. (2012). Time is money: Polychronicity as a predictor of performance across job levels. *Human Performance, 25*(2), 114–137. doi:10.1080/08959285.2012.658926
König, C. J., Buhner, M., & Murling, G. (2005). Working memory, fluid intelligence, and attention are predictors of multitasking performance, but polychronicity and extraversion are not. *Human performance, 18*(3), 243–266. doi:10.1207/s15327043hup1803_3
Lee, J. D., & See, K. A. (2004). Trust in automation: Designing for appropriate reliance. *Human Factors, 46*(1), 50–80. doi:10.1518/hfes.46.1.50_30392
Lim, J., & Dinges, D. (2008). Sleep deprivation and vigilant attention. *Annals of the New York Academy of Sciences, 1129*(1), 305–322.
Macy, M. W., & Willer, R. (2002). From factors to factors: computational sociology and agent-based modeling. *Annual Review of Sociology, 28*(1), 143–166.
Mark, G., Iqbal, S. T., Czerwinski, M., & Johns, P. (2014). Bored Mondays and focused afternoons: the rhythm of attention and online activity in the workplace. In *Proceedings of the SIGCHI Conference on Human Factors in Computing Systems* (pp. 3025–3034). New York, NY: Association for Computing Machinery. doi: 10.1145/2556288.2557204
Marques-Quinteiro, P., Curral, L., Passos, A. M., & Lewis, K. (2013). And now what do we do? The role of transactive memory systems and task coordination in action teams. *Group Dynamics: Theory, Research, and Practice, 17*(3), 194–206. doi:10.1037/a0033304

Mathieu, J. E., Heffner, T. S., Goodwin, G. F., Salas, E., & Cannon-Bowers, J. A. (2000). The influence of shared mental models on team process and performance. *Journal of Applied Psychology, 85*(2), 273–283. doi:10.1037/0021-9010.85.2.273

Mayr, U., & Keele, S. W. (2000). Changing internal constraints on action: The role of backward inhibition. *Journal of Experimental Psychology: General, 129*(1), 4–26.

McGrath, J. E., & Kelly, J. R. (1986). *The Guilford social psychology series. Time and human interaction: Toward a social psychology of time.* New York, NY: Guilford Press.

McGrath, J. E., Arrow, H., & Berdahl, J. L. (2000). The study of groups: Past, present, and future. *Personality and Social Psychology Review, 4*(1), 95–105.

Mesmer-Magnus, J., Viswesvaran, C., Bruk-Lee, V., Sanderson, K., & Sinha, N. (2014). Personality correlates of preference for multitasking in the workplace. *Journal of Organizational Psychology, 14*(1), 67–76.

Monge, P. R., & Contractor, N. S. (2003). *Theories of communication networks.* New York NY: Oxford University Press:.

Monk, C. A., Trafton, J. G., & Boehm-Davis, D. A. (2008). The effect of interruption duration and demand on resuming suspended goals. *Journal of Experimental Psychology: Applied, 14*(4), 299–313.

Morgan, B., D'Mello, S., Abbott, R., Radvansky, G., Haass, M., & Tamplin, A. (2013). Individual differences in multitasking ability and adaptability. *Human Factors, 55*(4), 776–788. doi: 10.1177/0018720812470842

Mortensen, M., Woolley, A., & O'Leary, M. (2007). Conditions enabling effective multiple team membership. In K. Crowston, S. Sieber, & E.Wynn (Eds.), *Virtuality and virtualization. IFIP International Federation for Information Processing* (pp. 215–228). Boston, MA: Springer.

O'Leary, M. B., Mortensen, M., & Woolley, A. W. (2011). Multiple team membership: A theoretical model of its effects on productivity and learning for individuals and teams. *Academy of Management Review, 36*(3), 461–478. doi:10.5465/amr.2009.0275

Payne, S. J., Duggan, G. B., & Neth, H. (2007). Discretionary task interleaving: Heuristics for time allocation in cognitive foraging. *Journal of Experimental Psychology: General, 136*(3), 370–388.

Poposki, E. M., Oswald, F. L., & Chen, H. T. (2009). *Neuroticism negatively affects multitasking performance through state anxiety* (No. NPRST-TN-09-3). Millington, TN: Navy Personnel Research Studies and Technology.

Pulakos, E. D., Arad, S., Donovan, M. A., & Plamondon, K. E. (2000). Adaptability in the workplace: Development of a taxonomy of adaptive performance. *Journal of Applied Psychology, 85*(4), 612–624. doi:10.1037/0021-9010.85.4.612

Pulakos, E. D., Schmitt, N., Dorsey, D. W., Arad, S., Borman, W. C., & Hedge, J. W. (2002). Predicting adaptive performance: Further tests of a model of adaptability. *Human Performance, 15*(4), 299–323. doi:10.1207/S15327043HUP1504_01

Railsback, S. F., & Grimm, V. (2012). *Agent-based and individual-based modeling: A practical introduction.* Princeton, NJ: Princeton University press.

Sanderson, K. R. (2012). *Time orientation in organizations: Polychronicity and multitasking* (Unpublished doctoral dissertation). Miami, FL: Florida International University.

Smith-Jentsch, K. A., (2015). *On shifting from autonomous to interdependent work* (Technical Report February). Houston, TX: National Aeronautics Space Administration.

Stachowski, A. A. (2011). *A model of time use at work: Individual differences, time use, and performance* (Unpublished doctoral dissertation). Fairfax, VA: George Mason University.

Stonedahl, F., & Wilensky, U. (2010, May). Finding forms of flocking: Evolutionary search in abm parameter-spaces. In *International workshop on multi-agent systems and agent-based simulation* (pp. 61–75).Berlin, Heidelberg: Springer.

Stuster, J. (2010). *Behavioral issues associated with long-duration space expeditions: Review and analysis of astronaut journals: Experiment 01-E104 (Journals)*. Houston, TX: National Aeronautics and Space Administration, Johnson Space Center.

Sullivan, S. D., Lungeanu, A., Dechurch, L. A., & Contractor, N. S. (2015). Space, time, and the development of shared leadership networks in multiteam systems. *Network Science, 3*(1), 124–155. doi:10.1017/nws.2015.7

Thiele, J. C., Kurth, W., & Grimm, V. (2014). Facilitating parameter estimation and sensitivity analysis of agent-based models: A cookbook using NetLogo and R. *Journal of Artificial Societies and Social Simulation, 17*(3), 11. doi: 10.18564/jasss.2503

Treem, J., & Leonardi, P. (2012). Social media use in organizations: Exploring the affordances of visibility, editability, persistence, association. *Communication Yearbook, 36*, 143–189.

Wickens, C., Gutzwiller, R., & Santamaria, A. (2015). Discrete task switching in overload: A meta-analyses and model. *International Journal of Human-Computer Studies, 79*, 79–84.

Wickens, C. D., Hooey, B. L., Gore, B. F., Sebok, A., & Koenicke, C. S. (2009). Identifying black swans in nextgen: Predicting human performance in off-nominal conditions. *Human Factors, 51*(5), 638–651. doi:10.1177/0018720809349709

Wickens, C. D., Santamaria, A., & Sebok, A. (2013, September). A computational model of task overload management and task switching. Proceedings of the Human Factors and Ergonomics Society Annual Meeting, *57*(1), 763–767.

Wilensky, U. (1999). *NetLogo*. Evanston, IL: Center for Connected Learning and Computer-Based Modeling, Northwestern University.

Wittenbaum, G. M., & Stasser, G. (1996). Management of information in small groups. In J. L. Nye & A. M. Brower (Eds), *What's social about social cognition? Research on socially shared cognition in small groups* (pp. 3–28). Newbury Park, CA: Sage Publications, Inc.

Zhang, J., & Norman, D.A. (1994), Representations in distributed cognitive tasks. *Cognitive Science, 18*(1), 87–122. doi:10.1207/s15516709cog1801_3

Zika-Viktorsson, A., Sundström, P., & Engwall, M. (2006). Project overload: An exploratory study of work and management in multi-project settings. *International Journal of Project Management, 24*(5), 385–394. doi:10.1016/j.ijproman.2006.02.010

11 The Human Factors of Design for Spaceflight

Kritina Holden
Leidos

Gordon Vos and Jessica J. Marquez
NASA

CONTENTS

Human Systems Integration (HSI) 205
Human-Centered Design Process and Core Human Factors Metrics 206
Spaceflight Case Studies 208
    International Space Station (ISS) 209
    Orion Multi-Purpose Crew Vehicle (MPCV) 214
    Exploration 218
Conclusion 221
Acknowledgments 221
References 221

Human Systems Integration (HSI) is an interdisciplinary technical and management process to design and develop systems that effectively and affordably integrate human capabilities and limitations. NASA implements HSI to ensure spacecraft and habitat designs support optimal human performance that leads to successful missions. We begin this chapter with an overview of HSI and the Human-Centered Design (HCD) process, followed by exemplars of successful HSI at NASA, facilitated by human factors practitioners. The spaceflight case studies described were selected from ISS, Orion, and Exploration development projects.

HUMAN SYSTEMS INTEGRATION (HSI)

Human Systems Integration (HSI) is a phrase that encompasses several concepts.

To fully describe HSI, we must first define a *system*, which essentially is an assemblage of components forming a complex whole, one that is greater than the sum of its parts. In the use of systems, humans are critical elements that contribute positively to system safety, reliability, and performance. Indeed, in many cases, their creativity, adaptability and problem-solving capabilities are key to resilient operations. HSI ensures that human capabilities and limitations are effectively considered in system design and development, so that that the human and software/hardware components of the system cooperate, coordinate, and communicate effectively.

This places human concerns on par with other aspects of system design. HSI uses process and technical disciplines to provide a successful and lower risk mission capability. The goal of this process is to reduce lifecycle costs by ensuring that designers consider operational costs, particularly those associated with users and maintainers of a system. It focuses on placing human concerns on par with other aspects of system design.

HSI repeatedly validates the original intent of the system from a human perspective, making sure that the true purpose of the system is not lost in the details. It considers the points where humans and systems interact, and brings together users, experts, designers, and engineers to make sure system demands are within the capabilities of its users. HSI also systematically infuses information from past designs, operational use, and user feedback into systems development, resulting in a continuous improvement loop. Ultimately, HSI aims to contain lifecycle costs by bringing operations-era experience to design and development with the intent of reducing manpower, skill demands, and training. Some of the key methods used by HSI integrators and practitioners include the Human-Centered Design (HCD) process; standardized usage of core human factors measures; the creation of standards, requirements, and guidelines that ensure use and consideration of these methods and measures during the design and development of new spaceflight vehicles and habitats; and inclusion of HSI personnel as members of the design and engineering teams.

Details regarding NASA's HSI philosophy, approach, and guidance on implementation are documented in NASA's Human Systems Integration Practitioner's Guide (HSI PG, NASA/SP-2015-3709), which is publicly available on the NASA Technical Reports Server (ntrs.nasa.gov). From the NTRS description of the HSI PG: "The HSI PG is written to aid the HSI practitioner engaged in a program or project (P/P), and serves as a knowledge base to allow the practitioner to step into an HSI lead or team member role for NASA missions." In other words, the HSI PG provides a resource that enables HSI implementation and action.

HUMAN-CENTERED DESIGN PROCESS AND CORE HUMAN FACTORS METRICS

The Human-Centered Design (HCD) process is one that is executed and iterated throughout the overall systems engineering lifecycle, so that the system matures over time. The metrics used to assess the design in each of these iterations include workload ratings, error rates, usability ratings, ratings of discomfort/fatigue/exertion, and assessment of compliance for considerations such as strength requirements, reach and range of motion, anthropometric accommodation, and time on task. At NASA, the thresholds or criteria values used for these assessments vary based on the design reference mission (DRM) for the system being developed and have changed over the years with a trend toward more end-user accommodation, less demands being placed upon the user's capabilities, and greater degrees of system flexibility being desired. The net result of this trend is the development of systems with better usability that enhance human performance while reducing lifecycle cost (by avoiding/reducing the need for late changes or redesigns).

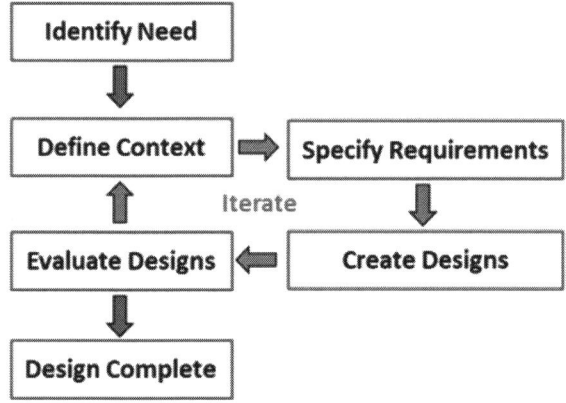

FIGURE 11.1 Flow of the human-centered design process.

The NASA Human Integration Design Processes (HIDP) document (NASA/TP-2014-218556) is an excellent reference for understanding how HCD is applied in human spaceflight contexts, though ultimately it is not much different than applying HCD in terrestrial environments, as described in the ISO document "Human-centered design for interactive systems" (ISO 9241-210:2010). According to both the documents, the general flow of HCD is described in Figure 11.1.

Each step of this continuous improvement loop engages human factors and HSI personnel in the assessment of the current design, at whatever level of fidelity it may be, determines if issues exist, and determines how best to mitigate them. These steps involve the following activities:

- Define the context of use: what are the tasks or objectives associated with the design.
- Specify requirements: what expectations or requirements must the design accommodate.
- Create design solutions:
  - Define design trades
  - Prototyping, rendering, mockup building
  - Develop alternative prototype solutions based on design trades
- Evaluate designs: test and evaluate the prototype designs for usability, workload, and design induced errors.
- Iterate: following testing and evaluation, fold the results back into the maturation and development of the prototype, after which this cycle repeats.

As stated in the HIDP, understanding the user and the operating environment (identifying needs and defining the context of use) is important to ensuring that design solutions meet the needs of the user within constraints of the operating environment. Understanding the user and environment means gaining a full awareness of the user (i.e., capabilities and limitations, skills and expertise), the work environment's constraints and challenges (e.g., microgravity, isolation, small enclosed volumes, etc.), and the tasks that will be performed to accomplish the mission (e.g., piloting, maintenance, eating, and sleeping). Understanding is gained through conducting the following activities:

- Develop missions and scenarios
- Develop concept of operations
- Allocate functions between user and system
- Perform user task analysis
- Conduct requirements analysis

In line with NASA's HSI process document, under "Visualize Design Concepts" and "Create Design Solutions," candidate design solutions should be visualized through graphical or physical representations based on information gathered in the Understanding the User and Environment activities. Design concepts may be communicated in many forms, depending on the maturity of the design, and may range from paper and pencil sketches, to interactive prototypes, to high-fidelity mockups, or computer-based simulations. It is important during this activity to communicate ideas and involve the user in focused design reviews to gather feedback. Designs and their physical representations should be iteratively improved based on user feedback until acceptable solutions are achieved. Designers should consider the use of available design data, models, and equipment when producing design solutions.

Finally, according to NASA's best practices, the HIDP states that in the "Evaluation of Designs," we evolve designs by identifying areas for design improvement through the gathering of quantitative and qualitative data. Intentional design iteration is a fundamental principle of HCD, which contributes to lifecycle development cost control by helping to identify risks and issues early in the design cycle when they are relatively inexpensive to fix. Evaluation of design concepts and alternatives is crucial to achieving optimal design solutions. Evaluations begin early and continue throughout system design. Evaluations can include a wide variety of activities, such as informal reviews with Subject Matter Experts (SMEs) or users, formal usability tests for gathering quantitative performance data or qualitative observations, assessments of design based upon Human-in-the-Loop (HITL) evaluation, or flight simulations to assess vehicular handling qualities and vehicle controllability by pilots.

SPACEFLIGHT CASE STUDIES

While standards and requirements for spacecraft crew interfaces exist that are appropriate for operational environments similar to the International Space Station (ISS), Exploration-class vehicles and habitats are anticipated to have very different crew interface characteristics, and operate under different environmental constraints than ISS. Exploration crews will have to effectively interact with new displays and controls under conditions of vibration, acceleration, and changing gravity levels. Missions will increase in length, increasing levels of autonomy and requiring newer technologies not yet proven in the space environment. Astronauts will face the challenges of physical deconditioning, prolonged isolation and confinement, significant communication latencies, environmental stressors, and increased responsibility. Autonomous crews may have to manage and control all aspects of the mission.

In missions to date, astronauts have been very successful; however, this statement must be qualified with the clause "with timely assistance from Mission Control personnel." The autonomous nature of future Exploration missions makes them very dissimilar to Space Shuttle and ISS operations. Consequently, there is uncertainty regarding the adequacy of design approaches for autonomous operations. We know that displays must provide all of the information needed by crew to operate autonomously, and in a form that is intuitive and promotes proper attention and cognitive load. Displays must also be usable in a variety of environmental conditions expected during the mission. Controls must be designed to provide automation when needed to compensate for the effects of the space environment. Research is ongoing to determine how displays and controls should be designed to best serve future autonomous space missions.

What follow in the sections below are a number of case studies from ISS, Orion, and Exploration (i.e., Mars-leaning work) that illustrate some of the space human factors design challenges and the work that has been done by the NASA human factors community of practitioners to address those challenges. Following the best practices of the Human-Centered Design process described above enabled practitioners to address these challenges with successful solutions.

INTERNATIONAL SPACE STATION (ISS)

The ISS is a microgravity research laboratory, in which astronauts from multiple nations conduct studies in a wide variety of disciplines. The first module of the ISS was launched in 1998, with the first long-term residents arriving in November, 2000. It has been inhabited continuously since that date. Since humans have lived and worked on ISS for some time, we continue to gain critical knowledge with each new expedition – knowledge that will help us safely send future crews beyond the low Earth orbit, and ensure their return from long-duration space missions in good health.

ISS Habitability. Due to its complexity and length of missions, ISS is the perfect environment for capturing habitability design lessons learned that can be applied to future Exploration spacecraft design. Given that habitability-related stressors will increase as the duration and level of isolation of a space mission increases (Celentano, Amorelli, & Freeman, 1963; Connors, Harrison, & Akins, 1985; Fraser, 1968; Harrison & Connors, 1990; Keeton, Schmidt, Slack, & Malka, 2012; Stuster, 1996, 2000, 2010; Whitmore, Adolf, & Woolford, 2000; Whitmore, McQuilkin, & Woolford, 1998), it is important to identify whatever we can from the longest duration spacecraft currently available – the International Space Station.

After each ISS mission (most lasting 6 months), the crew participates in a detailed post-mission debrief to answer questions about their experience and describe any issues they had, or any suggestions they might have for future crew or future vehicles. Critically important design information is obtained at these debriefs, as the design of space vehicles and habitats can greatly affect habitability and overall well-being. Astronauts can experience discomfort when their living and working spaces have inadequate volume, noise that interferes with privacy and tasks, odors, and poorly designed hardware and software, causing frustration (Beaubien & Baker, 2002). That frustration, over time, can lead to increased errors and reductions in crew satisfaction and safety.

Currently, real-time (or near real-time) subjective human factors and habitability data collection during space operations is limited. Interview data from the *Crew Comments Database* (an internal repository of data from the debriefing of astronauts after they return from a space mission) reveal that many crewmembers consider call-downs to Mission Control Center (MCC) to be a primary means of reporting human factors and habitability concerns. While critical problems are addressed using this method, complete data, including details of smaller issues or complaints, may not be fed back to the human factors and habitability practitioners or designers who need the information for enhancing efficiencies and effectiveness and/or feeding into next generation spacecraft design. There have been some habitability questionnaires on Skylab (Johnson, 1975), Mir (Novak, 2000; Whitmore et al., 2000), and Shuttle (Mount et al., 1994; Mount & Foley, 1999; Mount, Whitmore, & Stealey, 2003), and one study on ISS, which asked astronauts to journal and record entries related to behavioral factors (Stuster, 2010, 2016).

The ISS Habitability study (Greene, Thaxton, & Adolf, 2018) was conducted with six crew subjects: one 1-year duration and five 6-month duration crewmembers. The goal was to characterize the current state of ISS habitability using tools to capture data near real-time, with particular emphasis placed on areas of interest defined based on knowledge gaps, known problem areas, and volume-driving tasks. Near-real-time habitability and human factors data were collected in this study with a NASA Johnson Space Center-developed tool: Space Habitability Observation Reporting Tool (iSHORT). The iOS-based tool provided a simple interface for the crew to report open-ended positive or negative observations about their environment, equipment, and general activities within the ISS habitat. A screenshot is shown in Figure 11.2.

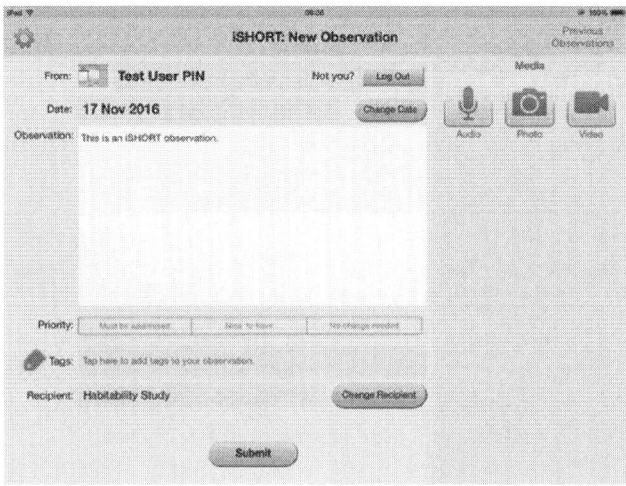

FIGURE 11.2 Screenshot from iSHORT.

Example comments recorded by the crew in iSHORT include:

- *The scratch pane only allows small access for the camera but the window itself is nice and large.*
- *There are cables all over the place, cables on cameras, cables on monitors, power cables, cables going into laptops, cables on racks. They are snag hazards, they are messy. [...] managing these things is a huge problem, time sync.*
- *If you can keep away from complicated alphanumeric codes and go to plain English or plain language names of parts, that helps a lot as well.*

iSHORT reports were pre-populated with the current date and time, but crew could adjust the date and time to report events that happened in the past. Participants could also select a priority-level to assign to the observation (*Must be addressed*, "*Nice to have*", or *No change needed*). In addition, crew could select tags to identify relevant human factors and habitability topics of interest that relate to the observation. The tags could also be used as memory joggers for expected entries. Observations could be recorded as text, entered with a keyboard, or audio or video recording. Photos or video could also be captured to further describe/support the entry. During the ISS study, another stand-alone application (iQ&A) was developed for survey administration and tested along with iSHORT. The iQ&A survey consisted of open-ended questions, plus satisfaction ratings for privacy, habitable volume, and layout.

Crew participants in the ISS Habitability study were asked to view an overview video (serving as the only training for the study). They completed an observation in iSHORT once every 2 weeks; created iSHORT walk-through videos (guided video tours of an area within ISS) once per month; created narrated task-based videos once per month; completed an iQ&A habitability and human factors survey three times during the mission; and participated in a real-time conference with the study principal investigator three times during the mission to answer follow-up questions based on crew inputs to iSHORT and iQ&A.

Overall, video emerged as the preferred method of reporting across participants, with four of the six preferring it over text or audio. Task-based videos were made on tasks, such as: food preparation activities, exercise equipment setup and use, payload setup, blood collection, and housekeeping. Walkthrough videos included tours of hygiene areas, translation paths from one ISS module to another, the robotic workstation, dining areas, and crew quarters.

A content analysis methodology (Stemler, 2001) was employed on the observations, following a similar methodology to that employed by Stuster (2010, 2016). A set of codes was defined with seven primary categories: Activities, Habitat environment, Equipment, Operations, Group interactions, Outcomes, and Study. Outcomes included satisfaction, effectiveness, efficiency, ease of use, and suggestions, among other options. The Outcomes category had the most entries, which indicates that the crew were able to provide observations that are valuable to human factors and habitability professionals, and hence to future space programs. Across the categories, the highest frequency comments dealt with hardware, layout, interface design, and stowage. Once all comments and videos were analyzed and grouped, the researchers

(Greene et al., 2018) were able to synthesize the inputs to create the recommendations shown in Table 11.1.

The importance of these recommendations is that they indicate areas where NASA requirements may be missing, or where requirements may need to be improved for the design of future space vehicles and habitats. In addition, ISS trainers and operational team members are in the process of using the results to improve current ISS operations.

Medical pack and cue card design. One of the spaceflight domains that is critically dependent on good human factors design is onboard medical operations. Currently on ISS, some astronauts are medical doctors, but most are not. Astronauts without a medical background receive only approximately 40 hours of medical training pre-mission. Much of the medical expertise comes from Flight Surgeon physicians in MCC remotely advising crewmembers.

ISS currently has a number of medical packs filled with hundreds of medical instruments, disassembled equipment components, and medications to address the most common, expected issues. In order to respond to a medical incident, crews must be able to find and follow the correct medical procedure, and then also locate,

TABLE 11.1
List of Recommendations Resulting from ISS Habitability Study

1. Increase the use of wireless technology.
2. Design stowage systems for efficiency and function
3. Give additional thought to placement and design of handrails and restraint systems
4. Increase the integration of software and hardware for tasks that are expected to be performed regularly
5. Provide highly usable interfaces for hardware and software that are intended to be reconfigured to support crewmember use
6. Design systems for consistency
7. Provide a dedicated volume for hygiene operations that is separate from toilet operations
8. Ensure labels are clear, visible, and accessible from multiple viewing angles
9. Design stowage systems for efficiency and function
10. Give additional thought to placement and design of handrails and restraint systems
11. Increase the integration of software and hardware for tasks that are expected to be performed regularly
12. Provide highly usable interfaces for hardware and software that are intended to be reconfigured to support crewmember use
13. Design systems for consistency
14. Provide a dedicated volume for hygiene operations that is separate from toilet operations
15. Ensure labels are clear, visible, and accessible from multiple viewing angles
16. Provide windows for crew recreation and operational tasks
17. Provide crew with the ability to control and modify environmental factors such as temperature, lighting, and ventilation
18. Ensure the trash management systems sufficiently control odor
19. Design packaging to facilitate activities and reduce trash
20. Ensure surfaces in areas that are likely to get dirty are easily cleanable and accessible.

correctly set up, and use the specified medical equipment within the time constraints of the situation. The incident to be addressed may have been trained up to a year ago, meaning training decay and loss of skills is a certainty. For this reason, it is critically important that the hardware and software associated with medical operations be well-designed and easy to use for those who are not medical doctors. While NASA medical operations groups design carefully and do preflight testing with crew, the involvement of human factors and the application of human factors methods have helped ensure safety and usability of some of the most critical medical components on ISS.

Smith, Byrne, and Hudy (2005) conducted a study of ISS medical packs to evaluate the organization of items and provide recommendations for redesign. The overall goal was to improve the efficiency of identifying and locating items in the medical packs, thereby, potentially increasing the survival rate of crewmembers in the event of a medical emergency. The medical pack assessment made use of scenario-based evaluations and eye tracking to identify the speed of identifying/accessing items needed for a medical emergency. As a result of the medical pack assessment, Smith and colleagues (2005) documented issues in several categories: Labeling, Location/Collocation of items, Clear Presentation of Information, Error Prevention, Stowage, and Equipment Design. For example, the assessment identified labels that were inconsistent and confusing, items frequently used together stored in separate locations, and dissimilar items that could be dangerous if confused – (e.g., Q-tips and silver nitrate sticks) packaged in very similar packaging. Recommendations for redesign of labels, packaging, and packing/location were provided to the ISS Program.

Medical pack cue cards, which are typically located in the lid of ISS medical packs, were assessed as part of another study involving the Respiratory Support Pack. The Respiratory Support Pack (RSP) is a medical pack onboard the ISS that contains much of the necessary equipment for providing aid to a conscious or unconscious crewmember in respiratory distress. Inside the medical pack lid pocket is a 5.5 by 11 in. paper cue card, on which is printed the procedure to set up the equipment and deliver oxygen to a crewmember in distress. In training, crewmembers expressed concerns about the readability and usability of the cue card, which was very text heavy, and included a complicated flowchart of actions. Byrne, Hudy, Whitmore, and Smith (2007) completed three iterations of redesign and study of the RSP cue card. The RSP medical pack was used in scenario-based evaluations in which participants were timed when completing the procedure with the medical pack equipment. The procedure involved assembling pieces of respiratory equipment and then treating a patient mannequin. Cue card redesigns were completed after each test to address the problems found, as well as to highlight opportunities for improvement. The final cue card design included reduced text, color cues, and a schematic of the equipment. In the final study, the time for a participant to complete the new RSP procedure and deliver oxygen to a patient in respiratory distress was reduced by 3 minutes, as compared to the original design. The benefit gained from this human factors work was highly significant and could mean the difference between life and death for a future astronaut. The redesigned cue card shown in Figure 11.3 was used for many years on ISS and strongly influenced the cue card design for the equipment used today. These types of studies highlighted the importance of human factors to NASA physicians,

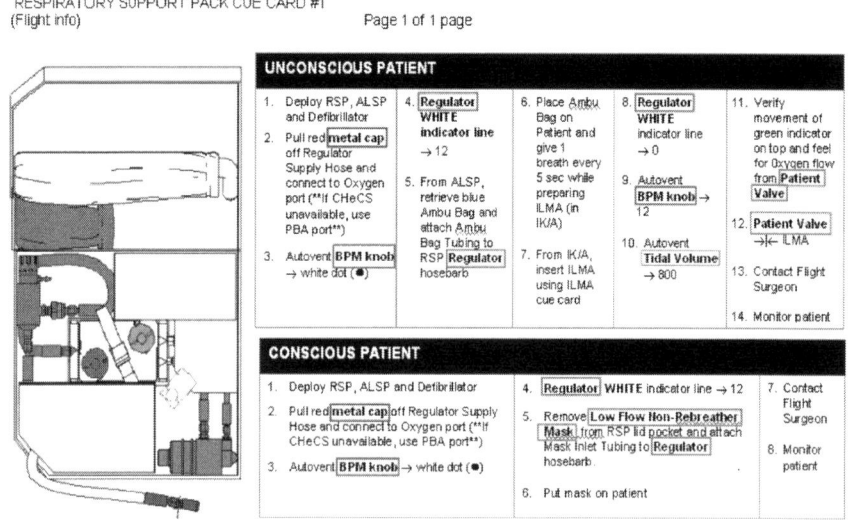

FIGURE 11.3 Redesigned respiratory support pack cue card in grayscale.

as well as the overall contribution human factors can make to ensure safety and mission success in extreme domains such as spaceflight.

ORION MULTI-PURPOSE CREW VEHICLE (MPCV)

The Orion Multi-Purpose Crew Vehicle (MPCV) is a new NASA spacecraft being developed to take astronauts to the moon and Mars. Although Orion has an appearance reminiscent of Apollo, this vehicle will be the most advanced spacecraft ever built. Determining the optimal habitable volume required for a long-duration mission, and the types of displays and controls that should be selected or developed to command this vehicle, have presented interesting human factors challenges.

Habitability: Net Habitable Volume (NHV). Volume within a space vehicle or habitat is a valuable resource for astronaut crews, yet one that is limited by numerous considerations, such as launch mass and production costs. For this reason, the internal volume within which the crew operates (the net habitable volume) is often less than desired, forcing careful assessment of volume needed to perform necessary tasks as well as how these tasks are performed when workspaces are adjacent or overlap.

Ideally, to review the volume needed for a specific vehicle or habitat design, a first step would be to perform a task analysis of all of the activities required for the design reference mission for the said vehicle or habitat. Then, the associated data for each task would be researched, based on past projects or on an evaluation of prototype ideas using a mixed methods approach (both qualitative and quantitative). The qualitative data associated with such a review would include ratings of acceptability, functionality, and applicability of the design for the mission at hand, including consideration of multiple factors, such as privacy needs, cleanliness/

hygiene requirements, possible overlap of volumes amongst differing tasks for collocated crew operations, and more. The quantitative data needed includes metrics such as location and orientation of the crew for each task, the volume used to complete tasks both at particular intervals in time and across the total task time, internal translation paths, flow of work amongst workstations or interfaces, and task completion times. These data can then be used for computational modeling of volume needs, industrial engineering time and motion studies, and finally, a detailed characterization of the net habitable volume required.

In addition to the restrictions on volume from both launch cost and operational considerations, due to differences in gravity, there are significant impacts to the way the environment is laid out and how human interaction with work areas occurs. In some ways, the microgravity environment may facilitate the inclusion of multiple work areas in a single volume due to the ability to use all three axes to place and orient the work stations; however, it also can result in challenges due to the need for the crew to be able to restrain/stabilize themselves, and the challenge of having multiple people working in a small space.

There have been many documents, workshops, studies and activities at NASA focused on net habitable volume, with some of the more recent notable examples shown below:

- Habitable Volume Workshop Results: Technical Products (NASA/TM-2014-217386) (Thaxton, Chen, & Whitmore, 2013)
- Minimum Acceptable Net Habitable Volume for Long-Duration Exploration Missions (NASA/TM-2015-218564) (Whitmire et al., 2015)
- Human Integration Design Processes (HIDP) document (NASA/TP-2014-218556), Chapter 4.9, Functional Volume Design (NASA, 2014)

The concepts, guidelines, and standards discussed in these documents have been put into practice multiple times in recent years, with NHV design considerations being key factors in development of Orion, as well as other recent and on-going spacecraft development projects (e.g., Commercial Crew Program, Gateway, and Artemis). For Orion, NHV evaluations were performed from the very beginning, in the mid-2000s, and have continued to the present (2019).

With each iterative NHV evaluation, the fidelity of the mock-ups being used has matured and increased, starting with a wood and foam low-fidelity mock-up, progressing to the medium/high fidelity mockup presently in the NASA JSC Space Vehicle Mockup Facility (SVMF). Figure 11.4 shows the evolution of the mockup. The evaluations are performed in such a way that simulated tasks are executed in as close to flight-like conditions as is possible, and data collected on the time to perform the tasks, error rates, usability ratings, volume acceptability, and observation of any obstructions of physical contact amongst the crew and the vehicle structure.

Displays and controls design for advanced spacecraft. In contrast to previous NASA vehicles (i.e., Space Shuttle), new spacecraft, such as the Orion Multi-Purpose Crew Vehicle (MPCV), will include "glass cockpits" where crewmembers will interact almost entirely with software and electronic procedures for vehicle flight operations and system monitoring, rather than hardware (e.g., switches, gauges).

 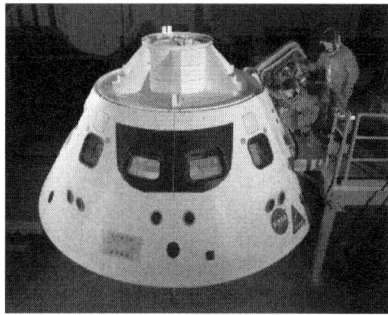

FIGURE 11.4 Low-fidelity mockup of Orion (2006), and medium-fidelity mockup of Orion (2017).

While the ISS is primarily controlled through software, a majority of the commanding is actually done by flight controllers in the Mission Control Center (MCC), rather than by the crew onboard. Future space vehicle and habitat crew will have to perform their missions with only software-based displays and controls available to them in their vehicle or habitat. As astronauts venture farther from Earth, crews will have reduced access to assistance from MCC due to communication delays and potential communication blackouts.

Although there are advantages to a glass cockpit design, there are also human factors challenges. Text and graphics need to convey a complex and vast amount of information on just a few display monitors, in a way that is readily understood by all crewmembers. Display formats need to meet requirements for usability, workload, and consistency. Having a software interface for commanding and monitoring necessitates a cursor control device (CCD). There are usability advantages to having a single device/method of interacting with space-based displays and controls, but the characteristics of this extreme environment vary greatly. For example, on the Orion spacecraft that will take a crew to the moon and Mars, a cursor control device needs to be operable with accuracy under the acceleration and vibration of launch and landing, and the microgravity of space. The device must also be operable with pressurized and unpressurized gloved, and ungloved, hands. There are many challenging design requirements for such a device.

Human factors researchers at NASA's Lyndon B. Johnson Space Center completed a number of research and development efforts to determine the best cursor control device (CCD) for spaceflight operations. During the early 1990s, several CCD evaluations were conducted in the laboratory, on the KC-135 reduced gravity aircraft, and during Space Shuttle missions STS-029 and STS-041 (Holden, Wilmington, & Whitmore, 1992; Adam, Holden, & Gillan, 1990; Holden & Beberness, 1993). The goal was to gather data to determine the best CCD design characteristics for use in microgravity. An optical mouse proved to be the fastest device in a number of environments, but it was not a good choice for the microgravity environment due to the number of separate pieces (mouse, cable, work surface, mouse pad). The trackball provided good performance and had the advantages of not requiring a work surface and being graspable for hand and body stabilization.

As the Orion program began, CCD research and development efforts resumed. In 2007, Sándor & Holden completed a laboratory study that compared performance of nine commercial and proprietary devices with and without EVA gloves. In general, the trackball devices showed the best performance, and data were used to down-select devices for future studies. An early concern was performance in a pressurized spacesuit, since pressurized gloves impact gripping ability and tactility. Thus, an engineering test was performed in a pressurized glovebox to identify basic types of hand and finger positions and motions that worked best under pressure (see Figure 11.5). Device components that were problematic with pressurized gloves were dropped from further consideration.

Toward the goal of having a standard way to evaluate cursor control devices, a CCD software test battery was developed (Sándor & Holden, 2008; Sándor, Holden, & Pace, 2011; Holden, Sándor, Pace, & Thompson, 2013). The test battery was used to evaluate standard commercial devices such as a trackball and mouse, as well as a variety of other commercial and prototype devices. The CCD test battery employed cursor control tasks described in the ISO 9241-9 standard, as well as tasks from previous studies conducted in microgravity. The test battery was used in many of the cursor control device tests conducted.

Multiple laboratory studies examined cursor movement type (continuous vs. discrete), and device (trackball, cursor knob, castle switch, scroll wheel, F18-like device, rocker switch) with gloved hands (Thompson, Sándor, & Holden, 2008; Thompson, Meyer, Sándor, & Holden, 2009). Additional testing was performed in a pressurized glovebox at the NASA's Lyndon B. Johnson Space Center (see Figure 11.5), and in a vibration test facility at NASA's Ames Research Center (Sándor et al., 2010). Of all the devices tested, the leading candidates in terms of performance (fast response times and low errors) were a trackball operated by the fingers and hand in continuous mode, a castle switch operated by the index finger in discrete mode, and a rocker switch operated by the thumb in discrete mode. Overall, the trackball always had faster response times, but a higher frequency of errors as compared to the other two devices. Given the

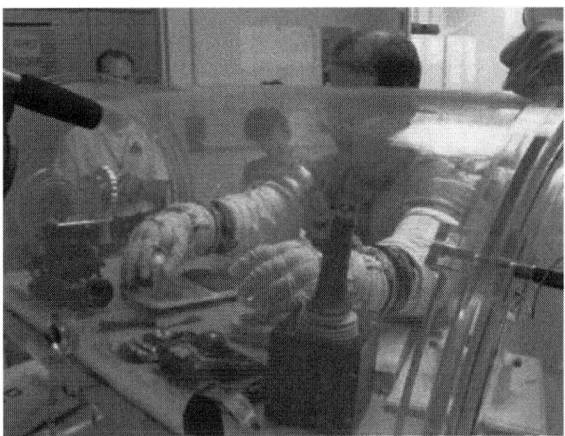

FIGURE 11.5 Evaluation of controls in a pressurized glovebox at Johnson Space Center.

importance of accuracy for the safety-critical environment of space, a custom CCD was designed for Orion that incorporated a rocker switch, castle switch, and pushbuttons; the device moved the cursor in a discrete, rather than continuous, fashion.

Exploration

Whether the next mission will be to the moon, a deep space asteroid, or Mars, there are many challenges yet to be solved to ensure that crew can remain healthy and capable of achieving their future Exploration mission. Research and development work is now beginning to determine what we need to know in order to ensure successful deep space missions. In addition to increased radiation and other deep space hazards, a key difference in these missions is the increasing autonomy of the onboard crew. We must make sure that they have the tools and resources needed to be successful without the full-time assistance of Mission Control.

Autonomous operations: Self-scheduling with "Playbook". Autonomous crews are required in future missions since communication with Earth will be both delayed (from seconds to minutes) and intermittent. The crew will only have limited opportunities to ask Mission Control teams for clarifications and guidance on assigned tasks. The crew may also have unique, in-situ knowledge about how to execute tasks, in which they may not be able to communicate to Mission Control in a timely manner.

One key factor in allowing astronauts to work more independently from Earth is to provide aids that allow them to dynamically replan and execute assigned tasks without depending on continual instruction from Earth. Currently, ground operators in the Mission Control Center (MCC) are largely responsible for ISS mission planning. The task of creating a week-long schedule for ISS crew takes dozens of people, multiple days to complete, and is often created months in advance of its execution. As such, re-planning or adapting to changing real-time constraints or emergent issues is taxing. With this current operational paradigm, shifting dynamic replanning responsibilities to crew (in other words, crew self-scheduling) is a daunting task. Removing the assistance that Mission Control provides will likely result in an overwhelmed crew with a higher workload. As NASA designs for future mission operations concepts to other planets or areas with limited connectivity to Earth, we need to consider how crew self-scheduling can be conducted seamlessly and with minimal Mission Control support intervention.

In order to study crew self-scheduling during long duration space missions, astronauts need a tool that allows them to manage their schedules without depending on interaction with Mission Control. "Playbook" (see Figure 11.6) is a user-friendly, mobile-ready, comprehensive software tool that enables astronaut crews to manipulate and execute mission plans (Marquez et al., 2013; Hashemi & Hillenius, 2013). At its core, Playbook is comprised of a mission Timeline that displays the scheduled activities for all crewmembers on any given mission day. Each activity can be selected to call up additional details, including associated procedures, execution notes for the crew, and operations notes for mission control.

Playbook is unique when compared to other schedule-viewers currently in use onboard ISS because it allows astronauts to edit the plan directly in the Timeline

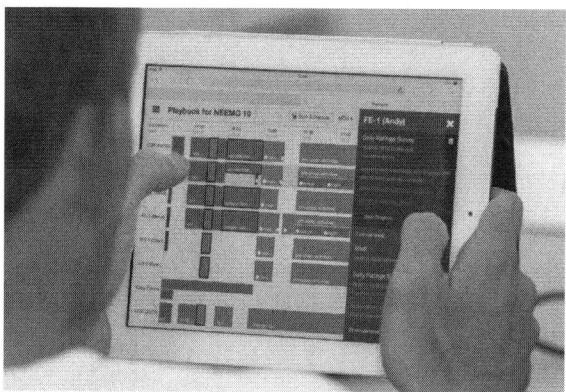

FIGURE 11.6 Playbook in use by astronaut during Earth analog mission.

without the need for intervention from Mission Control personnel. When self-scheduling is enabled, crewmembers can simply drag and drop flexible activities to another time or day (i.e., reschedule), and flexible activities can be reassigned as well. The crew can also create new activities and schedule them as appropriate within the Timeline. The crew may also add Task List activities, non-critical activities that astronauts are free to schedule into their Timelines when they have the availability to do so.

Self-scheduling has been evaluated as a new concept of operations analogs and onboard ISS. Several analog missions in NASA Extreme Environment Mission Operations (NEEMO) and Human Exploration Research Analog (HERA) have conducted self-scheduling evaluations. Analog crews were given planning problems of varying complexity and were asked to schedule and re-plan using Playbook. Furthermore, they were given the option to reschedule any flexible activity in their operational timeline, which the crew regularly took advantage of. Collective evidence suggests that self-scheduling is a feasible operational concept (Marquez et al., 2017). Furthermore, the crew is able to handle more complex planning problems than originally anticipated.

Playbook and self-scheduling have also been evaluated onboard ISS as part of the Crew Autonomous Scheduling Test (CAST) demonstration. NASA's Ames Research Center and the ISS Flight Operations Directorate (FOD) collaborated to investigate autonomous planning and replanning in the real, spaceflight operational environment of ISS. As part of CAST (Hillenius et al., 2016; Marquez, Hillenius, & Healy, 2018; Marquez, Hillenius, Healy, & Silva-Martinez, 2019), for the first time, an ISS astronaut scheduled their own tasks that were executed as planned. It was also the first time an ISS astronaut managed their own operational schedule to reflect an as-run timeline. Demonstration of the crew self-scheduling concept of operations in spaceflight was successful, despite the challenges imposed by the complexity of ISS operations. Future work remains in improving the simplicity of self-scheduling, be it at the planning level or at the scheduling interface, and developing operational processes and workflows that support crew as well as mission support teams.

Autonomous operations: Integrated science and astronaut teams. Mars exploration presents a unique challenge – not only do astronauts need to perform science exploration in a relatively autonomous manner, they need to do so with some guidance from Earth-bound science team. Astronauts will not necessarily have all the expertise required to conduct Mars exploration – as the topics range from chemistry, to biology, to geology. They will need to rely or receive feedback from a large team of scientists back on Earth with respect to, for instance, inquiry direction, scientific work processes, and sample collection. Unfortunately, there will be one-way communication delays ranging from a few minutes to up to about 20 minutes. As such, NASA has investigated the concepts of operation that potentially enable an integrated science and astronaut team to cooperate between planets.

NEEMO and Desert Research and Technology Studies (RATS) initiated studies specifically exploring various concepts of operations for Extravehicular Activities (EVA) (Chappell, Abercromby, & Gernhardt, 2013; Chappell et al., 2013, 2016; Abercromby, Chappell & Gernhardt, 2013; Bleacher, Hurtado, Young, Rice, & Garry, 2013). Their research laid the ground work for establishing measures for comparing the different concepts. Key measures center around establishing acceptability, capability assessment, and simulation quality rating scales. They set out to compare, for example, the effect of crewmember configurations and the capabilities that enabled or inhibited operations. For instance, would it be better to have one or two crewmembers on EVA? Who should the EVA crewmember communicate with? However, one limitation remained in their studies – would their concepts of operation translate to real, science-driven exploration?

A different NASA-funded analog emerged to investigate this question – Pavilion Lake Research Project (PLRP, Lim et al., 2011). It was driven by scientists who performed exploration in a spaceflight-like environment, namely an extreme environment (underwater submarine) and under some communication delay. Initial research indicated that some concepts translated (Miller et al., 2016), but further study was required to simulate the various capabilities that enabled the proposed concepts of operations. In 2015, the Biologic Analog Science Associated with Lava Terrains (BASALT) allowed the rare opportunity to investigate both operational and scientific questions about human Mars exploration.

BASALT investigated the habitability of terrestrial volcanic terrains as analog environments for early and present-day Mars while conducting scientific exploration under Mars-like operational conditions (Darlene et al., 2019). A team of diverse scientists set forth a variety of research goals and objectives, requiring data and sample collection on volcanic terrain. Analog astronauts were tasked to collect the data and samples in coordination with a science team. The science team was only available across a communication delayed of 5 or 15 minutes. Additionally, some excursions were bandwidth communication limited, i.e., not all the data could be transmitted (under delay) between analog astronauts and science team. This analog required a communication infrastructure that allowed analog astronauts to communicate and share scientific data collected (from images, video, voice, instrument readings) and operational data (time on task, traverse tracking). Furthermore, all this data and information was made available to the science team, requiring novel software to assimilate the large amount of information in order to make real-time scientific decisions affecting exploration. As a result of three deployments, we have learned and identified the essential capabilities that support scientific exploration under Mars-like operational conditions (Beaton et al., 2019; Payler et al., 2019), evaluated strategic and tactical planning concepts of operations (Brady et al., 2019; Stevens et al., 2019; Kobs Nawotniak et al., 2019), and delineated needs for EVA planning and execution (Marquez et al., 2019). Future work will focus on understanding the capabilities required to improve multi-team collaboration between EVA exploration excursions.

CONCLUSION

We are about to embark on many new ventures in human spaceflight: new commercially built spacecraft that will take astronauts to the ISS, a new deep space vehicle more advanced than any of the past, and missions that will put humans and habitats on other planets. Astronauts will need to be prepared to operate autonomously due to deep space communication delays and potential blackouts, and will need to be equipped with intelligent systems to aid them on their journey. This is a brand new model for NASA, a new concept of operations. The success of these future endeavors will be dependent on the continued involvement of human factors practitioners, and continued emphasis on HSI at all levels of development.

ACKNOWLEDGMENTS

The research described in this chapter was funded by the NASA Human Research Program (HRP), the ISS Program, and the Orion MPCV program. Except as cited otherwise, work was performed by civil servants or contractors as part of the Human Health and Performance Contract NNJ15HK11B (or former Bioastronautics Contract NAS9-02078) through the National Aeronautics and Space Administration.

REFERENCES

Abercromby, A. F., Chappell, S. P., & Gernhardt, M. L. (2013), Desert rats 2011: Human and robotic exploration of near-earth asteroids. *Acta Astronautica*, *91*, 34–48.

Adam, S., Holden, K., & Gillan, D. (1990). *Microgravity cursor control device evaluation for space station freedom workstations*. Proceedings of the Space Operations Applications and Research (SOAR) symposium, Albuquerque, NM.

Beaton, K. H., Chappell, S. P., Abercromby, A. F. J., Miller, M. J., Kobs Nawotniak, S. E., Brady, A. L., ... Lim, D. (2019). *Astrobiology*. doi:10.1089/ast.2018.1912

Beaubien, J. M., & Baker, D. P. (2002). A review of selected aviation Human Factors taxonomies, accident/incident reporting systems, and data reporting tools. *International Journal of Applied Aviation Studies*, *2*(2), 11–36.

Bleacher, J. E., Hurtado, J. M., Jr., Young, K. E., Rice, J. W., Jr., & Garry, W. B. (2013). The effect of different operations modes on science capabilities during the 2010 Desert RATS test: Insights from the geologist crewmembers. *Acta Astronautica*, *90*(2), 356–366.

Brady, A. L., Kobs Nawotniak, S. E., Hughes, S. S., Payler, S. J., Stevens, A. H., Cockell, C. S., ... Lim, D. S. S. (2019). *Astrobiology*. doi:10.1089/ast.2018.1850

Byrne, V., Hudy, C., Whitmore, M., & Smith, D., (2007). *Human factors assessment and redesign of the International Space Station Respiratory Support Pack (RSP) cue card*. Biennial Research & Technology Development Report. Houston TX: Johnson Space Center.

Celentano, J. T., Amorelli, D., & Freeman, G. G. (1963, May 2). *Establishing a habitability index for space stations and planetary bases*. Paper presented at the AIAA/ASMA Manned Space Laboratory Conference. Los Angeles, CA.

Chappell, S.P., Abercromby, A.F., & Gernhardt, M.L. (2013). NEEMO 15: Evaluation of human exploration systems for near-Earth asteroids. *Acta Astronautica, 89*, 166–178.

Chappell, S. P., Abercromby, A. F., Reagan, M., Gernhardt, M. L., & Todd, W. (2013, July). *NEEMO 16: Evaluation of Systems for Human Exploration of Near-Earth Asteroids*. Paper presented at the 43rd International Conference on Environmental Systems. AIAA 2013-3508. Vail, CO.

Chappell, S. P., Beaton, K., Miller, M. J., Halcon, C., Michael, G., & Abercromby, A. F. J. (2016). *NEEMO 18–20: Analog testing for mitigation of communication latency during human space exploration*. In 2016 IEEE Aerospace Conference. Piscataway, NJ: IEEE,

Connors, M. M., Harrison, A. A., & Akins, F. R. (1985). *Living aloft: Human requirements for extended spaceflight* (NASA-SP-483). Washington, D.C.: National Aeronautics and Space Administration. Retrieved from https://ntrs.nasa.gov/search.jsp?R=19850024459

Fraser, T. M. (1968). *The intangibles of habitability during long duration space missions* (NASA CR-1084). Washington, D.C.: National Aeronautics and Space Administration. Retrieved from https://ntrs.nasa.gov/archive/nasa/casi.ntrs.nasa.gov/19680017230.pdf

Greene, M., Thaxton, S., & Adolf, J. (2018). *Habitability assessment of International Space Station*. Unpublished internal document, National Aeronautics and Space Administration.

Harrison, A. A., & Connors, M. M. (1990). Human factors in spacecraft design. *Journal of Spacecraft and Rockets, 27*(5), 478–481.

Hashemi, S., & Hillenius, S. (2013, March 10) *"@NASA: The User Experience of a Space Station." SXSW interactive 2013*. SXSW. Austin, TX: SXSW Interactive. Speech.

Hillenius, S. R., Marquez, J. J., Deliz, I., Kanefsky, B., Korth, D., Healy, M., ... Zheng, J. (2016) *Designing and building a crew-centric mobile scheduling and planning tool for exploring crew autonomy concepts onboard the International Space Station*. International Space Station R&D Conference, July 12–14. San Diego, CA.

Holden, K., Sándor, A., Pace, J., & Thompson, S. (2013, May). Cursor control device test battery. *NASA Tech Briefs, 37*(5), 6–7.

Holden, K. L., & Beberness, B. J. (1993). *Cursor control device evaluations for space station freedom: Detailed test objective 1206-STS-41* (LESC-29975). Houston, TX: Lockheed Martin.

Holden, K. L., Wilmington, R. P., & Whitmore, M. (1992). *Cursor control device evaluations for space station freedom: A summary, NASA contractor report 185690* (NASA Johnson Space Center).

International Standards Organization (ISO), I. 9241–9 (2000). *Ergonomic requirements for office work with visual display terminals (VDTs)-Part 9: Requirements for non-keyboard input devices (FDIS-Final Draft International Standard)*. International Organization for Standardization. Retrieved from: https://www.iso.org/standard/30030.html.

Johnson, C. C. (1975). *Skylab experiment M487: Habitability/Crew quarters* (TM X-59136). Houston: Johnson Space Center.

Keeton, K. E., Schmidt, L. L., Slack, K. J., & Malka, A. A. (2012). The rocket science of teams. *Industrial and Organizational Psychology, 5*(1), 32–35.

Kobs Nawotniak, S. E., Miller, M. J., Stevens, A. H., Marquez, J. J., Payler, S. J., Brady, A. L.,... Lim, D. S. S. (2019). Opportunities and challenges of promoting scientific dialog throughout execution of future science-driven extravehicular activity. *Astrobiology*, 426–439 (published online: March 6). doi:10.1089/ast.2018.1901

Lim, D. S. S., Brady, A. L., Abercromby, A. F., Andersen, D. T., Andersen, M., Arnold, R. R., ... Winter, C. (2011), *A historical overview of the Pavilion Lake Research Project— Analog science and exploration in an underwater environment*. Geological Society of America Special Papers, vol. 483, pp. 85–115.

Marquez, J. J., Deliz, I., Kanefsky, B., Zheng, J., Hillenius, S., & Reagan, M. (2017) *Increasing crew autonomy for long duration exploration missions: Self-scheduling.* IEEE Aerospace Conference, Big Sky, MT.

Marquez, J. J., Hillenius, S., & Healy, M. (2018) *Increasing human spaceflight capabilities: Demonstration of crew autonomy through self-scheduling onboard International Space Station.* International Space Station R&D Conference, San Francisco, CA.

Marquez, J. J., Hillenius, S., Healy, M., & Silva-Martinez, J. (2019, July). *Lessons learned from International Space Station crew autonomous scheduling test.* International Workshop for Planning and Scheduling for Space, Berkeley, CA.

Marquez, J.J., Miller, M.J., Cohen, T., Deliz, I., Lees, D.S., Zheng, J., Lee, Y.J., Kanefsky, B., Norheim, J., Deans, M., and Hillenius, S. (2019, March). Future Needs for Science-Driven Geospatial and Temporal Extravehicular Activity Planning and Execution. *Astrobiology,* 440–461. doi: 10.1089/ast.2018.1838

Marquez, J. J., Pyrzak, G., Hashemi, S., Ahmed, S., McMillin, K., Medwid, J., ... Hurtle, E. (2013, July). *Supporting real-time operations and execution through timeline and scheduling aids.* 43rd International Conference on Environmental Systems, Vail, CO.

Miller, M. J., Lim, D. S., Brady, A. L., Cardman, Z., Bell, E., Garry, W. B., ... Abercromby, A.F. (2016). *PLRP-3: Operational perspectives conducting science driven extravehicular activity with communications latency.* In 2015 IEEE Aerospace Conference, IEEE, Piscataway, NJ. doi:10.1109/AERO.2016.7500643

Mount, F. E., Adam, S., McKay, T., Whitmore, M., Merced-Moore, D., Holden, T., ... Wolf, S. (1994). *Human factors assessments of the STS-57 SpaceHab-1 mission* (NASA-TM-104802).

Mount, F. E., & Foley, T. (1999). Assessment of human factors. In C. F. Sawin, G. R. Taylor, & W. L. Smith (Eds.), *Extended duration orbiter medical project: Final report* (NASA/SP-1999-534). Houston, TX: National Aeronautics and Space Administration.

Mount, F. E., Whitmore, M., & Stealey, S. L. (2003). *Evaluation of neutral body posture on shuttle mission STS-57 (SPACEHAB-1)* (NASA/TM-2003–104805). Houston, TX: National Aeronautics and Space Administration. Retrieved from https://ntrs.nasa.gov/search.jsp?R=20040200967

National Aeronautics and Space Administration [NASA]. (2014). *Human Integration Design Processes (HIDP)* (NASA/TP-2014-218556). Houston, TX: National Aeronautics and Space Administration. Retrieved form https://www.nasa.gov/sites/default/files/atoms/files/human_integration_design_processes.pdf

Novak, J. B. (2000). Human engineering and habitability: The critical challenges for the International Space Station. *Aviation, Space, and Environmental Medicine, 71*(9 Suppl), A117–A121.

Payler, S. J., Mirmalek, Z., Hughes, S., Kobs Nawotniak, S. E., Brady, A. L., Stevens, A. H., ... Lim, D. S. S. (2019). *Astrobiology.* doi:10.1089/ast.2018.1846

Sándor, A., Adelstein, B., Holden, K., Thompson, S., Beutter, B., Pace, J., & Anderson, M. (2010). *Performance with continuous and discrete cursor control device under vibration frequencies and amplitudes.* Unpublished internal document, National Aeronautics and Space Administration.

Sándor, A., & Holden, K. L. (2007). *Determining desirable cursor control device characteristics for NASA exploration missions.* Unpublished internal document, National Aeronautics and Space Administration. Retrieved from https://ntrs.nasa.gov/search.jsp?R=20070018168

Sándor, A., & Holden, K. L. (2008). *Cursor control device test battery: Development and application.* In Proceedings of the Human Factors and Ergonomics Society meeting, New York, NY.

Sándor, A., Holden, K. L., & Pace, J. (2011). *Cursor control device test battery.* Technical demonstration at the Human Factors and Ergonomics Society meeting, Las Vegas, NV.

Smith, D., Byrne, V., & Hudy, C. (2005). *Human factors assessment of International Space Station (ISS) medical equipment packs.* Proceedings of the Human Factors and Ergonomics Society annual meeting, 49 (1). Human Factors and Ergonomics Society. Retrieved from https://journals.sagepub.com/doi/abs/10.1177/154193120504900102

Stemler, S. (2001). An overview of content analysis. *Practical Assessment, Research & Evaluation, 7*(17), 137–146.

Stevens, A. H., Kobs Nawotniak, S. E., Garry, W., Payler, S., Brady, A., Miller, M., ... Lim, D.S.S. (2019). *Astrobiology.* doi:10.1089/ast.2018.1837

Stuster, J. (1996). *Bold endeavors.* Annapolis, MD: Naval Institute Press.

Stuster, J. (2010). *Behavioral issues associated with long-duration space expeditions: Review and analysis of astronaut journals experiment 01-E104 (Journals): Final report* (NASA/TM-2010-216130). Houston, TX. National Aeronautics and Space Administration. Retrieved from https://lsda.jsc.nasa.gov/lsda_data/dataset_inv_data/ILSRA_2001_104__1740256372_.pdf_Expedition_8_ILSRA-2001-104_2011_31_010100.pdf

Stuster, J. (2016). *Behavioral issues associated with long duration space expeditions: Review and analysis of astronaut journals* experiment 01-e104 (journals). Phase 2 finall report. NASA/TM-2016-218603. Houston, TX: National Aeronautics and Space Administration.

Thaxton, S., Chen, M., & Whitmore, M. (2013). *2012 habitable volume workshop results: Technical products* (NASA Technical Memorandum – TM-2014-217386). Houston, TX: National Aeronautics and Space Administration.

Thompson, S., Meyer, A., Sándor, A., & Holden, K. (2009). *A functional evaluation of cursor control devices for space vehicles under discrete modes of operation* Unpublished internal document, National Aeronautics and Space Administration. Houston TX: Johnson Space Center—NASA

Thompson, S., Sándor, A., & Holden, K. (2008). *Orion cursor control device functional evaluation* Unpublished internal document, National Aeronautics and Space Administration.

Whitmore, M., Adolf, J. A., & Woolford, B. J. (2000). Habitability research priorities for the International Space Station and beyond. *Aviation, Space, and Environmental Medicine, 71*(9 Suppl), A122–A125.

Whitmire, A., Leveton, L., Broughton, H., Basner, M., Kearney, A., Ikuma, L., & Morris, M. (2015), *Minimum acceptable net habitable volume for long-duration exploration missions* (NASA-TM-2015-218564). Technical report JSC-CN-32284. Houston, TX: National Aeronautics and Space Administration.

Whitmore, M., McQuilkin, M. L., & Woolford, B. J. (1998). Habitability and performance issues for long duration space flights. *Human Performance in Extreme Environments, 3*(1), 64–74.

Zumbado, J. R. (2015). *Human Systems Integration Practitioner's Guide.* NASA/SP-2105-3709. Houston, TX: NASA Johnson Space Center.

12 Introduction
The Power of Higher-Order Goals for Space Exploration

Kathryn E. Keeton
University of Texas at San Antonio; Minerva Work Solutions

David Musson
McMaster University and Northern Ontario School of Medicine

CONTENTS

The Power of Higher-Order Goals for Space Exploration 225
    Alignment of Higher-Order Goals: Addressing Issues of
    Increasing Complexity 226
    Alignment of Higher-Order Goals: Common Vision 228
    Alignment of Higher-Order Goals: Shared Common Values 230
    A Look to the Future 232
References 232

THE POWER OF HIGHER-ORDER GOALS FOR SPACE EXPLORATION

The presence of higher-order goals within an organization has been shown to meaningfully impact organizational success. We know this to be especially true in organizations where such higher-order goals help align critical organizational factors, including teams, work units, departments, and divisions within those organizations (Kozlowski & Bell, 2003). Alignment within the organization and buy-in on part of the individual employees with higher-order goals set by leadership has been shown to serve as a strong competitive and strategic advantage (Powell, 1992; Joshi, Kathuria, & Porth, 2003). Researchers posit that, at the individual level, aligned goal strivings can foster an increase in perceived meaningfulness in one's work, which in turn can improve overall motivation and attainment of work outcomes (Barrick, Mount, & Ning, 2013). Taken together, these research findings make a strong case for why higher-order goals are important to organizations (even while acknowledging that most organizations do not do this well) and demonstrate the critical impact these factors have on an employee's own identification in meaningfulness in their work and their own success of work attainment (Britt, Jennings, Goguen, & Sytine, 2016).

We believe that the existence of higher-order goals also serves to foster positive impact across national space agencies. The collective, and mostly collaborative, international efforts of the world's national space agencies working together have helped accomplish incredible human feats in both the human and non-human exploration of space. Indeed, some argue that the collective higher-order goals between international agencies have both fueled the competitive and collaborative efforts that have propelled the exploration of space forward to the extent that currently we see with the International Space Station and planetary exploration, and influenced amazing accomplishments that many believe could have not been done successfully alone.

Similar to what we have seen within organizations, benefits can extend to the level of individuals involved in national space agency efforts, perhaps most easily demonstrated in the experience of astronauts. While today's astronauts spend much of their time maintaining the International Space Station (ISS), they also have the opportunity to perform research and other impactful operational activities for the benefit of the science community back on Earth (e.g., science lab experiments, specific research experiments, extra-vehicular activities (EVAs), etc.). Such activities go above and beyond daily maintenance activities and provide an opportunity for astronauts to contribute to the greater goal of contributing to human scientific understanding. According to qualitative data collected by Dr. Jack Stuster, through his studies of astronaut diaries and personal logs, this type of work was highlighted as most meaningful and rewarding to many of the astronauts, helping buffer many of the stressors that astronauts experience during the course of their missions. This is especially powerful when considering that "work" as a topic or theme, as captured in diary entries, was the second most frequent topic discussed by astronauts in flight (Stuster, 2010). Astronauts also often reference their contribution to humanity or the overall mission among the international collaborative partners as a source of great pride and connection (Britt et al., 2016). As Astronaut Anne McClain stated, "Every vehicle that has been built and every flight that has been taken is an [international collaborative] accomplishment in and of itself." (Cutshaw, 2018).

In reflecting on these accounts of how higher-order goals impact spaceflight, we can examine how higher-order goals have served and continue to serve as a way to align (1) international space agency activities across activities characterized by increasing complexity, (2) efforts to set an inclusive vision for exploration endeavors of different space agencies, and (3) shared common values of these diverse national space agencies. As we discuss each aspect of higher-order goals, we will review some highly relevant accomplishments of the international space program at large. We will also look to the future and set the stage for following chapters in this section, where authors representing various national space agencies share the impact of higher-order goals of their own space program.

ALIGNMENT OF HIGHER-ORDER GOALS: ADDRESSING ISSUES OF INCREASING COMPLEXITY

Higher-order goals help integrate issues of complexity within and across organizations. A powerful example of this in the setting of outer space can be seen when examining the history of crewed space stations over the last half century. The first crewed space station was Salyut 1, launched by the Soviet Union in 1971 (https://spaceflight.nasa.gov/history/shuttle-mir/; https://history.nasa.gov/SP-4225/mir/mir.htm). Six Salyut space stations followed as each station was launched complete with all supplies and experimental equipment; once expended, these stations were then abandoned. These stations represented both a primary focus for the Soviet Space Program following the race to the moon and a lasting legacy of program success. It was during this era, in 1975, when the Apollo-Soyuz Test Project (referred to by the Soviets and later Russians as Soyuz-Apollo) was conducted. Though this was a stand-alone program of collaboration between two competing superpowers, it represented a significant collaboration both politically and technically. Some have described this project as the formal end to the space race that began with Sputnik in 1957 (see Samuels, 2005), but the logistical, political, and organizational challenges that were addressed and overcome were to be a harbinger of future cooperation and collaboration.

The Salyut stations were then followed by space station Mir, launched by the Soviet Union in 1986 and operated by the Soviet and later by the Russian space programs. Mir was the first modular space station, was larger and more massive than any of its predecessors, and offered significant opportunity for international cooperation. The feat of assembling and launching a long-term space station is a technologically and monetarily daunting undertaking and one that many other international space agencies at the time could have not realized on their own. However, the decision to transition Mir to a space station inhabited by astronauts from multiple countries helped overcome ever increasing issues of complexity including operations, logistics for training, scheduling, etc. and perhaps most notably, cost. Over the course of Mir's 15-year life, it became an international space home to over 125 cosmonauts and astronauts representing over 12 different countries over the course of 17 space expeditions, including 28 long-term crews (history.nasa.gov). As a result of the many successes and lessons learned during its operation, Mir paved the way for its successor, the International Space Station (ISS).

ISS presented even greater technological and operational challenges and included multiple partners in its design, development, and construction. As of January 2018, over 320 individuals representing 18 different countries have stayed on board, with contributions (either through modules or robotics) from NASA, Roscosmos, the European Space Agency, the Canadian Space Agency, and the Japanese Aerospace Exploration Agency (https://www.space.com/16748-international-space-station.html). Missions on ISS can last 6 months or even longer, with a handful of astronauts living on board for upwards of a year. Such individuals will typically train for 18–24 months, spending a significant portion of their training away from home, often training at other international partner locations. In addition, the ISS crews are often comprised of six individuals, with three individuals rotating out approximately every 3 months. These additional mission-related factors in both coordination and logistical operations of crew training and composition among international partners (and their direct impacts on other important factors like team cohesion and collaboration) highlight the magnitude of complexity the mutual partnership of the ISS creates for successful operations and mission execution.

And yet, this international partnership has successfully completed 58 Expedition missions to date (www.nasa.gov) despite ever increasing complexities in mission design and logistical considerations for the selection, training, and support of the astronaut crew. Here again we see the power of higher-order goals helping to align efforts from the international partners to make these expeditions possible. Specifically, we posit that the international partners' ability to address these complexities is due to their ability to align both within teams (i.e., within complex individual national space agencies) and within the overarching multiteam system (MTS) (i.e., the international partnership at large) (Marks, DeChurch, Mathieu, Panzer, & Alonso, 2005). If supported, this alignment and focus on the higher-order goal will continue to be critical (both within each agency and within the overarching MTS) to future success of international spaceflight collaborations. This is particularly true when considering that longer-duration missions, such as to lunar stations or expeditions to the planet Mars, hold the potential for an exponential increase in complexity. For such missions, their future success will entail additional factors that must be considered including delayed communications between ground control and the flight crew, a paradigmatic shift for autonomous operations for the flight crews, and of course, additional physiological and psychological risks to the crew for deep space exploration.

ALIGNMENT OF HIGHER-ORDER GOALS: COMMON VISION

Higher-order goals also help align a common vision, especially when multiple stakeholders are at play. In 1962, when President John F. Kennedy gave his famous 'We choose to go to the Moon' speech, this open challenge and public commitment helped integrate and unify NASA and the US population to a higher-order goal, which would be realized just seven short years later.

> Yet the vows of this nation can only be fulfilled if we in this nation are first, and, therefore, we intend to be first. In short, our leadership in science and in industry, our hopes for peace and security, our obligations to ourselves as well as others, all require us to make this effort, to solve these mysteries, to solve them for the good of all men, and to become the world's leading space-faring nation. We choose to go to the moon. We choose to go to the moon in this decade and do the other things, not because they are easy, but because they are hard, because that goal will serve to organize and measure the best of our energies and skills, because that challenge is one that we are willing to accept, one we are unwilling to postpone, and one which we intend to win, and the others, too.
>
> **John F. Kennedy**
> *September 12, 1962 at Rice University*

This commitment served to focus efforts and provide direction for NASA for the next 20 years. And its singular focus helped NASA build a similar central focus in terms of organizational structure, execution, and lower-level goals within the organization.

Since the 1960s, we have seen a common vision being used again as a vehicle to establish and successfully execute higher-order goals within the international space partners. As described above, the ISS has been an impressive success, primarily because the national space agencies, working together, were able to align behind a singular vision of developing and operating the ISS for the purpose of research and space exploration (https://www.nasa.gov/audience/forstudents/5-8/features/nasa-knows/what-is-the-iss-58.html). During its tenure, the ISS has produced a wealth of scientific research, spin off technologies, and impressive space exploration discoveries both because of an extensive on-board science program and due to the space telescopes maintained and constructed during EVAs performed by ISS astronauts (Evans et al., 2009).

Now the collective international space agencies are charged with pursuing a common vision for the future of space exploration. This future vision may entail long-duration missions to the moon, Mars, and perhaps beyond. Indeed, the majority of the research funded by NASA's Human Research Program focus on enabling long-duration mission expeditions (defined by specific criteria included in various design reference missions, or DRMs) by mitigating or addressing specific "risks" identified as factors that must be first resolved in order to make long-duration flight possible (https://www.nasa.gov/hrp/about). Many other research programs for other national space agencies have a similar focus, and this sponsored research is often carried out in analog environments, or environments that try to mimic specific physical, environmental, and/or psychological characteristics of what would be expected in a long-duration mission. These factors may include communication delays, disconnection from ground control, other ground-based support systems, social isolation, or physical confinement. These analogous environments are especially important when trying to understand the impact of team- and leader-related behaviors, like team cooperation and collaboration, decision making, effective communication, and psychosocial support. Addressing, studying, and developing solutions and countermeasures to the challenges represent one of the most identifiable higher-order goals that drives national research programs and international collaboration in space sciences.

And yet, with the uncertainty of future space-related funding across national space agencies, some have argued that it is increasingly difficult to pursue these higher-order goals (i.e., realization of a crewed Mars mission by a specific target date) if there is a lack of continuity and alignment around a singular, common vision. As we have seen in the past, this connection around a common vision has proven integral to the success of the achievement of the higher-order goals set by the international partners. Research supports the notion that the ability to achieve set goals within a team relies heavily on a common shared vision among those within the MTS. This has been shown to be especially true when a team is exposed to a traumatic or extreme environment even when led by a strong, transformational leader (Eberly, Bluhm, Guarana, Avolio, & Hannah, 2017). Extreme environments similar to space likely require a robust and well-defined vision among team members in order to achieve the set higher-order goals. Let us hope, as the different international partners present in their individual chapters following this introduction, that we can continue to push for a common vision that is inclusive of higher-order goals and that will allow us to achieve and realize long-duration mission success in this international partnership.

ALIGNMENT OF HIGHER-ORDER GOALS: SHARED COMMON VALUES

The impact of higher-order goals on aligning national space programs may be most apparent when considering the concept of a shared common value. As with the other areas we have examined, we can look back historically to understand how shared common values have played an important role in the achievement of higher-order goal success. As has been the case for early explorers, including the likes of Magellan, Zheng He, Shackleton, Columbus, or Lewis and Clark, many would argue that space exploration exists for the sake of *exploration* itself. While we acknowledge many other drivers contribute to the propensity to discover and explore, a common thread along human history, the value of exploration as pure justification in its own pursuit. We can find examples from ancient history: 'Leave no stone unturned.' – Euripides, 428 BC. More recently, we can look to the experiences and reflections of some of the 20th century's greatest explorers and adventures:

> The explorers of the past were great men and we should honour them. But let us not forget that their spirit lives on. It is still not hard to find a man who will adventure for the sake of a dream or one who will search, for the pleasure of searching, not for what he may find.
>
> **Sir Edmund Hillary**

And furthermore, we see examples from fiction and science fiction, where writers project these philosophies on the characters they create:

> That may be the most important thing to understand about humans. It is the unknown that defines our existence. We are constantly searching, not just for answers to our questions, but for new questions. We are explorers. We explore our lives day by day, and we explore the galaxy trying to expand the boundaries of our knowledge.
>
> **Benjamin Sisko**
> *(as scripted by Michael Piller, Screenwriter, Star Trek Deep Space 9, 1993).*

In the human exploration of new frontiers, higher-order goals provide further support for this commitment to exploration as a common value. Historical documentation from early explorers, including the likes of Ernest Shackleton and his crew who sought to reach the South Pole in the early 1900s, describes expeditions filled with desolate landscapes, hostile environmental conditions, insurmountable trials, and tribulations including lack of food, water, or both, and feuding teams. Similar accounts can be found in memoirs of Nansen (1897), Peary (1907), and many others. Despite the challenges, these remarkable individuals pressed on with a singular focus completing the exploration, with those challenges serving only to fuel their commitment to the mission goals and motivation to succeed (Shackleton, 1919).

Similar to these early explorers, astronauts, representing a diverse range of cultures and nationalities, face high-level risks in extreme environments. They must overcome these challenges, face the risks of launch and spaceflight, and work together as a crew effectively to succeed. Many of the high-level objectives for spaceflight missions involve the successful completion of scientific experiments, studies, and observations. The role of scientific study as a higher-order goal is also true for research conducted on behalf of space exploration in analogous environments on Earth. Here too, international partners must collaborate and coordinate research projects effectively to glean important findings from conducted research that will inform the design and implementation of future space missions and to support the value of continued space exploration (Landon, Slack, & Barrett, 2018). True to this common shared value, NASA's own perspective rings true for all international partners:

> Humans are driven to explore the unknown, discover new worlds, push the boundaries of our scientific and technical limits, and then push further. The intangible desire to explore and challenge the boundaries of what we know and where we have been has provided benefits to our society for centuries.
>
> *NASA (2019)*

The current international space community is characterized by many interagency working groups: teams dedicated to solving the challenges of spaceflight faced by all agency partners. For example, key interagency working groups have been formed in response to the biomedical challenges of human spaceflight, challenges which are faced by astronauts from all spacefaring nations. The Multilateral Medical Policy Board (MMPB), the Multilateral Medical Operations Panel (MMOP), and the Multilateral Space Medicine Board (MSMB) all exist to help coordinate and align spaceflight medical issues across agencies. The boards include representation from NASA, RSA-IMBP (Russian Space Agency – Institute for Biomedical Problems), GCTC (Gagarin Cosmonaut Training Center), ESA (European Space Agency), JAXA (Japanese Space Agency), and CSA (Canadian Space Agency). The Multilateral Medical Operations Panel (MMOP), which coordinates medical system support for International Space Station (ISS) crews, has multiple sub-working groups, each focused on specific challenges of spaceflight. These include sub-groups dedicated to acoustic issues, biomedical training requirements, environmental health, countermeasure development, human behavior and performance issues, in-flight clinical medicine requirements, medical standards, nutrition, and more. Similar multinational working groups exist for operations and for research activities on ISS. These groups work together to develop international standards, policies, practices, and solutions to the multitude of complex challenges faced by ISS crews and mission operators. All of these teams are clearly aligned under the higher-order goal of overcoming the multiple risks and challenges to maintain health and crew well-being in space.

On the frontline of operations, Mission Control Centers (MCCs) from NASA's Christopher C. Kraft Jr. Mission Control Center and the Mission Control Center of the Russian Federal Space Agency (also known by its acronym "TsUP") must collaborate, along with Launch Control Centers (LCCs), with MCCs from other international partners, including the Columbus Control Center (Col-CC) at the German Aerospace Center (DLR) that controls the European Columbus research laboratory at the International Space Station and JAXA's JEM Control Center and HTV Control Centers. Coordination across all of the Centers can involve challenges due to communication technologies, language differences, time zone separations, and differences in operational and organizational cultures. ISS crews themselves are inherently multicultural, multilingual, and diverse. However, it is the high-order objective of mission success that serves to unify, align, and foster collaboration necessary to achieve mission success.

A Look to the Future

We have reviewed how higher-order goals serve multiple purposes, from addressing complexities, to defining a common vision or defining shared values. We see the power of the international partnership in achieving these goals. What now follows are the individual international partners' perspective of how their current and future work will continue to support higher-order goals among the collaborators.

REFERENCES

Barrick, M., Mount, M., & Ning, L. (2013). The theory of purposeful work behavior: The role of personality, higher-order goals, and job characteristics. *Academy of Management, 38*(1), 132–153.

Britt, T. W., Jennings, K. S., Goguen, K., & Sytine, A. (2016). *The role of meaningful work in astronaut health and performance during long-duration space exploration missions* (NASA Technical Manuscript (TM), 2016-219276). Houston, TX: NASA.

Cutshaw, J. (2018). *Army astronaut prepares for December launch to International Space Station.* https://www.militarynews.com/peninsula-warrior/news/army_news/army-astronaut-prepares-for-december-launch-to-international-space-station/article_7908134c-b6dd-11e8-bfd2-f3a506baff08.html

Eberly, M. B., Bluhm, D. J., Guarana, C., Avolio, B. J., & Hannah, S. T. (2017). Staying after the storm: How transformational leadership relates to follower turnover intentions in extreme contexts. *Journal of Vocational Behavior, 102*, 72–85.

Evans, C. A., Robinson, J. A., Tate-Brown, J., Thumm, T., Crespo-Richey, J., Baumann, D., & Rhatigan, J. (2009). *International Space Station Science Research Accomplishments during the assembly years: An analysis of results from 2000–2008* (NASA/TP-2009-213146-REVISION A).

Joshi, M. P., Kathuria, R., & Porth, S. J. (2003). Alignment of strategic priorities and performance: An integration of operations and strategic management perspectives. *Journal of Operations Management, 21*, 353–369.

Kozlowski, S. W. J., & Bell, B. S. (2003). Work groups and teams in organizations. In W. C. Borman, D. R. Ilgen, & R. J. Klimoski (Eds.), *Handbook of psychology (Vol. 12): Industrial and organizational psychology* (pp. 333–375). New York, NY: Wiley.

Landon, L. B., Slack, K. J., & Barrett, J. D. (2018). Teamwork and collaboration in long-duration space missions: Going to extremes. *American Psychologist, 73*(4), 563–575.

Marks, M. A., DeChurch, L. A., Mathieu, J. E., Panzer, F. J., & Alonso, A. (2005) *Teamwork in multiteam systems. Journal of Applied Psychology, 90*, 964–971. https://pdfs.semanticscholar.org/72ba/d9f4ab87c79f81539c31cfe56a43b763c4fe.pdf

Nansen, F. (1897). *Fram over Polhavet. Den norske polarfærd 1893–1896.* Kristiania: H. Aschehoud Co. Forlag.

NASA. (2019). *Beyond earth: Expanding human presence in the solar system. Why we explore.* https://www.nasa.gov/exploration/whyweexplore/why_we_explore_main.html#.XL4gjC8ZOWg

Peary, R. (1907). *Nearest the pole.* Doubleday: Page and Company.

Powell, T. C. (1992). Organizational alignment as competitive advantage. *Strategic Management Journal, 13*(2), 119–134

Samuels, R. J. (Ed.). (2005, December 21). *Encyclopedia of United States National Security* (1st ed., Volume II, p. 669). SAGE Publications. ISBN 978-0-7619-2927-7.

Shackleton, E. (1919). *South*. London: Century Publishing. ISBN 0-7126-0111-2.

Stuster, J. (2010). *Journal flight experiment: Expedition 31/32 science symposium* (NASA Technical Manuscript (TM), 2010-216130). Section 3 (Results), pp. 9–10. Retrieved from https://ntrs.nasa.gov/archive/nasa/casi.ntrs.nasa.gov/20120003494.pdf.

NASA. (2001). The history of Shuttle-Mir. Washington, DC: NASA. Retrieved from https://history.nasa.gov/SP-4225/mir/mir.htm

O'Shea, P.G. (2016). Ernest Shackleton overcame more than geographical challenges. https://www.irishexaminer.com/viewpoints/analysis/ernest-shackleton-overcame-more-than-geographical-challenges-389306.html

13 Behavioral Health and Performance for Long-Duration Missions

Christopher F. Flynn
Federal Aviation Administration

CONTENTS

Introduction 235
Part 1: Crawl. Phase I (NASA-Mir, 1993–1998) 236
    Relationships (People) 236
    Rules (Culture, Systems) 237
    Reforms (Technology, Knowledge) 238
Part 2: Walk. Phase II (Initial ISS Missions 1–22, 1999–2009) 242
    Relationships (People) 242
    Rules (Culture, Systems) 244
    Reforms (Technology, Knowledge) 247
Part 3: Run. Phase II (ISS Missions 23 to Present, 2010–Present) 248
    Relationships (People) 248
    Rules (Culture, Systems) 248
    Reforms (Technology, Knowledge) 249
Conclusion 249
References 250

INTRODUCTION

In 2019, the International Space Station (ISS) has been manned for more than 6600 days by 58 Expeditionary crews. Multiple advances in technology and medical knowledge have created a strong connection between ISS crews and spaceflight operational medical support staff on Earth. This now-trusted connection has been earned over years of hard work by NASA Behavioral Health and Performance Group (BHPG) and international Spaceflight Human Behavioral Health Working Group (SHBPWG) partners who (through countless hours of listening and dialogue in each country's space medicine and operations committees) advocated for stronger relationships between partners, changes in spaceflight operational rules, and reformed "the way things had been done." In 1994, when the first NASA-Mir astronaut arrived for long-duration mission training in Russia, what are now called behavioral health and performance (BHP) concepts were thought to be largely "unnecessary" for NASA astronauts. The success in maintaining the behavioral health and performance of 58 ISS expeditionary crews has its foundation in more than two decades of advocacy by each SHBPWG partner representing BHP factors in their spaceflight organizations. We might consider the progress over these years as a "crawl, walk, run" of international collaboration that created new "relationships, rules and reforms" in spaceflight medical and mission operations. I had the privilege to participate in this progress as: a NASA flight surgeon and psychiatrist, NASA Crew Surgeon for NASA-Mir Mission 6 and for ISS Expedition Four, and as a behavioral health crew support officer for long-duration missions helping to develop our BHP programs from 1996 through 2004. In this chapter, we will review *relationships* between people, *rules* creating new systems and *reforms* in technology, and knowledge that has solidified BHP requirements as crucial to the health and performance of long-duration mission (LDM) astronauts and those who will one day man space exploration missions.

PART 1: CRAWL. PHASE I (NASA-MIR, 1993–1998)

Relationships (People)

The first NASA-Mir astronaut Norman Thagard, MD, arrived at the cosmonaut training center in Star City Russia with his flight surgeons, David Ward and Michael Barratt in February 1994. By the time of Thagard's launch in March 1995, Drs. Ward and Barratt (NASA's flight medicine ambassadors of operational medicine to the Russian Space Agency (RSA)) had solidly established that the NASA crew surgeon should be part of the NASA-Mir preflight astronaut support cadre. At NASA Headquarters, Dr. Arnauld E. Nicogossian, MD, MS, was Associate Administrator for Life and Microgravity Sciences (the position now called Chief Medical Officer) who had longstanding personal relationships with senior RSA space medicine leaders including Dr. Anatoly I. Grigoriev, MD. Although these were early positives to build from, our Russian Space Agency (RSA) space medicine colleagues initially felt intruded upon by NASA crew surgeons' presence. With years of experience flying international visitors to Mir, the simplest way to manage US astronauts was for NASA to follow RSA medical rules and countermeasures. However, the NASA space medicine culture was built upon a different model. It emphasized data-driven change as useful and tremendous constraint in medical intrusiveness on astronauts. To succeed, the Phase-I (or NASA-Mir) program would have to survive a clash of national, as well as organizational cultures.

For more than a decade (starting in 1982), NASA spaceflight medical operations had focused on supporting Shuttle missions up to 17.5 days on orbit. From February 1994 to June 1998, NASA completed seven astronaut missions on Mir with on-orbit stays of 115–188 days. It was a steep learning curve. As the NASA-Mir crew surgeons began work with their astronaut, we were determined to "live up" to the high regard that had been earned by Shuttle crew surgeons from their mission astronauts. Joining our crewmembers in pre-/in-/post-flight Russia, the NASA-Mir crew surgeons (Mike Barratt, David Ward, Gaylen Johnson, Tom Marshburn, Terry Taddeo, Pat McGinnis, and myself) learned "first-hand" about the multiple difficulties experienced by our NASA-Mir astronauts. For NASA medical operations leaders, an important first surprise was the much greater time demands placed on the crew surgeon caring for an LDM astronaut.

RSA space medicine experts were initially skeptical of the NASA-Mir crew surgeons. This was completely understandable, given their many years of experience in LDM's compared to NASA's short-duration flights. A cultural difference was quickly apparent: age and experience are highly valued in Russian medicine and NASA-Mir crew surgeons were younger (equating to observing rather than directing care). English and Russian language skills were shallow on both sides which created communication difficulties. Another cultural difference was the reluctance of Russian professionals to openly share information (especially any past problems in spaceflight operations). Only through trust, earned by time spent together as colleagues, could information flow. For NASA crew surgeons who were used to accessing information easily in the US, there were a lot of hurdles to overcome to be part of the RSA space medicine team.

Another difference between RSA and NASA space medical support was the separation of care of the astronaut between pre-/post-flight and on-orbit phases of the LDM. The NASA crew surgeons create a relationship with our crewmembers starting in pre-flight training, continuing through the on-orbit mission and finishing after post-flight rehabilitation. The RSA Star City medical experts only worked with their crewmembers before and after the spaceflight mission, while the RSA on-orbit medical team members were based in Moscow at Mission Control and the Institute of BioMedical Problems (IBMP). The RSA Star City medical team was led by Dr. Valery Morgun, MD, along with psychologists and neuropsychiatrists: Dr. Rostislav B. Bogdashevskiy, PhD; Dr. Oleg O. Ryumin, MD; and Dr. Yuri A. Spatenko, MD. Dr. Ryumin especially assisted the NASA-Mir crew surgeons because he had experience as an RSA surgeon working in Houston for his crewmember on a prior shuttle mission. At RSA mission control, NASA-Mir crew surgeons were assisted by Dr. Irina V. Alfeorova, MD, the Lead Crew Surgeon for each mission, along with the psychologists and neuropsychiatrists: Dr. Olga P. Kozarenko, MD; Dr. Svetlana I. Stepanova, MD; and Dr. Vyacheslav P. Salnitskiy, PhD.

Rules (Culture, Systems)

NASA medical operations staff learned to overcome several cultural and systems barriers in supporting the NASA-Mir crewmembers, including language challenges and shared medical decision making. While some NASA-Mir crew surgeons had a gift for learning the Russian language, most of us had to rely on translators to assist them in their interactions with their Russian space medicine colleagues. Thankfully, NASA created an Operations Office at the Cosmonaut Training Center in Star City with a Director of Operations who could represent Washington and Houston during Russia working hours (a 9-hour time difference) and work "on the ground" issues for astronauts in training and their families. Wonderfully accommodating translators worked in the NASA Operations office, but they were often overtasked and not always able to go to meetings with the NASA-Mir crew surgeon. At times, the NASA-Mir astronauts who were proficient in Russian could help bridge a brief interaction between NASA and Russian physicians, but they had a strict training schedule. If a NASA-Mir crew surgeon "officially" objected to a training or medical event/protocol, this would require a translated discussion and/or documents in Russian and English, that would be reviewed by medical leaders both in Russia and the US.

It was crucial that the two medical teams learned how to reach sometimes thorny medical agreements. Otherwise, the astronaut would be left "stuck" between conflicting opinions. NASA medical decisions tend to be based on open access to data, whereas RSA medical decisions utilized data but emphasized conclusions reached by a senior physician. At times, it was correct for a NASA-Mir crew surgeon to further question the medical safety or validity of a required event. This would require a call back to a NASA senior medical leader in the US, who would then request a translated call with an RSA senior medical leader for discussion. Those high-level relationships would frequently lead to a compromise agreement but required at least a 2-day turnaround. Key Johnson Space Center (JSC) senior medical operations leaders during Phase I were Sam L. Pool, MD, JSC Assistant Director of Space Medicine/Space and Life Sciences and Roger D. Billica, MD, Lead for Phase-I Medical Operations. They worked closely with RSA senior medical operations leaders Dr. Valery V. Bogomolov, MD and Dr. Valery V. Morgun, MD.

As NASA-Mir 1 crew surgeon Mike Barratt said regarding the Phase-I period of joint NASA/RSA medical operations, "American and Russian medical teams have different philosophies on astronaut selection and certification, and on the medical monitoring of astronauts. More than anything, the two medical teams learned how to make their two systems work together." (Morgan, 2001a) These years would give NASA and RSA space medicine professionals much greater insight into how to overcome these cultural and organizational challenges. Although some thought this relationship would end after the final NASA-Mir mission, in January 1998 officials from 15 countries ratified an agreement to design, develop, operate, and utilize an International Space Station. Led by the US, the ISS would become the largest, most complex international cooperative science and engineering program ever attempted. NASA space medicine leaders had already started learning how to join with participating medical experts and would now need to create management systems to select, train, care for, and recover LDM astronauts and their families. (NASA.GOV, 1998)

REFORMS (TECHNOLOGY, KNOWLEDGE)

One of the great challenges faced by NASA-Mir crew surgeons was communication with the on-orbit crewmember. For the Shuttle, communication was relatively easy based upon orbiting satellites with relatively few and brief periods without a connection. In contrast, the Mir required a link through Ground radio stations which left periods of time without an active voice or data link. NASA-Mir 4 astronaut Jerry Linenger, MD, found voice communications too frustrating and tried only using email with the Ground team (Morgan, 2001b). Text information was sent to Mir using the Packet system, which required very specific formatting of the file from the Ground to orbit. NASA-Mir 1 astronaut Thagard stated,

> The cultural isolation is extreme. There were times when I went 72 hours without speaking to an English-speaking person. I didn't get a lot of news up there. ... All of those things start to weigh heavily after a while. If I had been looking at six months [mission] I would have been really worried at about three months that I wasn't going to make it.
>
> *Harwood (1995)*

While it was difficult for a NASA-Mir astronaut to have voice communications with NASA operations staff in Moscow Mission Control, it was even more challenging to speak reliably to their family in the US. Implementing communications that connected the NASA-Mir astronaut to their team and family was a high priority of the mental health support team because of the powerfully positive response for on-orbit crewmembers (Bluth & Helppie, 1986d).

Russian LDM cosmonauts were connected to their families and to spaceflight psychological support professionals as a routine part of their care while on orbit. NASA spaceflight mental health professionals began to develop a psychological support team, as well. For our NASA-Mir astronauts/families, the team consisted of Al W. Holland, PhD, Steve Vander Ark and Kelly Curtis. Building on relationships with Russian mental health experts in Star City, IBMP, and Mission Control, the team helped to implement more English-based communications for NASA-Mir astronauts. A second crucial psychological support factor was the launch of comfort items to the NASA-Mir astronaut in a crew care package. To be allowed any volume and weight for an astronaut's crew care package on a cargo resupply vessel to Mir, something else had to be subtracted from requested equipment or supplies for the station. Because emergency re-supply requirements were frequent, protecting that volume and weight required strong support from the senior NASA-Mir program leaders. The mental health team was indebted to Phase-I program leaders NASA astronaut Frank L. Culbertson, Jr. and RSA astronaut Valery V. Ryumin who supported these crew care packages as essential to the missions.

NASA medical operations was adapting and learning from the NASA-Mir mission astronauts. If a Shuttle mission felt like a medical operation's "sprint," NASA-Mir missions had to be treated more like a "marathon" by the LDM crew surgeon and team. With a shuttle mission, we knew the astronaut would return "in a week or two" to Earth-bound medical evaluation and care. There were frequent enough off nominal/emergency events on the NASA-Mir missions that NASA medical operations leaders questioned how to assess an astronaut's cognitive functioning over the course of an LDM. Our Russian space mental health colleagues used psycholinguistic analysis of their crewmembers' communications with the Ground teams to judge neurological status. From the US perspective, the US crew surgeon (and LDM astronaut) needed a tool to decide if a toxic exposure, such as the smoke and ethylene glycol release on Mir (Morgan, 2001b), or a decompression event (Morgan, 2001c), or a head injury (Morgan, 2001a) was severe enough to warrant an emergent evacuation from Mir. Developing a repeatable measure of an astronaut's cognitive performance became an urgent operational need. After NASA-Mir 6, I was fortunate to lead a small team of volunteer scientists to develop, test, and implement a cognitive assessment tool for orbit that became WinSCAT (Kane, Short, Sipes, &

Flynn, 2005). The tool was first tested by astronaut Andrew Thomas, PhD, AO on NASA-Mir Mission 7 and was then implemented beginning with ISS Mission 1.

As the NASA-Mir flights continued, the NASA mental health team promoted the idea that NASA would have to provide "more" for LDM astronauts and their families. As the NASA-Mir missions began, NASA's longest spaceflight had been 84 days in 1973 on Skylab 4. During that mission, the crew turned off communications with the ground control team due to severe frustrations with task overload and lack of negotiation about their on-orbit schedule (Eschner, 2017). Twenty-two years later, NASA Mission leaders and Medical leaders were skeptical that mental health concerns would need as much medical attention as cardiovascular and muscle deconditioning. Thankfully, NASA astronaut Ellen Baker, MD, was talking closely with our NASA-Mir astronauts and families. She became an ardent and vital advocate of expanding mental health support for LDM missions from within the NASA Astronaut Corps. The mental health team also benefitted from years of trust-building by prior NASA psychiatrist Royden Marsh, MD, (a highly experienced US Air Force pilot-physician and flight surgeon/psychiatrist) and community psychiatrist Camis Milam, MD (who had created a trusted connection with astronaut families).

The NASA mental health team also needed to explain the challenges faced by LDM astronauts and their families with more than just our opinions. NASA mission and medical leaders needed data to help them weigh the risks of the mental health needs of these astronauts and families against many other demands on budget and valuable time in training and on orbit. Data came from multiple researchers who had studied information on long-duration space missions or isolated/confined terrestrial missions. US Navy submarine crews were one analogue suggesting psychiatric conditions could arise during a mission (Weybrew & Noddin, 1979). US and Soviet space medicine experience suggested that LDM cosmonauts could experience "exhaustion, asthenia, euphoria, depression, hostile interpersonal reactions, anxiety and accentuation of negative personality traits" (Myasnikov & Zamaletdinov, 1993). Our NASA-Mir Russian colleagues advised our NASA mental health team to expose LDM astronauts to difficult survival training events, sleep deprivation, and isolation. Any of our proposals would need to be acceptable to Mission senior leaders, Medical senior leaders, especially the current/future LDM astronauts and their families.

By mid-1997, a structure for a spaceflight mental health program to support LDM's began to take shape: Holland brought years of operational psychology knowledge; Vander Ark and Curtis brought knowledge about the operational support of the astronaut and their family and I brought years of flight surgeon/operational psychiatry knowledge. Together, we framed the Four Factor Model, which focused the many problems of LDM's into a consistent framework and language to our NASA Mission and Medical leaders (Figure 13.1). This model had a number of strengths. It opened a path to developing psychological prevention strategies (psychological support and advanced selection and training concepts). It defined how behavioral health prevention and treatment (psychiatry and sleep/circadian concepts) contributed to performance. It created a "home" in medical operations to advocate for certain human factors areas that contribute to performance (habitability, individualized training/retraining/ergonomics, and workload/scheduling). It "fit" with NASA research concepts. The model focused on maintaining astronauts' performance, which aligned

Behavioral Health and Performance

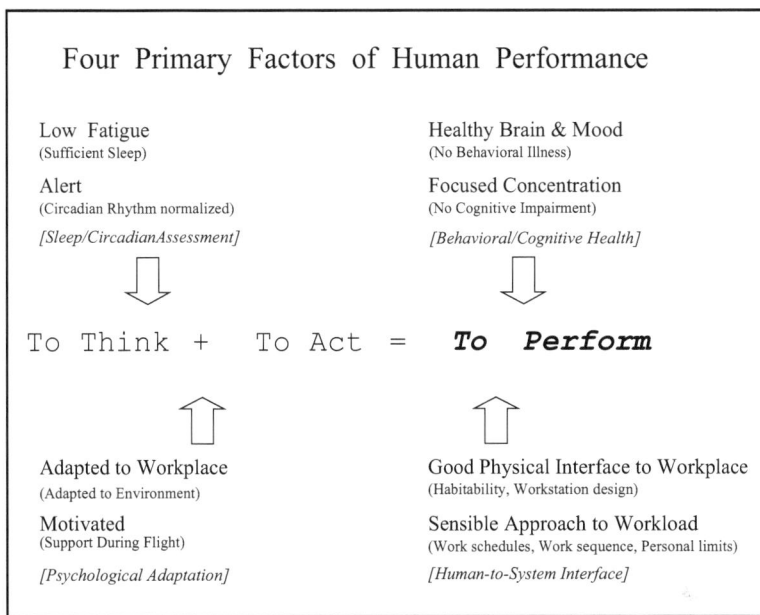

*(Flynn, 2008); used with permission from *Principles of Clinical Medicine for Space Flight*.
[Alt text: Four factors of cognition and behavior affect human performance.]

FIGURE 13.1 Four primary factors model of human performance ((Flynn, 2008); used with permission from *Principles of Clinical Medicine for Space Flight*).

well with the Corps' goals. As the model became accepted, our mental health team was newly named: the Behavioral Health and Performance Group (BHPG). In June 1998, NASA-Mir 7 astronaut Thomas completed the final Phase-I mission. By Fall 1998, BHPG and the Four Factor Model was approved into the NASA Medical Operations "critical path" requirements to ensure the health of LDM astronauts.

In December 1998, the first meeting of the ISS partner's mental health experts from Russia, Canada, Europe, Japan, and the US occurred in Moscow. A great challenge was before that team: to understand the goals and constraints of at least five partner countries who would select, train, and support their astronauts on future ISS LDMs. Despite the relative "seniority and experience" of Russia and the US, the first group members chose to make its decisions based upon consensus. This was costly in time to fully discuss pros/cons of recommendations, followed by final member decisions already being approved by each country's medical leaders. Yet, consensus had the advantage of making each partner's voice carry equally in agreements, creating very strong bonds of trust, and very durable agreements. Through intent listening and determined collegiality, the international Spaceflight Human Behavior and Performance Group (SHBPWG) members overcame difficult cultural and organizational obstacles to approve its foundational structure of mental health care for LDM astronauts and their families. As the first two ISS modules (Zarya/November 1993 and Unity/December 1998) launched into orbit, the SHBPWG group had begun.

With expectations high on what was needed, the BHPG now faced the daunting challenge of justifying a substantial budget for travel/training/development, necessary time with astronauts pre-/in-/post-flight, and recruiting talented personnel.

PART 2: WALK. PHASE II (INITIAL ISS MISSIONS 1–22, 1999–2009)

Relationships (People)

As ISS missions began in 2000, BHPG was one of many groups requesting assistance from NASA space Medicine and Missions leaders to care for ISS astronauts and families. Fortunately, there were NASA astronauts who understood that ISS crews needed a robust mental health support system. Within the Astronaut Corps, there were nine NASA-Mir astronauts/backups, eight prior astronaut Directors of Operations in Russia and seven ISS 1–4 astronauts/backups who spoke to the hardships of LDM training/missions. Crucial support came from experienced astronauts/physicians Ellen Baker, MD, and Dafydd Williams, MD. In 1998, Dr. Williams became the Director of the JSC Space and Life Sciences Directorate (the highest decision maker for medical operations in Houston). These astronauts helped BHPG advocate for resources that provided needed medical and mental health capabilities for ISS crews/families.

When ISS-1 astronaut William Shepherd launched in October 2000, there were now eight NASA crew surgeons who had supported US NASA-Mir astronauts (who had flown 966 days on orbit). NASA senior medical leaders were convinced that mental health support was an essential part of caring for LDM astronauts/families. All involved had learned that significant emotional stressors would occur during the LDM (Table 13.1). However, opinions varied greatly on *how much support* would be needed. Agreeing upon implementable solutions depended upon the sound reasoning and support of many space medicine leaders during this decade. Two Apollo-era NASA flight surgeons, Sam L. Pool, MD, and Craig Fisher, MD, along with Nitza M. Cintron, MD, PhD; Roger Billica, MD; James M. Duncan, MD; and J.D. Polk, DO were significant JSC senior spaceflight medical decision makers. As Dr. Williams completed his leadership as Director of Space and Life Sciences at JSC in 2002, Jeffrey R. Davis, MD, began his tenure as Director. In 2001, Frank D. Carpenter, MD, became the Chief of Behavioral Health and Performance; followed by Gary E. Beven, MD, in 2008 (both USAF flight surgeons and psychiatrists), and later joined by psychiatrist Ronald Moomaw, MD. Remarkably, in 2009, now astronaut Michael Barratt, MD, (prior NASA-Mir 1 and ISS-1 crew surgeon) flew 199 days in space for ISS Expedition 19/20.

BHPG/SHBPWG also needed senior Mission managers and Headquarters senior medical managers to assist approving and implementing LDM mental health support requirements. William "Bill" Gerstenmaier and Michael Suffredini were senior ISS Program/Mission leaders who always gave BHPG a "fair hearing," encouragement, and support. At NASA Headquarters, Dr. Nicogossian engaged with Russian senior medicine colleagues until 2002; when Richard S. Williams, MD, began his leadership guiding spaceflight medical policy for ISS. Senior RSA medical leaders Dr. Grigoriev, Dr. Bogomolov, and Dr. Morgun continued their collaboration.

TABLE 13.1
BHPG and SHBPWG Factors Confirmed Important in Long-Duration Missions (Lengyel & Newman, 2014)

Factor	Recommendation
Psychological Adaptation	Crewmembers need flexibility, resiliency, and sense of humor due to unexpected mission extensions.
	Crew selection for deep-space missions will become more critical to mission success.
	Provide team building and development activities to evaluate compatibility for long-duration missions.
	Behavioral support program elevated morale while on orbit; using family contact (IP phone), telecons, and leisure activities.
Behavioral health	Medical evaluation of individual crewmember stress and compatibility will be important.
Psychological adaptation, behavioral health	Crews must be carefully selected, and be prepared for difficulties, deprivation and long separation from loved ones.
	Astronauts should be observed and evaluated in stressful training scenarios for their interactions and behaviors.
	Crews need training to detect psychological decrement using multiple methods, including advanced behavioral assessment technology.
Fatigue management	Mission planning must consider crew mental health and incorporate exercise as part of the strategy.
	Future spacecraft designs should have individual private sleep quarters for: personal time, privacy, and decoration including family photos.
Human-System-Interface (H-S-I)	Providing crewmembers with flexibility for planning their day-to-day schedules would benefit exploration programs.
	The training organization, in conjunction with the crew office, may consider a library of "just-in-time" training videos for use on-board.
	Habitability must be evaluated by a multi-skilled team of reviewers including operators, behavioral scientists, system + subsystem designers.
	Habitability, layout, and consideration of crew comfort/privacy must be "front and center" in earlier phases of design for long-duration missions.
All four factors	The flight surgeon, behavioral health team, and ISS crews have developed trust based upon the medical team's crew advocacy (e.g. crew rest cycles) and is a model for deep space missions.
BHPG + SHPBWG	Governance by consensus is beneficial in major international projects: agreements should encourage consensus decisions while allowing for a means of resolution in extreme cases.
	The collaboration between the NASA medical team and the International Partners should serve as model for deep space exploration.
BHPG, SHBPWG + International/ National Partner Researchers	The collaboration between the medical operations and research teams created synergies for the ISS Program and should serve as a model for deep space exploration.

Two additional physicians were crucial in facilitating solid interactions between senior spaceflight medical leaders at NASA and RSA: Ashot E. Sargsyan, MD, and Oleg L. Navinkov, MD, PhD.

For a strong foundation in LDM astronauts' and families' mental health care and support to be created, international partnership was needed. The SHBPWG members soon found plenty of pressures, as each ISS partner was challenged with questions about astronaut selection, astronaut training, pre-/in-/post-flight mental health status evaluations, and certification for LDMs. The two co-chairs of the SHBPWG were initially Vacheslav Salnitskiy, PhD (RSA) and myself (NASA), and I was replaced by Leena Tomi, PhD (CSA) in 2005. Steve Vander Ark steadfastly supported the SHBPWG as Executive Secretary keeping documents and communications flowing between members and the various committees where new start requirements would be defended. As time pressures on members grew, the group forcefully debated the option to shift from consensus decision making to majority voting. In 2004, SHBPWG maintained consensus as its decision process and went on to successfully gain approval (by the end of that year) for 40 of 46 (85%) of SHBPWG's recommended LDM mental health requirements. Key SHBPWG members from 1998 to 2018 are shown in Table 13.2.

Rules (Culture, Systems)

The medical changes requested in spaceflight culture and operational systems during the initial years of ISS operations required extensive review by the senior Medical and Mission operations leaders. The BHPG/SHBPWG generally followed a systems concept of "predict difficulties, identify potential problems early, monitor status and respond to correct problems." The "predict-identify-monitor-respond" model fit well with the NASA engineering culture. On the other hand, the BHPG/SHBPWG proposals could be viewed as "muted in scope" or "shocking to the spaceflight system" based upon the senior reviewer. One of the most dramatic requests from the BHPG/SHBPWG was requesting a new private psychological conference (PPC) visit for the LDM astronaut. The PPC would allow all aspects of the "predict-identify-monitor-respond" model to be assessed while the LDM astronaut was on orbit. But, this request would ask for a major change in spaceflight communications and culture.

This additional official communication from Ground team to astronaut was not used by RSA experts (who listened and only talked to astronauts if severe concerns were noted) and could be viewed by NASA crew surgeons and NASA astronaut Capsule Communicators as unnecessary. It was a giant step of collaboration, collegiality, and confidence when the NASA Flight Surgeon corps, the NASA Astronauts Corps, senior spaceflight medical leaders, and the ISS Program mission managers approved the PPC. Although implemented by NASA with ISS-1, the PPC was fully approved by documentation in 2003. The PPC became a powerful tool to the BHPG/SHBPWG professionals because it continued the relationship between the BHP team and the crewmember through the flight, allowing a discussion on concerns in any of the Four Factor areas in a non-recorded/confidential visit (Figure 13.1).

Behavioral Health organized the approach to maintain a healthy brain, on orbit. The BHPG/SHBPWG had several high-priority concerns, identifying and treating:

TABLE 13.2
Key Spaceflight Human Behavior and Performance Working Group Members, 1998–2018

Year	CSA	ESA	GCTC	IBMP	JAXA	NASA	Exec. Secretary	Co-Chair	Chair
1998–1999	L. Tomi, M. Lange	D. Manzey	O. Ryumin, Y. Spatenko	S. Stepanova, O. Kozarenko	C. Sekiguchi	A. Holland	S. Vander Ark	V. Salnitsky IBMP	C. Flynn NASA
2000–2002	L. Tomi, M. Lange	D. Manzey	O. Ryumin	S. Stepanova, O. Kozarenko	N. Inoue	A. Holland	S. Vander Ark	V. Salnitsky IBMP	C. Flynn NASA
2003–2004	L. Tomi, M. Lange	D. Manzey	A. Vasin	S. Stepanova, O. Kozarenko	N. Inoue	F. Carpenter, A. Holland	S. Vander Ark	V. Salnitsky IBMP	C. Flynn NASA
20052008	M. Lange	D. Manzey	A. Vasin, D. Baranetz	S. Stepanova	N. Inoue	W. Sipes, G. Beven	S. Vander Ark	V. Salnitsky IBMP	L. Tomi CSA
2009–2011	M. Lange	D. Manzey, Y. Pecena	A. Vasin		N. Inoue	W. Sipes, G. Beven	S. Vander Ark	S. Stepanova IBMP	L. Tomi CSA
2012	M. Lange, G. Gray	D. Manzey, Y. Pecena	O. Ryumin		A. Matsumoto	W. Sipes, S. Johnston	S. Vander Ark	S. Stepanova IBMP	L. Tomi CSA
2013	M. Lange	D. Manzey, Y. Pecena	O. Ryumin	M. Baranova	T. Anzai, K. Ogata	W. Sipes, G. Beven	S. Vander Ark	S. Stepanova IBMP	L. Tomi CSA
2014	M. Lange	D. Manzey, Y. Pecena	O. Ryumin		G. Suzuki, Y. Yamamura	G. Beven, S. Whitmire	S. Vander Ark	S. Stepanova IBMP	L. Tomi CSA
2015	M. Lange, W. Sipes	D. Manzey, Y. Pecena	O. Ryumin		G. Suzuki, Y. Yamamura	G. Beven, A. Holland	S. Vander Ark	S. Stepanova IBMP	L. Tomi CSA
2016	M. Lange	D. Manzey, Y. Pecena	O. Ryumin	O. Karpova	G. Suzuki, K. Ogata	G. Beven, R. Moomaw	S. Vander Ark	S. Stepanova IBMP	L. Tomi CSA
2017	P. Sedge, M. Lange	D. Manzey, Y. Pecena	O. Ryumin	O. Karpova	G. Suzuki, K. Ogata	G. Beven, A. Holland	S. Vander Ark		L. Tomi CSA
2018	P. Sedge	D. Manzey, Y. Pecena	O. Ryumin	O. Karpova	G. Suzuki, Y. Yamamura	G. Beven, A. Holland	S. Vander Ark		L. Tomi CSA

depression (a generalized fatigue was already considered likely) (Kanas et al., 2001), head injury (weightless items still have mass on orbit), severe toxin and/or decompression exposure (already experienced on Mir). Additionally, in 2006 and 2007, the death of a former astronaut by apparent suicide and the arrest of an active astronaut also reinforced that astronauts deserved care for their mental health needs in all phases of their career (Newman & Hauser, 2007; Whitesides, 2007). In this decade, visits with a NASA BHPG psychologist or psychiatrist were approved for each phase of the LDM (preflight, inflight-PPC, and postflight) plus during an active NASA astronaut's career. Most ISS partners elected to fly WinSCAT as part of their brain monitoring plan for on-orbit astronauts. Medications to treat depression (and even psychosis) were added to the on-orbit medical kit.

Psychological Adaptation focuses on the astronaut's "adaptation" to LDM isolation and confinement, as well as his/her social "fit" with the crewmembers on orbit and Ground professionals to accomplish the mission's goals. The adaptation of the family to LDM stressors is vital to mission success, as well. As NASA-Mir 7 astronaut Thomas reflected, "You have to use your own resources to make the life interesting, to keep your motivation going. It's undeniably a challenge because you're in a confined space. So, there are great challenges of taking on a mission like this. There is no doubt about it." (Morgan, 2001e). Assisting each LDM astronaut to develop their own psychological strategies to succeed in an extreme environment is necessary, since these skills are not "innate." An astronaut's ability to create strong relationships between crewmembers on orbit significantly reduces crew tension in an LDM. NASA-Mir 6 astronaut Wolf explained, "There is no small or unimportant job on the space station." While on Mir, a failure of the condensation system caused "bowling ball size or beach ball size… gooey, slimy ice-cold fluid… track[ing] down the structure and into the wiring." Wolf decided he was going to take on this cleaning task to show his support of the crew, saying to his crewmate Pavel Vinogradov, "You'll never have to do this again." (Morgan, 2001d).

Developing these adaptation skills led RSA mental health experts to implement extensive psychological testing and evaluation of potential crewmembers premission and inflight (Garshnek, 1989). During this decade, BHPG/SHBPWG members evaluated a number of advanced psychological training platforms as each country looked for features that would also "fit" with their organizational and national cultures. Psychological support professionals would meet with the LDM astronaut and their family starting 2 years before launch. Weekly family conferences, calls to Earth using the internet protocol (IP) phone from orbit, and family surprises in crew care packages all became standardized. New tools to choose astronaut applicants who might adapt more easily to LDM stressors were also being developed and tested. Debriefs of the mission with psychologist and psychological support professionals also became requirements.

Sleep and Circadian deficits on orbit can create a negative impact on performance; as can requesting astronauts to perform critical operations during their circadian rhythm "trough." Sleep/circadian disruptions have strong connections between terrestrial aircrew fatigue and poor performance (including mishaps) (Caldwell, 1997; Luna, 1997). Studies of on-orbit sleep revealed decreased sleep on Shuttle missions (Monk, Buysse, Billy, Kennedy, & Willrich, 1998) and disruption of the circadian rhythm and sleep stages on Mir (Gundel, Polyakov, & Zulley, 1997) reducing an astronaut's performance. "The main consequences of inadequate sleep are decrements of performance, sporadic emotional flareups, and extensive (up to 50%) use of hypnotics. However, there are large individual differences in the vulnerability to sleep loss" (Tobler & Borbely, 1993). BHPG/SHBPWG worked to assure at least two mechanisms existed to assist with crewmember fatigue: defending schedules that provided adequate time for sleep and avoids work at circadian nadir and providing medications for sleep.

Human-System Interface factors affect astronaut performance primarily in the areas of work/rest schedules, and in ergonomics/including the value of privacy, as well as individualized methods for LDM training/retraining. Task overload is a scheduling problem that leads to a breakdown of astronaut morale, tension between the Ground teams and the on-orbit crew. On a 150-day Salyut-7 mission (1983–1984), by the 4th month the crew was asking for an end to the experiments so they could have more free time. During this mission, sleep time was cut from 9 hours to 8 hours, and an hour was added to the work schedule. After 100 days, Aleksandr P. Aleksandrov said they were tired and that their fatigue was building (Bluth & Helppie, 1986c). In addition, task overload reduces sleep time and creates exhausted astronauts, who need to be able to respond effectively to critical emergencies that can take days to resolve (Bluth & Helppie, 1986b). After the Spektr depressurization mishap on NASA-Mir 5, astronaut Michael Foale, PhD, CBE reported, "The station fell dark and silent. According to Foale, this was the hardest time he experienced on board MIR; but that hardship was mainly because they all got so fatigued. Lazutkin went two full days without sleep" (Morgan, 2001c). On orbit ergonomics also add a risk for injury when design of workstations do not accept a broad range of male and female astronauts; increasing fatigue, risk of injury, and decreasing performance (Mount & Foley, 1999). Periods of privacy are also crucial for LDM crewmembers, with cosmonauts isolating in the Soyuz for short time periods (Bluth & Helppie, 1986a) which on ISS can occur with crewmembers' private sleep quarters. The PPC became the primary tool to evaluate an astronaut's scheduling pressures on orbit, while post-flight debriefs were the tool for better understanding of the impact of design for on-orbit operations.

Reforms (Technology, Knowledge)

As NASA decision makers required data to inform policy and operational changes in spaceflight medical support, BHPG became the center-point to brief internal and external reviewers about plans to support the mental health of US LDM astronauts. Our BHPG also became the group that would request, advocate for, and implement any approved NASA LDM mental health requirements. While JSC was focused on operational support, NASA Headquarters had been developing connections to US scientists who could help research and develop LDM countermeasures for LDM medical problems. Led by Jeffrey Sutton, MD, PhD, the National Space Biomedical Research Institute (NSBRI) was created in 1997 and by 1999 had seven teams advancing space countermeasures research. Two teams were directly tied to BHPG: Neurobehavior and Performance (led by David F. Dinges, PhD) and Human Factors and Performance (led by Elizabeth B. Klerman, MD, PhD). During this decade, BHPG relationships with NSBRI scientists created a dynamic bi-directional flow of information: BHPG providing operational insights to the NSBRI teams and NSBRI teams providing recent research data to BHPG informed better care for ISS astronauts and their families.

PART 3: RUN. PHASE II (ISS MISSIONS 23 TO PRESENT, 2010–PRESENT)

Relationships (People)

Albert Holland, PhD continues to lead the BHPG's Psychological Adaptation efforts and has been joined by operational psychologists James Picano, PhD and occupational psychologist Kelley Slack, PhD. In 2011, the Space and Life Sciences Directorate (still led by Dr. Jeff Davis, MD) became the Human Health and Performance Directorate, reflecting the growing emphasis on astronaut performance. In 2012–2013, astronaut Thomas Marshburn, MD, (prior NASA-Mir 4 and ISS-7 crew surgeon) completed 146 days on orbit for ISS Expedition 34/35. At NASA Headquarters, JD Polk, DO assumed the leadership role as Chief Health and Medical Officer in 2016. William Gerstenmaier continues as Associate Administrator of Spaceflight Operations; while Michael Suffredini turned over leadership as ISS Program Manager to Kirk Shireman in 2015.

Rules (Culture, Systems)

In early 2010, the ISS international partners agreed to continue supporting ISS missions at least until 2020. SHBPWG continues to promote each partner's spaceflight BHP-related programs. At NASA, Behavioral Health evaluations are fully integrated into annual astronaut medical examinations. An updated WinSCAT (modified from ISS inflight data and ground studies) continues to be flown, recording both nominal (92%) and off-nominal (8%) data from on-orbit evaluations (Kane, Seaton, & Sipes, 2011). Private Psychological conferences occur every two weeks to support NASA LDM astronauts. Advances in psychological selection at initial astronaut selection ("Select-In" focus) now highlight variables that will likely help astronauts meet the demands of LDM missions, such as agreeableness, conscientiousness, empathy, sociability, and flexibility, among others (Paris, 2014). The psychological support team greets the ISS astronaut and their family starting 2 years before launch and builds individualized programs to support them during the LDM. The weekly private family conference (PFC) continues, as does the crew care package that flies favorite items/family surprises on each resupply for each crewmember (Beven, Holland, & Sipes, 2008).

Crew scheduling and sleep guidelines remain central to managing LDM crewmembers' fatigue. In 2011, BHPG/SHBPWG professionals began a close review of complex scheduling guidelines in order to reduce circadian disruptions. In 2013, ISS crew surgeons were provided with standardized recommendations for helping astronauts manage fatigue during all phases of the LDM. (Evans-Flynn, Gregory,

Arsintescu, Leveton, & Vessey, 2015) In 2016 a review of the crew schedules continued the 6.5-hour ISS workday during nominal non-docked mission days for astronauts to perform systems and research work.

REFORMS (TECHNOLOGY, KNOWLEDGE)

The NSBRI provided dynamic collaboration between BHPG and US researchers. NSBRI researchers conducted studies in analog environments and aboard the ISS using already established tools (e.g., the Psychomotor Vigilance Task, an objective measure of performance) and newly developed prototype tools (e.g., a mathematical model measuring individual fatigue affecting performance and a self-directed training and treatment tool for high levels of stress). In a 520-day simulation of a mission to Mars, BHPG/SHBPWG partner country's investigators evaluated the risks to performance from behavioral health status, cognitive and behavioral conditions, and psychosocial adaptation within a team (NSBRI.ORG, 2015). The close collaboration between NASA Operations and NASA Human Factors and Behavioral Performance (HFBP) continues to produce advances for on-orbit health. The HFBP research team is intently focused on developing countermeasures for near-earth and distant space missions. In 2014, as NASA looked toward future space exploration missions, the "lessons-learned" from 38 ISS and 7 NASA-Mir expeditions emphasized many BHPG/SHBPWG factors as a crucial foundation for the health and performance of LDM astronauts. (Lengyel & Newman, 2014) (Table 13.1). As the NSBRI era ended in September 2017, the new Translational Research Institute for Space Health (TRISH) began spearheading the ongoing search for novel spaceflight crew health countermeasures.

CONCLUSION

From its quiet beginnings as NASA entered long-duration space missions in 1994 until today, the NASA Behavioral Health and Performance Group (BHPG) and the ISS international partners Spaceflight Human Behavior and Performance Working Group (SHBPWG) programs have created a foundation to support the behavioral health and performance of LDM astronauts and their families. A Four Factor model informed the early years of research/development/ implementation of countermeasures and the groups have continued to focus efforts on: behavioral health and psychological adaptation, while sleep and circadian health and human-system interface issues have shifted to other advocates. From 1997 to 2018, international, NASA, and NSBRI (now TRISH) researchers have collaborated with BHPG/SHBPWG partners to develop and deliver new BHP countermeasures for LDM missions beyond low Earth orbit. Over the past 25 years, through good-will and persistent negotiations, BHPG and SHBPWG partners have advanced operational requirements and programs that delivered hands-on care and support to their LDM crewmembers and families. This was an era when NASA space operations shifted from Shuttle missions to LDMs, and spaceflight medicine senior leaders recognized the importance of BHP factors for success in LDMs, highlighting Performance as it reshaped its JSC space medicine operational and research organization into the Human Health and

Performance Directorate. From decades of BHPG/SHBPWG operational experts diligently caring for LDM astronauts/families and collaborative research by international partners, behavioral health and performance spaceflight requirements are no longer debated if important but are recognized as crucial to the success of current LDMs and future space exploration missions (Scimemi, 2017).

REFERENCES

Beven, G., Holland, A., & Sipes, W. (2008). Psychological support for U.S. astronauts on the international space station. *Aviation Space and Environmental Medicine, 79*, 1124.

Bluth, B. J., & Helppie, M. (1986a). *Soviet space stations as analogs* (2nd ed., I-7) (NASA Grant NAGW-659). Washington, DC: NASA Headquarters.

Bluth, B. J., & Helppie, M. (1986b). *Soviet space stations as analogs* (2nd ed., I-54) (NASA Grant NAGW-659). Washington, DC: NASA Headquarters.

Bluth, B. J., & Helppie, M. (1986c). *Soviet space stations as analogs* (2nd ed., III-50) (NASA Grant NAGW-659). Washington, DC: NASA Headquarters.

Bluth, B. J., & Helppie, M. (1986d). *Soviet space stations as analogs* (2nd ed., III-88) (NASA Grant NAGW-659). Washington, DC: NASA Headquarters.

Caldwell, J. A. (1997). Fatigue in the aviation environment: An overview of the causes and affects as well as recommended countermeasures. *Aviation Space and Environmental Medicine, 68*, 932–938.

Eschner, K. (2017, February 8). *Mutiny in space: Why these skylab astronauts never flew in space again.* Retrieved from http://www.smithsonianmag.com/smart-news/mutiny-space-why-these-skylab-astronauts-never-flew-again

Evans-Flynn, E., Gregory, K., Arsintescu, L, Leveton, L. B., & Vessey, W. (2015, January). *Risk of performance decrements and adverse health outcomes resulting from sleep loss, circadian desynchronization, and work overload* (JSC-CN-34196). Washington, DC: NASA Scientific and Technical Information Office.

Flynn, C. F. (2008). Chapter 17. Psychological & psychiatric disorders and support. In M. B. Barratt & S. L. Pool (Eds.), *Principles of clinical medicine for space flight*. (pp. 391–412). New York, NY: Springer Verlag.

Garshnek, V. (1989). Soviet space flight: The human element. *Aviation Space and Environmental Medicine, 60*, 695–705.

Gundel, A., Polyakov, V. V., & Zulley, J. (1997). The alteration of human sleep and circadian rhythms during spaceflight. *Journal of Sleep Research, 6*, 1–8.

Harwood, W. (1995, July 10–16). Thagard: changes needed before next six month mission. *Space News, 26*, 8. Retrieved from https://spacenews.com/download/2019SNAWARDS.pdf

Kanas, N., Salnitskiy, V., Gushin, V. Weiss, D. S., Grund, E. M., Flynn, C., & Marmar, C. R. (2001). Asthenia—Does it exist in space? *Psychosomatic Medicine, 63*, 874–80.

Kane, R., Seaton, K., & Sipes, W. (2011, May). *Cognitive assessment during long duration spaceflight* (JSC-CN-21764). Washington, DC: NASA Scientific and Technical Information Office.

Kane, R. L., Short, P., Sipes, W., & Flynn C. F. (2005). Development and validation of the spaceflight cognitive assessment tool for windows (WinSCAT). *Aviation Space and Environmental Medicine*, 76(Suppl.), B183–B191.

Lengyel, D. M., & Newman, J. S. (2014, September). *International space station: Lessons learned for space exploration* (NASA Public Lessons Learned Database: Entry 12603). Washington, D.C.: NASA. Retrieved from https://www.nasa.gov/iss-lessons-learned-report

Luna, T. D. (1997). Air traffic controller shift work: What are the implications for aviation safety? A review. *Aviation Space and Environmental Medicine, 68*, 69–79.

Monk, R. H., Buysse, D. J., Billy, B. D., Kennedy, K. S., & Willrich, L. M. (1998) Sleep circadian rhythms in four orbiting astronauts. *Journal of Biological Rhythms, 13*, 188–201.

Morgan, C. (2001a). NASA-1 Norm Thagard: An end and a beginning, March 14–July 7, 1995. *Shuttle-Mir = [Mir-Shuttle]: The United States and Russia share history's highest stage* (pp. 16–31) (NASA SP; 4225). NASA: Johnson Space Center.

Morgan, C. (2001b). NASA-4 Jerry Linenger: Fire and controversy, January 12–May 24, 1997. *Shuttle-Mir = [Mir-Shuttle]: The United States and Russia share history's highest stage* (pp. 86–101) (NASA SP; 4225). NASA: Johnson Space Center.

Morgan, C. (2001c). NASA-5 Mike Foale: Collision and recovery, May 15–October 6, 1997. *Shuttle-Mir = [Mir-Shuttle]: The United States and Russia share history's highest stage* (pp. 104–117) (NASA SP; 4225). NASA: Johnson Space Center.

Morgan, C. (2001d). NASA-6 David Wolf: Recommitment to Mir, September 25, 1997– January 31, 1998. *Shuttle-Mir = [Mir-Shuttle]: The United States and Russia share history's highest stage* (pp. 120–135) (NASA SP; 4225). NASA: Johnson Space Center.

Morgan, C. (2001e). NASA-7 Andy Thomas: Smoother sailing, January 22–June12, 1998. *Shuttle-Mir = [Mir-Shuttle]: The United States and Russia share history's highest stage* (pp. 138–151) (NASA SP; 4225). NASA: Johnson Space Center.

Mount, F. E., & Foley, T. (1999). Assessment of human factors. In C. F. Sawin, G. R. Taylor, & W. L. Smith (Eds.), *Extended duration orbiter medical project final report*(NASA/ SP-1999-534). Washington, DC: NASA Scientific and Technical Information Office.

Myasnikov, V. I., & Zamaletdinov, I. S. (1993). Chapter 19. Psychological states and group interactions of crew members in-flight. In A. E. Nicogossian, S. R. Mohler, O. G. Gazenko, & A. I. Grigoriev (Eds.), *Space biology and medicine: Joint US/Russian publication in five volumes*. Reston, VA: American Institute of Aeronautics and Astronautics.

NASA.GOV. (1998, January 29). *Partners sign ISS agreements. International space station: Space station assembly*. Retrieved from https://www.nasa.gov/mission_pages/station/ structure/ elements/partners_agreement.html

Newman, M., & Hauser, C. (2007, February 6). *Astronaut charged with attempted murder*. Retrieved from https://www.nytimes.com/2007/02/06/us/06cnd-astronaut.html

NSBRI.ORG. (2015, May). *NSBRI accomplishments*. Retrieved from http://nsbri.org/wp-content/uploads/2016/02/NSBRI-Principal-Accomplishments.pdf

Paris, A. (2014). Physiological and psychological aspects of sending humans to Mars: Challenges and recommendations. *Journal of the Washington Academy of Sciences*, Winter, 3–20.

Scimemi, S. (2017, November). *Committee on biological and physical sciences in space: ISS transition and deep space gateway concept*. Irvine, CA: National Academies.

Tobler, I., & Borbely A. (1993). Chapter 12. Twenty-four hour rhythm of rest/activity and sleep/wakefulness: comparison of subjective and objective measures. In S. L. Bonting (Ed.), *Advances in space biology and medicine* (Vol 3, pp. 163–183). Greenwich, CT: JAI Press.

Weybrew, B. B., & Noddin, E. M. (1979). Psychiatric aspects of adaptation to long submarine missions. *Aviation Space and Environmental Medicine, 50*, 575–580.

Whitesides, L. H. (2007, September 20). *Even astronauts commit suicide: A tribute to a friend and a plea*. Retrieved from https://www.wired.com/2007/09/suicide-and-hom

14 The Canadian Space Agency and Human Behavior and Performance in Space
Historical Overview

Leena Tomi and Marvin Lange
Canadian Space Agency

CONTENTS

Introduction 253
Selecting Canadian Astronauts 255
CSA Contribution to Human Behavior and Performance Training 258
Supporting Canadian Astronauts 261
Future Challenges 265
References 265

INTRODUCTION

Canada has a long history in space exploration going back to 1962 when it became the third nation to put an artificial satellite, Alouette I, into space. Canada was also the first nation to establish its own domestic geostationary communications network with the launch of the Anik A satellite in 1972. The contribution of the Canadarm, a remote-controlled mechanical arm for the Space Shuttle, resulted in the National Aeronautics and Space Administration (NASA) inviting a Canadian to fly aboard the Shuttle. This invitation led to the establishment of the Canadian astronaut corps. In 1983 the first six Canadian astronauts were selected, and in 1984 Marc Garneau flew aboard the Challenger (STS 41-G) becoming the first Canadian in space. In that same year, the United States invited Canada, Japan, and the European Space Agency (ESA) to join in the building of a space station. Canada signed on to this endeavor in 1986, marking the beginning of its long-term commitment to human exploration of space.

In 1989 the Canadian Space Agency (CSA) was established to coordinate civilian space-related activities on behalf of the Government of Canada. Its mandate, "to promote the peaceful use and development of space for the social and economic benefit of Canadians," has been the guiding principle of the Agency ever since. Achieving the goal of being involved in space exploration would not have been feasible if Canada had not been a part of an international consortium, as it did not have the financial resources required to undertake such a large endeavor alone. Hence, the CSA is a dedicated proponent of international cooperation in space exploration.

In 1993 the CSA selected four more astronauts. A growing astronaut corps, and the establishment of the CSA Operational Space Medicine Program (OSM) that same year, necessitated the development of a Canadian capability in the provision of human behavior and performance (HBP) countermeasures. However, the impetus for an organized effort in this area only came in 1998 when Canada signed the revised Intergovernmental Agreement to build the International Space Station (ISS) with the United States, Japan, the ESA, and two new partners – Russia and Brazil. That same year, the ISS Spaceflight Human Behavior and Performance Working Group (SHBP WG) of the Multilateral Medical Operations Panel (MMOP) was established as the primary working body for coordinating partner inputs and activities in the areas critical to astronaut behavior and performance in spaceflight. Figure 14.1 shows ISS partner representatives at the second SHBP WG Meeting in Hamburg, Germany, 1999.

The CSA has been a member of the ISS MMOP SHPB WG since its first meeting in Moscow in December 1998, actively collaborating with other ISS partner agencies in developing and standardizing human behavior and performance countermeasures. While implementing common standards in this area vis-à-vis selection, training, monitoring, and support, the CSA has to also consider its policies, Canadian medical practice guidelines, Canadian culture, as well as the specific circumstances of Canadian astronauts. This is done following the SHBP WG principle of striving for common objectives with the understanding that some approaches may differ among agencies.

FIGURE 14.1 Second ISS MMOP SHBPWG Meeting, Hamburg, Germany, 1999. From left to right: Oleg Ryumin, Leena Tomi, Marvin Lange, Natsuhiko Inoue, Anka Putzka, Dietrich Manzey, Albert Holland, Stephen Vander Ark, Chris Flynn, Regina North, Larissa Smirnova, Svetlana Stepanova.

SELECTING CANADIAN ASTRONAUTS

To date, there have been four astronaut recruitment campaigns in Canada. The first one was conducted in 1983 by the National Research Council of Canada (NRC) after NASA invited a Canadian to fly aboard the Space Shuttle. Since then the Canadian Space Agency has held three more Astronaut recruitments, in 1992, 2008–2009, and 2016–2017. In the 1983 and 1992 recruitment campaigns, the core selection criteria used reflected the requirements and standards specific to the agencies providing the flight opportunities (NASA and Russian Space Agency), while for the 2008–2009 and 2016–2017 campaigns the ISS internationally agreed standards were used. Typically, additional criteria regarded important for the CSA were also considered.

When the NRC published its call for astronauts in 1983, the primary selection criteria were determined by their intended role as payload specialists aboard the Space Shuttle. Consequently, priority was given to candidates with scientific and technical skills required to conduct experiments in space during short-duration missions. The home base for the astronauts and their families was expected to be Ottawa, Canada. At that time, the space agencies had not yet studied in depth the attributes that would define the ideal astronaut candidate. As a result, the first Canadian astronaut selection did not include any psychological or psychiatric screening, except for a very few basic questions in the general medical screening questionnaire about the previous history of mental illness (select-out criteria). There was no specific assessment of personality qualities or interpersonal skills (select-in criteria). Irrespectively, the one female and five males selected performed well in the program, with five of them flying eight shuttle missions and one long-duration mission aboard the ISS. One of the six selected served as a back-up payload specialist, but left the CSA before having flown.

Some societal considerations were already present in the first selection campaign. There was an aspiration that the candidates would represent different regions of Canada, reflect Canadian social and gender diversity, and could communicate with and inspire the Canadian public in both official languages, English and French, all the while being fully qualified to carry out the required operational tasks. These considerations have been part of all subsequent selections as well. However, the small number of candidates selected by Canada and the very stringent nature of professional, physical, and medical criteria continue to challenge these aspirations.

In 1992 NASA opened its astronaut mission specialist training to the countries participating in the building of the International Space Station. This opportunity changed the focus for the CSA 1992 recruitment campaign from selecting payload specialists to selecting candidates capable of conducting operational tasks related to building and maintaining a space station. It also meant that most of the astronauts chosen would eventually be based in Houston, Texas, to train at the Johnson Space Center (JSC). Relocation to Houston was to add another level of adjustment for the candidates and their families, as well as an added challenge to the CSA to stay connected with its astronaut corps.

At the time of the 1992 selection, there still was no international agreement on the desirable psychological attributes for astronauts. In planning behavioral evaluations, the CSA elected to use some data from NASA, some published data from analogue environments, and recommendations from psychiatry consultants. As the CSA Operational Space Medicine Section was only formally established in 1993, the medical and psychological screenings were outsourced to external consultants without medical oversight. The psychology screening was conducted in relative isolation from the rest of the process, and there was little communication between the psychology and psychiatry consultants. This led to some inconsistencies between their evaluations that could have been prevented by the sharing of psychological test and interview outcomes. In this selection, one female and three male candidates were chosen. However, one of the four selected withdrew his candidacy soon after the announcement for personal reasons. The three remaining astronauts ended up participating in six shuttle missions and one long-duration mission aboard the ISS.

By the time of the third astronaut selection in 2008–2009, the roles of the Canadian astronauts as mission specialists and flight engineers were well defined, as were their posting and training locations. Most of the missions were expected to be of long-duration aboard the International Space Station. These certainties allowed a more detailed job analysis to be conducted to guide the selection process. Also at this time, the CSA OSM team under the leadership of Dr. Jean-Marc Comtois, managed and coordinated the entire medical assessment process, including psychological and psychiatric assessments. The human behavior and performance assessment team consisted of four consultants, including three Canadian psychologists and one psychiatrist, as well as a NASA psychologist and a psychiatrist. The psychology and psychiatry assessments included tests (select-in and select-out) and interviews. Each interview was done jointly by a psychologist and psychiatrist with access to the results of the psychological testing before the interviews.

By 2008 the behavioral medicine criteria were well established by the ISS Program (ISSP) and outlined in its Medical Evaluation Document Volume A, SSP 50667 (MED Vol. A). Moreover, with the increasing mission length, the ISS partner agencies had recognized that long-duration crewmembers needed to possess certain behavioral competencies to ensure the success of international missions. This recognition had led to the development of the first comprehensive behavioral standards for long-duration missions, the ISS Human Behavior and Performance Competency Model by the Human Behavior and Performance Training Working Group. The Model was primarily developed to form the basis for the ISS HBP training curriculum. However, it also included recommendations for selection criteria, based on the acknowledgment that it may not be possible to instill some desired behavioral attributes by training alone. The CSA was the first agency to use these standards in evaluating candidates in the 2008–2009 selection campaign. They were used to guide the psychological interviews by the CSA HBP evaluation team, and an attempt was also made to conduct behavioral observations based on them. For this selection, the CSA had partnered with the Canadian Department of National Defense (DND) to have the candidates tested at one of their naval damage training facilities, and behavioral observations by the CSA observers were made during two of the DND test scenarios. However, it soon became evident that the CSA selection team did not have enough people with necessary training and experience to conduct such assessments and apply the standards reliably enough. Instead, the CSA ended up relying mostly on the separate behavioral observations by the DND team, made using their own standards.

In the 2008–2009 campaign, the CSA selected two male candidates, and both started their training at the JSC almost immediately after the campaign ended. Only one of them has been assigned to a mission at the time of writing. Such a long waiting time for a mission assignment reflects another reality for Canadian astronauts. Flight frequency is based on the agency's contribution to the ISS Program, and for the CSA this translates into a Canadian astronaut flying only every 4–5 years.

The most recent CSA campaign took place in 2016–2017. For the second time, the medical selection process was managed and coordinated by the CSA Operational Space Medicine team. In determining the human behavior and performance selection criteria, the ISS MED Vol. A and the ISS Human Behavior and Performance Competency Model were again used. Jointly with DND, the CSA also conducted a new comprehensive job analysis with the assistance of past and current CSA astronauts, as well as some NASA astronauts. The CSA HBP evaluation team was also able to consult the results of a recent NASA job analysis for 6-12 month missions including missions to ISS, Asteroid, Moon.

This time, the CSA partnered with DND to take advantage of their expertise in assessing military personnel using their Assessment Center process. In two such assessment centers, the DND experts created a series of job-related exercises to measure distinct skills, abilities, and attributes considered to be critical to the success of space missions. The candidates also worked in small groups where, in addition to displaying their ability to manage various unexpected problems, they also demonstrated their ability to work together as a group, either as a leader or as a member of the group. With the support of the experienced DND team of observers, behavioral observations were made in a more coordinated manner than in the 2008–2009 campaign. A separate team of CSA consultants conducted psychological tests and interviews. This team consisted of two psychiatrists and three psychologists, as well as one NASA psychiatrist. Before the interviews, the psychology and psychiatry consultants were able to consider the information from the tests (select-in and select-out) as well as the results from the behavioral observations. In this campaign, as in the previous one, the psychological tests were chosen to be primarily the same as those used by NASA. This way, over the years, it may be possible to accumulate a more substantial database for a closer study of the validity of the tests used in the selection of astronauts. In this campaign, as in the previous one, French-speaking candidates were offered the opportunity to take their tests and interviews in French.

In 2017 two astronaut candidates, one female and one male, were selected and both started their training at the JSC soon after being selected. The last two selections were timed by the CSA to coincide with the NASA selections, in order to have the new CSA astronaut candidates join their NASA counterparts in the NASA Astronaut Candidate (ASCAN) training. After the ASCAN training, the CSA astronauts work out of the NASA astronaut office, only occasionally visiting the CSA headquarters. To ensure the compatibility of selection objectives, and for a better exchange of information, it has been significantly advantageous for the CSA human behavior and performance team to work closely with its NASA counterparts during these past two selections. Not only have the NASA specialists participated in the

CSA selections, but the CSA consultants have been invited to observe and participate in the NASA selections.

During the last two selections, the CSA personnel and active Canadian astronauts and their spouses gave briefings to the candidates and the candidates' families about the realistic living and working lives of CSA astronauts, including details about the terms for government employees posted outside Canada. In the 2016-2107 campaign, these briefings were more formally integrated into the selection process as Realistic Job Previews and closed-door meetings with experienced astronauts and spouses.

The fact that the psychological and behavioral assessment of candidates has evolved and expanded over the four selection processes reflects the increasing emphasis that has been placed by the space agencies on human factors. They have been recognized as being of more significant consequence as missions are extending in duration and possibly outside of the low Earth orbit. Specific to the CSA, there has also been an increasing recognition that circumstances specific to CSA astronauts dictate that, in addition to the internationally agreed-upon expeditionary competencies, behaviors, and desired personality traits, some additional criteria should be considered or given more weight in case of CSA candidates. Such criteria include candidates' adaptability to living outside Canada, away from extended family support, an ability to cope with extensive travel, as well as readiness to endure long wait times for mission assignments. CSA-specific factors have also led the human behavior and performance assessments to probe candidates' motivation in more detail, as well as such traits as resilience and cross-cultural competency.

CSA CONTRIBUTION TO HUMAN BEHAVIOR AND PERFORMANCE TRAINING

Since 1992 Canadian astronauts have done most of their professional training at the Johnson Space Center in Houston, Texas, alongside their NASA colleagues. This training includes the same human behavior and performance training provided to NASA astronauts.

The fact that the CSA currently provides no HBP training at the CSA does not mean that the CSA has no involvement in the ISS astronaut training. Since the establishment of the ISS MMOP Spaceflight Human Behavior and Performance Working Group, the CSA has worked in close collaboration with its international partners in planning and monitoring behavioral training. In 2001, in response to a request by the Multilateral Crew Operations Panel (MCOP) to assist in evaluating behavioral training of astronauts and cosmonauts, the SHBP WG and the International Training Control Board (ITCB) initiated multilateral curriculum design meetings, using a structured approach to establish competency requirements in this area. The ITCB Human Behavior and Performance Training Working Group (HBPT WG) was established to continue the process and consisted of representatives from all the international partner agencies, including astronauts/cosmonauts, human behavior and performance specialists, and training specialists. The results of this multi-year effort were published in 2008 in two NASA publications, International Space Station Human Behavior & Performance Competency Model Volume I and Volume II (Human Behavior and Performance Training Working Group, 2008). These documents outlined eight human behavior and performance competency categories, 25 competencies, 96 behavioral markers, and provided details, examples, and cognitive and affective teaching points for the behavioral markers. The ITCB HBPT WG also conducted a detailed evaluation of HBP team training offered by the ISS partners and prepared recommendations for an ISS team training flow. The NASA and other partner human behavior and performance training curricula are based on the recommendations outlined in these two volumes. The MMOP SHBPWG routinely reviews any changes to training curricula and flows.

One of the team training elements evaluated by the ITCB HBPT WG was the Astronaut Team Training in Canada (ATTIC) offered by DND. It was the result of a direct arrangement between the NASA Astronaut Office and the Canadian Aerospace Training Project International Training Programs (CATP ITP), with some facilitation by the CSA. ATTIC was developed to provide individual, team, and leadership skills training to prepare astronauts for long-duration spaceflight. The first training session was conducted in Cold Lake, Alberta in January 2000, and the second in January 2003 in Valcartier, Québec. It was conducted for groups of 6 astronauts at a time and was to be one of the four training elements of NASA's Astronaut Expedition Interpersonal Training Program. The members of the ITCB HBPT WG were invited to observe this training in 2003, to assess whether it could become part of the advanced ISS team training. The finding of the HBPT WG observer team was that ATTIC was beneficial, "allowing it to be developed into an advanced HBP training for ISS astronauts without major changes." However, ATTIC was not continued mainly due to financial constraints.

In terms of training development, the CSA has been specifically interested in cross-cultural training given Canadian expertise in this area. In support of the international training definition effort, a survey was conducted by the CSA in 2003–2006 to identify cross-cultural challenges facing the ISS personnel, as well as to define cross-cultural training requirements for both crewmembers and ground personnel. The results of this survey informed the recommendations by the ITCB HBPTWG regarding the cross-cultural competencies for long-duration missions. Part of the survey results have been previously reported elsewhere (Kanas & Manzey, 2008, pp.124–125; Tomi, Kealey, Lange, Stefanowska, & Doyle, 2008).

Survey participants included astronauts and support personnel from all the ISS partner agencies and organizations. All together 75 astronauts and 106 members of the ground support teams participated in the survey by filling out a questionnaire. Interviews were also conducted with most of the participants to get additional information and to gain a deeper understanding of the ISS operational environment and challenges. Astronaut participants included 23 astronauts with long-duration mission experience (>30 days), including 16 ISS expedition astronauts (eight Russian and eight NASA astronauts), and seven with experience from Mir, Shuttle-Mir and Euromir missions. The majority of the ground personnel participants included personnel with direct support roles in human missions.

Given the continued relevance of the results of this extensive survey, a summary of them is worth inclusion. They include the importance of training both astronauts and support personnel, the importance of learning about organizational culture differences in addition to national differences, as well as the importance of investing in the creation of a culture of trust between the organizations. Notably, among the problems facing ISS personnel, both the crewmembers and ground support personnel rated "insufficient coordination and/or mistrust among organizations" among the top two. The perceived lack of trust between the ISS partners was also reflected in the high ratings given to such problems as "miscommunication and/or mistrust among ground control and support teams" by both groups, and "mistrust of the motives and behavior of team members from other cultures" by support personnel. Answers to the open-ended questions also included comments about the need for the organizations to "foster an environment of trust," "coordinate their goals," and "coordinate operational standards and processes." Participants also mentioned the need for the organizations to respect the international nature of the ISS operations by selecting personnel who can function in a multicultural environment, and especially in case of the ground personnel, by doing more to facilitate employee-to-employee and team-to-team contacts. Table 14.1 shows the ten highest rated issues for the astronauts and support personnel surveyed.

TABLE 14.1
Highest Rated Cross-Cultural Problems Identified by Astronauts and Support Personnel, in Order of Importance

Astronauts	Support Personnel
1. Insufficient coordination and/or mistrust among organizations responsible for planning and managing the mission.	1. Difficulty in communication due to misperception, misunderstanding.
2. Difficulty in communication due to misperception, misunderstanding.	2. Insufficient coordination and/or mistrust among organizations responsible for planning and managing the mission.
3. One member feeling culturally isolated as a minority.	3. Miscommunication and/or mistrust among ground control and support teams.
4. Difficulty in communicating due to language differences.	4. Differences in work and management styles (attitudes to authority, decision-making, role of the team leader, task versus relationship balance, etc.).
5. Miscommunication and/or mistrust among ground control and support teams	
6. Differences in work and management styles (attitudes to authority, decision-making, role of the team leader, task versus relationship balance, etc.).	5. Difficulty in communicating due to language differences.
7. Being separated from one's family and home culture.	6. Mistrust of the motives and behavior of team members from other cultures.
8. Decreasing team morale, withdrawal and scape-goating due to an inability to cope with cultural differences.	7. Decreasing team morale, withdrawal and scape-goating due to an inability to cope with cultural differences.
9. Differences in attitudes with respect to gender roles, norms, and responsibilities.	8. Differences in attitudes with respect to gender roles, norms, and responsibilities.
10. Different attitudes with respect to needing and taking direction from ground control.	9. Different standards (values and expectations) of work performance during spaceflight.
	10. One member feeling culturally isolated as a minority.

When questioned about potential countermeasures for alleviating the adverse effects of cross-cultural differences, both support personnel and crewmembers rated the provision of cross-cultural training as the most important countermeasure. The majority of the participants supported the training of key support personnel and astronauts together to facilitate crew-ground interactions.

The CSA survey resulted in more emphasis on training for ground personnel, as well as on the importance of coordination and trust between organizations than did previous similar studies (Lozano & Wong, 1996, pp. 1–4; Santy, Holland, Looper, & Marcondes-North, 1993, pp. 196–200). This was likely a reflection of the increased complexity and international nature of space operations since the previous surveys. The adequacy of training and support provided for multicultural ISS teams is worth continuous monitoring by the agencies. As the space historian Oberg has noted, international spaceflights and collaborations have historically been the consequences of, not the causes of, improved international relationships, even though the rhetoric in space communities often tends to reverse this relationship.

SUPPORTING CANADIAN ASTRONAUTS

For Space Shuttle missions, most of the human behavior and performance support for the Canadian astronauts was provided by NASA. Only after the CSA signed onto the International Space Station Program did it start developing a framework of its own in this area. In supporting ISS missions, the CSA follows medical support standards outlined in ISS Program documents, such as the ISS Medical Operations Requirements Document, SSP 50260 (ISS MORD, and the Medical Evaluation Document Volume B, SSP 50667 (MED Vol. B). The implementation frameworks, processes, and procedures are defined in the International Space Station Joint Medical Operations Implementation Plan SSP 50480 (ISS JMOIP). The behavior and performance standards outlined in these documents are based on the recommendations of the Spaceflight Human Behavior and Performance Working Group. This Working Group also monitors the practical implementation of the support measures, with the primary goal of ensuring approximately the same level of support for all the ISS astronauts and cosmonauts, and their families.

At the CSA, medical support, including HBP support, is provided by the Operational Space Medicine section. This group is directed by the CSA Chief Medical Officer and consists of three teams: the Flight Surgeon team, the Medical Operations/Project Management Team consisting of non-physicians who provide discipline-specific support, and External consultants who provide discipline-specific information, expertise, advice, and services. The areas of HBP support can be divided into Behavioral Medicine Support, In-Flight Support for crewmembers during missions, and Family Support.

Behavioral Medicine Support refers to the support provided by psychologists or psychiatrists. While some of this support is available for the CSA astronauts and their families by NASA specialists at the JSC, the CSA OSM and its behavioral medicine consultants have primary responsibility for this care. It is essential to have support providers who are familiar with the crewmember and who understand the Agency, Canadian culture, and are familiar with Canadian medical standards.

To date, all of the CSA consultants providing Behavioral Medicine support have been involved with the selection of the astronauts under their care. Such an early involvement has given them a beneficial early knowledge of the astronauts. This support continues through astronauts' careers. Importantly, it also includes care for the families, as the astronaut's wellbeing is tied to the welfare of the family. The CSA consultants typically keep in touch with the astronauts and their families through visits and electronic and telephone contact. Regular contact is essential for the building of trust between the astronaut and the support provider, and also allows the support provider to know the astronaut's family and stay current with their life circumstances. Each astronaut and their families have their own unique needs, and it is crucial for the support team to be aware of them early in the astronaut's career.

Once assigned for a mission, the Behavioral Medicine specialist monitors the performance of the astronaut and their behavioral health through regular assessments, before, during, and after the mission, as stipulated in the MED Vol. B document. Monitoring during the ISS missions includes biweekly Private Psychological Conferences (PPC). The areas of special attention during PPCs include work-rest schedules, sleep and circadian issues, and any evidence of interpersonal difficulty. For some areas of concern, the agencies have developed common guidelines of care. For example, in the case of sleep, circadian, and workload issues, these are contained in an internal ISS document entitled, Guidelines for Management of Circadian Desynchrony in ISS Operations, SSP 50480-ANX3. This document was a culmination of a multi-year effort by the ISS Fatigue Management Team (FMT), a sub-group of the MMOP SHBP WG, and was finalized in 2014. This document also stands as a good example of agencies recognizing the importance of having common objectives while respecting different national standards and methods. For example, in the case of medication intervention for fatigue, it was agreed by the FMT that when it comes to sleep countermeasures, "each agency may refine them and manage and oversee the implementation of any such countermeasures for their own personnel."

Throughout the mission, the Behavioral Medicine specialist also stays in regular contact with the astronaut's family and provides support as required. Post mission, the support continues for the astronaut and the family and begins as soon as practicable after the landing. This support involves monitoring their psychological wellbeing, and assistance with family reintegration.

In-Flight Support is provided to astronauts during ISS missions to promote their psychological wellbeing, by alleviating the effects of isolation, monotony, and separation from friends and family. In practical terms, this is done by helping the astronauts to stay connected with their family, friends, and their home culture and society, as well as supporting recreational activities. At the CSA, this support is managed by the Operational Space Medicine HBP Team, in close collaboration with KBRWyle, a NASA contractor. Such an arrangement has allowed the CSA to take advantage of the experience and frameworks built by KBRWyle with NASA, while at the same time prioritizing crewmembers' connection with Canada and the CSA. The same arrangement has been successfully used for all three Canadian long-duration missions to date, Expeditions 20/21 (2009), 34/35 (2012–2013), and 58 (2018–2019).

The In-Flight Support measures the CSA provides are the same as those by all the ISS Partners. They include support for maintaining contact between the astronaut and the family via private video conferences, delivery of personal care packages from family, and up-linking of greetings, photos, and videos from family and friends onto the astronaut's personal onboard website. They also include sending of news and recreational videos (movies, sports, cultural events), and organizing private communication events with persons and groups of interest to the crewmember. This support also includes the provision of onboard recreational resources, for example, musical instruments, like the guitar the Canadian astronaut Chris Hadfield is shown to play in Figure 14.2. Communication between the crewmembers and their friends and extended family is also typically facilitated via a restricted social media or other websites. Many of these support measures require close collaboration with the immediate family. Therefore, the pre-flight briefings and training on In-Flight Support routinely involve not only the astronaut but also the family.

All the Canadian support content in this area is coordinated and provided by the CSA. To help with this effort, the CSA routinely hires students. This has offered a welcome opportunity to introduce Canadian social science students to this area. The provision of this support for the three long-duration astronauts to date has also allowed the CSA HBP to build successful collaborative connections with Canadian media and entertainment producers, who have graciously provided content for the astronauts' personal onboard websites. It has also allowed the CSA HBP to work with Canadian cultural icons in arranging private conferences for the astronauts. The dedication and support of such groups and individuals have been of extreme importance for the success of the missions. Even though this side of the mission support is not widely known, being of a confidential and private nature, it has brought in people who may not otherwise be involved with space missions and has increased awareness of space travel in a very personal way.

Family Support pertains to practical assistance provided to the astronauts' families mainly during missions. It overlaps with parts of the In-Flight Support involving families, but is separate from and in addition to family support provided by the behavioral medicine consultants. At the CSA, it is managed and coordinated by the Operational Space Medicine HBP Team, in close collaboration with their KBRWyle counterparts, as well as with the CSA administrative staff. Even though most of the support in this area is currently mission-focused, an effort is made to expand

FIGURE 14.2 CSA Astronaut, Chris Hadfield, relaxing aboard the ISS (Expedition 34/35).

its scope to include practical support outside mission assignment periods. As with all the agencies, the concrete implementation of this support is subject to internal guidelines and budgets.

In 2006 the CSA HBP started participating in Family Support operations alongside NASA for Shuttle launches involving Canadian astronauts (STS-115, STS-118, STS-127) to build CSA capacity in this area. For ISS missions, the primary Family Support objectives and plans are defined by the ISS Program and monitored by the MMOP SHBP WG. The general objectives are tailor-made to the individual family's needs as much as possible. Where there is overlap with In-Flight Support, Family Support is aimed at supporting the families to support the astronauts in space, for example, in assisting families to prepare content for astronaut's webpage (e.g., family videos), in preparing care packages sent to the astronaut, in coordinating private family conferences, and other special events involving the family. It also involves support provided to the families during critical moments of the mission, especially during launch and landing. The OSM HBP provides this support with the assistance of the CSA mission logistics personnel, and naturally with the NASA and KBRWyle personnel involved with the coordination of the launch and landing guest operations. Crucially, it also involves the readiness to provide support in contingency situations and making sure the families are kept informed of any critical situations affecting the crewmember.

Outside of mission-specific support, Family Support at the CSA has also included some practical assistance with daily matters. For such matters, the Operational Space Medicine HBP team works closely with the CSA administrative staff and with other CSA departments, given that many of the issues in this category fall outside the direct mandate of the OSM HBP. One of the factors affecting the everyday lives of Canadian astronaut families is their long-term relocation to Texas. Even though they are entitled to Canadian government allowances and benefits aimed at ensuring that posting outside Canada does not lead to any financial or other disadvantages, the system does not always appear to work sufficiently well for astronauts, who are typically posted for more extended periods than these benefits were designed to cover. Moreover, claiming the benefits can demand a significant amount of time in filling the required documentation. Relocation can also be disadvantageous for the careers of spouses, and maintaining the Canadian cultural identity of children has been a concern for some astronaut families. Being posted outside of Canada also means that family members are away from their established networks of family and friends, and have to cope with little support during astronauts' frequent and often long absences from home due to training. The support measures by the OSM HBP have included the provision of more concrete information on relocation to Houston, including briefings during the selection process, and compilation of practical information on moving, living, and working in Texas. The OSM HBP has also provided some practical assistance with relocation-related documentation. However, even though these and some other measures have been implemented by the CSA to alleviate the concerns and strain stemming from relocation, more assistance is required in this area. It is clear that the wellbeing of the family is essential for the behavioral health and performance of the astronaut. The spouse is an integral part of the role played by the astronaut for the benefit of Canada, and their wellbeing should be supported and their contribution recognized.

FUTURE CHALLENGES

Future international exploration plans involve extended missions beyond low Earth orbit, including missions to Mars. The current human behavior and performance countermeasures will need to be rethought and redeveloped to meet the novel challenges astronauts and their families assigned to these missions will face. The work that has been done over the past 20 years in support of the ISS crews will provide a solid foundation. Moreover, international partners have been able to develop a well-functioning framework of cooperation in the area of ISS medical support, including behavior and performance. The success the agencies have achieved in coordinating their goals, standards, and processes has been remarkable. This accomplishment can act both as an example and as a good starting point for supporting future exploration programs.

REFERENCES

International Space Station Human Behavior & Performance Competency Model Vol. 1 & Vol. 2. (2008). *Mission operations directorate. ITCP human behavior and performance training. Working Group* (NASA/TM-2008-214775, Vol. 1 & NASA/TM-2008-214775, Vol. 2). Available online: http://ston.jsc.nasa.gov/collections/TRS/

Kanas, N., & Manzey, D. (2008). *Space psychology and psychiatry* (2nd ed.n). El Segundo, CA: Microcosm Press and Springer.

Lozano, M. L., & Wong, C. (1996). *Concerns for a multicultural crew aboard the International Space Station* (CSERIAC Gateway, 7).

Oberg, J. (2005). The real lessons of international cooperation in space. *The space review*, July 18. Available online: http://www.thespacereview.com/article/413/1

Santy, P. A., Holland, A. W., Looper, L., & Marcondes-North, R. (1993). Multicultural factors in the space environment: Results of an international shuttle crew debrief. *Aviation, Space and Environmental Medicine, 64*: 196–200

Tomi. L., Kealey, D., Lange M., Stefanowska, P., & Doyle, V. (2008). Cross-cultural training requirements for long-duration space missions: Results of a survey of astronauts and ground support personnel. *International Symposium on Space technology and Science*. https://archive.ists.or.jp/upload_pdf/2008.-p-04.pdf

15 Astronaut Selection at JAXA – from the BHP Perspective

Natsuhiko Inoue
Japan Aerospace Exploration Agency

CONTENTS

Astronaut Selection Carried Out by JAXA 267
JAXA Fourth Astronaut Selection (1999) 268
    The Selection System 268
    The Entry Requirements 268
    Steps Taken in the Selection 271
    Establishing Items for BHP Assessment 271
    Long-Duration Mission Aptitude Examination 271
JAXA Fifth Astronaut Selection (2009) 274
For the Future Selection 277
References 278

ASTRONAUT SELECTION CARRIED OUT BY JAXA

JAXA has carried out astronaut selection five times, in which nine men and two women candidates were selected (Table 15.1). The astronaut candidate is certified as an "astronaut," after completing basic training.

Among the above five selections, the first through third selections were mainly intended to select a Mission Specialist or a Payload Specialist to fly onboard NASA's Space Shuttle, therefore the Behavioral Health and Performance (BHP) component in the astronaut selection was consisted primarily on interviews and examinations. This differed significantly from the later fourth and fifth selections that were intended to select astronauts to serve onboard the International Space Station (ISS).

Notable in the last two selections was an observational assessment of the applicants conducted by experts in various fields during a stay of six nights and seven days by utilizing the isolation and confinement facility (Figure 15.1) at JAXA's Tsukuba Space Center (TKSC) as part of the third stage – the final phase of the selection process. This was a unique method compared with other selection methods adopted by other space agencies, thus this chapter focuses on the fourth and fifth astronaut selections.

TABLE 15.1
JAXA Astronaut Selection

No.	Year of Selection	Total Number of Applicants and Details	Selected Astronaut Candidate
1	1985	533 applicants 488 men (92%) and 45 women (8%)	Mori, Mukai*, Doi
2	1992	372 applicants 331 men (89%) and 41 women (11%)	Wakata
3	1996	572 applicants 511 men (89%) and 61 women (11%)	Noguchi
4	1999	864 applicants 780 men (90%) and 84 women (10%)	Furukawa, Hoshide, Yamazaki*
5	2009	963 applicants 839 men (87%) and 124 women (13%)	Yui, Onishi, Kanai

Note: The asterisk (*) denotes women candidates, as per an excerpt retrieved from http://www.jaxa.jp/press/2008/06/20080624_select_j.html

JAXA FOURTH ASTRONAUT SELECTION (1999)

This marked the first astronaut selection made by the National Space Development Agency of Japan (NASDA, the predecessor of JAXA) under the name of "Astronaut candidate recruitment for future ISS missions."

THE SELECTION SYSTEM

The selection was carried out by two committees set up under the JAXA Astronaut Review Board, which makes a comprehensive judgement on the suitability of applicants. The Competence Review Committee was responsible for the vocational ability examination, and the Medical Review Committee for medical and psychological assessment, particularly with the Psychiatric/Psychological Review Subcommittee (PPRS) for BHP assessment, where JAXA had invited external experts in clinical psychology/psychiatry (Figure 15.2).

THE ENTRY REQUIREMENTS

The following requirements were set for applicants:

A. General Requirements
  1. Having Japanese nationality
  2. Having graduated from a university (category of natural sciences[1])

---

[1] Faculties of science, engineering, medicine, dentistry, pharmacy, agriculture, etc.

Astronaut Selection at JAXA

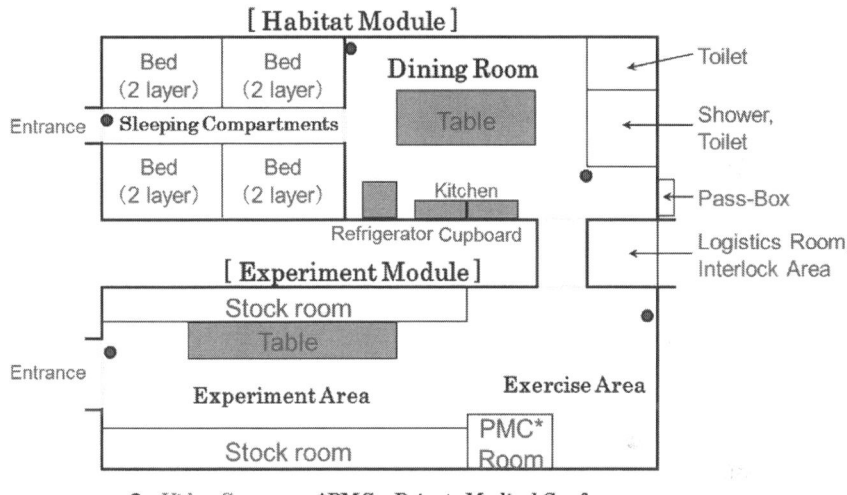

FIGURE 15.1 JAXA isolation and confinement facility.

3. Having at least 3 years of practical experience in research, design, development, manufacturing, or work experience in a field of natural science (as of June 20, 2008)

    (Candidates with a master's degree are deemed as having 1 year of practical experience, and candidates with a doctoral degree as having 3 years of practical experience.)
4. Having sufficient abilities (scientific knowledge and skills) for flexibly responding to astronaut training and space navigation activities in a wide range of fields
5. Having sufficient English-speaking ability for training among a team of international astronauts and being capable of smooth communication with other team members

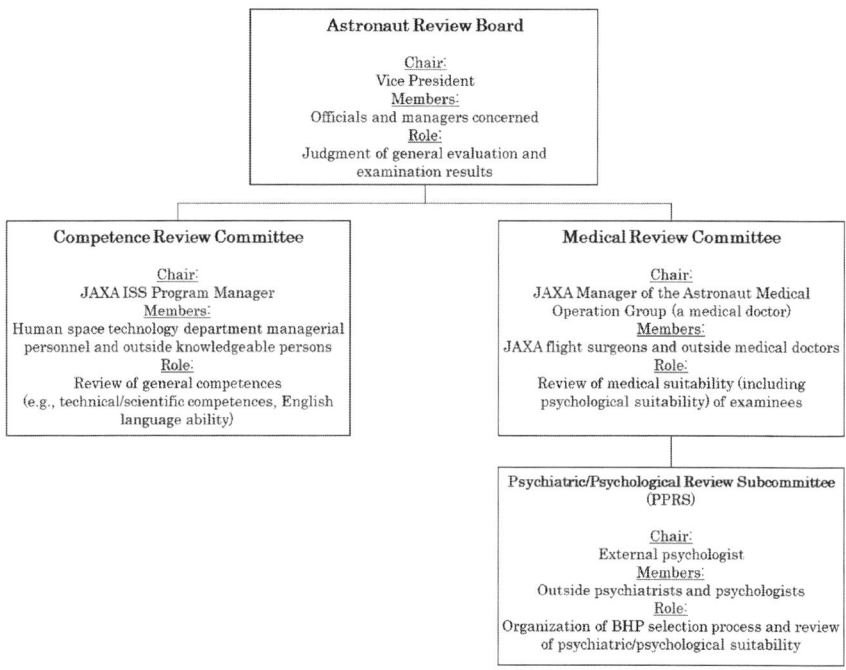

FIGURE 15.2 Organizational chart.

6. Having the medical and psychological characteristics necessary for adapting to astronaut training and a long-term stay in the space environment, specifically as follows:
B. Medical characteristics
   1. Body height: At least 158–190 cm (~62 to ~75 in.) in height.
      (Note: Extravehicular activities in a space outfit require a body height of at least 165 cm (65 in.).)
   2. Weight: At least 50 kg to <95 kg (~110 to ~210 pounds)
   3. Blood pressure: Systolic BP not exceeding 140 mmHg; diastolic BP not exceeding 90 mmHg
   4. Vision: Corrected vision of at least 20/20 for each eyeball
      (Note: No requirements are specified for uncorrected vision)
   5. Color vision: No defects
   6. Hearing ability: No defects
C. Psychological characteristics and others
   1. Having psychological characteristics suited for being engaged in long-term astronaut activities among an international team, including cooperativeness, adaptivity, mental stability, and willpower.
   2. Having a cultured personality (e.g., knowledge of one's own culture and foreign cultures, effective communication skills, especially

in describing personal experience in an impressive way) befitting a Japanese astronaut.
3. Being capable of working for NASDA (currently JAXA) for at least 10 years and perhaps longer periods of time, especially in foreign countries.
4. Possessing a Japanese automobile driving license necessary to obtain an international driving license required for the initial work in the United States before being recruited.
5. Having been recommended by the organization to which the candidate belongs or any other organization.

Steps Taken in the Selection

In the fourth astronaut selection, applicants were assessed in four stages with BHP assessment at each stage.

- Screening of application documents: Screening based on medical certificate/health condition questionnaire
- The first stage: Primary medical examination and psychological aptitude test (questionnaire)
- The second stage: Secondary medical examination, psychological aptitude test (questionnaire and work test), psychological interview, structured psychiatric interview, etc.
- The third stage: Comprehensive screening based on the results of the long-duration mission aptitude examination and from medical and psychological aspects

Establishing Items for BHP Assessment

To establish items for BHP assessment, the sub-items for assessing competencies required for Japanese astronauts were developed with reference to the Mission Specialist Suitability Requirement established by NASA (NASA, n.d.). The PPRS experts determined the methods and measures for assessing with the competency sub-items, including examinations, tests, and interviews. Then a matrix table with its vertical axis for the competency sub-items and its horizontal axis for assessment methods was prepared to ensure that the overall assessment covered all items to be assessed without fail at each stage.

Long-Duration Mission Aptitude Examination

The PPRS considered how crew members maintain their BHP in good condition as the largest risk factor for mission completion after their work environment markedly changed to 6-month long-duration ISS missions from 2-week Space Shuttle missions. JAXA explored the means for assessing the detailed BHP backgrounds of the examinees that cannot be acquired solely with questionnaires and assessment interviews for a limited time, in considering the constraints in assessment (i.e., facility, cost, accuracy of assessments), and then proposed introducing an aptitude examination of a long-duration mission for six nights and seven days at the final stage where the examinees are narrowed down, by using an isolation and confinement facility that allows experts to directly and continuously observe the behavior of the examinees.

The unprecedented examination method proposed raised the following concerns and objections from the personnel concerned.

- NASA has never had that kind of examination.
- Can the capability of the examinees for long-duration missions in space be assessed through a 1-week stay at the isolation and confinement facility?
- Is there any other possible way of conducting an accurate BHP aptitude assessment other than having the examinees stay at an isolation and confinement facility?
- Has the examination method been proven to be academically effective?
- Isn't an interview with JAXA astronauts by NASA in Houston more effective in assessing examinees' competencies (as always conducted in the final stage of JAXA's astronaut selection)?

The responses of the PPRS experts were as follows:

- The tests and interviews we conduct to assess examinees can never be perfect. Selecting Japanese astronauts who are able to endure long-duration missions in space requires another step for assessing the overall humanity of each examinee in the end.
- The purpose of the proposed examination method is to maximize the judging source for assessment by continuously observing the behavior of examinees, and not to assess an examinee who endures a 1-week stay at the isolation and confinement facility as being able to stay in space for a long term. Securing an opportunity for behavioral observation to a certain extent is the point of the examination.
- It must be avoided to select astronaut candidates without observing their behavior in any actual stressful situation. They should be observed directly by multiple experts at the final selection stage.
- The isolation and confinement facility is a facility where induced stress can be homogenized and multiple experts can observe the examinees in an ideal facility for assessment.
- In terms of academic effectiveness, there is no evidence to support the contention that active astronauts can properly assess astronaut candidates. Astronaut selection is a kind of work for the general public, which should value the assessment by multiple experts for BHP competency to select candidates having the right stuff.

In parallel with the above discussion, JAXA's external advisory committee members and external experts were asked for their opinions about whether examination using the isolation and confinement facility would be appropriate and thus avoid excessive impact on the examinees. They made positive comments and recommendations for the examination as follows:

- Staying at the isolation and confinement facility is a means of inducing stress to the examinees, who should be assessed based on an interview given by experts.
- Reference data that give less stress on examinees, such as actigraphy, should be used. Physiological and biochemical data including electrocardiograms (ECG) and blood/urine sampling are not options because such data clearly lack defined criteria and may give excessive stress to examinees.
- Providing a sufficient preliminary explanation of the examination to examinees, obtaining their consent, and imposing strict control of the data obtained are essential.

Based on the above, the long-duration mission examination at the isolation and confinement facility is established to select-out disqualified examinees, with the following essential assessment components.

- Interview by psychiatrists: Conducted before/after staying at the isolation and confinement facility
- Interview by psychologists: Conducted before/after staying at the isolation and confinement facility, and daily during their stay
- Behavioral observation by psychiatrists and psychologists: Performed daily during the stay
- Acquiring reference data: When necessary (Actigraphy is used daily during the confinement to assess insomnia or sleep disturbance that may affect performance in the next daytime.)

For this purpose, each examinee was given, during the period of being placed in a closed environment, personal tasks (work instructed to be accomplished by an individual separated from other examinees) and collective tasks (work instructed to be accomplished in a competitive situation at times, by one or two groups of examinees).

The assessment protocol was set as follows:

- An examinee who shows a BHP-related finding (problematic behavior) is disqualified.
- An examinee who exhibits inappropriate behavior as an astronaut is disqualified.
- An examinee who is found to have a problem in long-duration missions in space based on behavioral observation or other means is disqualified.

The time schedule at the isolation and confinement facility during the stay is provided in reference to the daily routine on the ISS: Getting up at 6:00; Working individually or in groups during the daytime; Psychological interview; Personal hygiene; Free time after 20:00; and Going to bed at 22:00.

In the fourth astronaut selection, eight examinees (seven men and one woman) participated in the long-duration mission examination and all completed the 1-week stay without leaving halfway during the week. With more steps that included specialized medical examinations (including an equilibrium test), interviews with US and Japanese astronauts at NASA's Lyndon B. Johnson Space Center, and interviews with executives, the fourth astronaut selection ended with three new astronaut candidates.

JAXA FIFTH ASTRONAUT SELECTION (2009)

The BHP assessment in the fifth astronaut selection is described in detail in my previous paper (Inoue & Tachibanta, 2013). The fifth astronaut selection, in particular, had the objective of choosing persons who have the potential to assume the key responsibilities of commander on the International Space Station. Emphasis was placed on the verification of strong leadership skills and suitable followership.

As for the Entry requirements, "Having the required ability for astronaut training to swim a distance of 75 m (3×25 m) wearing swimming gear and clothing, and to tread water for 10 minutes." was added due to the training program for the astronaut candidates required swimming ability.

With the BHP assessment system through the stages and the overall protocol which generally followed the fourth astronaut selection, the selection was divided into four stages from the screening of application documents to the third-stage selection.

The PPRS requested that the long-duration mission aptitude examination continue in the fifth astronaut selection, based on the positive feedback given by experts as retrospective assessment after the fourth astronaut selection.

- Psychiatrists: The examination should continue in later selections as it revealed information about the examinees, including their stability under mental stress and behavioral styles and lifestyles while in groups, which had not been acquired by interviews and other methods.
- Psychologists: The examination is effective as the final assessment step, which allows us to confirm by directly observing scenes where the examinees' psychological features are assessed at the first and second stages. It should also be effective in later selections.

While the assessment method was being examined at JAXA (2007–2008), the situation surrounding the ISS and crews changed as described below.

- Once the decision was made to retire the Space Shuttle, "judging astronauts' competency for long-duration missions in space with flights onboard the Space Shuttle" was no longer possible.
- A case of injury involving an active astronaut occurred.

Accordingly, the Multilateral Crew Operations Panel (MCOP) in charge of approving astronauts to become ISS crew members examined possible means (including training and testing) that would serve astronaut selections for long-duration ISS missions, and then received proposals from space agencies. JAXA determined that the examination of staying at the isolation and confinement facility was the most suitable means for experts to judge examinees with "leadership, followership, and team building skills," which JAXA considers essential for future ISS crew members.

Based on the above background, the long-duration mission aptitude examination using the isolation and confinement facility was planned for the third stage in the fifth astronaut selection from the beginning. Furthermore, an assessment of "the ability of examinees to accomplish tasks in space" by the Competence Review Committee members was added to the examination, which had included observation and assessment made only by psychiatric/psychological experts following the fourth selection. Then a minor change was made in the examination schedule by adding a daily group task to accomplish issues at certain times of the day during their stay. (Except for that task, the general schedule largely remained the same as that of the test in the fourth selection where the behavior of examinees during the daily group task was also observed and assessed by experts; Figure 15.3.)

In addition, the BHP assessment details have been updated by reflecting internationally coordinated content. From 2005 through 2007, astronauts, trainees, and BHP experts from ISS partner agencies gathered regularly to discuss and examine carefully "Behavioral Health and Performance Competencies that ISS crew members are required to acquire before being launched." They recognized the Eight Competencies that were summarized in an international document (ISS Mission Operations Directorate ITCB HBP Working Group, 2008).

Based on the Eight Competencies, JAXA has developed five items for fundamental competencies, which are included in the assessment items for observing examinees during their stay at the isolation and confinement facility (Table 15.2; excerpted from Inoue and Tachibana, 2013). While the general tasks (the combination of personal tasks and collective tasks) during the isolation was almost the same as the 4th selection, the emphasis was on the demonstration of five competencies in a stressful environment.

In the fifth selection, the long-duration mission aptitude examination included not only the select-out of disqualified examinees, but also a three-grade rating (A: Excellent, B: Normal, and C: Unsatisfactory).

In the psychiatric assessment, an examinee was given a grade of "C" when disqualified on a psychopathological basis under the astronaut medical criteria (defined

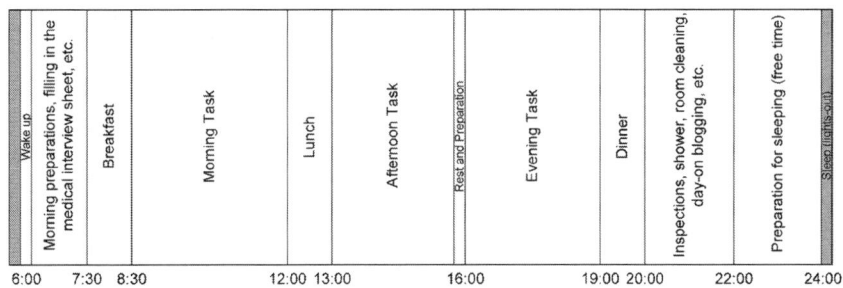

FIGURE 15.3 General daily schedule of the long-duration mission aptitude examination.

TABLE 15.2
Behavioral Competencies

Multilateral BHP Competencies	JAXA's Fundamental BHP Competencies
Self-care/Self-management	Emotional Stability
Team Work and Group Living	Aptitude for Group Living
Leadership	Leadership and Followership
Communication	Communication
Decision-making and Problem-solving	Decision-making and Problem-solving
Conflict Management	
Situational Awareness	
Cross-cultural	

as an ISS document named "ISS Medical Evaluation Document") in any pre- and post-stay interviews, and for multiple items for assessment based on the behavioral observation during his or her stay at the isolation and confinement facility; given a grade of "B" when passing the astronaut medical criteria; and given a grade of "A" when assessed as being particularly excellent in all of them. As a result, an examinee even with a single grade of C in any of the interviews and for observation assessment items was rated as C; one even with a single grade of B in any of them was rated as B, and only an examinee with a grade of A in each of them was rated as A.

In the psychological assessment, an examinee with half of his or her grades in the multiple assessment items higher the mean was rated as A; one with half of his or her grades lower than the mean was rated B; and only an examinee whose behavior was found not suitable as an astronaut while being observed or interviewed was rated C.

As a result, throughout the confinement, the psychiatrists/psychologists group found neither excessive character trait or tendency that might adversely affect the psychodynamics of the group, nor tendency toward insomnia or sleep disturbance.

The fifth astronaut selection also had additional specialized medical examinations and interviews following the long-duration mission aptitude examination, ending with three newly selected astronaut candidates. Despite being conducted completely independently, the assessment by the Competence Review Committee and that by the PPRS highly rated the same examinees in their respective scales. Even though this is a narrative information, this result implies that the assessment setting of the long-duration mission aptitude examination using the isolation and confinement facility was appropriate.

Essentially, the appropriateness of the astronaut selection result can be assessed only in a retrospective way based on the result achieved by the selected astronauts in their ISS missions. As of December 2018, the three selected astronaut candidates, Yui, Onishi, and Kanai, all completed their long-duration ISS missions, steadily performing difficult tasks including the capture of the H-II Transfer Vehicle (HTV) and extravehicular activity (EVA) during their missions, and now have resumed regular work toward their next mission assignment. This fact certainly proves the appropriateness of the method for BHP-related selection.

FOR THE FUTURE SELECTION

The author believes that JAXA need to continue such isolated-environment testing as long as each country assumes the selection of astronauts of its nationality.

The main reason is that this method is more important than any other method used in the selective examination of astronaut candidates, because it offers the following advantages in terms of mental and psychological evaluation:

- Precise observation of examinee behavior in a stressful environment;
- Homogeneous application of stress to the entire population of examinees; and
- Easy safety management.

Dramatic technological sophistication in recent years has brought about various wearable sensors capable of monitoring human-to-human distances and stress reactions. However, such devices for the time being will not surpass the ability of experts to evaluate collective coherence, the ability to respond to sudden emergency conditions, and the relationship between inner negative stress reactions (e.g., tension, mental fatigue, emotional stability) and expressions in the form of physical behavior.

Even though such closed-environment facilities will further be used, will it be the same evaluation criteria in the future selection for the Moon/Mars mission? The answer should be "No." This is because the workplace for astronauts will be no longer the ISS. As stated in this paper and in ISS Mission Operations Directorate ITCB HBP Working Group (2008), the BHP competencies required in the preceding (4th and 5th) selection were used as those needed for accomplishing missions on the ISS. In the future Moon/Mars missions, people will obviously have to cope with different work environments (e.g., operations, term of a mission, number of crew members) unlike that of the ISS. For example, NASA assumes 3 years for a Mars mission, and a crew of four members. Other environmental factors include few supply opportunities, a communication lag hindering real-time telecommunications, and a long loss of communication with personnel on Earth (when Mars comes into conjunction with the Sun).

Next question. So, what will be the BHP competencies needed in such novel environments? Although the BHP competencies such as "Communication" and "Aptitude for Group Living" will probably not lose their importance, both may lose some significance in the future. For example, astronauts going on a mission to Mars must have an autonomous judging ability and the mental makeup to be able to boldly enter an unknown world like seafarers in the Age of Exploration. Participating international organizations will again have to discuss jointly and to reach agreement on the definition of competencies required in the new mission environments.

Then, JAXA will identify specific items one-by-one related to evaluation in a future astronaut selection that correspond to such competences. To summarize, our future tasks will be these three points, as stated in this chapter:

- To design total selection procedures;
- To decide the scenarios and test items to be used during examination including isolated-environment testing; and
- To define evaluation criteria, points of evaluation, and evaluation flow.

REFERENCES

NASA. (n.d.). International mission specialist personal suitability selection guidelines (unpublished).

ISS Mission Operations Directorate ITCB HBP Working Group. (2008). *Volume I. Human behavior and performance model, working group document.* Houston, TX: Johnson Space Center. Retrieved from https://ntrs.nasa.gov/search.jsp?R=20080018552

Inoue, N., & Tachibana, S. (2013). An isolation and confinement facility for the selection of astronaut candidates. *Aviation, Space, and Environmental Medicine, 84,* 867–871.

16 Selected Russian Contributions to Spaceflight

CONTENTS

Introduction 279
Part 1: Russian Psychological Support, Monitoring, and Inflight Studies............ 280
    Methodology of Russian Inflight Psychological Support 280
    Methodology of Space Crew Psychological Status Control 282
Part 2: Russian Space Experiment "CONTENT" 284
    Method 285
    Results 286
    Conclusions 289
Part 3: Russian Space Experiment "INTERACTIONS-2" 289
    Theoretical Background 290
    Methodology 291
    Results 291
    Conclusions 293
Part 4: Russian Space Experiment "PILOT-T" 293
Method 294
    Scope of Research 295
    Results 296
    Conclusions 298
Conclusion 298
References 299

INTRODUCTION

Institute for Biomedical problems (IBMP) was established in 1963 by the Ministry of Health of the Soviet Union upon the request of the Constructor General of the Soviet space rockets, Sergei Korolev. The prime objective of the IBMP was execution of ground-based and inflight research in the area of human health and working capacity under extreme factors of extended spaceflight. Later on, when the duration of space mission increased, Ministry of Health required IBMP to be responsible for the medical support of the Soviet space crews. During a period of 55 years, IBMP, upon requests of Soviet and Russian space industry, executed numerous works in the areas of space medicine and biology, gravitational physiology, radiobiology, life support systems, and psychophysiology. Still Institute's activities in the areas of inflight medical support, maintenance of health and working capacity of the Russian cosmonauts remain the prime objective of IBMP. This chapter is devoted to the small area of inflight medical support – to the psychophysiological control, support, and research that has been carried out by the IBMP during recent period of execution of Russian Space Program.

Part 1: Russian Psychological Support, Monitoring, and Inflight Studies

Vadim Gushin, Dmitry Shved, Alla Vinokhodova, Yuriy Bubeev, Daria Schastlivtceva, Anna Yusupova, Olga Karpova, and Angelina Chekalina

SRC RF – Institute of Bio-Medical Problems of RAS, Moscow, Russia

METHODOLOGY OF RUSSIAN INFLIGHT PSYCHOLOGICAL SUPPORT

In spaceflight, humans experience sensory deprivation and monotony, which means a long-term significant deprivation (or heavy limitation) of extrinsic stimuli. The reason for sensory deprivation and monotony in a spaceflight is the situation of being isolated within a small confined environment (space station, spacecraft) where environmental conditions: temperature, humidity, barometric pressure, gas composition, etc. are created by life support system and maintained at a fairly constant level. So, in spaceflight a person is deprived of the impact of natural time setters, most part of biological organisms, seasonal climate fluctuations, and of impressions connected with a change of a person's whereabouts, so their perceptive sensors function in an environment rather poor in extrinsic stimuli. Besides that, a gravity-sensing mechanism switches off in space which leads on to an even greater impoverishment of afferent currents – and serves as yet another source of sensory deprivation. Bright picturesque images might appear in sleep or sleep-like condition as a "substitute" for a reality poor in external stimuli. Such images simulate habitual scenes of everyday life on Earth, family life, contact with nature, etc. This is one of the numerous vivid confirmations of the significant impacts of sensory deprivation and monotony on central nervous system, which got a provisory name of "deprivation phenomena" (Kozerenko, Sled, & Mirzadjanov, 2001).

As the duration of the current spaceflight increases, cosmonaut's emotional sphere also comes to be affected predominantly by limitation of social contacts. The influence of the social isolation factor in a confined hermetic cabin is a result of compulsory socializing of cosmonauts – obligatory communication with a limited circle of people in the crew and Mission Control. As Novikov (1981) stated, limited social contacts which are at the same time excessive (socializing too closely with a limited circle of people), necessity to reconsider many conventional social notions and elaborated role orientations, and impossibility to satisfy some social needs could cause serious psychosocial problems. Social deprivation phenomena observed in a spaceflight manifest themselves in an increasing persistent need to maintain audio and visual contacts with family members and friends. Limitation of social contacts also can induce negative emotional reactions linked with professional activity, for instance with communication with the ground services. Such reactions may complicate the process of crewmembers' communication, becoming a source of conflict.

Their incrementing intensity manifests itself in cumulative weariness and central nervous system asthenization due to an inadequate reaction of the nervous system to stimuli. In asthenization, strong extrinsic stimuli may evoke a poor response, while on the other hand minimal stimuli may produce a strong reaction (Myasnikov & Stepanova et al., 2000). A sign of deterioration in cosmonauts' psychic condition is a frequent appearance of frankly negative emotional responses especially if they leave a lasting negative track behind themselves in the form of low mood. Normally emotional responses (defined as emotional component of response to various external and internal stimuli) are transitory, clearly oriented and extremely diverse, and, most important, are not very strong. If however negative emotions predominate and become stagnant, establishing a steadily negative mood background together with irritability, aggressiveness, constant complaints of feeling unwell, of fatigue, headache, etc., and if at the same time we observe paradoxical forms of emotional reactions with inadequate outbursts of irritation in response to insignificant stimuli, then this should be regarded as evidence of intense psychological trouble. In such condition a person often manifests speech peculiarities which are not normally characteristic of him or her, such as swearwords, expletives, sounds and words filling pauses, unusually loud or, on the contrary, unusually low speech with increased/decreased tonality and speed (Myasnikov, Uskov et al., 1982). So, individual speech style changes. It should also be pointed out that asthenization of cosmonauts' nervous and psychic sphere which mostly affects controlling systems, may have a negative impact on the interpersonal relationships in a space crew and on the crew-ground interaction, as well as affect performance of each crewmember.

These problems caused, for 40 years, the necessity for the Soviet medical support specialists of Moscow Institute for Medico-Biological Problems to elaborate the system of psychological countermeasures called psychological support. The prime objective of this system is maintenance of the space crew's psychic state, working capacity, and team spirit (Kozerenko et al., 2001). The main principle of the activities of the psychological support group in Russian MCC is reconstruction of the usual information media for the astronauts in order to prevent the effects of sensory deprivation, monotony, and social isolation. To compensate the lack of incoming information, psychologists provide the crew with the fresh country and world news, especially related to the description of their Mission, as well as the news about events in the Russian Astronaut Core. So now cosmonauts get through the Crew Web Page electronic versions of papers magazines; TV and radio news programs including sport; and movies, entertaining shows, and documentary films. Psychological support group is trying to compensate the lack of sounds and visions of nature, composing special audio and video programs. Greenhouse aboard also is regarded not only as a research target but also as an object that is providing the opportunity to contact and to take care of the piece of nature that they miss in the mechanical surrounding of the hermetic volume with artificial life support system. All these pieces of data and logistics delivered, including books, movies, musical instruments, etc. help the crew to spend free time actively that helps to keep good mood and recreate.

These electronic data and logistics are prepared by psychological support group relying on individual tastes and preferences, cultural differences (gender, national, religious, professional, etc.) detected before the flight, transmitted aboard, and stored at the file server. Certainly, during the Mission the crewmembers could ask something additional, and not planned before, in accordance with their current needs, i.e. audiobooks, new film releases, or nutrition. According to our experience, provision of food and drinks variety is an important countermeasure to prevent negative impact of sensory deprivation and monotony.

Another important concern is compensation of social deprivation. Now the crewmembers can participate in private family videoconferences from their homes in the Star City, can call them utilizing IP-telephone. To keep contact with non-professionals that they miss due to forced character of the most part of their communication in space, cosmonauts actively participate in radio séances with amateurs around the world. For the same purpose our cosmonauts are expressing themselves through social Internet networks. During especially stressful events during the Mission (like delay in cargo ship or accidental crewmates' substitution) special videoconferences with friends and colleagues from the astronaut core are organized where colleagues could share their experience of coping. Psychological support group recommends Russian cosmonauts to take initiative in preparation of joint free time spending (including social events like national holidays and birthdays) with foreign partners to enhance socialization aboard. For this purpose, special deliveries by cargo ships provide cosmonauts with souvenirs, gifts, and national food to share in the crew. Finally, to keep crew motivation and morale Russian psychological support group invites national VIPs from government, clergy, and artistic circle to communicate with the cosmonauts.

In order to give necessary individual psychological support and to reduce stress level Russian psychological support system acquired NASA's experience of private psychological conferences. Once in 2 weeks, utilizing private communication channel, a psychologist, determined by the cosmonaut before the Mission, spends time talking with the crewmember. That provides cosmonaut opportunity to transfer or drain out negative feelings and emotions, share some ideas that he cannot express to his teammates. These regular talks and recommendations given by the specialist help not only to reduce individual stress level but also to improve group interaction.

We want to stress that psychological support inflight is based not only on the knowledge acquired by psychologists during long training period. Permanent distant monitoring of their psychological status and relations in the crew, carried out by another group of psychiatrists and psychologists, working in Russian MCC, is the fundamental of all psychological support measures.

Methodology of Space Crew Psychological Status Control

Psycho-diagnostics in the medical support system of manned space missions aims at the identification of various forms of adaptive behavior of people under extreme conditions of life and work. In other words, psycho-diagnostics of cosmonauts' health status is a synthesis of behavioral and professional performance evaluations made conjointly by physicians and psychologists who are using approved procedures, evaluation scales, and terminology. Monitoring of the crew's health is done in a complicated professional environment which differs from the normal clinical environment in several ways. In a spaceflight, unlike clinical conditions, expert evaluation and diagnostics are performed on the basis of a remote observation (no direct contact with a "patient"), with a scarcity of diagnostic data and impossibility in certain cases to make some necessary additional studies. Medical practice on Earth presupposes such relationship as "curing doctor and suffering patient," who is mostly motivated to disclose the patient's status. In the frame of a spaceflight, physicians and psychologists, who fulfill a role of a distant observer (and not of a proximate helper), have to deal with healthy people who have passed a careful medical selection and are not inclined to complaint. Moreover, due to the fact that cosmonauts are highly motivated to continue the Mission and take part in a subsequent flight, they are likely to deny any health or psychological problems which they might be suffering from. On the one hand, such behavioral strategy allows to keep up their self-confidence and efficiency and is necessary to cope. On the other hand, it leads on to a denial of actually existing medical and psychological problems. So classic methods of direct interviewing which have proved to be reliable on Earth, both oral and written ones (tests), yield a so-called "socially desirable" result meaning: "we are OK" – which ensures the image of a superhero capable of enduring any hardship. Therefore inflight diagnostic decisions have to be taken on the basis of insufficient information or, alternatively, new approaches toward medico-psychological diagnostics have to be developed.

Psychological control of cosmonauts at Space Station performed by IBMP, led the IBMP specialists to the development of a method which allows remotely controlling and evaluating the crew's psycho-emotional status. It is based on the expert evaluation of the content of their communication with Mission Control Center (TCOUP). Information exchange is an intrinsic part of the professional activity of cosmonauts and MCC, and the communication efficiency directly determines the appropriateness of MCC and crew decisions for the accomplishment of Mission Protocol. Combining engineering, technological, medical, and psychological aspects of this professional activity makes communication of the crew and Mission Control an important source of unbiased current information. Adequate, open, and friendly contact between the ground and the space professional groups determines, on the one hand, emotional tonus and performance of the cosmonauts, and, on the other hand, precludes the development of so-called deprivation effects caused by the impact of factors of a prolonged spaceflight. The level of personal disclosure in communication during prolonged flight, including emotions and conflict tension, is not complete for the abovementioned reasons, but is still better than during official interviews and reports. Research conducted during flights at "Mir" space station (Myasnikov, Shaposhnikov, & Zamaletdinov, 2001) revealed that various parameters of verbal activity (length of communication session, semantics, thematic variety of speech, emotional expressiveness of voice messages, etc.) are relatively stable indicators of the individual verbal behavior of a cosmonaut. Due to this, a record and a later detailed analysis of communication of a space crew and Mission Control have been an intrinsic part of the

IBMP's medical support group activities starting from the 70s of the past century (Myasnikov et al., 1982).

Until recently such analysis was a descriptive procedure made by specially trained experts with medical background. According to this procedure the specialists, analyzing crew-MCC talks, on the basis of their expert opinions have to complete on the daily basis a list of individual and group-related indicators of the psychoneurological status of crewmembers (Orbital Station "Mir", 2001, 2002). The authors of this list of criteria – Myasnikov and Zamaletdinov (1997) – distinguished 14 individual and five group-related indicators used in the dynamic evaluation of the cosmonauts' mental state. The individual indicators are: dominant interests, proposals (complaints), deprivation phenomena, emotional response, mood, general behavior, health, sensorial sphere, motor performance, sleep, psycho-physiological tension, and professional activity. In order to estimate accompanying individual workload of the crewmembers another scale of expert evaluations has been developed, which helps to render the work-rest distribution in quantitative characteristics ranged by number of points. A special cluster of scales describes efficiency of group interaction thus allowing to conclude about the small group's structure (formal and informal leaders, scapegoats) and about the presence of tension in the space-crew interaction. Monitored signs of a conflict in the crew are: narrowing of the contacts within the crew and the exclusion of the scapegoat from it, or limiting interaction with such partner to the formal minimum, determined by the need to participate in a common activity. Later B.I. Myasnikov and I.S. Zamaletdinov added into the above-described procedure 7 degrees of intensity for each diagnostics indicator. The diagnostics scale was subdivided into three zones: optimal (from the 1st to the 3rd degree of the qualitative evaluation), transitional (from the 4th to the 5th degree), and unfavorable (from the 6th to the 7th degree). A precondition for a correct assessment of an indicator is the fact that this indicator has appeared in at least two successive communication sessions.

So, quantitative values representing qualitative changes along all or the majority of indicators make up quite an informative system of a dynamical remote evaluation. The main advantage of the usage of the crew-MCC communication for the evaluation of the cosmonauts' psychological status is its "noninvasiveness," since the board-ground communication is a regular procedure in a spaceflight. Diagnostic technique developed by psychologists from IBMP allows to evaluate quantitatively the psychic status of cosmonauts as well as "psychological climate" in a space crew without compelling the crewmembers to undergo additional test procedures which would demand extra time and without installing additional equipment at the space station. On the basis of the elaborated criteria of communication's content analysis psychologists from IBMP can provide flight directors on the daily and weekly basis with their conclusions about the psychological status of the crew.

Part 2: Russian Space Experiment "CONTENT"

Vadim Gushin, Dmitry Shved, Anna Yusupova,
Natalya Supolkina, and Angelina Chekalina
SRC RF – Institute of Bio-Medical Problems of RAS

Remote psychological monitoring has shown its efficiency in diagnostics and prediction of the psychological status of Russian space crews (Myasnikov et al., 1982). However, to perform such monitoring an expert needs years of working experience in MCC for the proper interpretation of the crew-MCC communication content, so the work of an expert has more to do with art than science.

One of the possible ways of resolving this issue is to use quantitative stress coping-oriented content analysis to reduce communication content to a limited reproducible set of categories (Krippendorf, 1980). Our approach to categorization in content-analysis of the cosmonauts' communications under space stress is based on stress coping theory of Lazarus and Folkman (1984). They stated that under stressful conditions, as a result of human resource mobilization, various coping-strategies are developed, which people use to adapt to difficult working situations, to gain necessary performance results and/or to keep emotional stability. The spaceflight situation with its limited instrumental resources, risks to life and health, high social responsibility for performed activities can be classified as imposing excessive requirements that exceed resources of an average human subject. In space psychology, P. Suedfeld became a pioneer in the studies of coping strategies, using this approach in analysis of astronauts' diaries and interviews (Suedfeld, Brcic, Johnson, & Gushin, 2015).

It was mentioned above that sensory and social deprivation in extended spaceflight can negatively influence crew communication as the prime source of new information and social support as well as an area where individual feelings are mostly expressed and shared. Therefore, signs of coping strategies in crew communication with Earth could confirm the appearance of stress caused by shortage of instrumental and psychological resources during the flight, and characterize the effectiveness ("good or poor contact") of information exchange between the crew and MCC. Also, non-effective coping strategies revealed in communication could be the reason for additional psychological support in flight. This approach to content analysis was in parallel tested in numerous space simulations held in Canada (Suedfeld et al., 2015), US (Stuster, 2010), and Russia (IBMP) continuously since 1971.

Pilot inflight study by Kanas and Yusupova (Kanas, Gushin, & Yusupova, 2008) held in 2003–2007 confirmed principal possibility of monitoring changes in astronauts' psychological state, relying on content analysis of the crew communication.

Method

The purpose of "Content" space experiment is testing in spaceflight support practice this new approach to remote monitoring of psycho-physiological status, in-group and intergroup (crew-MCC) interaction, as well as effectiveness of data exchange between the crew and MCC. This goal was set due to several negative opinions concerning communications with MCC during spaceflights that were expressed in private conversations by American astronauts and Russian cosmonauts (Myasnikov, Shaposhnikov, & Zamaletdinov, 2001).

To assess the reproducibility of the content analysis methodology, a study was conducted on the consistency of the opinions of four independent experts. They evaluated 1-month data set containing transcripts of communications between Russian segment of ISS crew and MCC. The opinions of each expert on 15 evaluation criteria (content analysis categories) were compared with the opinion of the group (three other experts) using correlation analysis. In order to reveal the most informative content analysis categories, factor analysis was used. In accordance with the study results, the method's reproducibility was considered sufficient enough for its further utilization (Yusupova, Shved, Gushchin, Supolkina, & Chekalkina, 2018).

The main experiment started in April 2015. Table 16.1 provides the full list of target statement categories including coping strategies detected by the three independent experts in Russian crews communication with MCC during first 3 years of "Content" experiment. It is divided into three groups corresponding to main functions of communication (information sharing, social regulation, and expression of emotions) according to Lomov (1981).

Participants of "Content" space experiment, up to date $N = 15$, were Russian cosmonauts from ISS expeditions 43/44–54/55. All subjects signed informed consent for participation in the experiment.

Results

During the first stage of data analysis we attempted to classify crew communication parameters into statistically distinctive groups. Content analysis categories in all subjects ($N = 15$) were clustered to visualize possible groups of categories (Figure 16.1).

The first cluster includes categories mainly consist of information exchange categories (see lower cluster in Figure 16.1) as well as *Subordination* (socio-regulatory function) and *Emotional Support* (affective function). This result allows us to conclude that cosmonauts' statements, attributed by experts to *Informing/information sharing*, prevail over all other contents of the crew communication with MCC. This significantly differs from the data obtained in chamber studies (Gushin et al., 2016) where information exchange function of communication was less pronounced. Chamber crews, especially after they adapted to the isolation conditions and Mission Protocol execution procedures, were more prone to express in their communication with MC statements attributed to social regulation (*Blaming, Avoiding responsibility,*

TABLE 16.1
Content Analysis Categories (Used in 2015–2018) and Lomov's Functions of Communication

Informative Function	Socio-Regulatory Function	Emotional (Affective) Function
Information sharing/request	Taking/avoiding responsibility	Positive/negative emotions
Planning/scheduling	Seek for support	
Requests/demands	Subordination/disobedience	Humor/sarcasm
Initiative	Confrontation	Self-control
Time utilization	Mistrust/Trust	Emotional support
Objects searching		

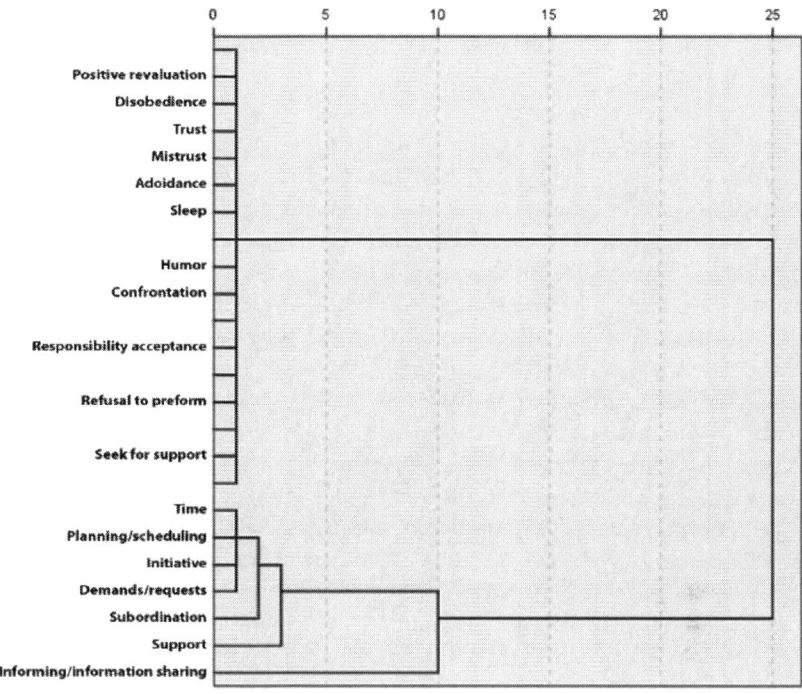

FIGURE 16.1 Clustering content analysis categories over a scalable distance according to communication inflight, using Ward method.

and *Confrontation*) and Emotions (mostly *negative*). This result clearly demonstrates a major difference in demands of working environments (real and simulated), crews' preparedness and motivation. Certainly, conditions of real spaceflight, with risks to life and health and high responsibility, require much more discipline, as well as everyday professional discussions of problems caused by complex flight Protocol.

The second cluster mostly consists of communicative parameters attributed to stress coping strategies (effective and ineffective ones). If *Subordination* and *Seek for support*, contained in the first factor, seem to be a natural part of crew communication, reflecting the commanding and consulting functions of MCC, other coping strategies observed, such as *Confrontation, Mistrust, Avoidance*, and Emotions may serve as the early markers of stress experienced in flight (Lazarus & Folkman, 1984; Suedfeld et al., 2015). We suppose that their appearance should be followed by the subsequent changes in psychological support.

As one of the experiment objectives is monitoring of dynamic changes of the crewmembers' psychological state on various stages of the extended spaceflight, two concepts of inflight impact were tested. In studies conducted during polar winterovers, negative effects of so-called "third quarter phenomenon" were described, expressed in depression, decrease of working capacity and motivation (Bechtel & Berning, 1991). However, N. Kanas found no changes in mood during third quarters in spaceflights (Kanas, 2015). According to the data from Russian space psychologist

O. Kozerenko (Kozerenko et al., 2001) – who also detected four stages of psychological adaptation in extended spaceflights – acute period of adaptation (first month of expedition) and fourth quarter (so-called "final rush" during the busy period of preparation for landing) are the most stressful to the crews.

Present data analysis confirmed O. Kozerenko's concept of the "final rush" period in the final part of the flight (the last 30–45 days), considered as critically difficult for the crew (Kozerenko et al., 2001). In all crewmembers, an increase in the total volume of communication was noticed, related to an increase in activity intensity in the final stage of the flight. The resolution of these problems led to significant growth of statements reflecting more attention to the *Planning* of the working process (the accuracy of the linear approximation, $R^2 = 0.983$). At the same time, there was an increase in the number of statements related to the manifestation of the crew's claims (*Requests/demands*) to MCC ($R^2 = 0.923$) and the common desire to *Avoid responsibility* for the problems ($R^2 = 0.934$). Coping during this stressful period was related to the increase of humor in verbal reactions to problem situations ($R^2 = 0.947$).

Among the results obtained, manifestations of the "third quarter phenomenon" were found on especially long (up to 340 days) ISS expedition, 43–46. Similar to polar winter-overs (Bechtel & Berning, 1991), general increase of copings in crew communication was found (Figure 16.2).

Crews who reacted to the problem situations using effective coping strategies, successfully completed the flight program during this period. This was confirmed by the increase in statements interpreted as *Initiative* and *Planning* ($R^2 = 0.935$) as well as Taking of Responsibility ($R^2 = 0.822$). We also detected the increase in statements attributed to Time utilization ($R^2 = 0.881$), which confirmed the existence of time deficit. We believe that this was due to the cosmonauts' initiative to plan their activities in a better way, proactively proposing the MCC more efficient ways of crew time management. In some cases, inefficient, from cosmonauts' point of view, planning of their work schedules by MCC led to rise of emotionally negative counter-proposals (*Confrontation* category, $R^2 = 0.837$), together with statements

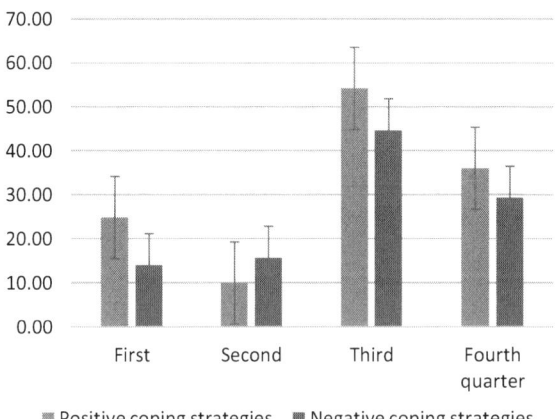

FIGURE 16.2 Coping strategies in cosmonauts' communication (amounts of coping strategies used by flight quarters).

interpreted as *Avoidance of responsibility, Mistrust*, and *Negative emotions*. Thus, a well-trained and experienced crew wanted to gain more trust, independence, and autonomy, which was not always supported by the Flight administration (Kanas et al., 2008; Kanas, 2015; Stuster, 2010). That was expressed during the expeditions of the ISS-43–56 in negative emotional "drainage," pronounced through communication with the MCC ("displacement" of negative emotions according to Kanas (2015). This data confirms results of US space experiments such as "Journals" by J. Stuster and "Reaction Self-Test" by D. Dinges and M. Basner, where similar results were obtained (Basner et al., 2014; Stuster, 2010). Thus, "Content" experiment allowed us to distinguish the third and fourth quarters of spaceflight as problematic.

Conclusions

Several identified trends in cosmonauts' communication seem significant after first 3 years of "Content" on-board experiment:

1. Within in-flight problem situations, crewmembers that successfully perform the flight program operations, express more coping in their communication with MCC. However, these coping strategies may be more or less effective, taking into consideration their impact on problem solving, emotional stress reduction, and data exchange with MCC. Most part of crew communication was effective with prevailing of statements attributed as *Informing/information sharing, Requests/demands, Initiative, Planning/scheduling, Time utilization*.
2. Period of the "final rush" (last month before landing) is the most difficult flight period for cosmonauts, which has a significant impact on the structure of their communication with ground services. Tendency to manifest the "third quarter phenomenon" was noticed in crew-MCC communication in spaceflight with increased duration (more than usual six months). During both periods amount of crew communications increases, as well as statements attributed to Social regulation (*Confrontation, Avoidance of responsibility, Mistrust*) and affective (*Negative emotions*) speech functions.
3. Emotional transfer phenomenon (displacement) was confirmed for the critical periods of the flight, showing patterns similar to N. Kanas and J. Stuster results.

Obtained results about crews' communicative behavior during critical stages of spaceflight have practical application to the psychological observation and support.

Part 3: Russian Space Experiment "INTERACTIONS-2"

Vadim Gushin, Alla Vinokhodova, and Anna Yusupova
SRC RF – Institute of Bio-Medical Problems of RAS

Gro Sandal
University of Bergen

The problem of cohesion in heterogeneous multinational crews can be a significant challenge in long-term spaceflight (Kanas & Manzey, 2008). Common norms and shared values are important conditions in order to avoid interpersonal stress and maintain group cohesion.

In 2014, the space experiment "Interactions-Attitudes" was completed, in which more than 20 Russian crewmembers of the ISS took part. It was shown that cosmonauts perceive their compatriots and foreign members of the ISS crews in different ways (Vinokhodova & Gushin, 2014). These differences are associated with the so-called "phenomenon of stereotyping": when an unfamiliar person, communication with whom proceeds only informally, all the more recognizing his strengths and weaknesses. For a part of the cosmonauts the estimates of other crewmembers were getting simplified to "black–white", "good–bad" under the influence of the long-term spaceflight. This can interfere with an adequate vision of themselves and others and complicate the interaction. In addition, the phenomenon of an increase of "psychological distance" between the crew and the Control Center (MCC) in the course of the flight was established.

Starting in 2015 with the flight of the 43rd ISS expedition, the space experiment "Interactions-2" continues the "Interactions-Attitudes" and is devoted to the study of the patterns of intra- and intergroup (communication with the MCC) interactions of the ISS crews. In addition to confirmation and statistical justification of the previously obtained results, the "Interactions-2" examines the impact of national differences on the value priorities of the crewmembers, their cohesion and identification with the group, the perception of key aspects of interaction as leadership, conflict resolution, the volume and quality of communication with MCC.

Theoretical Background

Recently, studies of values priorities have become an important trend in the development of group space psychology both in Russia and other countries. Suedfeld (2006) conducted a quantitative content analysis of the memoirs of seven male, three female astronauts, and two NASA employees using the basic human values by Schwartz (2006) as categories for detection. The author concludes that the participation in spaceflight has a pronounced positive effect on the personality and value system of astronauts, in particular, contributes to the so-called salutogenesis, or personal growth (Suedfeld Brcic, Johnson, & Gushin, 2012). In the experiment of Stuster (2010), the diary entries of 10 American astronauts, men and women, working on board the ISS were studied. It has been shown that the key differences between the diaries of the astronauts and the winterers reveal the increased importance of astronauts' dedication to work. The role of personal values for the formation of a cohesive group was studied in an experiment with prolonged isolation, simulating a manned flight to Mars (Sandal & Bye, 2015). The results showed that differences in values are the sources of interpersonal tension, especially with increasing crew autonomy. A joint Russian-Canadian study of interpersonal perception in participants of international crews who performed 1–5 spaceflights and completed an active career (Suedfeld et al., 2015; Vinokhodova & Gushchin et al., 2017), showed the presence of a specific hierarchy of values, similar for cosmonauts and astronauts. The existence of positive ethnic stereotypes has been established – the idealization of foreign crewmembers for that part of the cosmonauts, whose perception was more integrated.

Methodology

For research, the computer-based PSPA method (Personal Self-Perception and Attitudes), developed by IMBP was used (Gushin Efimov, Smirnova, Vinokhodova, & Kanas, 1998). PSPA is a system of subjective attitude analysis based on the semantic differential of Ch. Osgood and G. Kelley's repertory grid technique. Starting from the 45th expedition, the CULT survey is used to assess the influence of cultural factors on interaction. It includes parts of the Flight Management Attitudes Questionnaire previously used in extensive studies of pilots, and the Crew Portrait of Values Questionnaire based on Schwartz' theoretical framework (Schwartz, 2006).

To date, 19 crewmembers have been involved in the experiment: 15 of them have completed the study, including two representatives of foreign space agencies; one Russian crewmember continues to perform it onboard; and three cosmonauts have conducted the baseline research phase.

Experiment schedule. Before flight: Twice – Training and Baseline Data Collection – not earlier than 60 days before launch; In flight: one time in 2 weeks, starting from the third week; After flight: once – +7 to +10 days after landing.

To study the values, the content analysis of interpersonal perception criteria was used (PSPA methodology). The list of criteria for content analysis included 60 constructs reflecting significant personal characteristics (3 constructs × 2 factors × 10 cosmonauts). Content analysis was carried out by three experienced experts using categories classification of values, according to S. Schwartz. Expert estimates coincided by 90%.

Results

Figure 16.3 shows the results from 10 subjects – ISS crewmembers. The percentage of the most significant evaluation criteria, relating to the categories of values by Sh. Schwartz, was calculated. The data aggregated for the group of subjects and for the whole period of spaceflight are presented.

The preliminary results of the "Interaction-2" space experiment allowed to identify categories of values, common to representatives of various space agencies participating in the experiment: *Achievement, Conformity,* and *Benevolence* (meaningful for all participants of the experiment). The values of *Self-Direction* and *Security* categories were also significant.

At the same time, differences in the value structure of the crewmembers of the ISS, which are related to cultural factors, were found. These differences were expressed, for example, in the relationship between the importance of *Achievement* category (it includes social recognition, success, dedication, professionalism) and *Conformity* (politeness, education, self-control, commitment, diligence). Many cosmonauts (but not all of them) showed the preference of group values over individual, which can

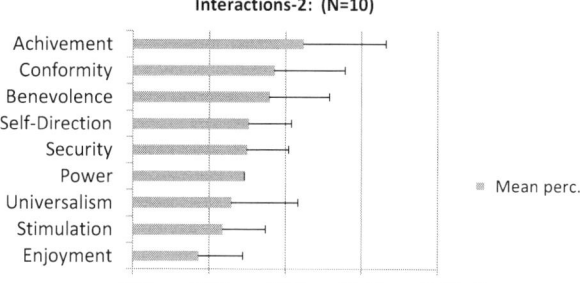

FIGURE 16.3 The results of "Interaction-2" experiment.

be explained by the collectivist nature of our culture. However, the individual values of *Achievement*, *Self-Direction*, and *Stimulation* were also important for them. These data can be compared with the results of the study mentioned above (Suedfeld, 2006), where male astronauts showed an increase in the importance of the categories *Achievements*, *Hedonism (or Enjoyment)*, and *Benevolence* after the completion of spaceflight.

To confirm our finding, the data of 20 cosmonauts on the space experiment "Interactions-Attitudes," which ended in 2014 is presented (Table 16.2). We can see that, both in the baseline and post-flight study, the group values dominate in the cosmonauts' value structure: *Conformity* – 18.8% of the list of criteria before the flight and 17.4% of the list of criteria after flight; *Benevolence* –13.8 and 12.3% before and after flight, respectively. After space flight, there was some increase in

TABLE 16.2
Space Experiment "Interaction–Attitudes" – The Results of Content Analysis of the Interpersonal Perception Criteria

Results of "Interaction–Attitudes"

Russian Crew Members of the ISS ($N = 20$)

Values	Before Flight (%)	After Flight (%)
Conformity	18.8	17.4
Benevolence	13.8	12.3
Universalism	13.0	10.9
Self-direction	12.3	17.4
Achievement	10.9	10.1
Enjoyment	10.1	11.6
Stimulation	10.1	10.9
Security	8.7	6.5
Tradition	1.4	1.4
Power	0.7	1.4

the importance of *Self-Direction* (from the group of individual values) to 17.4% of the list of categories. It can be explained by the end of the stressful spaceflight, which requires a lot of self-restraint and self-control, respect for the priority of social over personal.

It becomes obvious that the most important value for the majority of astronauts and cosmonauts, regardless of nationality was *Benevolence*. This category is described by such characteristics as "friendly, sincere, non-conflicting, working for the benefit of others, devotee to the friends or group." The domination of these values is undoubtedly an important condition for the formation, despite the existing cultural diversity, of ISS crews, of a cohesive team, which is able to successfully overcome the adverse factors of a long spaceflight.

CONCLUSIONS

The study of interpersonal perception in the international space crews showed the existence of value priorities, representing a specific professional culture common to cosmonauts and astronauts. Values such as hard working, maintaining standards of social behavior, are based on high self-esteem, enterprise, and spirituality, peculiar to this group of people. This culture is international and was formed as a result of compliance with certain professional requirements during the selection and preparation for work in specific extreme habitat conditions in long-term spaceflight. Further studies within the framework of the space experiment "Interaction-2" will allow statistically validating the results obtained, as well as studying in more detail the changes in the value priorities of the ISS crewmembers under the influence of long-term spaceflight factors, for example, related to changes in the crew composition.

Part 4: Russian Space Experiment "PILOT-T"

Daria Schastlivtceva, Tatyana Kotrovskaya, Yuriy Bubeev,
Alexander Dudukin, and Angelina Chekalina
SSC RF – Institute for Biomedical Problems-RAS

Bernd Johannes
Institute of Aerospace Medicine (German Aerospace Center)

"Pilot-T" is a continuation and development of a series of experiments "Pilot" since 1987. Nevertheless, there is still no complete understanding of the influence of the long-term negative factors of spaceflight on the cosmonaut's professional reliability, especially when landing on another planet. To a certain extent, this is due to the lack of use of the neurocognitive approach, which, in a general sense, means the study of the connection between the specific features of neural activity and cognitive behavior. The main hypothesis is that professional reliability is the correlation of activity performance indicators and the functional state of the central nervous system. The psychophysiological reactions are the indicators of the complex reaction – the psychophysiological "cost" of activity. Thus, when predicting a cosmonaut's professional reliability, it is necessary to take into account neurophysiological parameters, reconstruct the functional structure of the brain according to encephalography, apply decoding technologies for controlling cognitive brain signals, and mathematical models of electrical brain activity (Komotskij & Salnitskij, 1977; Ryzhov & Salnitskij, 1983).

The objective of the experiment is to improve methods and hardware of assessing and predicting the reliability of crewmembers' professional activities when performing complex operator tasks (piloting a spacecraft and controlling transport and robotic means on the surface of a space body) at various stages of a long spaceflight (LSF).

Since 2014, the first stage of the "Pilot-T" space experiment (SE) has been held on the RS of ISS. The model of professional operator activity is the program "Six-degrees-of-freedom (6df)," which simulates the manual control of objects with six degrees of freedom and which contains secondary cognitive tests. The quality parameters of professional activity are compared with the physiological indicators obtained using the "Neurolab-2010" hardware complex. With the help of "Neurolab-2010," we register the electrocardiogram; pulse wave, electric resistance, and skin temperature of the little finger (left); and speech signal. At the moment, 16 cosmonauts have completed the full experiment cycle.

METHOD

The study took place from 2015 to 2018; the crews of expeditions 43/44–53/54 (13 cosmonauts) took part in the study during working hours in GMT. Inflight: 43/44–50/51 ISS – the SE "Pilot-T" were carried out two times a month, and for expeditions 51/52–53/54 ISS – one time a month. Figure 16.4 shows the cosmonaut-operator place on board of the Russian segment of ISS during the SE "Pilot-T."

The SE "Pilot-T" consists of 2 protocols: (1) the "6df" protocol aimed at the study of the reliability of the professional activity of a crewmember when performing the simulation of manual control of the docking of two spacecraft; (2) the "Cognitive

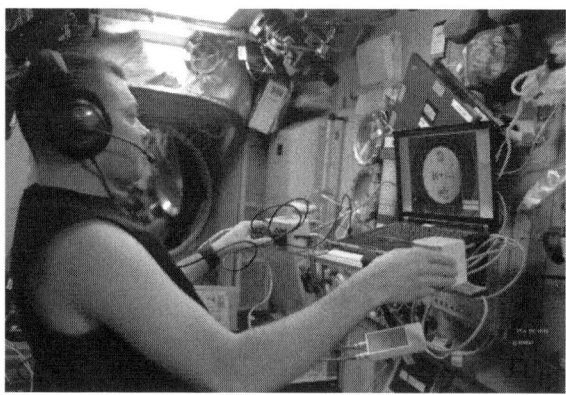

FIGURE 16.4 Photo FE-4 ISS 44/45 on board of the RS of ISS during the SE "Pilot-T".

tests" protocol was conducted for the study of the neurocognitive processes of a human operator at various stages of the LSF (a series of tests is used, aimed at evaluating working memory, intellect, attention switching, speed, and accuracy of sensory-motor response) (Ushakov, Ivanov, Kvasovets, & Bubeev, 2015).

When implementing the experimental program of the SE "Pilot-T," the cosmonaut performs manual control of complex dynamic objects with the six degrees of freedom joystick. The characteristics of the ISS spatial motion, as well as the system of manual control of the the spacecraft, are simulated close to the actual docking process. The cosmonaut manages the spacecraft with the help of joystick, one of which (left) specifies linear movements of the center of mass of the spacecraft along three axes, and the other (right) – the rotation around the center (also along three axes.) The trajectory of the spacecraft is visualized on the computer monitor, and, thus, the moving object is navigated. After performing each task, the crewmember has the choice: to increase, reduce, or keep the previous difficulty level of the docking task. During piloting, the physiological parameters: ECG, skin conductance, pulse wave velocity, and peripheral skin temperature of the little finger are recorded.

To study the cognitive functions and state of the central nervous system, we used the "Module Compact," which includes the following tests (Ushakov et al., 2015):

1. working memory test ("Visual memory");
2. calculation test ("Even-Odd");
3. visual perception test ("Simple visual-motor reaction");
4. CSTR – eye-motor coordination test ("Reaction to a moving object" test); and
5. "State-self-esteem" questionnaire.

For data analysis the non-parametric Kruskal-Wallis criterion was used, which makes it possible to identify significant differences in the dynamics of the cognitive functioning of cosmonauts during the periods before the flight, during the LSF, and after the flight. We also used Ward's cluster analysis to group the subjective assessment of the psycho-emotional state into groups of data, describe them, and construct a scale of emotional stability/instability. This scale is designed to assess the mobilization of resources during the implementation of complex operator activities during training, flight, and after its completion.

Scope of Research

Protocol: two training sessions for teaching the methodology for performing the SE and getting familiar with the scientific equipment. They are held within half a year before the start individually with each cosmonaut (110 minutes each); two test sessions to collect background data. They are held no later than 30 days before the start individually with each cosmonaut (90 minutes each). Inflight: two times a month (duration of each session is 100 minutes), postflight: two examinations (60 minutes each with cosmonaut). The first examination should be conducted in third to fifth days after landing, the second – ten to fifteenth days after it.

RESULTS

Figure 16.5 shows examples of docking simulation task results and the distance traveled by the spacecraft for two types of tasks (the first is the static system for manual control; the second is a dynamic task with the maximum possible degrees of freedom). Each task difficulty level contains several options; they are selected randomly from a variety of equivalently difficult tasks.

The histograms (Figure 16.6) of the individual statistical characteristics (m and S) of the main parameters, obtained from the results of cosmonauts performing simulation tasks are presented below. Allowable (regulated by the constructive specialty of the spacecraft) contact parameters for docking in the performance of simulation tasks corresponded to the conditions for real docking of two spacecrafts (Johannes et al., 2017):

- longitudinal relative speed of approach (V_x) – modulo $0.07 \div 0.15$ m/s;
- lateral relative speed (V_y; V_z) – modulo no more than 0.057 (m/s);
- relative angular mismatch by roll (Gamma) – modulo no more than 4 degrees;
- the total relative angular misalignment in pitch and yaw (Theta1 + Theta2), (Phi1 – Phi2) – modulo no more than 6 degrees.

Due to the change in the flight program, two groups were allocated to the SE "Pilot-T": group 1 performed an experiment on board the RS of ISS two times a month, group 2, one time a month.

It can be seen from Figure 16.6 that these two groups do not differ statistically reliably in the docking results, which indicates a high professional level of all the crewmembers participating in this SE. Comparing the pre-flight data with inflight and post-flight data, a relative decrease in such performance parameters as fuel consumption, time of task execution, spacecraft speed during docking, and error

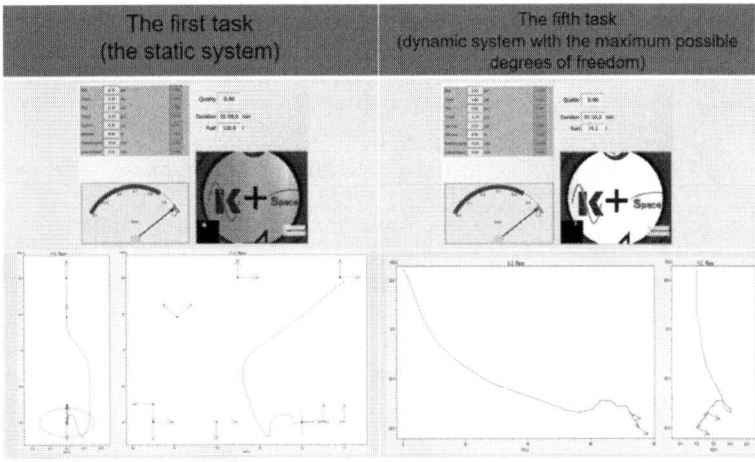

FIGURE 16.5 Examples of two task of docking results.

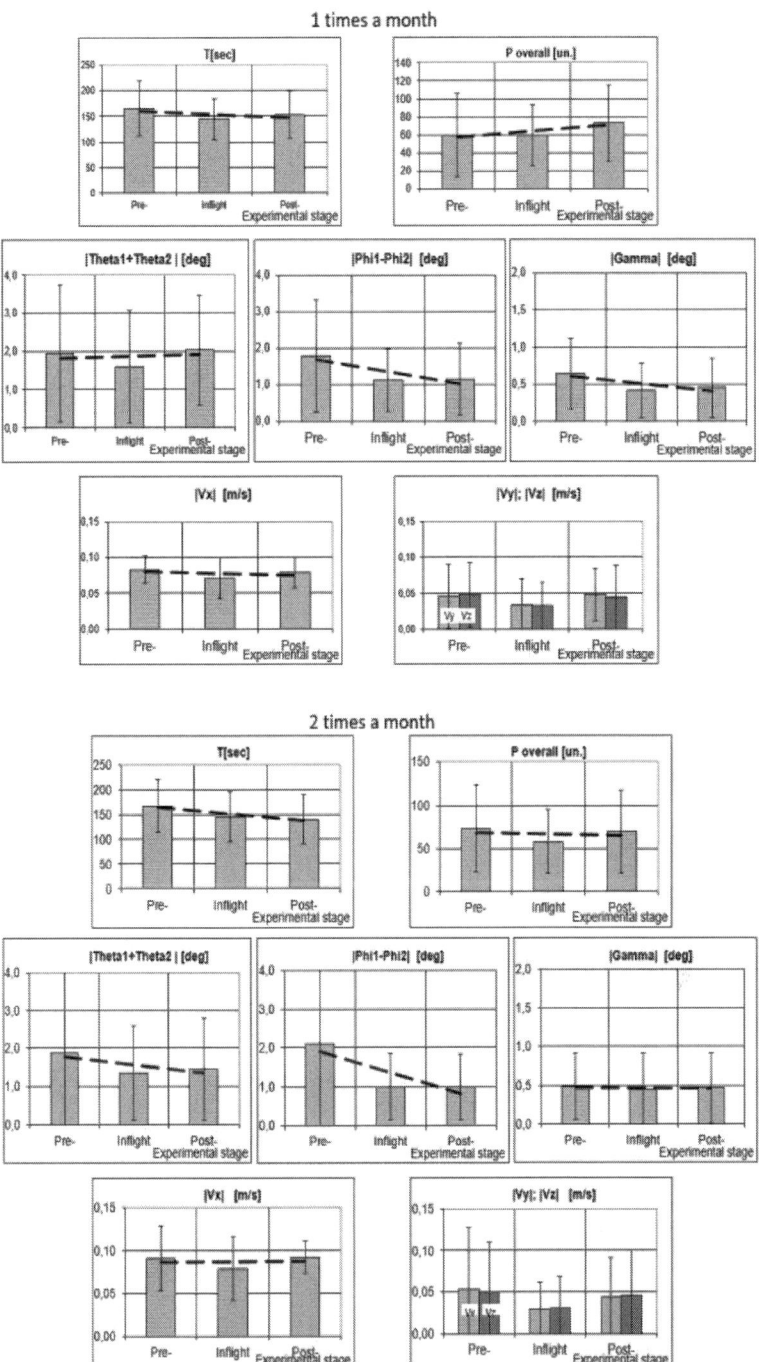

FIGURE 16.6 Histograms of the individual statistical characteristics (m and S) of the main parameters.

angles of the associated axes of interacting objects was revealed. However, no statistically significant changes were detected, which may testify about a high level of qualification in all crewmembers.

The physiological data showed changes similar to former results collected on the MIR station and the ISS. The heart rate was significantly decreased inflight; also the post-flight heart rate was lower than preflight. The indicator of parasympathetic control of the heart rate RMSSD decreased significantly from preflight to inflight. The pulse transit time decreased significantly from pre to inflight; however, the correlation between PWT and blood pressure is not known under weightlessness. A highly significant decrease was also found for periphery finger skin temperature indicating serious vasoconstriction as far as the environmental temperature was rather increased than decreased. Finally the changes of the sympathetic correlate skin conductance did not reach significance level. None of the physiological measures showed significant differences between the five flight tasks of different difficulty level (Bubeev et al., 2016).

On the contrary, cognitive tests for working memory, SVMR, and CSTR, proved to be informative for assessing the changes of the working capacity of cosmonauts during the flight. An increase in the level of attention and a decrease in the subjective feeling of fatigue during the flight diagnosed by the battery of tests can be used can be used for the prediction of crew motivation and cognitive resources before the execution of real docking and other inflight key operations.

Conclusions

1. The data obtained during the implementation of the pilot program "Pilot-T" indicated a high level of professional skills in docking the spacecraft on the ISS. Regardless of the cycle of the experiment on board the RS of ISS, the group of cosmonauts demonstrated a tendency of reducing the time and fuel consumption while performing flight imitation tasks.
2. At all stages of the space experiment, the crewmembers' fulfillment of imitation tasks for manual control and docking of two spacecraft did not cause an increase in the functional costs with increasing complexity of the operator's activity.
3. In flight, the cosmonaut's mental resources are mobilized, which leads to an increase in his mental performance. This is reflected in the overall improvement in cognitive tests results, compared with preflight and postflight. Cognitive tests for working memory, SVMR, and CSTR, proved to be informative for assessing the changes of the working capacity and motivation at different stages of spaceflight.

CONCLUSION

Peculiarity of Russian space medicine culture is the close relationship between medical support itself and researches made inflight. The obligatory claim for the applied nature of these studies was established by Sergei Korolev. So, on the one hand, every biomedical experiment should be targeted at the practical needs of space medicine, on medical support of current and future crews. On the other hand, its background arises from the existing space practice, the real problems about which cosmonauts and crew surgeons are informing the scientific community. That differs our study design, because the scientists, if they require, mostly have access to the inflight data, related to their particular study (certainly, all the international bioethical standards should be followed) to interpret properly their own results. Another distinguishing feature of Russian approach is that many testing procedures are designed especially for space practice. That is why they have to be mostly non-invasive, take minimal time and effort from the cosmonaut, being naturally embedded into the already existing operations, like crew communication ("Content" experiment) or training ("Pilot" experiment). From our point of view, this approach allows to get more reliable and valid biomedical data from space.

REFERENCES

Basner, M., Dinges, D. F., Mollicone, D. J., Savelev, I., Ecker, A. J., Di Antonio, A., ... Sutton, J. P. (2014). Psychological and behavioral changes during confinement in a 520-day simulated interplanetary mission to mars. *PLoS One, 9*(3), e93298.

Bechtel, R. B., & Berning, A. (1991). The third-quarter phenomenon: Do people experience discomfort after stress has passed? In A. A. Harrison, Y. A. Clearwater, & C. P. McKay (Eds.), *From Antarctica to outer space* (pp. 261–265). New York, NY: Springer-Verlag.

Bubeev, Yu. A., Bronnikov, S. V., et al. (2016). *The first results of the experiment "Pilot-T" on board the ISS//Aviakosmicheskaya i ehkologicheskaya meditsina: XVI conference on Space Biology and Medicine* (pp. 38–39). Moscow: Nauchnaya kniga.

Gushin, V. I., Efimov, V. A., Smirnova, T. M., Vinokhodova, A. G., & Kanas, N. (1998). Subject's perceptions of the crew interaction dynamics under prolonged isolation. *Aviation, Space, and Environmental Medicine, 69*(6), 556–561.

Gushin, V. I., Yusupova, A. K., Shved, D. M., Shueva, L. V., Vinokhodova, A. G., & Bubeev, Y. A. (2016). The evolution of methodological approaches to the psychological analysis of the crew communications with Mission Control Center. REACH-Reviews in Human Space Exploration. *Mars, 520,* 3–9.

Johannes, B., Bronnikov, S., Bubeev, Y., Dudukin, A., Hoermann, H. J., Frett, T., Gaillard, A. (2017). A tool to facilitate learning in a complex manual control task. *International Journal of Applied Psychology, 7*(4), 79–85.

Kanas, N. (2015). *Humans in space*. New York, NY: Springer.

Kanas, N., Gushin, V., & Yusupova, A. (2008). Problems and possibilities of astronauts—Ground communication content analysis validity check. *Acta Astronautica, 63*(7–10), 822–827.

Kanas, N., & Manzey, D. (2008). *Space psychology and psychiatry* (2nd ed.). New York, NY: Springer.

Komotskij, R. V., & Salnitskij, V. P. (1977). Evaluation of ergatic control processes. *Optimizatsiya professional'noj deyatel'nosti kosmonavta M.: Nauka., 34,* 72–92.

Kozerenko, O. P., Sled, A. D., & Mirzadjanov, Y. A. (2001). *Crews' Psychological Support//Orbital Station "Mir", 1,* 365–377.

Krippendorf, K. (1980). *Content analysis: An introduction to its methodology*. Newbury Park, CA: Sage.

Lazarus, R. S., & Folkman, S. (1984). *Stress, appraisal, and coping*. New York, NY: Springer.

Lomov, B. F. (1981). *The problem of communication in psychology*. Proceedings of the problem of communication in psychology, Moscow, Nauka.

Myasnikov, V. I., Shaposhnikov, E. A., & Zamaletdinov, I. S. (2001). Inflight pychoneurological control. *Orbital station "Mir", 1,* 322–333.

Myasnikov, V. I., Stepanova, S. I., et al. (2000). *Problem of psychological asthenisation in long-duration space missions*. Moscow: Frim Slovo.

Myasnikov, V. I., Uskov, F. N. et al. (Eds.). (1982). *Distant observation and expert assessment*. Moscow: Nauka.

Myasnikov, V. I., & Zamaletdinov, I. S. (1997). Mental state and cosmonauts group interaction in flight. *Kosmicheskaya biologiya I medicina. T.3. Chelovek v kosmicheskom polete. Kn.2, gl.19*. Moscow: Nauka.

Novikov, M. A. (1981). Psycho-physiological and eco-psychological aspects of interpersonal interaction under autonomous conditions. In B. F. Lomov (Ed.), *Problem of communication in psychology* (pp. 178–217). Moscow: Nauka.

Orbital station. (2001). "*Mir*".

Orbital station. (2002). "*Mir*".

Ryzhov, B. N., & Salnitskij, V. P. (1983). Methods of assessing the level of psycho-physiological tension among operators. *Kosmicheskaya biologiya i aviakosmicheskaya meditsina*, 5, 83–84.

Sandal, G. M., & Bye, H. H. (2015). Value diversity and crew relationships during a simulated space flight to Mars. *Acta Astronautica*, 114, 164–173.

Schwartz, S. H. (2006). Value orientations: Measurement, antecedents and consequences across nations. In R. Jowell, C. Roberts, R. Fitzgerald, & G. Eva (Eds.), *Measuring attitudes cross-nationally: Lessons from the European Social Survey* (pp. 161–193). London: Sage.

Stuster, J. (2010). *Behavioral issues associated with long-duration space expeditions: Review and analysis of astronaut journals* (Experiment 01-E104 (Journals)). Houston, TX: National Aeronautics and Space Administration, Johnson Space Center.

Suedfeld, P. (2006). Space memoirs: Value hierarchies before and after missions—A pilot study. *Acta Astronautica*, 58(11), 583–586.

Suedfeld, P., Brcic, J., Johnson, P. J., & Gushin, V. (2012). Personal growth following long-duration spaceflight. *Acta Astronautica*, 79, 118–123.

Suedfeld, P., Brcic, J., Johnson, P. J., & Gushin, V. (2015). Coping strategies during and after spaceflight: Data from retired cosmonauts. *Acta Astronautica*, 110, 43–49.

Ushakov, I. B., Ivanov, A. V., Kvasovets, S. V., & Bubeev, Yu. A. (2015). Neurosemantic and psychophysiological correlates of rhythmosuggestive correction of stress conditions. A*viakosmicheskaya i ehkologicheskaya meditsina*, 49(6), 55–60.

Vinokhodova, A. G., & Gushin, V. I. (2014). Study of values and interpersonal perception in cosmonauts on board of international space station. *Acta Astronautica*, 93, 359–365.

Vinokhodova, A. G., Gushchin, V. I., et al. (2017). Retrospective analysis of interpersonal perception of experienced cosmonauts – members of multinational missions to the orbital stations "MIR" and the ISS. *Aviakosmicheskaya I Ecologicheskaya Meditsina (Russia)*, 51(5), 22–30.

Yusupova, A. K., Shved, D. M., Gushchin, V. I., Supolkina, N. S., & Chekalkina, A. I. (2018). Preliminary results of space experiment "Content". *Aviakosmicheskaya i Ekologicheskaya Meditsina (Russia)*, 52(3), 28–37.

17 The Blue Dot

Don Pettit

A Space mission, by its very nature, is a microcosm submerged within a megacosm. The megacosm is the solar system, the microcosm is this small metal can that makes up your diminutive universe. Based on our experience with dissention between individuals within societies, one would think that living in a metal can with 5–6 crewmates for 6 months at a time would be a recipe for disaster; that we would fragment and thus perish together with our mission. The fact that this rarely happens, historically and now, is a testimony to innate human behavior in small groups when there is a well-defined purpose that is larger than yourself. For those who volunteer to venture into the frontier, I believe there is an internal realization that the mission takes precedence over personal desires and that survival depends on the crew working together as a cohesive unit. Technology has softened the arduous nature of the frontier so that no one alive today has experienced the conditions of a 16th-century explorer. Expanding into the solar system, we may find ourselves again in circumstances similar to those 16th-century explorers. The feeling of isolation will have no earthly parallel when we look back and realize everybody you ever knew, everybody that ever existed, is on that small blue dot.

When venturing into the space wilderness, your crewmates become a surrogate family filling the roles of your abstracted kin. You share your stuff; food, clothing, special treats from home, and most important, personal stories. You accommodate the small annoyances that inevitably arise.

Wilderness expeditions are always mass- and volume-limited. Supplies for maintaining the crew – food, water, clothing, medical equipment – and supplies for achieving the mission itself, including vehicle maintenance, have priority. There is little room for anything else. At most, each crewmember can bring one small bag of personal items. In spite of this, expeditions, both present and past, have reserved precious mass and volume for items of no operational significance. Robert Scott, in his 1910-1913 Terra Nova Expedition to Antarctica (Scott perished after having reached the South Pole second to Amundsen), brought a voluminous and fragile piece of then state-of-the-art technology that had absolutely no operational utility. He dragged a gramophone all the way to his Antarctic base camp so that his crew could have musical entertainment (this gramophone is displayed in the EMI Music Archives in London). On the International Space Station, precious up-mass and volume are allocated for items like musical instruments, video projectors for watching group movies, Christmas decorations, and special letters/treats from home. A significant fraction of the space-to-ground communications bandwidth is reserved for crew support via radio-link internet connections including streaming of music, movies, and two-way video with your family. It is possible to order flowers from space for those special family occasions back on Earth. Wilderness exploration will continue to utilize state-of-the-art technology for maintaining crew psychological health as we venture into deep space.

One fascinating psychological impact for past oceanic explorations is that the crew had no idea what to expect from the big picture; were they going to fall off of the edge, find a new continent, an island, other people (warlike or friendly, you must be prepared for both), be consumed by disease, or sea monsters? No one knew what they were going to find as well as *when* or *if* they were returning. They would set sail from port knowing the previous expedition had been gone for 5+ years with no word as to outcome. Good chance they had all perished. To sign up for a voyage like that took a special mind set.

Exploring our solar system will be psychologically different. We will know exactly where we are going and what the landing zone will be like down to the size and composition of the local boulders. The basic chemistry and local resources will be known. All thanks to remotely operated robotic probes. You will know *exactly* when your return is scheduled due to the clockwork nature of orbital mechanics. Radio contact will give you access to numerous experts to help solve problems as well as connections to your family. The big unknowns will be with the hardware that keeps you alive; will your rockets work, will your life support equipment continue to function, will your food/water last? There will be a backup plan for every aspect. What is left for discovery will be the details; observations of such a nature that only a human can make, the sort of details that tickle our imagination, enrich our minds, and ultimately lead to new knowledge that improves life for everyone back on Earth.

Historically, missions into the wilderness require those members to operate in a highly autonomous fashion. There will be no spare parts, no supplies, there will be nothing more than what can be gathered along the way. And possibly more critical than supplies are the necessary decisions on how best to proceed. Decisions made in the wilderness can make or break an expedition. And the members flourish or suffer based on the nature of their decisions. Like their 16th-century predecessors, members on these types of missions require a special mindset with matching skills for operating over long periods without the supporting framework of civilization. Earthly exploration has shown that autonomy works.

Our space program began and continues to be the opposite of autonomy. Every orbital action is painfully scripted by ground-based teams and executed by astronauts on a timeline scheduled down to every period of 5 minutes (interestingly, no time is ever scheduled for toilet breaks). Astronauts are chosen in part for their ability to follow such tight orders and then trained over years in a manner to ensure such orders are followed. Nobody on Earth, even for military operations, works under this level of scrutiny. Crewmembers that stray too far from completing the timeline will never fly a second time. If more than a few hours go by without direct contact from mission control, a near emergency is declared (by mission control). Designing space missions in this way imparts a clear and not necessarily healthy psychology upon the crew, but has worked so long as the radio link allows direct real time communication.

Optimizing space exploration as well as astronaut selection in this way may present problems for space missions beyond Earth orbit. The very nature of distance and time will force deep space missions into autonomy and will require crew with a wilderness-mechanic aptitude empowered to make both large and small decisions without prior approval or guidance from Earth. And such decisions with skill-backed implementation will once again determine the outcome. And the crew will flourish or suffer based on their own decisions.

Stories of exploration are filled with risk and danger, failures, and triumphs. This story will continue but with a cast of new perils. On Earth, these perils are from exposure to well-understood life-giving but life-taking elements: heat, cold, wet, water, toxins, nasty plants, insects, aggressive animals, and inhabitants. However, the basics for sustaining life are found everywhere: air, water, food, useful raw materials, and shelter. In the case of adversity, the time constant for death is days, weeks, or months. During that time, it may be possible to resurrect the situation. In space, there are none of the basics for sustaining life. Everything for life will need to be provided by, or made by, a machine. Maintaining adequate supplies of food and water will be trying. Space radiation, not a factor for life on Earth, could be deadly. Only the very basic raw materials will be locally available, typically in their fully oxidized and most difficult to utilize form (rocks, sand, regolith). The time constant for death varies from seconds (failure of pressurization) to months (slow starvation, radiation poisoning). Due to the non-life supporting environment and the sheer distances from Earth, survival from major malfunctions may be doubtful. The psychological relief from knowing where, when, and what for your expedition will be nulled by the uncertainty of how your machines will operate.

Oceanic explorations began by sailing with the ebbing tide. In 1670, the British scientist Harry Hyrne wrote to the Royal Society with a letter titled "Hypothesis of the Tydes" where he proposed that the tides were caused by the Moon and thus were determined with the precision of orbital mechanics. For our future missions, orbital mechanics will once again dictate when we will set sail into our solar system. Throughout history, the Moon has dictated when humans can explore and this will continue. The Moon is the gateway to human expansion into the solar system.

If it weren't for humanity's innate urge to explore, we as a species would probably be yet one more fossil layer slowly eroding from some Ethiopian cliff side. The propensity for a small fraction of our numbers to venture off into the unknown ultimately yields new places to live and new resources to use. History proves that civilization thrives in the wake of exploration. In the long term, exploration is one of many human elements needed to ensure our survival. It is clear from the fossil records that the history of life on Earth is that of extinction. Subliminally, we realize that having our DNA on more than one planetary body increases our species' chance of survival.

When we begin to expand into our solar system, the shrinking blue dot of Earth will place us into an exploration category that we as a society have not experienced for generations. We have done this before and so we shall continue. We are human and this is what we do to survive.

Halfway to Pluto

Don Pettit, Exp 31 to ISS, May 2012

I'm halfway to Pluto and Earth doesn't know
the trials of travel in space as we go
With thrust to our backs while we speed on our way
the blue dot of Earth gets fainter each day
When earthly horizons slip from your view
the color of loneliness changes its hue
And a radio call to our mission control
takes nearly a day to just say hello
Yet our boss back on Earth abstract from our flight
has no understanding of our minds in this plight
The Sirens of Space, singing songs for our souls
try to tempt us to ruin on the reef of black holes
Over ears with wax patches, we resist Siren's call
thus avoiding the reef and escaping the fall
Our families back home make do while we're gone
with or without us their life does go on
For the future of Earth and the human race
the final frontier we seek will be space
Our kind thus expands into places unknown
I'm halfway to Pluto but never alone

Index

actigraphy 273
adaptability 20, 45, 88, 95, 165, 184, 205, 258
adaptation 87, 115–117, 120–127, 129, 135, 156, 159–160, 172, 184, 241, 243, 246, 248–249, 288
adaptive behavior 282
adaptive task switching 183–184
adverse impact 22, 27, 29
agent-based model 192–195, 200
analog environment xiii, 6–7, 10–13, 18, 86, 93, 102, 158, 220, 229, 249
Anderson, Clayton 120, 143, 148
Antarctica 10, 18, 25, 87, 119–120, 134, 156, 301
anxiety 88, 118, 125–126, 157, 163, 165, 240
Aquarius 67, 108, 110–112, 146
Arctic 18, 50
assessment xiii, 10–11, 17, 20–23, 25, 28–29, 36, 85, 89, 91–92, 94–95, 98, 125–126, 157–158, 162–165, 167–168, 206–208, 213–214, 220, 239, 241, 243, 255–258, 262, 267–268, 271–276, 284, 295; *see also* measurement
   behavioral anchors 29
   dynamic 92, 95
   intelligent technology 91, 94–95
   mental state 284
   neurocognitive 116, 119, 125, 126
   real time 11, 27–28, 82, 85, 89, 95
   unobtrusive 91, 92, 95
asthenia 120, 123, 240
Astronaut Medical Board 19
Astronaut Office 26, 47, 133, 136, 145, 146, 147, 150, 257, 259
Astronaut Selection Board 19
astronaut selection *see* selection
Astronaut Spouses Group 145–146
asynchronous communication *see* communication, asynchronous
automation 47, 158, 187, 209
autonomy 64, 68–69, 78, 101, 128, 161, 168, 171–172, 182, 191, 198–200, 208, 218, 289–290, 302–303
   diminished 5

Baker, Ellen 240, 242
bandwidth 141, 220, 301
Barratt, Michael 236, 238, 242
behavioral health 116–119, 122–125, 127–129, 139, 150, 240–241, 243, 248–250, 262, 264

behavioral medicine 116, 125, 128, 134, 256, 261–263
behavioral observation 256–257, 272–273, 276
behavioral training *see* training, behavioral health
Belmont Report 1, 4–6, 8, 13, 14
Beneficence 5, 7–8, 11, 13
Benevolence 291–293
biodata *see* biographical data questionnaires
biographical data questionnaires 25, 208
Biologic Analog Science Associated with Lava Terrains (BASALT) 220
bio-marker 171; *see also* biomedical data
biomedical data 299
bonafide job qualification 22
boredom 157–158, 162–167, 171–172, 187
Bowersox, Ken 148–149
Bresnik, Randy 112

Canadian Space Agency xiv, 66, 144, 231, 244–245, 253–259, 261–264
Capsule communicator (CAPCOM) 67, 102
CAVES *see* cooperative adventure for valuing and exercising
Challenger 81, 117, 253
circadian rhythm 116, 123, 150, 240–241, 246–249, 262
coaching, leadership 90, 93
coercion 5–8
cognitive ability 21–22, 25–26
cognitive ability test 22, 25–26
cognitive decrement 5, 119, 157, 241
cognitive demand 104, 113, 181, 187, 198, 209
cognitive function 239, 247, 295
cognitive load *see* cognitive demand
cognitive process 40
cognitive reappraisal 165
cognitive resources 169, 184, 198–199, 298
cognitive test 27, 239, 294, 298; *see also* Neurocognitive test
Coleman, Cady 140
Columbia 9, 81, 117, 138, 148–149
commercial crew 147, 215, 223
commercial spacecraft 147–148, 221
commercial space program 24
communication 93, 124, 146
   anaphora 104
   asynchronous (*see* delay)
   blackout 63, 157, 216, 221, 240 (*see also* loss of)
   competency 22, 48, 56, 74, 269–270, 276–277

305

communication (*cont.*)
  compartmentalization 124
  cultural differences 290 (*see also* language)
  delay 30, 55–56, 63, 68, 90, 101–102, 104–105, 108–109, 111–113, 128, 150–151, 157, 171, 188–191, 194, 196–197, 199–200, 209, 216, 218, 220–221, 228–229, 277
  effectiveness 108–110, 112, 161, 205, 229, 289
  efficiency 105, 107–108, 188, 283
  family and friends 124–125, 136, 138, 141, 143, 149, 239, 263
  infrastructure 220
  language 237, 239, 255, 260, 270
  limited 18, 167, 280–281, 285
  loss of 69, 277 (*see also* blackout)
  medium 102, 105–108, 111–113, 144, 161, 238–239
  message lag 104, 151, 160
  message management 102
  problems 81, 93, 104, 118, 260, 281
  process 102, 105
  protocol 72, 102, 105, 107–109, 111–113, 220, 244
  proximity bias 104, 107
  psycholinguistic analysis 239, 283–289
  psychological support 138, 148–149, 238–239, 263, 280, 282, 301
  quality 102
  real-time 55, 92, 102, 104, 109, 112, 157, 194, 196, 302
  simultaneous 102
  synchronous (*see* real-time)
  technology 113, 138–139, 141, 187, 231, 253
  time-critical 102
  thread 105, 111, 113
  training 69–71, 84, 89, 108–109, 112–113, 127
  turn sequence 104, 110
compartmentalization 124
competencies 22–23, 27–28, 36, 39–41, 44–46, 48–58, 83–84, 86, 89–90, 95, 123, 127, 162–163, 165–168, 172, 256, 258–259, 271–272, 274–277
competency model 22, 59, 256–258
competency modeling 22, 38, 40, 44, 47, 59
complexity 2, 5, 7, 11, 71–72, 128, 209, 219, 226–228, 261, 298
concentration camp 3
confinement 30, 45, 87, 93, 108, 118, 128, 144, 158, 196–197, 200, 208, 229, 246, 267, 269, 272–273, 275–276
conflict management 89, 93, 127, 166–167, 172, 276
conflict resolution 290; *see also* conflict management
consent 3–7, 13, 273, 286

context 2, 18–23, 28, 36, 38–39, 44–46, 48, 53, 64, 69–73, 75–77, 81, 84, 86–90, 92–93, 127, 156–170, 172, 183, 186–187, 189, 192–193, 207
contingency action plan 146–147, 150
cooperation 52, 89, 227, 229, 254, 265
Cooperative Adventure for Valuing And Exercising (CAVES) 67, 146
coping strategies 88, 95, 127, 163, 285–289
coping techniques 167
cosmonaut 19, 21, 23, 67, 115–121, 123–124, 137, 140, 148, 227, 231, 236–237, 239–240, 247, 258, 261, 280–286, 288–296, 298–299
cost/benefit analysis 12–13
countermeasures 41, 44, 46, 58, 90, 92, 94, 108, 116, 118, 122–124, 126, 129, 138–139, 152, 157–158, 163, 184, 200, 229, 231, 236, 247, 249, 254, 261–262, 265, 281–282
Crew Care Packages (CCP) 139–141, 144, 151, 239, 246, 248
crew cohesion 141
crew composition *see* team, composition
Crew Discretionary Events (CDE) 143
crew dysfunction 165, 168
crew medical officer 68, 116, 125, 128–129, 131
crew performance 158, 162–163, 181
Crew Resource Management (CRM) 83; *see also* spaceflight resource management
crew roles 68
crew self-scheduling 218–219
Crew Support Astronauts And Casualty Assistance Calls Officer (CACO) 147
crew surgeon 116, 236–239, 242, 244, 248, 299; *see also* flight surgeon
crew webpage 140–141, 142, 264
criterion-related validity evidence 22–23, 37–38, 40, 44, 48–49
critical incident 91, 127
cross-cultural competency 21, 28, 258–259, 276
cross-cultural differences 261
cross-cultural problems 127, 259–260
cross-cultural training *see* training, cross-cultural
Culbertson, Frank 137, 140, 150, 239
culture, national 21, 26, 120, 122, 161, 168, 230, 246, 248, 254, 260–262, 270, 292
culture, organizational 26, 122, 161, 232, 236–237, 244, 246, 259, 293, 298

de Laurentiis, Giada 143
debriefs 44, 71, 73, 85, 89, 91, 93–94, 117, 123, 144, 169, 171–172, 209–210, 246–247; *see also* feedback
Declaration of Helsinki in 1964 3–4
deep-level characteristics 88, 95
deliberate practice 77–78

Index

depression 118–119, 121, 157, 163, 165, 171, 240, 246, 287
deprivation effects 158, 188, 240, 243, 280–285
deprivation phenomena 280, 284
design adequacy 209
Design Reference Missions (DRM) 54–55, 206, 229
discrimination 20, 22
disparate impact 25
distributed team *see* team, distributed
diversity 26, 38, 90, 93, 255, 293
Dunn, Jocelyn 10–11

earth-out-of-view phenomenon 157
emotion regulation 163, 165, 167, 172
emotional exhaustion 161, 169
emotional stability 24, 45, 48, 168, 189, 276–277, 285, 295
emotional transfer phenomenon 289
environment, isolated, confined, and extreme (ICE) 87–89, 116–117, 119–122, 124, 134, 156
ergonomics 38, 40, 240, 247
errors 18, 21, 37, 45, 51, 81, 83, 85, 90, 93, 102–103, 206–207, 210, 213, 215, 217, 296
ethical foundation 6
ethical guidelines 1–3, 7–11, 13
ethical requirements 9
ethical research 3, 4
ethics 2–3, 7, 10
Euripides 230
EVA *see* extra vehicular activity
evacuation 19, 21, 144, 239
evaluation of
    behavioral health 117, 125–126, 243–244, 246, 261, 282–284, 286, 291
    competencies 48
    ethics 2, 8
    event 165
    habitability 214–215
    medical emergency 213
    performance 48, 50
    risk 9–11, 14
    selection 19–20, 23, 53, 255–257, 276–277
    self-scheduling 219
    team training 259
    technology 7, 207–208, 216–217
exercise
    health 73–75, 137–138, 211, 243
    selection 20, 26–28, 86, 257
    training 74, 85
expedition training requirements integration panel 21
expeditionary training 46, 146
expeditionary workshop 127
experiments 8, 136, 192, 199, 226, 230, 247, 255, 289, 293; *see also* research
ethics 2–4, 6
exploration 1–2, 6–14, 23, 28, 54–55, 58, 63–64, 66, 68–69, 79, 82, 86–89, 93–95, 101, 108, 112–113, 123–124, 128–129, 156, 162, 166, 186, 188, 199, 205, 208–209, 215, 218, 220–221, 226, 228–231, 236, 243, 249–250, 253–265, 302–303
explorers 2, 6–7, 128, 230, 235, 301
extra vehicular activity (EVA) 66–67, 77–78, 110–112, 118, 217, 220–221, 226
extreme environment research 3, 14

face validity 21, 25–27
fairness 6–8, 17, 22, 26–27, 29, 42, 127, 242
family issues 45, 165, 168, 171
family separations 139, 145
family support 116–117, 147, 150, 258, 261, 263–264
Family Support Office (FSO) 125, 134, 136, 145, 152
fatigue 11, 120, 123, 125–126, 157, 165, 168, 170, 206, 241, 243, 246–249, 262, 277, 281, 298
federal regulations 6
feedback 27–28, 55, 73, 77–78, 82, 84–85, 89–91, 93–95, 104–105, 107, 132, 160, 171, 206, 208, 220, 274; *see also* debriefs
fidelity 26–27, 65–66, 74, 207–208, 215–216
firefighter 8, 10, 18, 78
flat astronaut 143
flight surgeon 116, 126, 128, 150, 212, 236, 240, 242, 244, 261; *see also* crew surgeon
focus of attention 77
followership 90, 93, 128, 172, 274–276
foods 12, 73–74, 124, 126, 138, 140–141, 147, 150–151, 158, 211, 233, 282, 301–303
food laboratory 150
frustration 121, 126, 138, 158, 162, 180, 210, 238, 240

Gagarin, Yuri 2, 117, 231
general mental ability 24; *see also* cognitive ability
generalizability 23, 86–87
goal alignment 225–226, 228–230
goals, high-order 13, 225–226, 228–232
grieving 148–150
guidelines 2–3, 6–11, 13, 28–29, 37, 43, 64, 71, 73, 134, 206, 215, 248, 254, 262, 264

habitability 45, 118, 126, 209–212, 214, 220, 240–241, 243
hallucinations 119
harm 5, 7, 11, 20, 118
health, behavioral *see* psychological well-being

health, mental 161, 169, 172, 231, 239–244, 246–247; see also well-being, psychological
health, physical 11
health, psychological 11, 152, 302; see also well-being, psychological
health standards 2, 8, 10, 11, 14
healthcare 83, 87, 241, 244
HI-SEAS 10, 155
human biological limitations 12
human experimentation 3
Human Exploration Research Analog (HERA) 88, 107–109, 111–112, 189–194, 199–200, 219
human exploration see exploration, human
human factors 91, 122, 183, 193–194, 200, 205–207, 209–214, 216, 221, 240, 247, 249, 258
human subjects 2–6, 285
Human Systems Integration (HSI) 205–208, 221
human-centered design 205–207, 209
human-system interface 123, 205–208, 221, 243, 247, 249
humor 25, 167, 243, 286, 288

ICE environment see environment, isolated, confined, and extreme
illness 6, 19–20, 116, 119, 121, 128, 241, 255
individual differences 88, 95, 163, 185, 188, 196–197, 200, 247
in-flight resource plan 139–140
informed consent 3, 5–7, 13, 286
Institutional Review Board (IRB) 6–7
interdependence 82, 86, 90, 92–93, 161, 180–183, 189, 194, 196–200
International Training Control Board (ITCB) 21, 258–259, 275, 277
internet protocol (IP) phone 125, 139, 141, 243, 246
interviews, structured 20, 26, 125
IRB see institutional review board
isolation 28, 30, 50, 87, 91, 93, 108, 118, 128–129, 156–157, 162–164, 188, 194, 196–197, 207–209, 229, 239–240, 246, 256, 262, 267, 269, 272–273, 275–276, 280–281, 286, 290, 301

Japan Aerospace Exploration Agency (JAXA) 21, 28, 66–67, 108, 144, 231, 245, 267–269, 271, 274–277
JAXA see Japan aerospace exploration agency
job analysis 22, 36, 38, 40–41, 47, 51, 54–55, 58, 256–257; see also work analysis
job change, requirements 29
job control 169
job performance 22–23, 25, 28, 37, 39, 46, 48–49, 51, 87, 122
justice 5, 7–8, 13

Kelly, Scott 11, 148, 155
knowledge
    strategic use of 74
    transfer of 19, 68–69, 71, 75, 77–78, 83–85, 87, 90, 184
Krikalev, Sergei 137

language 23, 40, 67, 94, 120, 133, 148, 173, 214, 236, 242, 245, 260
leadership 24, 27, 30, 46, 74, 89, 91, 94–95, 120, 129, 148, 161, 164, 188, 189, 198–199, 205, 227, 229, 237, 247–248, 256, 259, 275–276, 290
leadership, shared 164
leadership training 91
leisure time 126, 138, 158, 172–173
level of analysis 11, 13–14
life cycle, astronaut 10
Linenger, Jerry 139, 243
living and working in space 22, 126, 140
Lopez-Alegria, Michael 145

Mars 500 88
MARS team simulation 27
Massimino, Mike 116
Mcarthur, William 143
Mccool, Willie 149
meaningful work 157–158, 225–226
measurement; see also assessment
    intelligent 91, 94
    nonobtrusive 129
    performance 48
    robust 91–92, 94
    selection 36–37, 50
    teams 82, 85–86, 88, 92–93
    wearable 166
medical cue cards 212–214
medical data 8, 11
medical standards 19, 126, 231, 261
medications 121, 123, 126, 212, 246–247, 262
mental health status evaluations 125, 244, 248
mental model, shared 21, 83, 186
military 3, 8, 19, 25, 81, 83, 87, 120, 122, 126, 145, 257, 302
mindfulness 14, 158, 163, 165, 172
mindset 19, 87, 124, 302
minimal group effect 138
Mir 20, 44, 47, 118–119, 124, 126–127, 136–137, 210, 227, 235–242, 246–249, 254, 259, 283–284, 298
Mission Control Center (MCC) 12, 63, 65–68, 71–72, 75, 90, 101, 109–113, 141, 182, 210, 216, 218, 231, 283
mission objectives 64–68, 79
mission specialist 30, 66, 255–256, 267, 271
mission success 25, 64, 69, 75, 79, 88, 92, 95, 141, 214, 229, 232, 243, 246

Index

mission to Mars 12–13, 18, 20, 29, 44, 48, 53–56, 68, 70, 78, 92, 101, 108, 128, 150–152, 156, 158, 188, 192, 229, 249, 277
mission types 53–57
mission-critical 92, 101
monitoring 8, 11, 70–73, 76, 84–85, 91, 94, 102, 116, 123, 149, 156–157, 159, 164, 166, 171, 179, 211, 215–216, 238, 244, 246, 258, 261–262, 277, 282–285, 287
monotony 118, 151, 156, 162–164, 167, 172, 280–282
mood 119, 125–126, 158, 165, 168, 171, 241, 281, 284, 287
Moon Base simulation 74
Multilateral Medical Operations Panel (MMOP) 123, 231, 254, 258–259, 262, 264
multi-method job analysis 22
multitasking 119, 189
multiteam system (MTS) 118, 192–193, 228–229
multiteam task 190, 193–194, 199

NASA extreme environment mission operations (NEEMO) xiii, 67, 104, 108–113, 146, 219–220
NASA medical standard 19
national oceanic and atmospheric administration 2, 10
national outdoor leadership school 127, 146
national research act of 1974 4
NEEMO *see* NASA Extreme Environment Mission Operations
Net Habitable Volume (NHV) 55, 214–215
neurocognitive 119, 125–126, 293, 295
Nuremberg Code 4
nutrition 231, 282

operational environment 7, 208, 259
operational memory 295, 298
operational psychology 116, 125, 133–136, 139, 240
Orion transport module 158

part-task trainers 65–66, 76
payload specialists 255
peer review 27
performance adaptation 184
performance criteria 17, 19, 23, 25
performance, crew 158, 162–163, 166, 181; *see also* performance, team
personal growth 290
personality 15, 21, 23–25, 28–29, 38, 40, 48, 88, 108, 118, 121, 163, 167–168, 189, 197, 240, 255, 258, 270, 290
Pettit, Don ix, xiv, xx, 87, 148–150, 301, 304
photography, earth 157
physical health xi, 11; *see also* well-being, physiological

physiological well-being 108; *see also* physical health
pilots 24, 30, 50, 64–72, 74, 76–78, 88, 149, 208, 240, 279, 285, 291, 293–296, 298–299
playbook 218–219
polychronicity 189
post-flight 125–126, 136, 139, 144, 147, 236–237, 242, 244, 247, 292, 296, 298
practice xvi, 3–4, 13, 18–20, 26, 28–30, 49, 63–71, 73–78, 84–86, 88–90, 93–94, 116–117, 127–128, 155, 157–158, 162–164, 166–169, 171–173, 187, 208, 215, 231, 254, 283, 285, 299
practice, variability of 63, 75
preflight 94, 116, 133, 135–136, 139, 146, 213, 236, 246, 298
prevention 123, 125, 213, 240
private family conference 73–74, 125, 138, 141, 144
private family video conferences *see* private family conference
private psychological conference (PPC) 126, 128, 151, 244, 246–247, 262
protection of human subjects 6
psychiatric 12, 15, 19–20, 26, 121, 123, 125, 128, 255–256, 268, 275
psychiatric screening *see* screening, psychiatric
psychological climate 284
psychological detachment 169–170, 172
psychological health xi, xiii, 11, 162, 302; *see also* well-being, psychological
psychological reactions 171
psychological risks 12, 228
psychological safety 84
psychological screening 20, 25, 256; *see also* screening, psychological
psychological selection vii, 17–19, 21–23, 25, 27–29, 45–46, 248; *see also* selection, psychological
psychological stressors 118; *see also* stressors
psychological suitability 26; *see also* suitability
psychological support vii, viii, xiv, 46, 122, 124, 133–141, 143, 145, 147–152, 239–240, 246, 248, 279–282, 285, 287
  program 122, 124, 134, 152, 281
  teams 239, 248
  types xiv, 136
psychological trouble 281
psychological well-being xi, xiii, xiv, 108, 118, 121, 138, 140, 143, 155, 157–158, 167–169, 171–172; *see also* well-being, psychological
psychometric tasks 20, 49
psychomotor vigilance task 249
psychopathology 20, 168

psychophysiological reactions 293
psychosocial adaptation 87, 120–124, 126, 127, 129, 249

radiation xi, 11–12, 19, 118, 128, 218, 303
radiation, acceptable exposure 11–12
range restriction 23, 49, 53
realistic job preview 26, 163, 167, 258
recovery 126, 158, 169–172
recruitment 8, 255, 268
rehearsal 65, 68, 75
reinstatement, contextual 63, 71, 74
reinstatement, procedural 63, 72, 74
relationships xv, 21, 26, 39, 43, 46, 48, 50–53, 83, 120, 125–127, 166, 170, 186–187, 200, 235–236, 238–239, 242, 246, 248, 261, 281
research environments 1–2, 6, 14, 86
research participants 7, 8, 10, 12–13
research protocol 3, 4
research subjects 1, 5–7
research *see* experiments
resiliency 88, 95, 243
respect for persons 5, 7–8, 13
re-supply 73, 124, 128, 138, 140, 151, 239, 248
retaliation 9
retrieval cues 74
return to earth 8, 65, 68, 118, 147
right stuff 24, 272
risk, assessment 11
risk, human life 2, 12
risk/benefit analysis 1, 10, 11
Robertson, Patricia Hilliard 150
role switching 90, 94
Roscosmos *see* Russian space agency
Russian space agency 45, 124, 231, 236, 255

safety xi, xix, xx, 10, 19, 22, 45, 50, 53, 83–85, 121, 125, 134, 158, 190, 205, 210, 213–214, 218, 238, 277
Salyut 115, 119, 123–124, 126, 136, 227, 247
sample sizes 22–23, 37, 51–53, 86
schedule, timeline 302
screening, psychiatric 19–20, 255
screening, psychological 20, 25, 256
select-in 248, 255–257; *see also* suitability
selection xxii, xxiv, xv, 5–8, 17–30, 35–38, 41, 44–49, 52–55, 57–58, 65, 86, 117, 123, 127, 141, 173, 228, 238, 240, 243–244, 248, 254–258, 262, 264, 267–269, 271–277, 283, 293, 303
   decisions 20–22, 26
   method 19–20, 27, 35, 48–49, 267
   process xiv, 8, 19–20, 22–23, 25–29, 48–49, 53, 55, 57–58, 86, 256–258, 264, 267
   standardized methods 28
   systems 17, 27, 38, 268

select-out 255–257, 273, 275
self-awareness 91; *see also* self-management; self-maintenance
self-maintenance viii, xiii, 91, 94, 155–162, 168–170, 172–173
self-management 46, 127, 276
self-regulation 158, 162, 172
self-select 158, 280–282
sensory deprivation 163–164, 280–282
Shackleton, Ernest 230
shared knowledge 94, 161
Shepherd, Commander William M. (Bill) 137–138, 242
short duration mission 69
shuttle xiv, 20, 30, 44, 48, 53–54, 56, 64–66, 68–69, 81, 117, 119, 123–124, 126, 136–139, 147–148, 209–210, 215–216, 227, 236–239, 246, 249, 253, 255–256, 259, 261, 264, 267, 271, 274
Shuttle-Mir 119, 124, 126, 137, 227, 259 *see* Mir
Silver Snoopy 148
simulation 21, 26–27, 65–67, 69–71, 73–78, 85, 88–89, 104–105, 108–109, 249
   a day in the life of an astronaut 27
   fidelity 26–27, 65–66, 74
   mission 66, 75–78, 88, 104–105, 108–109, 249
   training 67, 71–72, 75–76, 78, 85, 89, 108–109
Skylab 65, 119, 123, 136–137, 183, 210, 240
sleep xv, 116, 118, 120–123, 125–126, 156, 163, 165, 168, 170, 188, 199, 208, 240–241, 243, 246–249, 262, 273, 276, 280, 284
social interaction 163
social isolation 30, 157, 163–164, 188, 194, 229, 280–281
social support 12, 87, 89, 93, 121, 167, 169–170, 180, 229, 285
sociometric badges 129; *see also* wearable sensors
Soyuz 66–67, 117, 119, 137, 144, 147–148, 227, 247
space fog 119
Space Habitability Observation Reporting Tool (iSHORT) 210–211
Spaceflight Cognitive Assessment Tool for Windows (WinSCAT) 126, 239, 246, 248
Spaceflight Human Behavioral Health and Performance Group (SHBPWG) xiii, 122, 235–236, 243–244, 246–249, 254, 259
spacewalk 65, 112, 118; *see also* extra vehicular activity
spacing 63, 74, 78 *see* training, spacing
stress coping 285, 287
stressors 20, 87, 108, 118–119, 121–122, 124, 127, 135, 138, 144–145, 156, 169, 209, 226, 242, 246

Index

physical 118
types of 118
submarine 156, 167, 220, 240
suitability 19–20, 26, 48, 268
support systems 18, 44, 47, 137, 156, 166–167, 172, 229
    four factor model 241, 243, 244, 249

Tani, Dan 150
task attractiveness 183, 196–197
task characteristics 72, 179, 185, 189, 196–197
task difficulty 183, 185, 200, 296
task interdependence 82, 161
task management 184, 189
task overload 240, 247
task routineness 161
task stickiness 184–185, 196, 199, 200
task success 101
task switching xiii 183–184, 186
team autonomy 161
team adaptation 159, 160
team cohesion 227
team collaboration 102, 221
team collective orientation 89
team composition 88
team context 156, 159, 183, 186
team coordination 84, 90, 94, 122, 182, 186, 220, 227
team definition 82
team dimensional training 83
team, distributed 18, 102, 107
team dynamics 86, 92, 171
team effectiveness xvi, 24, 83, 88, 161, 183, 184–185
team environment 18
team exercise 27–28, 86
team healthcare 83
team resilience 159
team self-maintenance 155–162, 168–170, 172–173
team skill decay 160
team task transitions 179, 181, 184
team training 64–65, 67, 69, 81–95, 259
    models 88–90, 94–95
teamSTEPPS 83
teamwork xv, xvi, 18, 20–22, 24–28, 30, 45–46, 56–57, 70, 81–92, 94–95, 127–128, 166, 168,–169, 180, 186
teamwork ABCs 84
teamwork reaction exercises 20, 26
technological advances 2
technologies, protective 12
technology 7, 13–14, 36, 44, 47, 53, 82, 91, 94–95, 101, 113, 136–139, 141, 144, 155, 166, 171–172, 179, 185, 187, 189, 191, 196–198, 212, 220, 235, 238, 243, 247, 249, 301–302
Thagard, Norm 137

third quarter phenomenon 287–289
thrive 19–20, 119, 152, 303
time constraints 105, 213, 218
timeline 64–74, 77, 118, 136, 140, 179–180, 218–219, 302
training xii, 7, 12, 21, 63–64, 66–78, 89, 91–93, 95, 117, 127–128, 139, 161, 163–164, 166, 168, 170, 172, 182, 191, 198–200, 213, 227, 257–261, 276
    ASCAN 66–67, 70–78, 117, 127, 139, 164, 257
    autonomy 64, 68–69, 78, 161, 172, 182, 191, 198–200
    behavioral health 127–128
    classroom 70, 76
    conflict management 89, 93, 127, 163, 166, 172
    content 12, 81, 84–85, 89–90, 95
    context 84, 86, 89, 92–93, 127, 156, 161, 168, 170, 172
    crew xii, 125, 163, 168, 213, 227
    crew-centered, mission-oriented xii, 63, 68–71, 74, 79
    cruise to Mars 74
    cross-cultural 28, 89, 122, 127, 163, 258–261, 276
    delivery-method 82, 84–86, 90–92
    demonstration 85, 89–91
    design 64, 68–70, 75, 86
    engagement 92
    flow 21, 65–67, 69–72, 74–76, 144, 259
    instructor-led 76
    measurement 82, 84–86, 88, 91–94
    Orion 70–73, 75–76
    practice 74–75, 77–78, 84–85, 89
    principles xii, 63, 69–70, 72, 74, 77, 79, 85–86, 92
    pre-flight 65, 82, 116, 125, 237
    retention 68, 69, 71, 74–75, 77–78
    schema 86
    single-flow-to-launch 21
    space flight 7, 63–65, 67–69, 72
    spacing 74, 78
    stress management 127, 163
    systems 89, 92
    tools 85, 91
    tools, delivery 85, 91
    transfer 68–69, 71, 75, 77–78, 83–87, 90
transitions viii, xiii, 179, 181–185, 187–192, 194, 198, 199

undue influence 5
USA vs Karl Brandt et al 3
usability 88, 94, 108, 206–208, 213, 215–216

validation 19, 22–24, 26, 29, 36–38, 41–43, 46–51, 53–54, 57, 195–196
    alternative 37, 38, 41–43, 46, 47, 49, 50–51, 53–54, 57

validation (*cont.*)
   synthetic validation 24, 29, 41–42, 48–53
   traditional validation 29, 37, 48–49, 53
validity generalization 29, 38, 40, 42, 44, 46, 48
values xiii, xiv, 12, 24, 88, 95, 121–122, 194, 196, 199, 206, 225–226, 230, 232, 260, 284, 290–293, 300
Vander Ark, Steve 239, 244
volition 187

Ward, David 236
wearable sensors 171, 277
well-being, physiological 108, 134
well-being, psychological 87, 108, 118, 121, 125–126, 134, 136–141, 143, 155–169, 171–172, 231
Williams, Suni 143

WinSCAT 126, 239, 246, 248; *see also* Spaceflight Cognitive Assessment Tool for Windows
winter-overs 288
withdrawal 8, 120, 189, 260
work analysis 35–36, 38–39, 40–41, 44–48, 50, 52–54, 57–58
   alternative 35–36, 38–41, 44, 46–47, 58
   astronaut 36, 54, 56–58
   traditional work analysis 36–38, 41, 58
work demands 41, 184
work design 180, 189, 192, 199
work recovery 169, 170–172; *see also* recovery
work samples 20, 26–28; *see also* job sample; realistic job preview
workload 102, 113, 118, 125–126, 161, 185, 207, 216, 218, 240–241, 262, 284
world medical association 3